GENDER AND SOCIAL PROTE
IN THE DEVELOPING WORLD

'*Gender and Social Protection in the Developing World* highlights a key gap in the current design of social protection programs and policies. Taking into account the barriers that women face in accessing resources, mainstreaming gender equality in social protection interventions is critical. This publication contributes to a rethinking of current interventions on social protection.'

Lilian Keene-Mugerwa, Chair, Africa Platform for Social Protection

'A timely and critical addition to the literature on this subject – the authors guide the reader to an approach to social protection that leads towards real transformation. Comprehensive yet context specific, this book provides an excellent balance of theory with practical guidance.'

Suzette Mitchell, UN Women (Vietnam)

'Holmes and Jones convincingly demonstrate that only social protection policies developed with a gender lens can alter the causes of poverty and vulnerability. Their prescriptions for programme change have the potential to transform lives on the ground. This book should be required reading for academics and practitioners alike.'

Liesl Haas, Department of Political Science, California State University

About the Authors

Rebecca Holmes is a Research Fellow in the Social Protection Programme at the Overseas Development Institute. Her research and policy work focuses on the linkages between social protection and social policy, and she has particular expertise in gender analysis. With a geographical focus on South and South-East Asia, her research includes studies on gender and social protection effectiveness, social protection and social inclusion, and social protection in fragile and post-conflict states. She has published widely for a range of governmental, non-governmental and donor audiences on social protection, and has spoken at a variety of public events and conferences on social protection.

Nicola Jones has a PhD in political science and is a Research Fellow in the Social Development Programme at the Overseas Development Institute (ODI). Her research, advice and public affairs work focuses on gender analysis, social protection and poverty reduction policies, child well-being, and the linkages between knowledge, policy and power. Since 2007 she has led a number of multi-country studies on the intersection between social justice and social protection in Africa, Asia, Latin America and the Middle East. She is currently a lead researcher in a cross-country study on citizen perceptions of cash transfers in sub-Saharan Africa and the Middle East, and is managing a regional review of gender-responsive social protection in Southeast Asia for UN Women.

Nicola has published widely for a range of academic, policy and practitioner audiences, including six co-authored books. The most recent are: "*Knowledge Policy and Power in International Development: A Practical Guide*" (2012) with Policy Press and "*Children in Crisis: Seeking Child-sensitive Policy Responses*" (2012) with Palgrave.

GENDER AND SOCIAL PROTECTION IN THE DEVELOPING WORLD

Beyond Mothers and Safety Nets

Rebecca Holmes and Nicola Jones

Zed Books
London & New York

Gender and Social Protection in the Developing World: Beyond Mothers and Safety Nets was first published in 2013 by Zed Books Ltd, 7 Cynthia Street, London N1 9JF, UK and Room 400, 175 Fifth Avenue, New York, NY 10010, USA

www.zedbooks.co.uk

Typeset in Sabon by Swales & Willis Ltd, Exeter, Devon

Index: rohan.indexing@gmail.com
Cover design by www.roguefour.co.uk
Cover photo © Aubrey Wade/Panos
Printed and bound by CPI Group (UK) Ltd, Croydon CR0 4YY

Distributed in the USA exclusively by Palgrave Macmillan, a division of St Martin's Press, LLC, 175 Fifth Avenue, New York, NY 10010, USA

A catalogue record for this book is available from the British Library
Library of Congress Cataloging in Publication Data available

ISBN 978 1 78032 042 7 hb
ISBN 978 1 78032 041 0 pb

Contents

Illustrations

Tables

Figures

Foreword

Social protection is arguably the great success story of development policy in the new millennium. Millions of poor people across Africa, Asia and Latin America are demonstrably better off because they have received cash or asset transfers, temporary employment during the annual 'hungry season', subsidised access to services, or other forms of social assistance and social insurance.

Yet social protection is often accused of being insufficiently gender-sensitive, or of dealing with gender only superficially. Female-headed households are routinely classified as a 'vulnerable group' in need of 'safety nets', perpetuating the treatment of women as 'dependents', alongside orphans and older people. In public works programmes, women are often under-represented because men take most of the work places – but if gender quotas are introduced insensitively, women can become over-burdened because they carry a disproportionate share of social reproduction responsibilities at home.

In this important book, Rebecca Holmes and Nicola Jones challenge the inadequate treatment of gender in social protection programming, highlighting the costs of this oversight and making a powerful case for moving 'beyond mothers and safety nets' towards a 'transformative' approach that will empower women and ensure more gender-equitable outcomes. Instead of just alleviating the consequences of poverty and vulnerability with social transfers for targeted 'vulnerable groups', social protection should recognise and address the underlying causes of poverty and vulnerability, many of which are driven by gendered inequities at the societal level.

The cross-country research on which this book is based reveals that there are instrumental as well as ethical justifications for applying a gender lens to social protection. Instrumentally, policies and programmes that are sensitive to gender are likely to achieve better outcomes in terms of their own objectives. The economic costs of gender gaps in education, health and employment can be quantified, so interventions that recognise and address these gaps are good not only for girls and women, but also for poverty reduction and economic growth. Ethically, I agree with the authors that 'equality between women and men – equal rights, opportunities and responsibilities – is a human right and a matter of social justice.' It follows that social protection that reduces inequalities between women and men, or between girls and boys, is also good for social justice.

One reason why social protection might have failed to develop a gender lens is that it has been appropriated by governments and some international agencies as a set of instruments for poverty reduction, and poverty is measured by economists at the household level. However, social protection addresses vulnerability as well as poverty – in fact I would argue that 'vulnerability management' should be its primary focus, with 'poverty reduction' a secondary objective – and vulnerability is experienced by individuals, not households. Differentiated vulnerabilities require differentiated interventions, so gender-specific and gender-intensified vulnerabilities and inequalities require gender-sensitive social protection.

Feminist theory has much to offer social protection that should inform the conceptualisation of policies and the implementation of programmes, but rarely does. For instance, social assistance typically targets 'poor households', the expectation being that resource transfers to the household head will be equitably allocated to those family members who most need support. However, this assumption ignores important work by feminist economists on intra-household bargaining models, as well as empirical evidence that men and women have different priorities and allocate incremental income in very different ways.

In practice, the design of social protection programmes often reflects assumptions about the gendered division of responsibilities between the 'productive' and 'domestic' spheres. Social protection programmes that are linked to economic sectors such as agriculture tend to be 'gender-neutral' in their design, and therefore benefit men, who are better positioned to take advantage of them. Conversely, social protection that is linked to social sectors – education, health and childcare – does take gender into account, but in ways that reinforce stereotypical gender roles. A classic example is conditional cash transfers, where the costs of compliance are borne by women in the household, in their role as mothers and carers, who ensure that their children attend school and clinic as required.

Some social protection programmes do attempt to address gendered inequalities – for instance, by nominating women as recipients of assets or cash transfers, even in male-headed households. However, the authors' in-depth analysis of a range of programmes reveals that 'gender-sensitive design does not always translate into gender-equitable impacts.' Delivering social transfers to women does not necessarily empower them within their families. It could instead expose them to gender-based violence. Similarly, inviting women to participate in community meetings about social protection programmes does not automatically translate into equality within patriarchal decision-making fora.

Other innovative interventions go further, aiming explicitly to challenge and change social norms that are harmful to girls and women. For instance, the authors report that some states in India offer financial incentives to delay marriage until girls reach 18 years of age. Also, school feeding programmes often target meals or take-home rations at female learners, in an effort to reverse gender imbalances in school enrolment. This does not address the reasons why parents allow their daughters to marry too young, or why they choose to send their sons rather than their daughters to school, but social protection has at least identified effective instruments for counteracting these practices.

How much further social protection can go – or should be expected to go – raises intriguing questions. Should social protection strive to empower women and transform gender relations? If social protection does not empower and transform, does it risk becoming a neoliberal tool that entrenches inequalities and dependency on safety nets, deferring rather than driving progressive social change?

Many other challenges and paradoxes remain. If social protection targets 'poor households' and delivers transfers to (mainly male) household heads, it stands accused of being gender-blind and reinforcing patriarchal power hierarchies. However, if social protection targets females as 'vulnerable groups' who need 'safety nets', it stands accused of paternalism and addressing consequences rather than structural causes of poverty and vulnerability. If public works programmes introduce gender quotas, this is critiqued for failing to recognise the skewed burden of social reproduction. If social protection assists women to meet their 'practical needs' by giving them cash transfers, it stands accused of failing to address their 'strategic needs' by empowering them. Clearly, applying a gender lens to social protection is not straightforward. It requires careful thought and sensitive design and implementation.

The evidence presented in this book leaves the reader in no doubt that gender considerations should be mainstreamed throughout social protection project cycles. The conceptualisation stage should incorporate a socio-cultural assessment to understand gender issues in each specific local context, and needs assessments should elicit the views and priorities and preferences of women as well as men. In terms of project design and implementation, if women and girls are generally poorer and more vulnerable than men and boys, the obvious implication is that interventions must be tailored to the specific needs of women and girls. Finally, monitoring and evaluation should incorporate gender audits, especially when programmes target women or girls, with ambitions to redress gendered inequities and transform relations and power hierarchies at household and community levels.

Some years ago I heard a radio announcer in Zambia introduce a female academic to a studio debate about women and human rights with the following remark: *'Doctor, I have heard you are very gender-sensitive – I hope that is not true!'* This book gives us hope that social protection will become much *more* gender-sensitive in future than it has been to date. Encouragingly, it even concludes with a series of 'good practice examples' that show us how this can be done.

Stephen Devereux
Centre for Social Protection
Institute of Development Studies
Brighton
UK

Preface

By mid-2000 a number of international conferences on social protection were being hosted around the world, bringing together academics, practitioners, governments and donors to share lessons from existing social protection programmes and to help inform the expansion of social protection across the developing world. These conferences reflected the trend of increasing domestic and international interest in social protection, and especially the potential applicability of social protection programmes to low-income and chronically poor contexts. However, what was striking at this time was the near absence of talk on gender in the discussions on social protection. While women's empowerment was emerging as a critical part of the debate on conditional cash transfers in Latin America, little attention was given to the importance of gender equity elsewhere, despite the significant increase in policy attention to social protection by donors and governments alike.

At the same time, more than a decade after the optimism of the UN Beijing Conference on Women in 1995, which galvanised a global and systematic approach to tackle gender inequality, political and financial commitment appeared to be waning. However, the Beijing Platform for Action had set up a variety of long-term institutional mechanisms to ensure that promoting gender equality would be mainstreamed through poverty reduction programmes, and there remained a strong base of knowledge, evidence and practice on promoting gender-equitable outcomes within international development policies and programmes. However, gender inequality – measured by indicators such as rates of violence against women, human capital attainment, access to resources, political voice and agency, and labour force participation – remained a pressing issue.

It was this continued urgency to address gender inequality, as well as the glaring gap between social protection and gender discourses, which prompted our research in this area. We took as our starting point the need to move away from the assumption that social protection was 'already addressing gender inequality' by targeting female-headed households and elderly women, and transferring income to mothers in the household. Instead we sought to interrogate the complexities of gender-related risks and vulnerabilities and assess how social protection could contribute to greater gender equity. When we began this research in early 2009, even more attention was turning to social protection as a potential policy tool for buffering the worst impacts of the food, fuel and financial crisis, which were reverberating throughout the developing world. Our research, based initially on primary data from eight country case studies, complemented by a detailed review of the global literature, sought to understand local and context-specific gender-based discrimination and inequality and their intersections with poverty and vulnerability, as well as to recognise the capabilities and coping mechanisms which men, women, boys and girls employed in the context of ongoing poverty (often exacerbated by the crisis). We looked to identify the mechanisms through which social protection programmes could strengthen gender-equitable and poverty reduction outcomes, and to understand political economy dynamics to explain why the divide between social protection and gender discourses existed, and how these issues could be more effectively tackled.

Throughout the research process we were often confronted with institutional resistance to promoting gender equity through social protection policy and programmes. This in itself highlights the need for continued advocacy for gender equity – not only as a right, but also as a means of achieving more sustainable poverty reduction outcomes. We also found significant under-investment in the gender machinery which had been put in place to ensure greater political, institutional and financial commitment to improving gender-related outcomes across all of our case study countries. Similarly, we encountered relatively limited involvement of civil society championing greater attention to gender relations within social protection debates.

That said, and bearing in mind that social change is seldom linear and often slow, our research highlights the importance of many social protection programmes in poor people's lives. We found not only an array of expected positive impacts – ranging from smoothing consumption to increased investment in girls' human capital development and broadening women's economic opportunities – but also a number of more indirect unexpected outcomes. These included improvements in women's household decision making, positive changes in intra-household relations and division of labour, and the creation of opportunities for women outside the home in employment and community decision making. These identified changes were admittedly often small-scale. However, it is our hope that by sharing innovative examples of good practice in programme design and implementation, and identifying a number of relatively straightforward steps to enhance the consideration of gender dimensions across the policy and programming cycle, that as an international community we can strengthen social protection policy and programming in order to achieve greater and more sustainable equitable outcomes for all – women, men, girls and boys.

Acknowledgements

This book has been a team effort on multiple levels, and we owe a profound debt of thanks to a considerable number of people. First, the primary research that informs a number of chapters as well as our overall thinking on gender and social protection was undertaken in partnership with the following very insightful colleagues from around the globe:

Fouzia Mannan in Bangladesh
Elydia Silva and Fabio Veras Soares in Brazil
Yisak Tafere and Tassew Woldehanna in Ethiopia
Christiana Amuzu in Ghana
Nidhi Sadana, Saswatee Rath and Abhay Xaxa in India
Sirojuddin Arif, Vita Febriany, Muhammad Syukri and Athia Yumna
in Indonesia
Paola Pereznieto and Mariana Campos in Mexico
Rosana Vargas in Peru
Shanza N. Khan and Sara Qutub in Pakistan
Tran Thi Van Anh in Vietnam.

We would not have been able to write this book without the time and openness of all the respondents in the communities and the participants of the social protection programmes during the fieldwork process, or without the insights of the programme implementers, designers, officials, analysts and activists whom we interviewed in each country. We are also grateful for the funding made available from the Department for International Development, UK (DFID) and the Australian Agency for International Development (AusAID) which enabled ODI to carry out the primary research data collection and analysis, and to the Social Protection Programme at ODI.

We benefited hugely from the expert peer review feedback from Stephen Devereux and Rachel Marcus on the full manuscript, as well as on individual chapters from Christiana Amuzu, John Farrington, Sri Wening Handayani, Samuel Hickey, Samantha Hung, Anna McCord, Keetie Roelen, Ashok Pankaj, Paola Pereznieto, Rachel Sabates-Wheeler, Nistha Sinha, Rachel Slater, Erika Strand, Rosana Vargas, Eliana Villar,

Cora Walsh and Jenn Yablonski, and from comments by an anonymous reviewer.

We have been very ably and cheerfully supported along the writing journey by a great group of research assistants, primarily Maria Stavropoulou, but also Hanna Alder, Evie Browne, Josiah Kaplan, Hanna Ketola, Hannah Marsden, Ella Page and Elizabeth Presler-Marshall, as well as by the excellent editorial input of Roo Griffiths and Kathryn O'Neil, and the encouragement and patience of the editorial team at Zed Books, especially Tamsine O'Riordan and Jakob Horstmann.

Rebecca is very grateful for all the encouragement and support she received from friends and family, especially her parents, Adrian and Katherine Holmes, as well as from Samantha Kuflik, Laura Robey and Vaijayanti Gupte. She particularly thanks her husband, Jaideep Gupte, whose consistent motivation and encouragement made completion of this book possible.

Nicola would also like to thank her parents, Allan and Sue Jones, for all their support, and her husband, Paul Presler, for his forbearance during yet more burning of the midnight oil.

Lastly, we would like to thank our little daughters, Eleya, Kirah and Shabanna, for their patience while their mothers were distracted by yet another early morning or evening at the computer…

List of abbreviations

ADB	Asian Development Bank
ADF	African Development Fund
AIDS	Acquired Immune Deficiency Syndrome
ASCRA	Accumulating Savings and Credit Association
AusAID	Australian Agency for International Development
BISP	Benazir Income Support Programme, Pakistan
BPFA	Beijing Platform for Action
BRAC	Building Resources Across Communities, Bangladesh
CCT	Conditional Cash Transfer
CEDAW	Convention on the Elimination of All Forms of Discrimination against Women
CFPR	Challenging the Frontiers of Poverty Reduction programme, Bangladesh
CLIC	Community LEAP Implementing Committees, Ghana
CPRC	Chronic Poverty Research Centre
CSA	Central Statistical Agency, Ethiopia
DAW	United Nations Division for the Advancement of Women
DFID	Department for International Development, UK
DLICs	District LEAP Implementing Committees, Ghana
ECLAC	Economic Commission for Latin America and the Caribbean
EPWP	Expanded Public Works Programme, South Africa
ESCAP	Economic and Social Commission for Asia and the Pacific
FAO	Food and Agriculture Organization of the United Nations
GAD	Gender and Development
ICRW	International Center for Research on Women
IDS	Institute of Development Studies
IFAD	International Fund for Agricultural Development
IFPRI	International Food Policy Research Institute
ILO	International Labour Organization
LEAP	Livelihood Empowerment Against Poverty, Ghana

LIPWP	Labour-Intensive Public Works Programme, Botswana
MDG	Millennium Development Goal
MGNREGS	Mahatma Gandhi National Rural Employment Guarantee Scheme, India
MoFED	Ministry of Finance and Economic Development, Ethiopia
MOLISA	Ministry of Labor, Invalids and Social Affairs, Vietnam
MoRD	Ministry of Rural Development, India
MPU	Micro Projects Unit, Zambia
NGO	Non-Governmental Organisation
NTPPR	National Targeted Programme for Poverty Reduction, Vietnam
ODI	Overseas Development Institute
OECD	Organisation for Economic Co-operation and Development
OFSP	Other Food Security Programme, Ethiopia
PSNP	Productive Safety Net Programme, Ethiopia
PWP	Public Works Programmes
RAFAD	Research and Applications for Alternative Financing for Development
RMP	Rural Maintenance Program, Bangladesh
ROSCA	Rotating Savings and Credit Association
SEWA	Self-Employed Women's Association, India
STUP	Specially Targeted Ultra Poor
UCT	Unconditional Cash Transfer
UNAIDS	Joint United Nations Programme on HIV/AIDS
UNDP	United Nations Development Programme
UNICEF	United Nations Children's Fund
UNIFEM	United Nations Development Fund for Women
UNISDR	United Nations Office for Disaster Risk Reduction
UNODC	United Nations Office on Drugs and Crime
WFP	World Food Programme
WHO	World Health Organization
WID	Women in Development

Introduction: why social protection needs a gender lens

Social protection programmes – programmes aimed at reducing vulnerability and promoting individual, household and community resilience to shocks and stresses–have spread rapidly across the developing world since the mid-1990s. Cash transfer programmes are now being rolled out in more than 36 countries, in some cases reaching millions of households (Hanlon et al., 2010), there are over 150 public works programmes in sub-Saharan Africa alone (McCord, 2009), and pro-poor insurance programmes are now estimated to reach hundreds of millions of impoverished households (Churchill and McCord, 2012).

This increased commitment to social protection policies and programmes heralds an important opportunity to tackle diverse experiences of poverty and vulnerability in a globalised world. Already there is strong evidence demonstrating the benefits of social protection interventions for poor people, namely increased income, improved food security, a reduction in seasonal work deficits and increased access to basic services (Barrientos et al., 2010). Nonetheless, a closer look at current social protection programming highlights an important gap. Beyond the shorter-term alleviation of income poverty and vulnerability through 'safety nets', social protection has yet to fully realise its potential to address the underlying causes of vulnerability and the drivers of inequality to achieve social justice and socially equitable outcomes. In particular, there has been a striking absence of a gender-sensitive approach to social protection design and delivery, despite growing evidence and awareness of the pivotal role that gender inequality plays in causing and perpetuating poverty and vulnerability.

It is this book's contention, therefore, that if a clear gender analysis informed social protection instruments and their rollout, this would in turn support individuals' and households' movement out of poverty in the longer term, while simultaneously encouraging the attainment of broader development goals. Central to our argument is the premise that, for social protection to constitute more than a safety-net approach – that is, for it to achieve its transformational objectives – it must be gender-sensitive. For this to happen, social protection must go beyond a narrow focus targeting women in their capacity as mothers, and also support women's and girls' empowerment and gender equity aims more strategically, including vis-à-vis domestic and care work within the household, access to income and asset generation opportunities, agency and voice within and beyond the household, and participation in community decision making.

Beyond mothers and safety nets: the argument for a gender-sensitive approach to social protection

In order to highlight the urgent demand for gender-sensitive social protection, we begin with a quote and a personal narrative to illustrate the reality of girls' and women's everyday experience of multi-dimensional poverty and vulnerability.

"If girls don't pass Grade 10, they generally don't retake the exam but instead sit at home and support the family and wait to get married. However, if boys don't succeed in education, they work in groups in trading activities. They have a good life – they get a job or can continue their education. Even if they start as daily labourers they can then earn enough money to trade in charcoal/ wood – they have a really good life – they can even buy a house in town. But girls, even if they earn 200–300 birr, this is usually absorbed by the family. They can't go off and be independent like boys. Supporting the family is in our nature, we can't take the risk of going independent. ... But men don't give you enough respect if your economic situation is weak ..." (Adolescent girl, Shibhta, Ethiopia, 2009, quoted in Jones et al., 2010).

Anu is from a Scheduled Caste community and lives in a poor household in rural Madhya Pradesh in India. She recently lost her job cooking midday meals at the local school, and received no compensation. Caste discrimination is still part of her daily experience in her village. There are limited income-generating opportunities, and Anu, as a Scheduled Caste woman, receives less payment for the same daily labouring work as men or higher-caste women. Anu cares for her mother- and father-in-law, as well as her blind brother-in-law. The latter receives a disability allowance of Rs. 150 (approximately $3) per month, but Anu says this is not sufficient to cover the costs of his care.

Anu and her family live in a mountainous area where crop production has suffered in recent years. In order to manage, her household employs a range of coping mechanisms, including migrating to Gujarat for employment and taking out loans, but these strategies are often detrimental in the long term. Interest rates are high and job opportunities and pay are low, particularly for Anu. Moreover, it is often Anu who bears the brunt of scarcity – for instance, she eats least and last when food is limited.

Like many other women in her village, although Anu is responsible for managing the household – caring for family members and carrying out the domestic chores as well as finding waged employment – she wields little power in her household over decision making beyond that on small household purchases, and requires permission from male family members to go to the market or the health centre. Whereas younger girls in her village now have greater opportunities to go to school and can marry later, girls are still more likely than boys to drop out of school as a result of domestic responsibilities or teenage pregnancy. This not only effectively limits their life choices but also contributes to women's lower status within the household.

Anu's personal narrative resonates with the lives of many women living in poverty in different parts of the world. Although there is significant context variation, in many countries women are represented disproportionately among the poor, with poor women and girls most likely to experience lifelong poverty as a consequence of gender inequality and discrimination (Chronic Poverty Research Centre, 2009). That is not to say that men and boys do not also suffer from inequalities and discrimination which trap them in poverty, but that more often, as a consequence of culturally and socially ascribed roles and responsibilities, women and girls not only have fewer income and asset generation opportunities, but also face greater social risks and vulnerabilities. These include early marriage, gender-based violence and traditional harmful practices such as son preference, limited physical mobility outside the house and greater time poverty, which all contribute to heightened poverty and vulnerability rates. Moreover, the strategies available to women to enable them to cope with such poverty and vulnerability differ from and are often more limited than those available to men.

Given these differential experiences of poverty and vulnerability, initiatives to promote gender equality are key for two reasons. First, gender equality is a basic human right and intrinsically important. Secondly, the promotion of greater gender equality can enhance economic efficiency and social development outcomes.

Evidence from around the world has demonstrated positive economic and social outcomes of tackling the barriers and constraints that women and girls face. Estimates suggest that, if women farmers were offered equal access to productive resources, agricultural output in developing countries could increase by as much as 2.5–4%; if barriers preventing women from working in certain occupations were eliminated, labour productivity could increase by 3–25% across a range of countries (Food and Agriculture Organization of the United Nations, 2011). Improving women's endowments, opportunities and agency can in turn promote more positive outcomes for the next generation. Enhanced decisionmaking power for women has been linked to a range of desirable outcomes, particularly those related to child well-being (Hoddinott and Haddad, 1995; Quisumbing and Maluccio, 2000; Thomas, 1990). And, at the beginning of the lifecycle, ensuring that girls are educated has numerous positive effects, including delayed marriage and pregnancy, a reduction in the risk of HIV and AIDS, increased household income, lower net fertility, better survival, health and education outcomes for future children, increased decision-making power within the household and community, and reduced gender-based violence rates (Agarwal, 1997; de Walque, 2004; Jones et al., 2010a; Khandkar, 1998; Kishor and Johnson, 2004; Lloyd and Young, 2009; Mathur et al., 2003; Morrison and Sabarwal, 2008; Pitt and Khandkar, 1998; UN Children's Fund, 2006b).

Many gender gaps have narrowed as a result of economic development where higher incomes and improved service delivery have, for instance, increased participation of women in the labour force or reduced the financial constraints on sending girls to school (World Bank, 2011b). However, not all gender gaps can be closed through economic measures alone, especially when poverty is combined with other forms of exclusion and deprivation, such as those related to geographical remoteness, insecurity and ethnicity (Bradshaw, 2002; World Bank, 2011b). Indeed, gender inequalities persist as a result of multiple constraints, including, for instance, institutional bias and embedded socio-cultural norms and gender roles (Kabeer, 1997; Sen, 2008). Promoting gender equity therefore requires that poverty reduction measures not only increase income but also tackle the structural and social causes of poverty and vulnerability. Recognising the impact of gender inequalities on women, men, girls and boys and addressing these are therefore critical to the effectiveness of policies and programmes that aim to reduce poverty and vulnerability.

In recent years, especially since the late 1990s, social protection has become an important policy response to high levels of poverty and vulnerability in developing countries, and has gained significant momentum among governments and donors as a result of demonstrating positive effects on reducing poverty and vulnerability, especially in the short term (Barrientos et al., 2010).

Social protection interventions have emerged in developing countries in particular as a buffer against severe economic shocks or continued chronic poverty, especially among vulnerable population groups. For instance, the rapid rise in poverty and vulnerability in Latin America and East Asia during the 1990s as a result of regional macroeconomic shocks, and the threat of social unrest and conflict that this presented, led to strengthened social protection policies and programmes (Barrientos and Hulme, 2008). In Latin America, governments inspired by the pioneering examples of Brazil and Mexico responded with a proliferation of conditional cash transfers across the region in response to the effects of the structural adjustment policies of the 1990s. The East Asian crisis during 1997–1998 prompted strong national policy commitments to social protection in several countries in the region, notably Indonesia, South Korea and Thailand. A number of countries in

South Asia have a longer history of social protection interventions, which are now being built on through a range of innovative and increasingly large-scale programmes, such as India's national public works programme. In comparison, coverage of social protection has been slower in sub-Saharan Africa. Recurrent food crises and the rise of HIV and AIDS have been major causes of vulnerability, pushing governments and donors alike to move away from emergency food aid programming to more predictable safety nets, including public works programmes aimed at building sustainable and resilient livelihoods (especially in Ethiopia and South Africa), as well as social transfers to those unable to work or with high household dependency ratios (including larger-scale initiatives in Ghana, Kenya and South Africa).

As such, social protection now constitutes an important component of poverty reduction approaches in many countries. However, most interventions focus on a shorter-term safety-net approach – smoothing income and consumption. Although this is of course an important objective, more recently there have been calls for social protection to go beyond this and to address the longer-term and structural causes of poverty rather than simply the symptoms. However, there has been very little attention to the importance of the social inequalities – such as gender inequality – that perpetuate poverty. Considerations of gender inequality too often focus only on women's immediate practical needs, are added on as an afterthought, or are left out of social protection programme design and implementation altogether. Moreover, although it is not expected that social protection can address all the root causes of gender inequality (for instance, tackling deeply embedded socio-cultural norms with regard to women's extra-household mobility, or inheritance practices that discriminate against women) our argument is that it could contribute to tackling a broader array of economic and social inequalities than has been recognised. Many social protection programmes have simply targeted women and/or girls without thinking through the possible change pathways that are needed to bring about empowerment and gender equity.

We aim to highlight the fact that the role of gender in social protection is more complex than this. Gender affects the types of risks that programmes seek to cushion people against, the choice of programme approach adopted, awareness-raising strategies, public buy-in and, arguably most important of all, programme outcomes. Indeed, simply targeting women or girls risks reinforcing traditional gender roles and responsibilities and overlooking important life-cycle and relational vulnerabilities that curtail economic and broader empowerment opportunities. This is not to argue that social protection should be seen as a magic bullet for addressing gender inequalities and their contribution to development deficits. Rather, there is an urgent need to approach existing shortcomings in social protection outcomes using a gender lens in order to strengthen programme impacts.

This may be achieved directly through more strategic programme design and rollout, or indirectly through coordinated and institutionalised linkages with complementary initiatives aimed at reducing gender inequalities and enhancing women's and girls' empowerment.

In order to better integrate a gender perspective into social protection programming, it is therefore vital to complement our collective understanding of the economic risks and vulnerabilities that cause and perpetuate poverty with a better appreciation of social risks and vulnerabilities, many of which are gendered (e.g. time poverty, gender-based violence, unequal intra-household and community decision-making power), and the ways in which these frequently intersect with and reinforce economic factors. Identifying the way that these gender dynamics across the lifecycle shape policy and programme impacts – both intended and unintended – is a complex endeavour. However, we argue that with relatively simple design changes and investment in implementation capacity there is the potential for social protection to contribute to transforming gender relationships at the individual, intra-household and community levels. Such changes do, however, need to be informed by an understanding of the way in which gender relationships are reflected within broader political economy dynamics that shape how programmes unfold on the ground in practice. This includes recognising the gendered assumptions that underpin the social protection goals and implementation approaches of national and local government actors, donors, non-governmental organisations and civil society groups.

Our starting premise, therefore, is that a strategic social protection framework and context-sensitive package of social protection instruments could make an important contribution to addressing men's, women's, boys' and girls' differential experiences of poverty and vulnerability, and should thus be embedded within longer-term social protection policy and programme aspirations. To this end, we identify six cross-cutting themes which emerge throughout the book and are explored further in the following chapters in relation to their importance in promoting a more gender-sensitive approach to social protection:

1   the relative influence of gendered economic and social risk analysis in informing social protection policy and programme design
2   implementation capacities of actors delivering programmes, including issues related to fiscal space
3   opportunities and challenges for institutional coordination and linkages
4   the quality and potential of the community–programme interface (i.e. regular interactions between community participants and implementing agencies' officers)
5   gendered political economy dynamics
6   monitoring and evaluation, knowledge exchange and lesson learning.

Methodology

Our book draws on primary evidence as well as a global review of secondary literature on gender and social protection in the developing world. Primary data was gathered over the course of a multi-year programme of research which explored the extent to which gender has been incorporated into the design, implementation and evaluation of a wide range of flagship social protection programmes that are reaching tens or hundreds of thousands of households, or in some cases even millions of families.

Together with national partners from eight countries (please see Acknowledgements section), we undertook primary qualitative and quantitative data collection with programme beneficiaries and programme implementers across four regions (Latin America, South Asia, South-East Asia and sub-Saharan Africa) between 2009 and 2012. In each of the country case studies,[1] four research sites (rural villages) in two districts (or the equivalent) were selected, drawing on a purposive matched sampling technique. This involved selecting two communities from each district with a similar poverty ranking, which was neither transient nor extreme poor (i.e. 'middling poor'), where the social protection programme in question was being implemented.

Our mixed methods approach included key informant interviews, focus group discussions and life histories with poor women, men and children across different stages of the lifecycle. In each country, 16 focus group discussions with women, men, girls and boys were used to tease out details of the impacts (both direct and indirect) of the social protection programme at individual, household and community levels. The use of in-depth life histories (with eight beneficiaries representing different life/social stages from adolescence to old age) allowed for a more detailed exploration of individuals' gendered experiences of risk and vulnerability, and provided insights into the relative importance of the social protection programme in diverse individuals' lives. Key informant interviews were also carried out using semi-structured questionnaires, while a small quantitative household survey was conducted in Ethiopia, Ghana, India, Indonesia, Peru and Vietnam, with 100 social protection programme households in each case.

Given the comparatively small sample size of the primary research methodology that was employed, a global review of secondary quantitative and qualitative data was used to triangulate the empirical findings. It is important to note, however, that there is significant variation in the availability of rigorous research across countries both on the gendered patterning of poverty and vulnerability, and on the impacts of social protection on gender equity and empowerment. With the important exception of analyses of cash and asset transfers, the relative dearth of rigorous impact evaluations of social protection in relation to gender means that, especially for some social protection instruments, including subsidy and pro-poor insurance programmes, the evidence base is very limited and fragmented.

Accordingly, although this book discusses a broad range of social protection programme initiatives, we focus on a smaller number of programmes in greater depth in order to assess in a more nuanced way how gender dynamics play out in social protection instruments implemented in a variety of political, socio-economic, cultural and spatial contexts. These include the following:

1. *Cash transfers* – conditional and non-conditional regular cash payments given to poor households, often caregivers:

   - Ghana's Livelihood Empowerment Against Poverty (LEAP) quasi-conditional cash transfer, reaching 68,000 households in 100 districts in March 2012
   - Peru's *Juntos* programme, reaching 492,000 households in 2012
   - Pakistan's Benazir Income Support Programme (BISP), reaching 2.8 million beneficiaries in 2010.

2. *Asset transfers* – transfers of productive assets (e.g. small livestock)to support income generation activities of poor households:

   - Bangladesh's Challenging the Frontiers of Poverty Reduction (CFPR) programme, reaching 412,700 households (1.44 million population) from 2002 to 2012.

3. *Public works programmes* – provision of cash or food payments in return for labour to build community assets, typically physical infrastructure:

   - India's Mahatma Gandhi National Rural Employment Guarantee Scheme (MGNREGS), reaching just over 50 million households in 2011–2012
   - Ethiopia's Productive Safety Net Programme (PSNP), reaching over 7.6 million chronically poor individuals in 2012.

4. *Subsidies* – subsidised or free services (e.g. health, education, childcare, agriculture) and/or food (e.g. rice rations):

   - Mexico's community child crèche system, *Estancias*, creating 9,500 day care centres, which 200,000 children are attending in 2012
   - Vietnam's National Targeted Programme for Poverty Reduction (NTPPR), reaching up to 6 million individuals in 2009
   - Indonesia's *Raskin* rice subsidy programme, reaching 18.5 million households in 2010.

Our discussion of these programmes is complemented by personal narratives of women, men, girls and boys, which are designed to illustrate the complex ways in which economic and social vulnerabilities affect people's experiences of poverty and vulnerability at different stages of the lifecycle, and to showcase the benefits – and the challenges – of current social protection

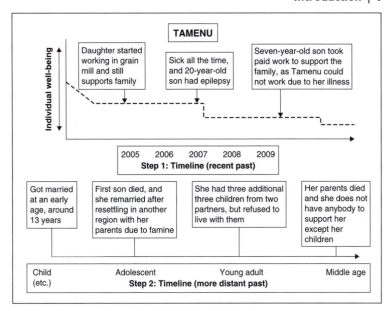

Figure 0.1 Life story of Tamenu (Ethiopian older woman)

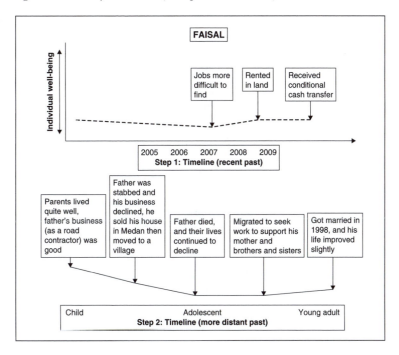

Figure 0.2 Life story of Faisal (Indonesian adult man)

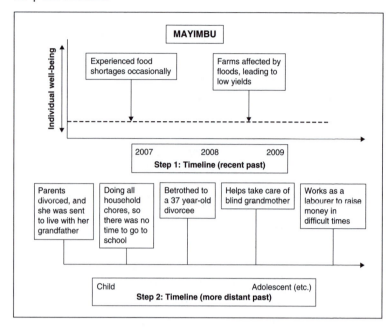

Figure 0.3 Life story of Mayimbu (adolescent girl, Ghana)

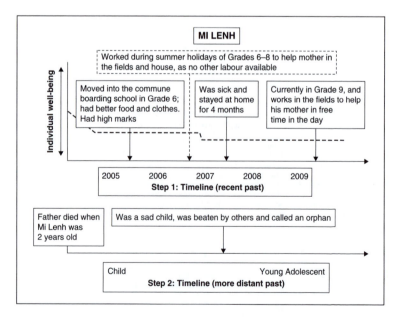

Figure 0.4 Life story of MiLenh (adolescent boy, Vietnam)

approaches to address these vulnerabilities. Figures 0.1 to 0.4 illustrate four of these life histories pictorially, giving a sense of the types of poverty traps and trajectories that women, men, girls and boys often face.

Structure of the book

The book is organised into two parts. The first part (Chapters 1 and 2) sets the context for understanding the importance of promoting a gender lens in social protection.

Chapter 1, entitled 'Key concepts in gender and social protection', discusses concepts relating to poverty, vulnerability, gender and social protection. It first explores what we mean by poverty, vulnerability and resilience, and then reflects on what feminist approaches to development have contributed to these debates. It next identifies key conceptual frameworks on the role of social protection in reducing poverty and vulnerability and the ways in which they have shaped our understanding of policy and programming instruments. We build on the Transformative Social Protection Framework, which recognises the interconnectedness of both economic and social risks, and extends the focus of social protection to arenas such as equity, empowerment and economic, social and cultural rights. We then consider the contributions of feminist theory to social protection policy and programme approaches. We argue that there is a considerable disconnect between gender and social protection, despite the importance of their integration in practice for poverty reduction and well-being outcomes. The rest of the chapter presents our framework which integrates a gender lens into social protection by looking at how economic and social risks are gendered from the macro-environment through to the individual level.

Drawing on this conceptual framework, Chapter 2, entitled 'The gendered patterning of vulnerability, risk and resilience', provides an overview of the ways in which poverty and vulnerability are gendered, paying particular attention to economic and social risks, how they intersect at the individual, household and community level, and how they are changing in the context of rapid globalisation at the national level. The chapter then discusses resilience and the differential coping strategies and resources that men and women have at their disposal. These include drawing on 'traditional' reciprocity and care, mutual assistance mechanisms, social capital, faith-based support and remittances, on the one hand, and resorting to adverse coping mechanisms such as indebtedness, adverse sales of assets, and risky behaviours, such as transactional sex, on the other.

The second part of the book discusses the evidence on the design, implementation and effects of social protection on gender equity and its role in promoting women's empowerment. It is divided into four chapters on social protection instruments – cash and asset transfers, public works, pro-poor insurance and subsidies – as well as a chapter on political economy dynamics, followed by conclusions and recommendations.

Chapter 3, entitled 'Transferring income and assets: assessing the contribution to gender-sensitive poverty reduction', looks at the evidence on cash and asset transfers to poor households. It examines the highly contested question: Have social transfers simply reinforced traditional roles for women as 'mothers at the service of the state', or are they a key tool for women's empowerment? The chapter argues that evidence from transfers targeting women has indeed been positive with regard to the promotion of gender equity in a number of areas, including girls' education and women's status within the household, but programmes have also had negative effects, such as exacerbating women's time poverty. In addition, although women have gained household status and respect, in only a few programmes has this change started to alter gendered divisions of labour, power imbalances and opportunities for women outside the household. The chapter looks at the reasons for this paradox, drawing in particular on case studies from Bangladesh, Ghana and Peru.

Chapter 4, entitled 'Working one's way out of poverty: public works through a gender lens', discusses the extent to which public works programmes – programmes which provide cash or food payments in exchange for labour inputs – have adopted a gender-sensitive approach in their design and implementation. It examines whether public works programmes can help to address gendered labour market inequalities, or whether they simply reflect and reinforce them. The analysis begins with a global review of public works programmes from a gender lens. It then focuses in more depth on two case studies, namely India's Mahatma Gandhi National Rural Employment Guarantee Scheme, which is the largest legally guaranteed labour-based programme in the world, and Ethiopia's Productive Safety Net Programme, which reaches over 7.6 million chronically food-insecure individuals.

Chapter 5, entitled 'Insuring against shocks: the gendered dimensions of insurance', begins by reviewing understandings of pro-poor insurance given limited consensus in the literature, and identifies a number of cross-cutting gender dimensions of pro-poor insurance programmes. It then assesses how gender dynamics play out in informal insurance mechanisms, including rotating savings and loans groups, non-rotating accumulated savings associations and burial societies. Finally, the chapter discusses the extent to which gender is considered in the programme design, implementation and impacts of formal insurance approaches – both social insurance, such as unemployment-based insurance, social health insurance and maternal health coverage, and micro-insurance programmes, such as life, health and disaster insurance. Reviewing existing good practices, the discussion focuses on what design and implementation features are necessary in order to help to mitigate general and gender-specific risks.

Chapter 6, entitled 'Ensuring access to state provision: towards more gender-sensitive subsidy schemes', uses a gender lens to discuss the design and implementation of subsidy programmes which support consumption and basic service access for the poor. Subsidies can include a wide range of objectives, including improving the real purchasing power of consumers, addressing calorie and nutrient deficiencies, supporting labour market participation, and assuring social and political stability. The chapter examines five types of subsidy programmes, namely food, agricultural, basic service (health and education), childcare and integrated subsidies. It highlights the challenges associated with incorporating gender-sensitive design and implementation into food and productive-oriented subsidies, while discussing the benefits of gender-sensitive subsidies in the social sector – that is, education, health and childcare.

Chapter 7, entitled 'Why politics matters: a gendered political economy approach to social protection', seeks to answer the important question of *why*, despite the evidence relating to the importance of gender equality, women's rights and women's empowerment, social protection has largely failed to sufficiently incorporate a gender lens. The chapter employs a framework that draws on political economy literature and a focus on the so-called 'three Is' – institutions, interests and ideas – to analyse why mainstream development actors have largely overlooked the role of gender in shaping these. We explore the opportunities or constraints that institutional arenas (such as elections and party politics, the legislature, the judiciary and informal politics) present in the negotiation of social protection policy and programme development. We also assess the interests of key actors and the relative balance of power between them in order to identify who is likely to gain or lose from policy shifts (e.g. political elites, bureaucratic agencies, donors and civil society champions). Finally, we explore the ideas held by elites and the public about poverty and its causes, the social contract between state and citizens, and the merits of particular forms of state support.

The concluding chapter, 'Conclusions and recommendations: advancing gender-sensitive social protection', synthesises the main arguments from across the chapters in the book and discusses their implications for more effective mainstreaming of gender in social protection policy and practice. We argue that relatively simple design changes and an investment in strategic implementation and evaluation practices will enhance the benefits of social protection in terms of promoting gender equity and girls' and women's empowerment, and by extension will improve the effectiveness of social protection, to reduce poverty and vulnerability and enhance resilience for all. Our book therefore aims to fill an important gap in the social protection evidence base and to serve as an essential resource for the increasingly diverse research, policy and programme actors in the international development field with an interest in social protection.

ONE

Key concepts in gender and social protection

Introduction

In recent decades, there have been considerable efforts to investigate the range of factors that may contribute to, and perpetuate, poverty across the life-course. This has resulted in increased understanding of whether and how policies to reduce pervasive poverty and inequality need to be broadened beyond those focused on consumption and income measures alone, to include objectives of social justice and well-being.

Indeed, international development discourse has become increasingly concerned with the multidimensional nature of poverty, including the role of social sources of risk and vulnerability – such as gender inequality, social discrimination, unequal distribution of resources and power and limited citizenship – in shaping how particular individuals and groups experience poverty (Chronic Poverty Research Centre, 2009). The inter- sections between economic and social sources of risks and vulnerabilities are also increasingly recognised as critical problems that need to be addressed in development policies and programmes by enhancing individual capabilities and promoting household and community resilience (Chambers, 1989; Nussbaum, 1995; Sen, 1999).

Gender inequality influences both economic and social sources of risk, at different levels – from the macro to the micro. Much work has been done by feminist economists and social scientists to further our understanding of the links and intersections between gender inequality and poverty, drawing attention to structural inequalities in, for example, the labour market, care economy and household (Chant, 2008; Folbre, 2006; Kabeer, 1994). The application of these theoretical insights to empirical research has generated sound evidence of the role that gender inequality at national, community and household levels plays in contributing to poverty and vulnerability and impeding economic growth. As such, promoting gender equity – which is the process of being fair to women and men – through strategies to compensate for the disadvantages that women face will lead to gender equality – that is, women and men will enjoy equal opportunities, resources and rewards (International Labour Organization, 2007a). Addressing gender inequalities through a range of legislation, policies and programmes, it is argued, is not only imperative from a rights perspective, but will also help to reduce poverty and vulner-ability, enhance capabilities and make it possible to meet the objectives of social justice and well-being (Chant, 2010). Unfortunately, however, the evidence base on the gendered dynamics of economic and social risks and vulnerabilities – and their intersection – has been only weakly reflected in social protection theory, policy and programming, despite the importance of gender equity for development outcomes (Molyneux, 2006; Sabates-Wheeler and Kabeer, 2003).

This chapter provides an overview of key concepts and analytical frameworks that are central to our argument about gender and social protection. We begin by discussing what we mean by poverty, vulnerability and resilience, and then reflect on what feminist approaches to development have contributed to these debates. Next, we identify key conceptual frameworks on the role of social protection in reducing poverty and vulnerability, and the ways in which they have shaped our understanding of policy and programming instruments, before finally considering the contributions of feminist theory to social protection policy and programme approaches. We argue that there is a considerable disconnect between these bodies of thought, despite the importance of their integration in practice for poverty reduction and well-being outcomes. Therefore, in the final section of this chapter, we reflect on the range of entry points through which a gender lens could be applied to social protection, and draw on this framework in our analysis of social protection instruments throughout the book.

Concepts of poverty and vulnerability

Until the 1990s, income and/or consumption were the main measures of poverty used by development actors and agencies. Money-metric approaches to measuring poverty were favoured for a number of reasons, including the fact that they are aggregates of multiple inputs, expressed in units that are of immediate and widespread relevance, relatively simple to calculate and theoretically objective (Dessallien, 1999). However, such approaches also have a number of limitations, relating not only to problems such as price and commodity differentials, but also to the exclusion of non-cash factors (Dessallien, 1999). As such, since the 1990s, there has been greater recognition of the multidimensionality of poverty and the importance of non-income indicators at the household and intra-household level (see, for instance, Ravallion, 1992). Indeed, increasingly, concepts and measurements of poverty have expanded to incorporate a view of the underlying structural inequities and inherent disadvantages that the poor face (Chronic Poverty Research Centre, 2009; UN Children's Fund, 2012). Therefore, even when resources are targeted at the poor, those individuals may not be able to take advantage of them because of structural constraints that impede access to productive assets (such as land and credit) as well as physical, social and human capital assets (such as health, nutrition and education).

The causes of these constraints lie in unequal power relations and weak governance structures, as well as inequities embedded in macro-policy frameworks and distributional systems (Dessallien, 1999). In promoting this perspective, Amartya Sen's capability approach (Sen, 1985) was pivotal. This approach is concerned with what individuals can do – what they are capable of – with poverty understood as capability deprivation. It focuses on opportunities, equity and well-being through the economic, social, political and cultural dimensions of life. Nussbaum (1995) took the approach further, also recognising the gendered differences of experiences of poverty and vulnerability. These conceptualisations advanced the understanding of poverty as well-being, which includes access to and control over resources, rights and freedoms, and sought to unravel the multiple deprivations and their underlying causes faced by poor households. They also led to advances in measuring aspects of human development in the 1990s (moving beyond income indicators) and, more recently, the Multidimensional Poverty Index of Alkire and Santos (2010), and the Social Institutions and Gender Index of the Organisation for Economic Co-operation and Development (2012), which is concerned with the role that socio-cultural norms and practices play in shaping women's economic productivity.

Much research has also been undertaken on the dynamic nature of poverty. Analysts have examined why some households move in and out of poverty while others remain in chronic poverty over generations. They have also explored the importance of life-course and intergenerational poverty (Bradshaw, 2002; Chronic Poverty Research Centre, 2009). Efforts to understand the factors that affect a household's vulnerability to poverty – that is, the likelihood that a household will become poor (or poorer) in the future – must therefore consider both the exposure to the risk that a household faces and the household's ability to cope with the risk (Chambers, 1989; Sabates-Wheeler and Devereux, 2008). Risk and vulnerability are critical concepts in social protection. Risks (or shocks and stresses) can be covariate (affecting whole communities, such as floods) or idiosyncratic (affecting individuals or households, such as illness). They are often regarded as exogenous and economic (such as the global financial crisis or food-price spikes), or environmental (such as floods or drought). However, not all adverse events come from outside, nor are they all shocks. Whereas shocks have a rapid onset and are unpredictable, such as sudden illness, stresses have a slower onset and can be more predictable, such as old age, or include events such as weddings or environmental degradation, deforestation and declining soil fertility (Farrington et al., 2007).

Vulnerability refers to the susceptibility of households to the risk of a shock or stress. While not all households are poor, all households may be vulnerable, but vulnerability to risk is influenced by numerous factors, such as individual and household demography, age, dependency ratios, location, social capital, ownership of assets and access to resources. Shocks are also not only economic or social, but also include physical (e.g. ill health), political (e.g. insecurity) and environmental events. Vulnerability is not just a factor of a household's income level, but is also shaped by underlying structural socio-political factors (Devereux and Sabates-Wheeler, 2004).

In addition to exposure to shocks or stresses, we are concerned with a households coping abilities in such contexts, and here notions of resilience – the ability to recover from or adapt to shocks – are key (Chambers, 1989; Sabates-Wheeler and Devereux, 2008; Drimie and Casale, 2009). Coping strategies have most often been proxied by income, consumption or asset profiles, resulting in an economic approach to vulnerability, risk and risk management (Sabates-Wheeler and Devereux, 2008). However, resilience is more complex than the capacity to cope with economic negative events (Sabates-Wheeler and Devereux, 2008). Indeed, Sen's capability approach also recognises the importance of social and cultural resources in shaping an individual's resilience. We return to these themes in our discussion on social protection frameworks below, but first we will review core concepts relating to gender and development.

Concepts of gender in development

What is gender?

Gender is a 'social relationship, historically varying, and encompassing elements of labour, power, emotion and language; it crosses individual subjectivities, institutions, culture and language' (Orloff, 2009:1). It is a socially constructed concept, referring to women's and men's different roles and responsibilities determined by social, economic, political and cultural factors. These are interpreted differently in different societies and cultures, but in many contexts they translate into inequality in resources, responsibilities, opportunities and constraints, especially for women (Pearson et al., 1984; Razavi and Miller, 1995). As Kabeer and Subrahmanian (1996) suggest, not all women are poor, and not all poor people are women, but all women have the potential to suffer from discrimination.

Feminist theory and practice have sought to explain and change systems of difference whereby 'women' and 'men' are socially constituted and positioned in relations of hierarchy. However, this is a complex endeavour. As with the poverty debate mentioned earlier, income poverty has often also dominated discussions on gender inequality. Increasingly, however, discussions are focusing on whether tackling income poverty is the most effective strategy for solving women's disadvantage. More 'robust' indicators of women's poverty include access to land, agency in decision making, legal rights within the family, vulnerability to violence, self-respect and dignity (Johnsson-Latham, 2004), as well as overwork, time deficiency, dependency and powerlessness (Chant, 1997; Kabeer, 1997; Sen, 1999). Such inequalities cannot be remedied by income alone, as they lie at the heart of deeper inequalities entrenched in patriarchal structures and socio-cultural norms (Molyneux and Razavi, 2002).

Why is gender important for development?

There is a dual rationale for promoting gender equality, and it is vital that both rationales feature as policy priorities. First, equality between women and men – equal rights, opportunities and responsibilities – is a human right and a matter of social justice. Equality between men and women is enshrined in international conventions such as the Universal Declaration of Human Rights and the Convention on the Elimination of All Forms of Discrimination Against Women (CEDAW). Secondly, greater equity between women and men can support economic growth and development outcomes, including well-being and resilience with regard to future poverty.

Box 1.1 Addressing gender inequality leads to poverty reduction, economic growth and enhanced household resilience

The costs of gender discrimination to economic growth and development outcomes are significant. Global evidence demonstrates that investing in gender equality and women's empowerment leads to enhanced productivity and improved social development outcomes.

Gender gaps in South Asia and the Middle East and North Africa cost up to 1.7% in growth (Klasen and Lamanna, 2009). The UN estimates that, in the Asian region alone, about $47 billion of yearly output are lost every year due to a lack of female participation in labour markets (Economic and Social Commission for Asia and the Pacific, 2007). If female labour force participation in India was similar to that in the USA, India's gross domestic product would increase by 4.2% a year and its growth would be 1.08% higher (Economic and Social Commission for Asia and the Pacific, 2007).

Eliminating barriers that prevent women from working in certain occupations or sectors would also have positive effects, reducing the productivity gap between male and female workers by one-third to one-half and increasing output per worker by 3–25% across a range of countries (Cuberes and Teignier Baqué, 2011; Hurst et al., 2011, cited in World Bank, 2011b).

Countries with educated and empowered women have higher rates of economic growth and gross national product (Dollar and Gatti, 1999). Conversely, countries with high gender disparities in education enrolment are estimated to have a gross national product up to 25% lower compared with countries where there is almost gender parity (Hill and King, 1995). If South Asia and sub-Saharan Africa had had more balanced educational achievements in 1960, and had done more to promote gender-balanced growth in education, their economic growth could have been up to 0.9% faster per year. Every year, Cameroon, the Democratic Republic of the Congo and Nigeria lose $974 million, $301 million and $1,662 million, respectively, as a result of failing to educate girls to the same standards as boys (Plan, 2008).

Gender inequality also impedes social development outcomes. Improving women's endowments, opportunities and agency can in turn promote more positive outcomes for the next generation. Enhanced decision-making power for women has been linked to a range of desirable outcomes, particularly those related to child well-being (Hoddinott and Haddad, 1995; Quisumbing and Maluccio, 2000; Thomas, 1990). Increasing women's control over household resources and the share of household income that is controlled by women changes household expenditure patterns in such a way as to benefit children in particular. In Brazil, women's own income has a positive impact on daughters' height, and in China, an increase in female income by 10% of the average household income increases the proportion of surviving girls by one percentage point and years of schooling for both girls and boys (World Bank, 2011b).

At the beginning of the lifecycle, ensuring that girls are educated has numerous positive effects, including delayed marriage and pregnancy, a reduced risk of HIV and AIDS, increased household income, lower net fertility, better survival, health and education outcomes for future children, increased decision-making power within the household and community, and reduced gender-based violence rates (Agarwal, 1997; de Walque, 2004; Jones et al., 2010a; Khandkar, 1998; Kishor and Johnson, 2004; Lloyd and Young, 2009; Mathur et al., 2003; Morrison and Sabarwal, 2008; Pitt and Khandkar, 1998; UN Children's Fund, 2006b). For instance, a large, cross-national study found that doubling the proportion of girls who completed secondary education (from 19% to 38%) would reduce infant mortality rates from 81 to 38 per 1,000 live births (Subbarao and Raney, 1995).

From 'women in development' to 'gender and development':
evolution of addressing gender in development discourse

Despite the importance of gender equity for development outcomes, it is only since the mid-1990s that national and international actors have taken a more strategic approach to promoting women's and girls' empowerment. The UN Commission on the Status of Women was established in 1946, but gender remained largely invisible in development discourse for several decades, beyond a focus on women as mothers or carers. Reflecting this, women's roles and responsibilities were seen solely in reproductive and domestic arenas in development policy and programming.

Starting in the 1970s, however, and influenced by the second international wave of feminism, attention was drawn to the importance of women in international development circles in a way that made their roles and needs visible to policymakers. This prompted the 'women in development' (WID) approach. For instance, Esther Boserup's seminal work, which was published in 1970, provided evidence of women's critical contributions to agricultural productivity, which in turn supported the economic efficiency argument that women should not be seen merely as passive recipients of welfare programmes (in their roles of mother and carer), but rather as active contributors to economic development (Razavi and Miller, 1995).

At the same time, the mid-1970s marked the beginning of a series of UN world conferences on women's issues,[1] and the establishment in 1979 of Convention on the Elimination of All Forms of Discrimination against women (CEDAW), heralding an important step towards the explicit prohibition of discrimination against women. However, although these conferences provided an opportunity to advance women's rights internationally, they also highlighted deep divisions in attempting to apply principles universally,[2] and weaknesses in the WID approach, especially an over-reliance on the economic efficiency argument at the expense of social justice, and insufficient attention to the relational nature of women's subordination. WID identified women's individual lack of access to resources as the key to their subordination without raising questions about the role of gender relations in restricting women's access to such resources in the first place.

As a response, and reflecting work underway within various social science disciplines suggesting the importance of power, conflict and gender relations in understanding women's subordination (Razavi and Miller, 1995), by the early 1990s the WID approach had been replaced with a 'gender and development' (GAD) lens, focusing on the socially constructed basis of differences between women and men. GAD emphasised the need to challenge existing gender roles and relations and the imbalance of power between women and men for both economic and social justice outcomes. This paradigm shift was signalled perhaps most clearly by the Fourth World

Conference on Women in Beijing in 1995, culminating in the Beijing Platform for Action (BPFA). Beijing reoriented attention towards gender inequality and poverty in an unprecedented way, resulting in the creation and strengthening of programmes to combat poverty among women (Chant, 2010). These programmes included, for instance, microfinance schemes for women and the integration of gender issues into the subsequent Millennium Development Goals (e.g. promoting gender parity in primary education, empowering women and reducing maternal mortality).

In practice, the BPFA galvanised both national and international commitments and resources to develop legal frameworks for gender equity and to mainstream gender within development policy approaches across all sectors – both economic and social. It also motivated the establishment of national and sub-national gender architecture, such as dedicated ministries of women's empowerment/gender equality. Furthermore, the BPFA promoted the implementation of gender mainstreaming tools, such as the integration of gender focal points in ministries and departments, gender budgeting, the collection of gender-disaggregated data, and gender training at all levels. It also galvanised efforts to build strategic alliances with non-governmental organisations and other women's organisations.

In policy and programming terms, the GAD approach prompted a focus on empowerment and moved beyond supporting women's 'practical needs'– that is, immediate needs linked to women's socially accepted reproductive, domestic and productive roles within existing power structures – to address women's 'strategic needs' or interests which challenge male privileges and seek to change women's status in society in relation to men (Molyneuvx, 1985: 232–3). Empowerment efforts – with empowerment understood as the need to transform the nature of power relationships – emphasised change in three interrelated dimensions (Kabeer, 1999), namely resources (defined broadly to include not only access but also future claims to material, human and social resources), agency (including that in decision-making processes, as well as less measurable manifestations of agency, such as negotiation, deception and manipulation) and achievements (well-being outcomes).

However, poverty interventions have tended to be more occupied with addressing the *condition* of poor women (i.e. their material circumstances) rather than their *position* (their place and power within domestic unity and in wider society) (Johnson, 2005 cited in Chant, 2010). Moreover, despite more recent attention to the importance of masculinities and 'men and boys' in the gender approach, 'steps to improve women's poorer condition have rarely challenged men's condition *or* position' (Johnson, 2005:57, cited in Chant, 2010; emphasis in original). Yet without tackling women's position in the economic and domestic spheres, access to power and decision making, poverty cannot be addressed in a sustainable manner (Baden and Goetz, 1997; Kabeer, 1995).

Conceptualising social protection

Certain types of social protection interventions (e.g. in-kind transfers, food and service subsidies, public works schemes) have been in existence since the 1960s in developing countries (Ellis et al., 2009), although the term 'social protection' has only garnered political traction since the late 1990s. Social protection plays an important role in smoothing income and consumption, but increasingly it is expected to take a longer-term approach to tackling the multiple factors that cause persistent poverty and vulnerability (Ellis et al., 2009).

Since the 1990s a number of social protection frameworks have emerged, often with distinct (but also overlapping) concepts and definitions of social protection. A common definition of social protection is that provided by Norton et al. (2001:7), namely 'actions taken in response to levels of vulnerability, risk, and deprivation which are deemed socially unacceptable within a given polity or society.' Perspectives and ideologies about the role of the state have shaped the nature of, and commitment to, social protection in developing country contexts (Barrientos and Hulme, 2008; see also Chapter 7). In some countries, social protection is embedded in understandings of a state – citizen contract and citizen rights to a minimum standard of well-being; in others, it is driven largely by donor agencies and non-governmental organisations and concerns about promoting improvements in human capital (see Box 1.2).

A core element across the range of social protection conceptual frameworks is their focus on vulnerability (not just poverty), thus highlighting the dynamic nature of poverty (Barrientos and Hulme, 2008). However, these frameworks differ in their conceptualisations of poverty and vulnerability and as such their social protection responses to this (addressing economic risks, meeting basic needs or redressing social inequities), and subsequently the types of social protection policy approach involved.

The framework proposed by Guhan (1994), which sets out social security options for developing countries, distinguishes between three social protection functions:

- protective measures, which have the specific objective of guaranteeing relief from deprivation
- preventative measures, which seek to directly avert deprivation in various ways
- promotional measures, which aim to enhance real incomes and capabilities.

Box 1.2 Approaches to social protection

Some governments have ensured a rights-based approach to social protection which entitles citizens to certain programmes and benefits. In Brazil, for instance, the *Benefício de Prestação Continuada*, a means-tested disability and old-age pension, is enshrined in the Constitution (although the conditional cash transfer, *Bolsa Família*, is not). In India, the Mahatma Gandhi National Employment Guarantee Act legally entitles poor rural households 100 days of employment a year. In South Africa, the right to social assistance is embedded in the Constitution.

Other countries have embedded social protection within broader social policy frameworks. In Brazil, Chile, Colombia and Peru, for instance, a single registry system tracks all services and programmes with which an individual interacts. The unification of beneficiaries under a single registry supports the integration of households into programmes such as food security, housing, banking and credit and judicial services. In Chile's *Chile Solidario* programme, for example, the conditional cash transfer fits within an integrated approach to eradicate extreme poverty through interventions in three main areas – psychosocial support (family support), monetary transfers and priority access to social programmes.

Meanwhile, in another cluster of countries, social protection programmes are implemented as more stand-alone programmes by governments or non-governmental institutions (such as donors or non-governmental organisations) to tackle specific vulnerabilities. The non-governmental Building Resources Across Communities, for instance, implements the asset transfer programme in Bangladesh, Challenging the Frontiers of Poverty Reduction, in order to address chronic poverty. In Ethiopia, the government and donors work together to deliver the public works programme, the Productive Safety Net Programme, in order to tackle chronic food insecurity and environmental degradation. In Malawi and Zambia, donors have funded pilot cash transfer programmes to ultra-poor labour-constrained households.

These categories usefully suggest a gradation of interventions, progressing from a more narrow approach (protection measures in the form of safety nets) to increasingly broad ones (preventative and even promotional measures).

In 2000, the World Bank developed the social risk management framework (Holzmann and Jørgensen, 2000:3), which defined social protection as 'public interventions to (i) assist individuals, households, and communities better manage risk, and (ii) provide support to the critically poor', presenting it as both a safety net and a springboard, similarly incorporating protective and promotive elements. This framework argues that mechanisms to reduce risk can enhance individual and social welfare, contribute to economic growth and development, and form a part of sustainable poverty reduction. The main elements of the social risk management framework are:

- risk management strategies (risk reduction, mitigation and coping)
- risk management arrangements by level of formality (informal, market based, and publicly provided or mandated)
- actors in risk management (from individuals, households, communities, non-governmental organisations, market institutions and government to international organisations and the world community at large).

The social risk management framework has been instrumental in driving thinking about social protection in development contexts, but has also been criticised for its narrow income-based understanding of risk and vulnerability and inadequate attention to the socio-political structures that contribute to chronic poverty (Devereux and Sabates-Wheeler, 2004; Guenther et al., 2007).

Sabates-Wheeler and Kabeer (2003) go some way towards addressing the need for a more integrated approach that integrates both the social and economic dimensions of risk and vulnerability, by adopting a gendered and life-cycle framework approach. They take as their starting point the disadvantaged position of women in relation to work opportunities vis-à-vis men from equivalent social groups, and argue that women are more likely to be excluded from social protection strategies. They present a framework for understanding gender segmentation of the workforce more fully, with three main categories:

- Gender-specific constraints to the participation of women in the labour market and household livelihood activities, which apply to either women or men because of their gender. For women, this reflects their biological role in reproduction as well as the social role of caring, which largely takes women's time away from being in paid employment.
- Gender-intensified constraints which arise from gender-specific beliefs and customs that reflect gender inequalities in opportunities and resources. For women, these constraints are shown especially in intra-household inequalities, which are sometimes reflected by community/society norms – for example, customary law (lack of inheritance rights, etc.).
- Imposed gender constraints are forms of disadvantage that reflect

external biases and preconceptions – for example, employers who refuse to recruit women, or who employ them only in stereotypical female jobs, trade unions which do not encourage women members, etc.

This approach makes an important contribution to placing social and structural inequalities at the centre of a social protection framework. However, its narrow focus on the labour force and extending social protection to informal workers limits its applicability beyond informal and formal workers. The authors note, though, that other programmes (such as land reform) that aim to provide security for households need to be considered in discussions of social protection.

Devereux and Sabates-Wheeler (2004) focus on the role of social and structural issues in more depth, adding a 'transformative element' to the approach of Guhan (1994) to 'address concerns of social equity and exclusion, such as collective action for workers' rights, or upholding human rights for minority ethnic groups' (Devereux and Sabates-Wheeler, 2004:10). Their transformative social protection framework emphasises the importance of the socio-political environment and includes changes to the regulatory framework to protect 'socially vulnerable groups' (e.g. people with disabilities or victims of domestic violence) against discrimination and abuse, to transform public attitudes and behaviour and to enhance social justice.

In our own analysis of social protection through a gender lens, which will be discussed further below, we draw on this transformative framework due to its focus on the social sources of vulnerability, the complexity of interactions between economic and social sources of risk and vulnerability, and a focus on well-being and equity as outcomes. It is this focus which moves social protection beyond constituting a mere safety net, which confines its scope to targeted income and consumption transfers, and extends it to arenas such as equity, empowerment and economic, social and cultural rights in order to better address chronic and structural vulnerability (Devereux and Sabates-Wheeler, 2004). The framework takes the position that the provision of consumption, income and asset insurance is only a partial response to vulnerability, and an expanded view of social protection must incorporate responses to both chronic and structural vulnerability (Sabates-Wheeler and Devereux, 2008). In terms of programming, therefore, the transformative social protection framework includes social justice measures, such as non-discrimination and equal opportunities legislation and campaigns. It also emphasises the potentially synergistic linkages between the four social protection instruments described in Table 1.1, and the value of considering social protection as a range of interventions rather than a one-off programme

(Devereux and Sabates-Wheeler, 2004). These instruments often overlap to achieve more than one objective and, as we argue throughout the book, well-designed social protection policies and programmes can mainstream transformative and equity objectives through protective, preventative and promotive measures. This may be through the design of programmes themselves, by creating strategic linkages to complementary programmes and services, and/or through the delivery of interventions. In summary, the transformative social protection framework aims to highlight the

Table 1.1 Social protection categories and instruments

Type of social protection	*Social protection instruments*	*Role in reducing poverty and vulnerability*
Protective (social assistance)	• Social transfers • Disability benefit • Pension schemes • Subsidised access to social services	Immediate protection and relief from poverty and deprivation
Preventative (insurance and diversification mechanisms)	• Social transfers • Social insurance • Livelihood diversification • Savings clubs, funeral societies★	Prevents deprivation and damage to coping strategies
Promotive (economic opportunities)	• Social transfers • Access to credit, transfers/protection • Common property resources • School feeding • Agricultural starter packs • Public works programmes	Promotes resilience through livelihood diversification and improves security
Transformative (addressing underlying social vulnerabilities)	• Promotion of minority rights • Anti-discrimination campaigns • Social funds	Transforms social relations to address concerns of social equity, social justice and exclusion

★ In many countries, informal community and household support networks continue to provide most support to the poor. Indeed, despite the increase in the formal provision of social protection to poor households since the 1990s, informal safety nets often remain relatively more important than government-led programmes, although in many countries these are under increasing pressure, given the effects of economic crises, chronic poverty, changing household demography and cultural norms, globalisation and migration. Informal mechanisms mirror the range of social protection instruments, including, for instance, transfers in the form of remittances, inter-household transfers of food, insurance mechanisms (e.g. community credit schemes, burial societies, mutual health schemes), sharecropping and labour-sharing arrangements, and protection for orphans and vulnerable children (e.g. through fostering). Informal mechanisms can be carried out by households and communities, and often by faith-based institutions. These are discussed in more detail in Chapter 2.

Source: Adapted from Davies and McGregor (2009); Devereux and Sabates-Wheeler (2004); Sabates-Wheeler and Devereux (2008).

potential of social protection measures to contribute to economic growth and productivity as well as social justice, either through achieving both objectives simultaneously or through linkages with other interventions (Sabates-Wheeler and Devereux, 2008).

Integrating a gender lens into the transformative social protection framework

Despite the increased focus on equity within the transformative social protection agenda, relatively little attention has been given to gender dimensions. Indeed, analysts and practitioners working in the area of gender and development and in social protection have had limited interaction. This is perhaps all the more surprising given the wealth of knowledge on the gendered patterns of vulnerability, risks and shocks. Gender dynamics affect vulnerability to shocks in a number of ways from the macro through to the micro level (see Table 1.2).

Meinzen-Dick et al. (2011) argue that:

- Women and men experience shocks differently depending on their different roles and responsibilities within the home and community. For instance, ill health is likely to have a disproportionately large effect on women, as women are not only often affected by their own illnesses, but also have responsibility for taking care of other sick family members.
- Women and men have differential abilities to withstand shocks. For instance, women typically have lower access to irrigation or water-harvesting methods to address the effects of droughts (World Bank, 2009), and fewer women have insurance to deal with extreme weather or pests (Meinzen-Dick et al., 2011).
- Women and men employ different coping strategies in the face of shocks. For instance, women's and men's assets are often used differently to respond to shocks. In Bangladesh, Quisumbing et al. (2011) found that women's assets were disposed of more quickly to respond to family illnesses, whereas men's assets were typically used to cover marriage expenses and dowry. This has important implications for gendered asset accumulation if the incidence and magnitude of both shocks and asset disposition vary over time.
- In addition to general shocks, there are also shocks that specifically affect women and lead to a loss of their assets and threaten their livelihood strategies. For example, divorce or death of their husband can lead to women losing their assets, especially where marriage is governed under customary laws that do not protect women's rights to property (Peterman, 2010).

Table 1.2 Examples of gendered economic and social risks and vulnerabilities

	Gendered economic risks	Gendered social risks
Macro-level shocks and stresses	Economic crisis: exacerbates women's time poverty and vulnerability to risky employment	Environmental disasters: women more vulnerable due to their caregiving role; socio-cultural mobility constraints; reliance on subsistence food production Social exclusion and discrimination informed by formal policies, legislation (e.g. lack of gender-equality legislation) and institutions (e.g. low representation of women in senior positions)
Meso-level shocks and stresses	Displacement, harvest failures or business failures affect women and men differently (e.g. higher male suicide rates during 2007–2009 Asian economic crisis) Gender-segmented labour markets, institutional discrimination (e.g. lack of affirmative action policies) Lack of tailored service delivery to poor women (e.g. extension services, credit, fertiliser)	Limited opportunities for women to participate and articulate views in community dialogues More limited social capital opportunities given time poverty and mobility constraints
Micro-level shocks and stresses	Sudden expenditure on health emergencies or funerals; women's assets are often the first to be sold and the last to be replaced in distress asset sales	Dearth of intra-household decision making and bargaining power for women, due to socio-cultural norms, time poverty and lack of economic empowerment

Moreover, the intersections between gender inequality, poverty and vulnerability, not only stem from exogenous economic-related factors, but also from structural and cultural factors. Gender inequality cannot be remedied through economic development and income alone. For instance, patriarchal structures and cultural norms and practices disadvantage women in a variety of ways, such as through exploitation, domestic violence, exclusion or marginalisation in public spheres and denial of full legal rights and equal protection (Fraser, 1997). By extension, then, policy that is designed to support a reduction in vulnerability should not focus simply on a shock or a 'vulnerable group', but should tackle and transform the context in which these vulnerabilities occur (Fraser, 1997). As Sabates-Wheeler and Koehler (2011) have noted, the implications of this for social protection are that although large-scale social protection instruments help to reduce poverty, they have limited value within a 'long-term progressive change model.' Such a model instead requires recognition that vulnerability is embedded in economic and social institutions and structures.

Here, insights from feminist economists, and especially analysts working on welfare state analyses, offer a useful perspective as to what this model may look like (Fraser, 1994; MacDonald, 1998). Fraser (1994), drawing on her work in post-industrial contexts on social welfare policies, argues for the need for such policies to foster gender equity by promoting women's employment and supporting informal care work. She argues that, for this to occur, attention must be given to gender equity through five normative principles:

1. Anti-poverty principle: In the context of high rates of female-headed household poverty, targeting goes some way towards addressing gender inequalities, but fails to respect several of the following principles which are also essential to gender equity in social welfare.
2. Anti-exploitation principle: Anti-poverty measures are important not only in themselves but also as a means to another basic principle – prevention of exploitation of vulnerable people. In guaranteeing relief from poverty, then, welfare provision should aim to mitigate exploitable dependency. The availability of an alternative source of income enhances the bargaining position of subordinates in unequal relationships. However, for welfare measures to have this effect, support must be provided as a matter of right. The goal should be to prevent at least three kinds of dependency, namely that on an individual family member, on employers and supervisors, and on the personal whims of state officials.
3. Equality principles in three spheres are also essential to gender equity in social welfare:

a. Income equality: This concerns the distribution of per capita income, when much of women's labour is not compensated at all, and when many women suffer from 'hidden poverty' due to unequal distribution within families.

b. Leisure-time equality: Many women do both paid work and unpaid primary care work, and women suffer disproportionately from time poverty. The leisure-time equality principle rules out welfare arrangements that would equalise incomes while requiring a double shift of work from women but only a single shift from men.

c. Equality of respect: This pertains to status and respect, ruling out social arrangements that objectify and denigrate women.

4. Anti-marginalisation principle: This promotes women's full participation on a par with men in all areas of social life – in employment, politics and the associational life of civil society.

5. Anti-androcentrism principle: Social policy should not require women to become like men, or to fit into institutions designed for men, but should enable them to enjoy comparable levels of well-being. This principle requires decentring masculinist norms – in part by revaluing practices and traits that are currently undervalued because they are associated with women. It entails changing men as well as changing women.

In addition to these principles, it is useful to consider here elements of the gender analysis of social security by Macdonald (1998), who emphasises the need to focus on three aspects within the intra-household sphere:

1. The importance of taking into account intra-household inequalities: By neglecting intra-household inequality and assuming that all members in the family are equal and share the benefits provided, programmes risk reinforcing women's disadvantageous position. Concerns are also raised if programmes simply target women as wives or mothers rather than as individuals.

2. Recognising the existing gender labour division at home and women's greater reproductive responsibilities, including unpaid family and care work: Programmes based on the traditional household gender labour division often fail to adequately consider women's responsibilities, and provide only minimal compensation for women's reproductive labour.

3. Allowing for a plurality of family arrangements: This principle is especially important when nuclear families are not the norm (see Chapter 2).

These principles can be applied to the transformative social protection framework in order to integrate a stronger focus on gender equity, but need to be approached through a careful context-specific lens (Holmes and Jones, 2009). Fraser notes that the goal should be to find approaches that avoid trade-offs and maximise the prospects of satisfying all, or at least most, of the five principles. Indeed, social protection – as a subset of social and economic policy – should not be expected to address gender inequality in its entirety. This is too big a task for any one policy domain. Indeed other policies, programmes and legislation are often more appropriate for tackling certain entrenched gender inequalities. That said, social protection programming needs to be cognisant of the gender dynamics of the context within which it operates and seek to promote gender-equitable outcomes accordingly. It can do this either directly within the parameters of its specific programme objectives, design and implementation practices, or indirectly by creating linkages to other programmes and services to help to overcome the multitude of constraints, many of which are gendered, that poor people face.

In summary, then, applying a gender-lens to the transformative social protection approach acknowledges:

1. that gender inequality is a source of risk and vulnerability embedded in the broader socio-political environment
2. that these risks and vulnerabilities are mediated through policy interventions, pre-existing political economy dynamics and socio-cultural norms, all of which have their own context-specific gender dynamics
3. that economic and social risks and vulnerabilities are inherently influenced by gender relations – women, men, girls and boys not only experience different types of risks, but also cope with the same risks and vulnerabilities differently (Holmes and Jones, 2009) (see also Chapter 2).

Figure 1.1 illustrates these macro- to meso- to micro-dynamics diagramatic-ally, and we discuss the importance of each of the levels further below.

- The *broader structural environment* includes the patterning of the care and productive economies, social institutions and regulatory frameworks, all of which influence the effect of policies in tackling gendered risks and vulnerabilities. In this regard, social protection needs to engage with the patriarchal context in which it operates and address the discriminatory practices that lead to inequitable outcomes. Accordingly, taking into consideration the care economy is of particular importance for women, as is recognising the inequalities found in productive economies and social institutions that discriminate against women. Regulatory frameworks, such as CEDAW, may support such anti-discrimination efforts (see Box 1.4 on gender-related policy and legislation implications for social protection).

- The *choice of different types of policy interventions* is highly political. Policy choices on social protection, on gender and on the integration between the two are influenced by institutions, interests and ideas held by national and international actors. Institutional arenas (e.g. elections and party politics, the legislature, the judiciary, informal politics) present opportunities or constraints in the negotiation of social protection policy and programme development. The interests of key actors are influential in designing policy, dependent on who is likely to gain or lose from policy shifts (e.g. political elites, bureaucratic agencies, donors and civil society champions) and the relative balance of power between them (e.g. power imbalances between ministries of finance/economics and of social welfare, which are often among the weakest). Ideas held by elites and the public regarding poverty and its causes also influence choices, including the role of the social contract between state and citizens.

- *Differential community, household and individual capacities and agency*: Targeting female-headed households is not sufficient to tackle gendered poverty and vulnerability. The ability of household members (including, importantly, women in male-headed households) to manage and cope with risks and vulnerabilities varies according to

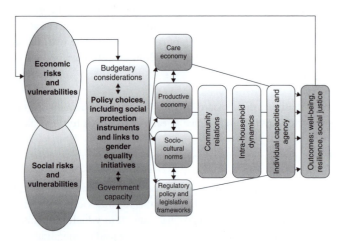

Figure 1.1   Pathways mediating the effects of economic and social risks on gendered well-being

Box 1.3 Gender-related policy and legislation implications for social protection

International and national laws and policies on equality and non-discrimination are important tools for supporting measures to promote social justice in social protection policy and programming. Although these links remain weak in practice in many countries (due to factors such as weak implementation capacities and unresolved tensions between constitutional laws and religious and customary laws, for example), they nevertheless offer important potential tools for strengthening a focus on equity within social protection design and implementation.

Many countries have ratified CEDAW, which defines what constitutes discrimination against women and sets up an agenda for national action to end this. The Convention defines discrimination against women as follows:

> any distinction, exclusion or restriction made on the basis of sex which has the effect or purpose of impairing or nullifying the recognition, enjoyment or exercise by women, irrespective of their marital status, on a basis of equality of men and women, of human rights and fundamental freedoms in the political, economic, social, cultural, civil or any other field.
>
> (UN General Assembly, 1979)

By accepting the Convention, states commit themselves to undertaking a series of measures to end discrimination against women in all forms.

National policies on women articulate ways in which gender equality can be achieved across sectors. These include promoting women's access to decision-making structures, incorporating women's issues in all levels of programmes and policies, changing discriminatory attitudes towards females, and encouraging research and awareness. National policies are often accompanied by action plans on gender equality, which provide mechanisms for gender mainstreaming which can be applied to the social protection sector. Gender focal points can help to facilitate cross-sectoral collaboration, while gender budgeting can be employed to highlight entry points for improving the use of existing financial resources and also expanding fiscal space to address gender inequalities.

numerous factors, including the composition of the household (e.g. dependency ratio, gender of the household head, number of girls and boys in the household), life-cycle status, individual and household ownership and control of assets (e.g. land, labour, financial capital, livestock, time), access to labour markets, social networks and social capital, and levels of education (see Chapter 2).

This gendered approach resonates with the essence of the transformative social protection framework insofar as it makes the case that by overcoming structural inequalities and injustice caused by social risks, people will be better able to engage in the economy and in social relations. Such an approach will also have positive spin-offs not only for individual livelihoods, but also for economic growth more broadly (Sabates-Wheeler and Devereux, 2008).

Therefore our central argument is that meeting the dual rationale for promoting gender equity – as a human right and as enhancing the effectiveness of programme outcomes – will support the success of social protection programmes in reducing poverty and vulnerability in a more sustainable way.

In the second part of this book we draw on this conceptual framework to guide our analysis of social protection instruments. We examine to what extent principles of gender equity have been considered in the design of social protection programmes, we discuss what the effects of these programmes have been at the individual, intra-household and community level, and we look at explanations of these effects through political and institutional drivers. We revisit and summarise the main findings in the concluding chapter of the book, identifying policy and programming implications for how to strategically integrate a gender lens into social protection.

TWO

The gendered patterning of vulnerability, risk and resilience

Introduction

This chapter focuses on the ways in which patterns of vulnerability, risk and resilience in developing countries are gendered. As Chapter 1 discussed, social protection concerns formal and informal measures to tackle vulnerability and risk and promote resilience. Vulnerability to and risk of poverty and deprivation are experienced differently by different social groups, particularly by age and gender – as are options for building resilience. Indeed, there is long-standing recognition that the incidence of male and female poverty and vulnerability is different, as underscored by the oft-quoted statistic that women constitute 70% of the world's poor.[1] However, as Box 2.1 highlights, the reality is considerably more complex.

Our starting point is that the diversity and complexity of gender-specific vulnerabilities are often overlooked in policy and programme documentation and debates, but that it is critical to capture these dimensions using a multi-layered framework. In the absence of adequate coping mechanisms and support structures, individuals often suffer from a series of shocks and stresses at the individual, intra-household and community levels. While one-off shocks might be surmountable, because they are often multi-dimensional, they serve to perpetuate long-term poverty traps (for an example, see Personal Narrative 2.1).

In this chapter, we use a gender lens to review the economic risks to which women are often vulnerable, and which they often shoulder disproportionately. We then address social risks and vulnerabilities, which women frequently identify as being even more important than economic risks (Chronic Poverty Research Centre, 2009; Narayan et al., 2000). Finally, we discuss resilience, and the different coping strategies and resources that men and women have at their disposal.

Economic vulnerabilities and risks

Gender-specific economic vulnerabilities and risks are shaped by various factors, including unequal labour markets, differential access to assets, environmental risks, and expenses incurred as a result of ill health and life-cycle events, such as weddings and funerals. We discuss each of these

---

Box 2.1 Poverty and vulnerability as a gendered experience

The gendered patterning of poverty and vulnerability across different countries is highly varied and much more complex than is often first assumed, as the following statistics illustrate:

- Chile: According to the Gendered Index of Indigence and Poverty, 123.9 women for every 100 men are living in poverty, rising to 132.2 for extreme poverty (Soares and Silva, 2010).
- Colombia: Poor rural female-headed households command only 40% of the total income of male-headed households (Soares and Silva, 2010).
- Ethiopia: Data from the early 2000s suggest that whereas male-headed households have greater consumption-expenditure capacity, female-headed households have higher per-capita food energy consumption (Lampietti and Stalker, 2000).
- Ghana: Female-headed households (30% of the population) have significantly lower levels of poverty (19.2% vs. 31.4%) (International Fund for Agricultural Development, 1999).
- Kenya: Although women's rural unemployment is lower than that of men, women's urban unemployment rate is 37.6%, compared with 13% for men (Kenya National Bureau of Statistics, 2009).

---

in turn, drawing on secondary literature as well as primary research from eight countries across Africa, Asia and Latin America.

Unequal labour-market participation

Due to household chores, child care-giving, and limited access to education, women face higher entry barriers to employment in the formal sector.
(Haggblade et al., 2001, cited in Cunguara et al., 2011:704)

Women face multiple barriers to income generation. They are less likely to participate in the wage-based labour market than men (48% vs. 72.8% as of 2009) (International Labour Organization, 2010b), less likely to have access to formal employment,[2] often excluded from the most lucrative positions, and paid less than men for the same work (Food and Agriculture Organization of the United Nations, 2011; World Bank, 2011b).

Personal Narrative 2.1: Tamenu's experience of multi-layered shocks in southern Ethiopia

When I was four years old, my parents sent me to my aunt in town who had no children. But when my father died, my aunt took me to the burial and left me there. I had to make ends meet for my siblings and so I accepted an offer of a man to live with his family. He made me his servant and exploited me heavily. After that I had three unsuccessful marriages. [...]

During the past five years, my house was burnt down and I lost many assets. My husband's brother gave us money to construct a house, but my husband is a drunken man and as a result he wasted some of the money. [...]

At the end of 2007, I came to know my positive HIV status. Now my interaction with community members is decreasing because of their attitude towards me, and the public works programme implementers have refused to give me a loan for oxen since they know my status. My son suffers from mental illness. I planned to take him to get holy water, but I cannot because I do not have enough money. [...]

I try to sell wood, grass, and use other sources of income to feed and buy second-hand clothes for my children. Now my only hope is to see the success of my children. Mine is already gone! I advise my children to focus on their education to save them from the challenges associated with dropping out of school which I face.

Source: Jones et al. (2010b:17).

There are multiple drivers of these phenomena. As discussed below, women disproportionately shoulder domestic responsibilities, which leaves them with less time for paid employment, and restricts how far they can travel to undertake such work (Cunguara et al., 2011). Furthermore, women are more likely to lack the human capital, financial resources and social ties that would facilitate waged employment. Facing multiple disadvantages, 'women thus tend to engage in informal activities that can be operated from home, require low capital investments, and build on skills they already have' (Eriksen and Silva, 2009, cited in Cunguara et al., 2011:704).

Women's employment opportunities are also more likely to be constrained by language, particularly when they lack opportunities to learn official languages, which often enable higher earnings (Chiswick and Miller, 1995). Indigenous and minority women – typically the least likely to receive formal education – may not be able to use their country's official (and business) language.[3] In Vietnam, for instance, ethnic minority women's reliance on their mother tongue 'renders them relatively isolated and also reduces income-generating opportunities' (Jones and Tran, 2010:25). Indigenous women in the Andes face similar constraints (Molyneux, 2011).

Even where women are employed, they typically earn less than men (International Labour Organization, 2009a; International Trade Union Confederation, 2008; Oostendorp, 2009). Lovell (2006) found that wage discrimination had actually increased between 1960 and 2000 for women working in urban São Paulo, in part because of women's growing segmentation in the service industry. In Bangladesh, this gap can be as high as 33% in the private sector and 27% in the public sector (Gunawardena, 2006, cited in Asfar, 2011). Although human capital levels certainly play a role in some contexts, this is not always the case. Fang and Sakellariou (2011:53), for example, note that in Thailand there is evidence of 'significant discrimination against women', particularly at the bottom end of the income ladder. They calculate that less than 25% of the gendered wage differential reflects differences in human capital.

In terms of agricultural work, the role of women varies significantly across the world. Women work as both market-oriented smallholders and subsistence-oriented farmers. In Ghana and Nigeria, female-headed households are more likely to be market- than subsistence-oriented. Within the household, market orientation can differ depending on the gender of the cultivator, with women often more likely to be engaged in subsistence farming and men more likely to cultivate cash crops. Market orientation can be conditioned by many factors, such as asset endowment, education, household composition and labour availability, land quality, access to markets and agricultural potential, affecting crop and livestock choice and productivity.

However, women face considerable gender-related constraints and vulnerabilities within the agriculture sector. Discrimination results in gender inequalities in assets and access to information, markets and financial services, which affect their ability to participate in market-oriented activities and the potential productivity of subsistence-oriented farming. Land ownership remains heavily skewed towards men – in many Latin American countries, 70–90% of formal owners of farmland are men (Deere and León, 2001), and similar patterns are seen in sub-Saharan Africa (Doss, 2006; Quisumbing et al., 2004). Strengthening women's land rights can significantly increase household income and families' welfare (World Bank, 2009).

Gender inequalities also occur because of institutional bias, mobility constraints and low literacy (which hamper the accessing of market information), poor access to credit and other financial services, and limited opportunities to participate in extension services, skills/training and leadership of rural organisations, and thus be in a position to influence policy. For instance, integrating gender into national plans and agriculture-sector strategies and ensuring women's representation remains a challenge (World Bank, 2005b). In many countries (such as Laos and the Philippines), providing title to land is not enough without complementary services to deliver change in other dimensions (World Bank, 2009). Moreover, inequalities in participation and power are also evident in the realms of land, labour, finance and product markets, and in the distribution of risks and gains along the value chain. For instance, small-scale producers, who are often poor women, may be excluded from lucrative high-value markets because they cannot compete with larger producers on costs and prices (World Bank, 2009).

Finally, migratory employment is also highly gendered. As Sassen (2008:462) notes, women are typically left behind while men seek waged employment, doing the 'invisible work of … the subsistence economy'. More recently, however, women have been increasingly migrating to urban areas, and to wealthier countries, to support their families (Masika et al., 1997; Morrison et al., 2008; Zlotnik, 2003). These women are much more likely than migratory men to be uneducated, poor, and the primary breadwinners for their families (Masika et al., 1997; Morrison et al., 2008; Zlotnik, 2003). In addition to facing the typical risks and hardships that migrant employees encounter, women are especially vulnerable to physical and sexual abuse and trafficking (Asfar, 2011), given the precariousness of their work situation (whether in agriculture, factory work, services or domestic work), especially if they are undocumented.

Male migrants are also exposed to a number of unique vulnerabilities. For example, they are at higher risk of contracting HIV and other sexually transmitted illnesses through risky sexual behaviours – illnesses that are often transmitted to their wives or partners on returning home (Saggurti et al., 2011; Wolffers et al., 2002). In certain male-dominated industries, such as construction work, migrant men are mistreated and exposed to occupational hazards, among a myriad of other abuses (Human Rights Watch, 2009). More subtly, the migratory experience can challenge men's traditional self-perceptions of their own masculinity, particularly when women lead the household during their absence. This renegotiation of gender roles has some positive aspects, but can also promote anxiety and a sense of identity loss among migrant men (Donaldson et al., 2009).

Differential access to assets

Women cannot sell assets if there is a disagreement with their husband. This is one reason for the disadvantaged position of women in the community. If she sells, her husband says she has robbed the household assets. And if her children back her he also complains that she destroys assets together with her children. … There is male dominance in decisionmaking on the common assets they have in the house. And yes, there are some women who suffer from domestic violence as a result.

(Married woman, Ethiopia, cited in Jones et al., 2010b:17)

Women's limited access to and control over productive assets such as land, credit and livestock is one of the main reasons for their lack of decision-making power in the household (Laddey et al., 2011; World Bank, 2009). For rural women, the fact that they do not legally own land is the keystone of this disadvantage (Grace, 2005; Varley, 2007).

Lack of access to title deeds as collateral can also limit women's access to credit. This can in turn restrict access to productive inputs, such as seed and fertiliser, which would enable them to improve their economic well-being and social status (Grace, 2005; Varley, 2007). It also reduces their interactions with extension agents (who tend to work only with land owners), and thus the techniques and information that can deliver higher productivity (Øvstegård et al., 2010).

Ownership of livestock is also gender differentiated: 'typically, men are responsible for the purchase, sale or pawning of large animals, such as cows, horses and oxen, while women tend to claim control over small animals, such as goats, sheep, poultry and pigs' (Fletschner and Kenney, 2011:3). Large animals not only have more intrinsic value, making them more suitable as collateral, but can also provide valuable labour, increasing productivity while decreasing human time requirements (Fletschner and Kenney, 2011). However, this dynamic is complex. Smaller animals can also prove easier for women to access and assert claims to, as well as to manage in profitable enterprise. As Miller (2001) notes, 'profits may be low, but so are the risks, and men are less likely to interfere.'

In Latin America, where women have possessed full legal rights for decades, many women still have difficulty registering joint land ownership (Food and Agriculture Organization of the United Nations, 2010). For rural women, as well as single women and female-household heads, this has led to significant constraints on access to credit (Fletschner and Kenney, 2011). In Vietnam, when long-term tenancies were assigned, 90% of land was handed out to men (Food and Agriculture Organization of the United Nations, 2010). In India, even where ownership rights are theoretically guaranteed by law, provisions that allow customary law to take precedence over statutory law have disregarded women's ownership rights (Food and Agriculture Organization of the United Nations, 2010). Women's access to land and other assets is even more problematic in sub-Saharan Africa, where traditionally widows lose access to family land on the death of their husband (Kimani, 2008). In many countries, legal reforms notwithstanding, the death of a husband renders his widow highly vulnerable (World Bank, 2011b; see also Figure 2.1).[4]

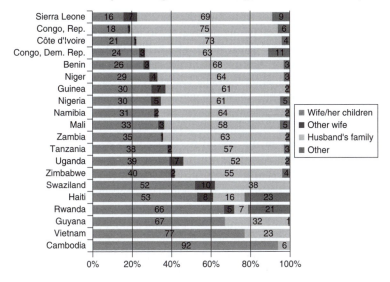

Figure 2.1 Asset distribution among women's marital and natal families

In urban areas, too, lack of assets is closely intertwined with poverty and vulnerability. Women (especially young mothers) without a male breadwinner often have more difficulty in securing rental accommodation (Kumar, 2010). A study on informal urban settlements in India, for example, found that some landlords were reluctant to rent to women because of doubts about female-headed households' economic security (Baruah, 2010). Moreover, women who move to urban areas on marriage often have to give up any potential claims to parental or ancestral property because they cannot afford to visit their natal families (Baruah, 2010).

Environmental risks

> ... *women are disproportionately vulnerable to climate change, because they are more likely to be found in the poorest sections of society, have fewer resources to cope, and are more reliant on climate-sensitive resources because of the gender division of labour.*

(Nelson, 2011:vi)

Climate change is already having a significant impact on the world's poor, particularly in Africa and Asia. The effects on women are particularly stark, given their high dependence on natural resources to provide food, water and fuel for the household, and care for its members (Nelson, 2011). In parts of Africa, prolonged drought has meant that women must travel further from home in order to meet their needs (Brody et al., 2008).[5] Not only is this very time-consuming, but it can also expose them to violence, including rape (Ngaira, 2007). Meanwhile, in the dry land regions of Africa's Horn, for example, women's options for diversification are constrained, as legal and/or cultural barriers restrict their ability to own land (Adenew and Abdi, 2005; Mwangi, 2009). In addition, women have less access to the technological innovations and capacity-building opportunities available through extension services that might enable them to sustain productivity in the face of the increasingly negative impacts of climate change.

Efforts to address climate change may have negative gendered impacts. For example, increased production of biofuel has contributed to rising food prices (Leturque and Wiggins, 2009; Food and Agriculture Organization and Organization for Economic Co-operation and Development, 2011), with detrimental impacts on food-insecure households in general and women in particular, given cultural norms which typically assign women responsibility for ensuring household food consumption.[6] In addition, women have less scope to respond; they have fewer financial options for coping with climate shocks and less access to policy fora to present their views and needs (Nelson, 2011).[7]

Natural disasters, which appear to be increasing in the face of environmental shifts, also have gendered effects. In the event of flooding, for example, women are less likely to be able to swim, are typically clothed in a manner that makes escape difficult, and are far more likely to 'stay behind to look for their children and other relatives' (MacDonald, 2005:474). In the 2004 tsunami, women in Sri Lanka and India were three to four times more likely to drown than men (MacDonald, 2005). Similarly, in the aftermath of the 2010 Pakistan floods, women faced unique socio-economic risks and barriers to medical, hygiene and nutritional support. Having shouldered the primary responsibility for water, sanitation and hygiene-related tasks prior to the flooding, many displaced women found themselves disproportionately burdened with more than half of the water collection, cleaning and garbage disposal tasks in camps (UN Women, 2010). Moreover, as women are often relegated to primarily reproductive and domestic household roles, their economic contributions are often less visible in the public sphere, and thus they are at higher risk of becoming unnoticed during post-disaster compensation processes (World Bank, 2010). Although related programming efforts have become more gender-sensitive in recent years (Green, 2008; UN International Strategy for Disaster Reduction, 2009), women's voices still go largely unheard in disaster prevention and response-related decision-making processes.[8]

Expenses related to illhealth

> Women and girls are the principal caregivers and bear the greatest degree of
> responsibility for the psychosocial and physical care of family and community
> members.
>
> (Ogden et al., 2006:333)

Expenses relating to illhealth—both direct and indirect—are one of the most serious risks faced by poor households (WHO, 2010), and because of women's role as primary caregivers, they typically face a disproportionate burden. Furthermore, while cross-country gender budgeting data on healthcare expenditure is rarely available (Chakraborty, 2010), we do know that because "(g)overnment policy also often equates 'women' with 'mothers' and 'reproduction'" (Klugman and McIntyre as cited in UNFPA and UNIFEM, 2006: 28) and tends to ignore women's other health needs, such as cancer screening, mental health and sexual violence, many women struggle to meet their basic health care (WHO, 2009). That said, because women are the primary caregivers in most situations, they typically utilise health care more than men. "As caregivers they come into contact with the health services both when bringing the sick, whether children or the elderly, to use health services, and in caring for them in the home" (as cited in UNFPA and UNIFEM: 28). Indeed, Sen and Östlin (2007: 3) observe that 'up to 80 percent of health care and 90 percent of HIV/ AIDS related illness care is provided in the home'—almost exclusively by girls and women at significant economic cost either through direct expenses (e.g. consultation fees, costs of medicines and transportation) or foregone income-generating opportunities. Having an ill family member requires not only 'sick care' but also more housework and transportation, as special diets, laundry and medical visits must be accommodated (ibid.; Akintola, 2005). This diverts time from 'food production, employment (and) education' (Blackden and Wodon, 2006: 21). It also leads to distress sales of an already limited asset base, as women are 'responsible for paying illness-related shocks' (Quisumbing et al., 2011:4).

Aside from reproductive health, where women's needs are obviously greater than men's, there is rarely an attempt, however, to consider gender in health care provision and financing. UNFPA and UNIFEM (2006:13) argue that even "50:50 in terms of health funds reaching men and women probably implies a bias against women". As it is, resourcing is much lower and in some cases even declining over time. In Mozambique, for example, the "budget allocated for 'gender'-related priorities (including those related to maternal health) is extremely low-below 1% of the total health expenditures in 2007" (UNIFEM, 2010: 18). Even sexual and reproductive healthcare, the most visible of women's needs, remains woefully underfunded—with MDG 5 unlikely to meet its 2015 target in part because funding levels as a proportion of total aid have declined over the past decade (UN, 2012).

Expenses related to life-cycle events

In some societies, women and girls are particularly disadvantaged by life-cycle events such as births, weddings and funerals (Holmes and Jones, 2010a). For Indian parents, 'the cost of a daughter's marriage is the single largest expense of their lives', and many start saving for it as soon as their daughters are born (Anderson, 2007:1). Dowries, which have inflated rapidly in real terms over recent decades, now represent up to six times the average annual salary, and weddings themselves are increasingly expensive (Anderson, 2007). Dowry expenses have led to discrimination against female children and violence against women (Rastogi and Therly, 2006). For example, in bride-price communities, poor parents who are suffering economic or nutritional constraints may marry their daughters very early to obtain cash from the marriage and reduce the number of mouths that have to be fed (Green, 2008). Bride burning in cases where dowry payments are delayed or inadequate has also become increasingly common (Maitra, 2007).

Expenses related to funerals also often have significant gender dimensions (UN Development Fund for Women, 2001). The immediate costs of funerals are prohibitive for poor populations in many developing country contexts, but present greater difficulties for women. As women generally have more limited income-generating potential and heightened socio-cultural vulnerability in widowhood, the negative economic spill-over effects combined with the loss of a breadwinner may also be longer-lasting. In South Africa, for example, estimates of funeral costs for households affected by HIV range from between 4 and 13 times the total monthly income prior to the loss of a breadwinner (Freire, 2004). Furthermore, although some attention has recently been paid to the financial impact of funerary customs, Mensah (2007:1) notes that few experts are addressing the often very negative psychological customs that accompany the expense: the 'funeral celebration is only an event that lasts for some few days, but the trauma for the widows and children persists long after.' In some societies, widows are stigmatised socially, while in others they are made to marry a relative of their dead husband. In many African countries, for instance, women are restricted to their households during the mourning rites, which are controlled by the dead husband's brother. Afterwards, they can also suffer the 'confiscation of their land and other property', forcing them and their children 'to survive on society's margins' (Kimani, 2008:1).

Social vulnerabilities and risks

Social risks and vulnerabilities are increasingly acknowledged as a critical component of poverty and deprivation (Chronic Poverty Research Centre, 2009). For women, these are often equally or even more important than economic sources of vulnerability (Holmes and Jones, 2010a). Jones et al. (2011) argue that social institutions – the collection of formal and informal laws, norms and practices that have an effect on human capabilities by either limiting or enabling individual and collective agency – have greater influence on developmental outcomes than is generally appreciated. Practices and norms such as son bias, discriminatory family codes, physical insecurity, restricted mobility and community participation all play a critical role in shaping and perpetuating girls' and women's experiences of poverty and deprivation.

In this vein, Sen (2004, cited by the Chronic Poverty Research Centre, 2009:39) argues that culture matters not just because it is a 'constitutive part of the good life', but also because it has an 'instrumental influence on the behaviours of individuals, firms and governments.' This translation of 'social' aspects into economic terminology has enabled a much wider understanding of its potential influence in development action. Social institutions are accordingly viewed as important because they are part of a wider culture that defines 'what is valued in terms of well-being, who does the valuing and why economic and social factors interact with culture to unequally allocate access to a good life' (Rao and Walton, 2004:4). Here, we focus on the gendered patterning of time poverty, gender-based violence, reproductive health vulnerabilities, and intra-household and community decision-making power.

Time use

> Women are dedicated to cooking and men work on the farm. Men play
> football when they rest, while we remain at home with household chores.
>> (Adolescent girl, cited by Vargas, 2010:9)

The multiple domestic sphere tasks for which women and girls are accountable in many societies result in what is widely known as time poverty. This limited say over their own time use can significantly limit women's and girl's life options, often from an early age (see Box 2.2). Reproductive and care duties, domestic tasks such as housekeeping and fetching water, and agricultural work on family farms and garden plots constrain the time that girls and women have for education and paid employment, particularly in rural areas (Blackden and Wodon, 2006). In Peru, for example, women are responsible for up to 80% of the family's work (International Fund for Agricultural Development, 2011). Similarly, in Mexico, women who are employed outside the home 'devote an additional 33 hours to domestic chores per week, while men's weekly contribution [is] six hours.'[10] In parts of Africa, such as Madagascar, Tanzania and Zambia, women and girls spend six hours each day simply collecting water.[11] Women's additional time burden limits their opportunities for wage labour, and forces many into lower-paying cottage industries that can be structured around domestic requirements (Seebens, 2011). Recent trends are worsening this situation. The HIV epidemic, for example, has added to women's time burden as the number of family members in need of care increases. Climate change is also impacting on women's and girls' time use with the collection of water and fuel increasingly involving longer travelling distances.

Gendered patterns of violence

> *Violence against women and girls continues unabated in every continent, country and culture. … Most societies prohibit such violence – yet the reality is that too often, it is covered up or tacitly condoned.*
>
> (Ki-Moon, 2007)[12]

Gender-based violence affects men and women differently. Men face significantly higher vulnerability to homicide (constituting 82% of all homicide victims) (UN Office on Drugs and Crime, 2011)) and to suicide (by a factor of three to one) (World Health Organization, 2002)). Women confront a range of different vulnerabilities to violence, starting before they are even born. Female feticide remains widespread throughout parts of Asia. India and China are 'missing' millions of girls, as a result of strong son preference, and in a number of countries sex ratios at birth are worsening (Sahni et al., 2008; World Bank, 2011b; see Table 2.1).[13] In addition, it is estimated that 130 million girls and women, most of them in Africa, have been subjected to female genital mutilation, putting them at risk of disability and even death (Sen et al., 2007).

Child marriage, which is still common in Asia, Africa and Latin America, increases girls' vulnerability to domestic violence. In Niger, 75% of girls are married before the age of 18 years, compared with just 3% of boys – as are 70% of girls in Bangladesh, compared with just 5% of boys (International Center for Research on Women, 2007).[14] Young brides often marry older men, and lack the education that could empower them to protect themselves; they are twice as likely to report being beaten than girls who marry later (International Center for Research on Women, 2006; Kishor and Johnson, 2004). Many girls and women have internalised their lower position in the social and family hierarchy, and believe they deserve this 'discipline.' The Demographic and Health Survey found that, on average, in 41 countries with available data, nearly 30% of women

Table 2.1 Worsening sex ratios at birth over time⋆

Country/region	Sex ratio at birth (male births per 100 female births)	
	1990	2010
China	110.4	121.2
Hong Kong, China (special autonomous region)	107.8	108.1
Singapore	107.4	107.3
Republic of Korea	112.6	110.0
Vietnam	104.0	105.9
Armenia	103.2	116.5
Azerbaijan	106.5	115.6
Georgia	105.5	110.7
Albania	108.2	107.0
Former Yugoslav Republic of Macedonia	106.0	107.9
Montenegro	106.4	107.9
Serbia	107.6	107.8
India	107.7	108.5
Micronesia, Federated States of	108.0	107.2
Papua New Guinea	106.3	107.8
Samoa	108.7	108.0
Solomon Islands	109.0	108.9
Suriname	106.4	107.2
East Asia and the Pacific	108.5	116.0
South Asia	106.8	107.5
Europe and Central Asia	104.4	105.6

Source: UN Development Programme (2010c) Human Development Report 2010. The Real Wealth of Nations: Pathways to Human Development. New York: UNDP.

⋆ Table includes countries where the sex ratio at birth was > 104 in 1990 and had increased further by 2010.

believed wife beating was justified for arguing with the husband, 25% considered it justified for refusing to have sex, and 21% believed it was justified for burning food (World Bank, 2011b).

Violence against women is widespread (Willman, 2008). It is estimated that at least one in three women worldwide experience physical or sexual abuse at some point in their life (Green, 2008). For example, more than 40% of Indian women report having been victimised by their husband, which is unsurprising given that '51% of Indian men think that hitting or beating their wives is acceptable.'[15] Similarly, in Uganda, 16% of men and

28% of women believe beatings are justified when a woman refuses to have sex with her partner, and 22% of men and 27% of women believe beatings are justified when a woman uses contraception without her partner's permission (Koenig et al., 2003). In the case of sexual violence, around 40% of female adolescents in Mozambique and nearly 50% of those in the Caribbean report that their first sexual encounter was forced (World Bank, 2011a). This has serious implications for the spread of HIV, as studies in Africa and Asia show that women who experience gender-based violence are up to three times more likely to be HIV-positive (Jewkes et al., 2010).

Gender-based violence also carries a longer-term cost to society. Not only does it take a physical toll on women's health (Kishor and Johnson, 2004), but also it makes them less able to work and care for children (Green, 2008), and saps their self-esteem. In addition, an increasing body of evidence shows that intra-household tensions and violence undermine social cohesion in a way that perpetuates cycles of insecurity and social risks. Children who grow up witnessing and/or experiencing violence are at heightened risk of involvement in violence within their own subsequent families and in the community, including gang activity (UN Children's Fund, 2006a; Watson et al., 2004). This reflects inadequate emotional support at home and the valorisation of violent masculinity; it makes communities insecure for all, and renders women especially vulnerable to sexual violence (Moser and van Bronkhorst, 1999).[16]

Neglect or structural violence is also a feature of many girls' and women's lives. Where resources are constrained, girls are less likely than their brothers to receive adequate nutrition or healthcare. In Pakistan, for instance, girls are nearly 8% less likely to receive immunisations, and in India the gap is nearly 15% (Gwatkin and Deveshwar-Bahl, 2001). Indian girls are often weaned earlier than boys, so their mothers can 'try again' for a son (Jayachandran and Kuziemko, 2011). This is reflected in a 40% higher child mortality rate in girls than in boys between 1 and 5 years, and accounts for up to 22,000 'missing girls' each year (Jayachandran and Kuziemko, 2011).

Reproductive health vulnerabilities

> *Children are a gift from God, but if I had thought about family planning I would have needed to get my husband's agreement to use it.*
>
> (Married woman, Ghana, cited in Amuzu et al., 2010:24)

Limited reproductive health rights emerge, as a significant source of social vulnerability. South Asian women, for example, are often marginalized in key decisions regarding their own health, with the majority of Nepalese (72.7%) and roughly half of Bangladeshi (54.3%) and Indian (48.5%) women excluded altogether from the decision-making process (Senarath and Gunawardena, 2009). Adolescent girls and young women are often especially vulnerable. Here, high teenage fertility rates are of concern because of greater health risks for both mother and child. Early pregnancy can lead to lower levels of schooling and training for teenage girls; it tends to be higher among poorer teenagers, a factor that can contribute to the intergenerational cycle of poverty; it compounds gender inequities, since most teenage mothers are single mothers who have to bear the responsibility for childbearing in the absence of the father; and it indicates that teenage reproductive rights are not effective, as most of these pregnancies are unwanted, and girls in most cases do not have access to contraceptives (ECLAC, 2007). Cultural attitudes (see Box 2.2), religious resistance and health system failures often underpin and perpetuate this vulnerability.

Women and young girls' limited decision-making power over their sexuality further compounds their reproductive health vulnerabilities. One of the main driving forces behind women's disproportionately high rates of HIV in Africa is their lack of socio-cultural and economic capacity to resist their husband's sexual demands (Farid, 2011; Santhya et al., 2007; Wagman et al., 2009). Young women in particular are often not able to refuse sex and cannot insist on using contraception, on account of unequal intra-household power relations and deeply embedded socio-cultural and religious norms (Haider et al., 2008; Hattori and DeRose, 2008; Seebens, 2006). Husbands often see larger families as evidence of their virility (Beyeza-Kashesya, 2010; Sethuraman et al., 2007; Varga, 2003). In Zambia, for example, contraceptive use declined among participants in a Harvard University-led randomized control trial looking at uptake of family planning services—even in the context of vouchers enabling access to free contraception—when men were included in the programme (Ashraf et al., 2010).

Unequal intra-household decision-making power

In many societies, women have little or no say in decision making, including decisions within their own families and even with regard to their own well-being (Jan and Akhtar, 2008). Women's needs are often accorded lower priority than those of men, or require male permission, as the following quotes demonstrate:

Husbands are the ones who take care of great matters [such as loans], so I can't say much. ... He didn't tell me anything about the loan. He thinks a wife knows nothing. I didn't talk to him about the [loan repayment] deadline or the interest because it would make my husband's family worry too, and I was afraid it would upset him. He says I don't know anything so I couldn't ask. I was too afraid to ask him.

(Married woman, Vietnam, cited in Jones and Tran, 2010:26)

Box 2.2 Life-course and intergenerational consequences of reproductive health vulnerabilities in Latin America

High and increasing rates of teenage motherhood in Latin America stem in part from cultural ambivalence – more liberal attitudes regarding sexuality in recent years on the one hand, and a denial of adolescent sexual autonomy on the other (Economic Commission for Latin America and the Caribbean, 2007; Näslund-Hadley and Binstock, 2010). In this regard, Latin American society presents an interesting mix of practices that reinforce traditional hierarchies in the family and religion, and modern rationality promoted through law and formal education, which emphasises individual freedom and equality (Fuller, 1998). The following quotes illustrate the difficult social position that many women, especially young women, face as a result of these value tensions:

It is sad that my daughter is a single mother, the man has forgotten his children, this is why my daughter is sick and cannot work well. ... Men deceive and leave young women, they don't take them seriously. ... They leave town and don't come back.

(Mother of a single mother, Peru)

When my father started drinking he abandoned us. We are 10 living siblings and my mother had to sacrifice herself – she went to the farm to work alone to wash the clothes of wealthier people. ... [My father] was there but he contributed little or nothing.

(Married man, Peru)

When I was a little girl, my parents left me and this caused me a great deal of pain. My mother said how can I have eight children? This was her concern so she took me to the jungle to work when I was six. ... My uncle and aunt forced me to cook for the agricultural workers. ... I was like a slave. ... In addition, my uncle tried to abuse me, so I decided to leave.

(Married woman, Peru)

[Most people in the community] ... think it's wrong for women to work outside the home and that if you go to work it's because you like another man or something.

(Married adolescent mother, Mexico)

Sources: Pereznieto and Campos (2010); Vargas (2010).

I may want to do something else later in life, such as learning how to sew and buying a sewing machine, but it will depend on whether my husband allows me to do so.

(Adolescent girl, Ghana, cited in Amuzu et al., 2010:23)

Women also generally lack the power to make decisions about their own resources. Most report that their husbands have significant control, and one in eight women say that their husband is in sole charge of spending their earnings (World Bank, 2011b). Traditional banking regulations, which typically call for deeds and collateral that women are unlikely to possess, have also made it more difficult for women to control their own money and make their own financial decisions (World Bank, 2011b). In part, this lack of financial control reflects women's lack of mobility in many countries, which is often imposed by restrictive norms tied to family honour and rigid gendered divisions between public and private spheres. Restricted mobility in turn often leads to women and girls becoming increasingly isolated from important political and economic processes and resources that are available only in public spaces, and reinforces dependence on male family members – spatial disadvantages which can both disempower them and contribute to poverty traps (Jones et al., 2010a). In Allahabad, India, 93% of boys compared with 22% of girls reported being able to travel unaccompanied to visit a relative (Sebastian et al., 2004),while in the urban slums of Nairboi, two-thirds of girls reported lacking a safe place to meet same-sex friends (Erulkar and Chong, 2005).

Intra-household dynamics are also critical in terms of nutritional security. As women are mainly responsible for managing the household's food, whether through purchase or production, their access to income and degree of household decision-making power significantly shape the family's nutritional outcomes. The more control that women have over family income, the greater the proportion of income spent on food (e.g. Haddad, 1992; Hopkins et al. 1994). Typically, however, women's lower status in the household means that food is not always distributed equally. In India, for instance, women and girls eat last and least in many families (Chorghade et al., 2009), and similar patterns were found during the 2007–2010 global food, fuel and financial crisis (Hossain et al., 2009). Maternal educational levels, which are in turn linked to women's empowerment, decision-making power and control over resources within the household, are also correlated with child nutritional outcomes, with low education often a contributing factor to inadequate caring practices (e.g. Smith and Haddad, 2000).

Although intra-household tensions between husbands and wives can be hard to endure, the risk of abandonment by a male partner may be even more detrimental. Male abandonment – be it real or resulting from a de facto absence due to migration or problems such as alcoholism – generally leads to women assuming full responsibility for children, thus increasing their domestic and productive burden. The effects on girls can also be very negative, including exposure to gender- and sexual-based violence, and potential exploitation within child marriages (UN Children's Fund, 2001).

Limited community decision-making power

The absence of women in decision making increases their vulnerability ... since their needs and concerns are not represented and are often inadequately addressed.

(Laddey et al., 2011:4)

Being able to participate in community decision making is often a critical pre-requisite for poor and vulnerable people to seek solutions to improve their livelihoods and well-being, but it is frequently an avenue closed to women, at both local and national levels (Hoare and Gell, 2009). In addition, community decision making typically relies more heavily on informal networks, thus disadvantaging women, who in many societies are typically either excluded from male-dominated networks or relegated to subordinate roles (e.g. Hicks, 2011).

Women's representation in decision-making bodies varies considerably around the world. Globally, women constitute 19.6% of national parliaments, with the lowest representation in the Middle East and North Africa (11.7%) and East Asia and the Pacific (12.4%).[17] There is also considerable variation in the level of representation at national versus sub-national levels. In Peru, women hold 21.5% of seats in the national Parliament (UN Development Programme, 2010b) but only 6% of all mayoral positions (Ward and Strongman, 2011). In Niger, women hold 13.3% of national seats (UN Development Programme, 2011), yet only 8% of women surveyed said they were included in community decisionmaking.[18] In Bangladesh, 19% of national seats are occupied by women (UN Development Programme, 2011), but less than 4% of government management positions are (Haque, 2008). These differential rates of representation are also partly shaped by whether quota systems are in place.[19] However, there does seem to be evidence that, although women may be gaining stronger representation at district and municipality levels, their representation as heads of local councils remains very low (UN Development Programme, 2010b).

Part of the problem is that quantitative representation is seldom supported by capacity-strengthening initiatives to ensure a qualitative shift in women's community participation. This is exacerbated by political elites' limited experience in exercising democratic mechanisms such as dialogue and negotiation. Underrepresentation is also exacerbated by social norms that devalue women and relegate them to the domestic sphere, with limited opportunities to access the education and income that are critical for building effective political influence (Khan and Ara, 2006). In Peru, for example, women have little say in participatory budgeting processes, even when they attend meetings (Ward and Strongman, 2011). Bolivia's Law of Popular Participation has been unable to increase women's voice, as it fails to address the burden of their other commitments and their lack of agency (Clisby, 2005). Similarly, in India, despite the fact that one-third of all governance seats are reserved for women, in most cases women have effectively been shut out of actual decision making because of the deeply patriarchal nature of the system, which continues to exclude them from the committees where decisions are made (Jayal, 2006).[20]

Resilience: gendered patterning of coping strategies and resources

Given the limited formal mechanisms for mitigating social and economic risks for the poorest in many developing country contexts, vulnerable populations often rely on informal coping strategies to secure their basic well-being. These strategies are varied, and can generally be classified as risk mitigation, self-insurance and risk transfer (Barnett et al., 2008). Other analysts divide coping strategies into problem-focused strategies (e.g. seeking treatment, changing lifestyle, joining support groups, acquiring new skills) and emotion-focused strategies (e.g. avoidance, fatalism, escapism) (Dageid and Duckert, 2008). The former are reflected in a growing body of literature on girls' and women's resilience and resourcefulness (e.g. working in community soup kitchens or setting up informal savings groups) in difficult times (e.g. Lind and Farmelo, 1996; Molyneux, 2007; Rai, 2008). The latter are largely considered to have negative long-term effects, although they might be protective in the short term.

However, there is an acknowledged gap in the data on household involvement in informal coping mechanisms and the relationship to poverty (Dercon, 2004). There is also limited literature on the gendered differentials and the ongoing and long-term impacts of these mechanisms on consumption smoothing or improvement of livelihoods (Quisumbing et al., 2011). However, as discussed in Chapter 1, the literature that does exist suggests that resilience to vulnerability and risk is gendered, with men and women having differential access to coping strategies and resources (e.g. Antonopolous and Floro, 2005; Meinzen-Dick et al., 2011). Here we discuss a number of coping strategies in more detail, including positive measures such as reliance on social capital, traditional reciprocity mechanisms, faith, and remittances. We also consider the gendering of adverse coping strategies such as distress migration and sale of assets, declining consumption patterns, reliance on low-risk but poorly remunerated forms of work, and risky behaviours such as transactional sex.

Social capital

Social capital refers to aspects of social relationships that can be converted into other forms of capital (e.g. economic, cultural) (Silvey and Elmhirst, 2003). It encompasses unorganised forms (e.g. links between family and neighbours) and organised forms (e.g. savings groups, religious associations), and entails both a behavioural component (i.e. what people do together) and a cognitive component (i.e. how people view their interaction with others – with trust, lack of anxiety, feelings of solidarity, etc.) (Bain and Hicks, 1998). As a means of facilitating cooperative action via norms, networks and associations, social capital is in turn integral to strategies aimed at improving livelihood options (Lévesque and White, 2001) and combating poverty (e.g. Woolcock, 1997) across a wide variety of contexts.

Analysts paint a mixed picture of the gender dimensions of social capital. On the one hand, the concept has helped to focus much-needed attention on the importance of moving beyond top-down development policies and including communities in the design and implementation of new initiatives. Group formation (e.g. microcredit groups that require regular meetings, social mobilisation efforts) can build women's human capital (particularly that of women with limited mobility) by providing opportunities to share skills and experience (Anderson et al., 2002; Kabeer et al., 2010).

On the other hand, work on social capital has been criticised on a number of fronts by gender analysts. This work has in part been informed by critics of the concept, such as Harriss (2002:12), who argues that it 'systematically evades issues of context and power.' Not only is there a 'dark side' (Harriss, 2002) of social capital in terms of groups such as gangs, the mafia, moneylenders and debt bondage brokers, which are antisocial and detrimental to the interests of society more generally, but it is also the case that strong groups may result in exclusivity and, in times of need, become associated with conflict. In the case of gender relations, the gendered power dynamics of social relationships and social networks are too often overlooked, including the expectation that community solutions to poverty reduction will rely on women's unremunerated work (e.g. Silvey and Elmhirst, 2003):

> *Social capital approaches might have the potential to render visible the importance of the reproductive or survival economy, but this activity should not be taken for granted and instrumentalised in ways that might be detrimental to*

the poor. Policies work best when, through redistributive and capacity building measures, they strengthen the capabilities of agents to enter into voluntary and mutually beneficial association, sustainable over time, rather than simply being short term and parasitic on the ties of solidarity that may exist.

(Molyneux, 2002: 180)

The specific gendered costs and benefits of participation in social networks need to be taken into consideration, as membership does not automatically create social capital (Cleaver, 2005). For example, while the poorest may initially be admitted to microcredit groups, their inability to make regular contributions or attend meetings regularly can lead to exclusion (Mayoux, 2001).

Very poor women may not have the time or resources available to build and maintain the relationships and associations required for social capital to function as a coping system (Bebbington, 2007). Furthermore, social capital has often been seen as a household asset, without consideration being given to intra-household relationships or the different forms of social capital that different household members might have (Mayoux, 2001). For example, women migrants in Indonesia are often pressured by their families to participate in networks that have high costs to them. One formal social organisation, which was designed to foster connections between female urban migrants and their rural families, implemented a rotating credit savings scheme designed to facilitate remittances from women's earnings back to their families, while also using regular meetings as an opportunity to assert moral pressure over participants' behaviour via appeals to family obligations and honour. This in turn both restricted their financial autonomy and extended the geographical reach of village kin-based control, even while simultaneously providing valuable support to the migrants (Silvey and Elmhirst, 2003).

At the community level, gender discrimination may also intersect with other forms of social exclusion, limiting opportunities to build up social capital. Indigenous and ethnic-minority groups, marginalised castes and displaced populations often have even more limited access to vertical forms of social capital (Woolcock and Narayan, 2000). An absence of effective linkages with political elites and/or a lack of identification documents such as birth certificates often exclude individuals from access to basic services, and from voting (Lin, 2000).

Traditional systems of reciprocity

Traditional systems of reciprocity and solidarity are an important subset of social capital and a key source of support for rural households in particular (Isham et al., 2002; Putnam, 1993). Reciprocity, or mutual aid, is a traditional institution in the Andes, for instance. *Ayni* provides support with building a house, farming or harvesting, as well as life-cycle events such as marriage and death. Social solidarity, or *minka*, refers to collective work to build and preserve communal assets. Similar social support systems are found in much of Latin America and in South Asia (Holmes et al., 2010; Vargas, 2010).

However, these mechanisms are coming under pressure as a result of a more individualistic approach towards mitigating social and economic risks per household, limited communal cohesion due to increasing financial pressures on families, and the competing demands posed by the need to be involved in remunerated work (Lourenço-Lindell, 2002).

In other contexts, especially Africa, mutual funeral associations are common and membership remains high. Around 87% of households surveyed in Ethiopia (Mariam, 2003) and around 95% of households surveyed in Tanzania (Dercon et al., 2006) belong to at least one indigenous insurance institution. In addition, a significant number of these provide assistance in the event of ill health or of a fire, crop loss or house destruction. However, as we discuss in Chapter 5, the poorest are often excluded from these mutual support mechanisms (Santos and Barrett, 2006).

Faith

Faith is a key coping mechanism for many vulnerable people, offering hope for a better tomorrow, a community to lean on in times of crisis and, in some cases, material support for short-term survival. Prayer can also serve as a powerful coping mechanism that helps to 'overcome the initial shock, sadness and anger' (Maman et al., 2009:965) experienced after a devastating event. Furthermore, as Green (2011) has noted, religion is a 'crucial part of identity formation' and is often at the root of how individuals deal with their problems.

Faith-based communities also represent a fundamental pillar of social support in many contexts. In the Democratic Republic of the Congo (DRC), for example, religious institutions were the second most cited source of support after family and friends (Bailey et al., 2011). Religious organisations, many with international affiliations, often also provide material support to vulnerable families, including offering care for orphans, running schools and training programmes, and serving as a distribution point for in-kind benefits such as food (Bailey et al., 2011).

Importantly for our focus on gender and social protection, faith-based institutions may be an important entry point for engaging with the gender dimensions of formal and informal forms of social protection. Studies have consistently shown that women are more religious than men, irrespective of age and belief system (Balachin, 2011; Miller, 1995), and faith and religion often play a major part in women's day-to-day activities. That said, it is also the case that religious teachings may be used by others, especially senior men, in ways that exacerbate women's social vulnerability (Chong, 2008; Raday, 2003). As Tomalin (2011) has noted, development organisations are increasingly strengthening their 'religious literacy', recognising the central role that religious leaders and institutions play in community well-being and recovery in the face of shocks. In this regard, social protection strategies aiming to tackle both economic and social vulnerabilities may need to consider engaging with religious institutions to improve their effectiveness.

Remittances

Transnational remittances are a critical coping strategy for many households, especially in low- and middle-income countries. In 2005, global remittances amounted to $167 billion; they represented as much as 70% of foreign direct investment in Latin America and the Caribbean (de la Fuente, 2008). Remittances are seen as an essential form of development finance (Brown, 2006), and were a key impact pathway in transmitting the effects of the 2007–2009 global economic crisis to impoverished populations in developing countries (Harper and Jones, 2011).

Given that gender is an under-researched area of migration studies in general (Mahler and Pessar, 2006), our understanding of the gendered patterning of remittance earnings and use remains limited. Indeed, the existing evidence on the gendered dimensions of remittances appears to be mixed (Kunz, 2006). Sernyonov and Gorodzeisky (2005) found that men from the Philippines remit more than women, and the income of households with men working abroad is significantly higher than that of households with women working abroad, based on different types of work and working destinations.[21] Male African migrants to Organisation for Economic Co-operation and Development (OECD) countries have also been found to remit more, particularly if they have a spouse remaining in their country of origin (Bollard et al., 2010). However, other analysts argue that women send disproportionately more of their earnings home than their male counterparts, even though they generally earn less than men (Orozco et al., 2006; Osaki, 1999; Silvey and Elmhirst, 2003; Vanwey, 2004). For example, female Salvadorian migrants to the USA were found to send more money home and to be more reliable in their remittance payments, despite earning less than male migrants (Abrego, 2009; Lindley, 2007:12).

Adverse coping mechanisms

Although poor people often use innovative and resourceful coping strategies, informal social protection mechanisms are not always positive, and can lead to a downward spiral of ill-being and chronic poverty (Chronic Poverty Research Centre, 2009). Here again, men and women resort to different approaches, including distress migration, sale of assets, declining consumption, and reliance on risky behaviours.

Distress migration, often from rural to urban areas, is a common coping strategy. Adolescent girls from highly food-insecure areas in rural Ethiopia are considerably more likely to migrate than boys (Erulkar et al., 2008), often undertaking domestic labour in others' households, which brings heightened risks of coerced and transactional sex and exploitative labour, as well as social isolation. Of young female migrants in a sample in Addis Ababa who were employed as domestic workers, 77% reported that their employers were abusive, sometimes physically and sexually (Erulkar et al., 2008). High levels of vulnerability have also been found among Ethiopian female migrants to the Gulf, and especially Saudi Arabia, where women generally enter into a form of bonded labour with very little scope for bargaining power to improve their working conditions (Fernandez, 2010).

Men's distress migration also brings risks for women, including reduced time for women's income generation, exploitation by moneylenders, increased vulnerability to HIV exposure, and abandonment. It also often results in girls taking on more domestic tasks, potentially at the expense of their education (Roy, 2011).

Declining food consumption (in terms of both quality and quantity) is another key coping mechanism that is strongly gendered. Women frequently become 'shock absorbers of household food security, reducing their own consumption to allow more food for other household members' (Quisumbing et al., 2008:1). In Bangladesh, for example, during the recent food-price crisis, the share of rice in total food expenditure increased, leaving a less diversified food basket. This resulted in a higher prevalence of wasting among girls aged 0–59 months (a statistically significant increase of 8.6%, compared with 7.1% among boys), and reduced weight among women in urban areas (Sulaiman et al., 2009).

The distress sale of assets such as livestock, furniture, jewellery and small businesses is also a strongly gendered coping mechanism. One study of Bangladesh and Uganda, reflecting differences in country and context, found that dowry and wedding expenses took their toll on wives' land in Bangladesh, with illness shocks also having a large detrimental impact, whereas death negatively affected wives' assets in Uganda (Quisumbing et al., 2011). In Bangladesh, however, husbands' land and assets were more negatively affected by covariate shocks (such as natural disasters) relative to wives' assets, whereas in Uganda, husbands' assets were relatively protected compared with wives' assets against covariate shocks. As the authors argue:

The differences in the relative impact of the shocks, and their impacts on different types of assets depending on whether these were owned by men or women, show that responses to shocks are context-specific, and that gendered responses to shocks are even more so.

(Quisumbing et al., 2011:34)

Lastly, resorting to risky behaviours (physical or social) is an adverse coping mechanism with important gender differences. Although the evidence is limited, research findings suggest that macroeconomic shocks often result in heightened gender-specific social risks at the micro level (e.g. Weiser et al., 2007). For example, the 1997–1998 Asian financial crisis highlighted gendered patterns of resulting emotional ill health (Friedman and Thomas, 2007; Jones and Marsden, 2009), increased gender-based violence (Heyzer, 2009; Knowles et al., 1999; Nooteboom and White, 2006), heightened time poverty and care work burdens (Hancock, 2001; Islam et al,, 2007), and women resorting to riskier sources of income, including commercial sex work (Wilopo, 1999 and Bronner, 2003, cited in Hopkins, 2006). Similarly, with increasing unemployment in Bangladesh stemming from the 2007–2009 global economic crisis, household tensions increased, resulting in more intra-household violence and increased addictive behaviours, such as chewing tobacco and alcohol consumption, with adverse health effects (Self-Employed Women's Assocation, 2009).

Growing poverty in the context of the recent global economic crisis has also made women and girls particularly vulnerable to trafficking, boosting the supply side of human trafficking worldwide (UN Office on Drugs and Crime, 2009). For example, among a sample of Cambodian sex workers, 58% entered sex work in the wake of the economic crisis, and 19% had previously worked in the hard-hit garment sector (UN Development Programme, 2009). Moreover, post crisis, conditions within the commercial sex work sector appear to be declining, as reflected in increasing reports of excessively long hours, increased debt bondage and more frequent cases of violence. There is evidence that young women and girls are increasingly vulnerable. For instance, activists warned that girls, especially those from poor regions who find themselves out of school, are likely to face strong pressures to find employment, which may put them at risk of exploitation and trafficking – either to domestic work or to commercial sex work (Federation of Free Workers, 2009).

Adverse coping strategies involving risky gendered behaviour are also common in fragile states (Colletta and Cullen, 2000). For instance, Bailey et al. (2011) analysed child-specific vulnerabilities in the Democratic Republic of the Congo and highlighted family breakdown and resulting risky social behaviours with important gender differences. Qualitative research from Kinshasa and Bas Congo provinces suggests that this is generally attributed to the failure of the main income earner (typically the father) to provide for the family, triggering a loss of authority, which frequently involves abandonment by the mother. Children and young people highlighted a lack of respect for authority due to inadequate parental support and resulting engagement in socially risky behaviours. For young women, these included paid sex from a young age, often resulting in early pregnancy; for young men, gang and criminal activity were common (mostly in urban areas).

Conclusions

This chapter has reviewed the gendered patterning of vulnerability, risk and resilience in order to provide an overview of the broader environment within which social protection systems, policies and programmes must engage. A central theme is that women, men, boys and girls are not only affected differently by the same risks or events, but also face different risks and have different coping strategies and resilience mechanisms available to them, depending on their gender. This shapes their experience of and ability to respond to economic and social vulnerabilities, as well as adverse coping mechanisms that they may have to employ in times of stress.

In the case of economic vulnerabilities, women face high wage differentials, employment insecurity because of culturally specific gendered work norms, constraints in balancing income-generating opportunities outside the home with domestic demands, and mobility constraints and language barriers. Women usually have to make the greatest sacrifices in terms of reduced quantity and quality of food consumption in times of economic difficulty, and they also often shoulder the burden of familial ill health disproportionately. Expenses related to life-cycle events (e.g. funerals, weddings) affect men and women differently, and are often major sources of economic stress.

In terms of social vulnerabilities, time poverty is a significant challenge for women and girls. Household decision-making power is often concentrated in a husband's hands, and this is sometimes reinforced by physical violence. Limited reproductive health rights are a significant concern, as is gender-based violence. In cases of male abandonment, single women are vulnerable, especially to labour shortages, social stigma and lack of access to assets. Women also suffer from limited opportunities to exercise meaningful voice and agency at the community level. This often intersects with other forms of social exclusion (e.g. of minority groups, marginalised castes and displaced populations) from linkages to political elites and access to identification documents.

Gender-specific economic and social vulnerabilities are frequently multiple and interlinked, undermining opportunities to achieve well-being and resilient livelihoods. In the absence of formal mechanisms to mitigate risks, social capital, including traditional systems of reciprocity and social solidarity, remittances and faith, constitutes an important source of support. As such, there is a growing body of evidence which highlights the resilience and innovativeness of many poor communities in times of crisis, including specific strategies adopted by women in a range of developing country contexts. This literature highlights the fact that policy and programming efforts need to be cognisant of and seek to build on these capabilities, rather than define marginalised social groups by their vulnerabilities and treat them as passive beneficiaries of support.

This said, in many contexts, many informal coping mechanisms are under increasing strain and are losing their efficacy, which means that households are often having to resort to negative coping strategies with long-term detrimental and gendered economic and social effects. Such strategies include indebtedness, distress migration, sale of assets, reduced consumption and risky social behaviours. Given this trend, formal social protection mechanisms are increasingly recognised as critical in promoting individual and community resilience. It is to such mechanisms that we shall turn in Chapters 3 to 7.

THREE

Transferring income and assets: assessing the contribution to gender-sensitive poverty reduction

Introduction

Social protection programmes that directly increase household wealth, such as cash and asset transfers, have gained political currency across the developing world. Since the 1990s, cash transfers paid directly to the poor – including non-contributory pensions, child and disability grants, and transfers conditional on school attendance and clinic visits – have reached millions of households. This approach has become increasingly important in the context of persistent poverty and the recent global food, fuel and financial crisis.

The growing popularity of cash transfers is due partly to their fungible nature, and to their empowerment effects where beneficiaries can spend the income according to their own priorities. In Latin America, conditional cash transfers (CCTs) have gained political acceptability, as they are contingent on beneficiary families sending their children to school and attending health clinics. This contractual approach between the state and citizens, combined with rigorous evaluation evidence demonstrating positive impacts in terms of reducing poverty and inequality, has encouraged many Asian and African countries to adopt cash transfers. In particular such programmes share an important design feature – they target the caregivers in the household, most of whom are women.

Yet income alone is insufficient to achieve sustainable poverty reduction (Chambers, 1989; Nussbaum, 1995; Sen, 1999). Increasing household income is only effective in reducing poverty when markets are functioning, quality basic services are available and accessible, and household members can engage in sustainable economic activities. Applying a gender lens to the transfer debate is important for a number of reasons. Even low-value payments can constitute an important contribution to daily expenditure, which women usually manage. Moreover, increasing women's control over income has positive effects on economic growth and development outcomes, including child well-being (e.g. expenditure on girls' education), as well as on women's own bargaining power within the household (Dollar and Gatti, 1999; Hoddinott and Haddad, 1995; Quisumbing and Maluccio, 2000; Thomas, 1990).

This is particularly important, given that, as we discussed in Chapter 2, women face greater constraints on earning an income, such as burdensome care responsibilities and labour market inequalities (International Labour Organization, 2010b). Furthermore, many women have little control over income beyond small household purchase decisions. Intra-household dynamics and women's lower status mean that they have little say in decisions, even about their own health (Jan and Akhtar, 2008; Sen et al., 2007).

Directing cash and asset transfers to women in the household has therefore sparked a considerable debate as to whether targeting women in poor households promotes women's empowerment and gender equity. On the one hand, it enhances women's economic empowerment; on the other, an instrumental approach simply targets women to achieve better programme outcomes, reinforcing their traditional roles – what Molyneux (2007), referring to CCTs, has coined 'mothers at the service of the state.' In this chapter we apply a gender lens to the debate on cash and asset transfer programmes, examining their role in reducing gendered experiences of poverty and vulnerability. Using secondary data from sub-Saharan Africa, Asia and Latin America, as well as primary research from Peru, Ghana and Bangladesh, we discuss the challenges and opportunities for enhancing the potential of gender-sensitive cash and asset transfers to move beyond gender stereotypes and safety nets.

Cash and asset transfers: an overview

The aim of cash transfers varies depending on the context, and this influences their design, targeting and implementation, but most have similar overarching objectives, namely immediate and direct alleviation of poverty and vulnerability by smoothing consumption and increasing access to basic social services. Cash transfers can also support longer-term poverty alleviation goals by breaking the intergenerational transmission of poverty (Department for International Development, 2011). Table 3.1 shows the different types of cash transfers that fall within the category of 'social assistance' in our conceptual framework (see Table 1.1 in Chapter 1). They include unconditional transfers (e.g. pensions, child grants, disability grants), transfers conditional on human capital development (e.g. attending health and nutrition check-ups, child vaccinations), perinatal care for mothers and attendance at health talks, enrolment of children in school and attendance targets, and labour force participation (e.g. public works schemes, as discussed in Chapter 4). The regular income received represents a proportion of household income ranging from a few percent of mean household consumption[1] to 20%.[2,3]

Unconditional cash transfers (UCTs) and CCTs also vary in coverage across countries. Social grants in South Africa reached 14 million people

Table 3.1 Typology of cash and asset transfer approaches

Type of cash transfer	Programme details	Main objectives	Target beneficiaries
Conditional cash transfers for human development	Regular income transfers, tied to behaviour conditions (e.g. school attendance, health visits)	To improve health, nutritional and educational outcomes	Children in poor households
Cash for work	Cash payment of wages for public works projects	To reduce seasonal vulnerability and increase household income	Able-bodied adults in poor households
Unconditional cash transfers	Regular income transfers to poor households, without any conditions attached	To increase household income to meet basic needs	Poor households, sometimes those with no available labour
Social pensions	Regular income transfers (non-contributory) to the elderly	To provide basic means of subsistence to the elderly	The elderly
Child grants	Income transfers to households with children	To provide support to meet basic needs of children	Children
Disability grants	Income support for people with disabilities	To support disabled people's access to services and basic needs	The disabled, especially those who cannot work
Asset transfers	Asset transfers combined with complementary programmes and services (economic and social)	To increase household income and graduate beneficiaries from poverty	Poor households

in 2009 (28% of the population), and in Brazil, *Bolsa Família* reaches 11 million families (20% of the population). In other countries, coverage is much more modest. For example, in Zambia in 2009 just 3% of eligible households received UCTs (McCord, 2009).

Asset transfers have been delivered on a much smaller scale, in some cases exceedingly small pilots.[4] For instance, In 2012, 412,700 households received an asset transfer from BRAC's Challenging the Frontiers of Poverty Reduction (CFPR) asset transfer in Bangladesh; 55,000 households benefited from the asset transfer programme, the Chars Livelihoods Programme (CLP) in Bangladesh from 2004–2010, and the pilot Trickle Up Ultra Poor Programme in India transferred assets to just 300 women in 2007, with the aim of scaling up to 4,450 participants by July 2015.

However, asset transfers are gaining attention from social protection actors, especially given the potential for beneficiaries to 'graduate' from poverty. They are seen as social assistance, but are designed to promote households' entrepreneurial and economic activities. For example, whereas most cash transfers provide regular but small amounts,[5] asset transfers represent a one-off but significant increase (as much as $150) to a household's wealth portfolio.[6] The aim is that households then generate a regular income from the asset. Asset transfer programmes tend to use an integrated approach, combining the transfer and related economic support (e.g. skills training, subsistence stipends), social development activities (e.g. awareness raising on inequalities, rights and discrimination) and healthcare.

The impacts of cash and asset transfer programmes have been relatively well documented compared with other social protection interventions. Rigorous impact evaluations demonstrate various positive effects on poverty and vulnerability at the household level. Evidence from UCT and CCT programmes shows positive impacts in terms of reducing the poverty gap and increasing per-capita consumption in middle-income countries (Department for International Development, 2011). For instance, the Child Support Grant in South Africa has reduced the poverty gap by 47% (Samson et al., 2004); in Brazil, the means-tested old-age pension and disability grant and the *Bolsa Família* CCT were responsible for 28% of the 2.7 percentage point fall in the Gini coefficient between 1995 and 2004 (Soares et al., 2007). Where transfers are well targeted to the poor and larger in value, and where the household can use additional income, there have generally been bigger reductions in income poverty (Department for International Development, 2011; Fiszbein and Schady, 2009).

The strongest and most consistent findings are that cash transfers improve consumption and food security, especially in low-income countries (Department for International Development, 2011). In seven programmes in sub-Saharan Africa, for instance, the majority of expenditure priorities are food based (Adato and Bassett, 2008). Moreover, recipient households spend on higher-quality nutrient sources than non-recipient households, although overall income or consumption levels are comparable (Fiszbein and Schady, 2009). Improvements in child nutrition are especially notable. The transfer duration and amount and the recipient's age (with the important window being birth to 24 months) are key factors determining these outcomes (Yablonski and O'Donnell, 2009). Similar positive effects on nutrition were found in Bangladesh's CLP, where beneficiary children were on average less stunted and underweight. Mothers' body index scores had also improved (Conroy et al., 2010).

Cash transfers can also increase access to health and education measured by increases in school enrolment and take-up of health services (e.g. preventative health services and health monitoring for children and pregnant women) (Department for International Development, 2011; Fiszbein and Schady, 2009). Critical debates over whether it is the *conditions* in CCTs that have resulted in increased service use remain inconclusive. While evidence suggests that the impact of CCTs on service use cannot be explained by the programme's cash component alone (Fiszbein and Schady, 2009), other studies have shown no significant differences in outcomes related to service utilisation between CCTs and UCTs (Baird et al., 2010; de Brauw and Hoddinott, 2008).

Despite positive effects on the use of basic services, there is little evidence that cash transfers improve final outcomes in health or education. This is likely because other factors such as initial enrolment rates, quality of available services, parenting practices, information availability and household perceptions, particularly of the returns of education and social-cultural issues are also important in determining final programme outcomes (Department for International Development, 2011; Fiszbein and Schady, 2009). This suggests that the potential for cash transfers to promote learning or improve health – without complementary interventions – is somewhat limited. Interventions that simultaneously seek to improve parenting practices and the home environment are particularly important (Fiszbein and Schady, 2009). For example, a number of CCTs condition transfers on participation in awareness raising and educational talks or fora. Some have increased the use of contraception by providing information previously not available to the poorest households (Lamadrid-Figueroa et al., 2010). Interventions that promote early learning opportunities are also important, as evidence from Ecuador and Nicaragua demonstrate (Macours et al., 2008; Paxson and Schady, 2007, cited in Department for International Development, 2011).

Moreover, investment in service provision is required if better outcomes in health and education are to be achieved. This may require empowering poor communities to make services more accountable. In Mexico, beneficiaries are now demanding better-quality services, forcing service providers to improve their performance (Barber and Gertler, 2010). In addition, a comprehensive programme that relies on more active and tailored interventions by social workers and others may be needed, as the case of *Chile Solidario* would suggest.

Finally, cash transfers can also contribute to economic productivity and growth. Although current evidence on the role of cash transfers in aggregate economic growth remains limited (Barrientos and Scott, 2008), they can strengthen 'micro-level outcomes which are intermediate to growth' (Barrientos and Scott, 2008:2). Again, the determinants are context-specific, but factors which support productivity include adequate, regular and reliable transfers that are appropriately channelled and complemented by asset accumulation and protection mechanisms (Bach, 2010), access to finance on better terms for poor people, and increased labour-market opportunities through, for example, lessening the burden of childcare, covering the costs of job seeking, and reducing the number of working days lost to ill health (Department for International Development, 2011). In essence, it is increasingly recognised that 'graduation' out of poverty through cash transfers is unlikely without complementary livelihood interventions (Hashemi and Umaira, 2011; Slater, 2009).

Here the asset transfer model, in which graduation is a key objective, offers more potential. For instance, in the CFPR in Bangladesh, which provides training alongside asset transfers, 90% of households reported improved earnings, and income increased from 40% to 56% between 2002 and 2005. Of the 54% of participants who owned land in 2005, 35% were landless in 2000, and 98% of participants had savings (a compulsory component) in 2005, compared with only 8% before joining the programme (Das and Misha, 2010; Department for International Development Bangladesh, 2006). Similar positive results have been found in the CLP. Even after the programme, participants increased their asset base significantly, reporting that programme beneficiaries increased their income and expenditure, on average, higher than the national extreme poverty line (Conroy et al., 2010). Increased investment in land and savings is also reported (Conroy et al., 2010). Das and Misha (2010) explain the positive findings from the CFPR programme as a result of determination and hard work, confidence, social networking and asset management skills.

Applying a gender lens to transfer programmes

Cash and asset transfers have the potential to address a range of gender inequalities, including those in human capital development (particularly health and education) and access to and control over income (including credit) and assets. They can also address the challenges that women face in balancing income-generating opportunities with domestic and care work demands, as well as the tensions that financial strains can put on household relationships (see Chapter 2). In addition, programmes are increasingly focusing on transformative objectives by promoting social and economic empowerment and more equitable gender relations at household and community levels. In this section, we look at the key features in terms of gender-sensitive design, the impacts on gender equity and the challenges that remain.

Gender-sensitive design features

A number of gender-related objectives have been made explicit in cash and asset transfer programmes, particularly those that improve demand for services through conditions to increase girls' school enrolment or women's attendance at health clinics. However, policymakers are increasingly looking at what other factors influence effectiveness in transferring income to households (Fiszbein and Schady, 2009; Teixeira and Soares, 2011). This refers not only to quality and availability of services, but also to the importance of intra-household dynamics, individual capabilities, and knowledge and agency to make decisions and change behaviour. While addressing gender inequalities has been an instrumental objective of many transfer programmes, an increasing number are incorporating design and implementation features to enhance positive gender-equitable outcomes. These include the following:

- *Empowering women as recipients of the transfer.* Many transfers target women as they are the primary caregiver so as to improve outcomes for children. However, increasing women's empowerment has most often been an instrumental goal, with limited explicit objectives and design features to promote empowerment. Exceptions include Bangladesh's CFPR and CLP asset transfers, which target women explicitly to strengthen their bargaining power and their position in the household (Building Resources Across Communities, 2009; Hossain and Blackie, 2011), and Egypt's CCT pilot, which focuses on mothers and female-headed households and has increased their capability to 'direct their lives' (Pathways of Women's Empowerment, 2010:2).
- *Reducing gender disparities in education*: A number of CCTs in particular have sought to address the gender gaps in education. Mexico's *Oportunidades* and Turkey's Social Risk Mitigation Project (both CCTs) pay higher benefits for girls, in recognition of their disadvantages in enrolment (Fiszbein and Schady, 2009; World Bank, 2008). Where boys are less likely to attend school, in Bangladesh, Cambodia and Jamaica, cash transfers explicitly promote their enrolment (Fiszbein and Schady, 2009).
- *Supporting women's access to reproductive health services*: A growing number of CCTs are tackling maternal mortality and promoting child well-being by requiring pregnant women to attend antenatal and postnatal visits and health and nutrition seminars, including Brazil's *Bolsa Família*, Bolivia's *Bono Juana Azurduy*, Egypt's *Ain El-Sira*, Indonesia's *Program Keluarga Harapan*, Peru's *Juntos*, the Philippines' *Pantawid Pamilyang Pilipino Program* and Ghana's Livelihood Empowerment Against Poverty (LEAP). Pilots in Ethiopia, Malawi and Uganda are comparing the effectiveness of CCTs with UCTs to reduce maternal mortality (Samuels and Jones, 2011).
- *Reducing the incidence of female infanticide and early marriage*: Delaying marriage has multiple direct and indirect benefits, including increased educational prospects, reduced fertility rates and improved health and child well-being (Jones et al., 2010a). Some states in India provide financial incentives for female births and for delaying girls' marriage until 18 years of age (e.g. *Apni Beti Apna Dhan* in Haryana).

- *Promoting family access to complementary services*: In Latin America, some CCTs have created links to other programmes and services (governmental and non-governmental). In some cases, this has involved introducing and institutionalising a single registry, enabling beneficiaries of one programme to access others. For instance, in Brazil, Chile and Colombia there is an explicit commitment to inter-sectoral working through CCTs (Soares and Silva, 2010), and a single registry supports the integration of households into programmes such as those dealing with food security, housing, banking and credit, and judicial services. In Colombia's *Familias en Acción*, this results in a commitment to empowering women and protecting them from domestic and sexual violence. *Bolsa Família* includes support for antenatal and postnatal care, although it has no specific objective relating to gender equality. *Chile Solidario*'s pillar on psychosocial support includes tackling intra-household violence. In Bangladesh, the CFPR and CLP promote women's savings accounts and aim to link women to credit sources as they graduate from the programme.
- *Providing skills training and knowledge*: A number of programmes have helped beneficiaries through training and awareness raising. For instance, the CFPR and CLP in Bangladesh and CCTs in Egypt and Ghana promote the interface between social workers and beneficiaries to increase women's knowledge on health, nutrition, rights and other social issues. In Mexico and Peru, *Oportunidades* and *Juntos*, respectively, strengthen women's leadership in local communities in their role as programme facilitators.
- *Addressing age-related vulnerabilities*: Non-contributory pensions are increasingly being implemented in middle- and low-income developing countries, including Brazil, India, Lesotho, Namibia, Nepal and South Africa. These recognise that women are more likely to experience a severe loss of income in their older years, and to risk losing their home and assets on widowhood. In regions such as Southern Africa, where HIV/AIDS has led to high numbers of absent middle-aged adults and vulnerable children, older women bear the brunt of additional childcare responsibilities.[7]

Impacts of cash and asset transfers on gender equity

The impacts of transfers on gender equity show varied results. Although there has been less rigorous research on and evaluation of the gendered effects (Department for International Development, 2011), this is now increasing. Here we provide an overview of the impacts from available evidence, with further discussion in the case studies that follow.

Women's empowerment and intra-household dynamics

Evidence suggests that targeting women with income transfers has important benefits for children's well-being and can also benefit women directly by enhancing their role in the household, provided that they control the transfer and make decisions about expenditure. In some cases, cash and asset transfers have contributed to improvements in women's confidence and status as they become less reliant on men for income for the household.

In CCTs in Latin America, women control the transfer, have improved self-confidence and mobility, receive greater respect from men, and in some cases have increased status in the household (Adato and Roopnaraine, 2010; Larrañaga et al., 2009, cited in Soares and Silva, 2010; Molyneux and Thomson, 2011; Vargas, 2010). In some cases, men are starting to take on domestic tasks, looking after children and sharing household decisions (Farah, 2009; Vargas, 2010). In the CLP asset transfer in Bangladesh, women have improved decision-making ability related to family planning, levels of self-perceived community respect and intra-household relations (Conroy, 2009).

However, these claims need to be treated with caution. In some cases, such as in Mexico, targeting women with cash transfers resulted in short-term increases in domestic violence (World Bank, 2011a). Subsequent programmes included measures to discourage domestic violence (in Brazil), training and awareness raising for mothers and families (in Colombia and Peru), and even the involvement of dedicated social workers (in Chile) (World Bank, 2011a).

Moreover, deeper investigation of the empowerment gains in targeting women demonstrates that, in practice, these can be quite limited (Molyneux and Thomson, 2011). Women cannot always increase their access to and control over household resources, their bargaining power in the household may not increase, and the traditional gender division of labour often remains unchanged (Arif et al., 2010b; Building Resources Across Communities, 2009; Conroy, 2009; Jenson, 2009; Molyneux, 2007).

Income and employment opportunities

Cash transfers can have an unintended effect on women's labour-market participation. In households in South Africa where women received the old-age grant, working-age women were significantly more likely to migrate for work as a result (Posel et al., 2004). The income from the pension helps to overcome two constraints on female labour migration, namely the resource constraint, with female pensioners sharing more from their income than male pensioners, and the childcare constraint. As such, women receiving pensions are correlated with positive impacts on child well-being (no similar effect is found for male pensions).

In terms of labour-market participation, especially for women, in Brazil *Bolsa Família* increased beneficiaries' labour-market participation by 2.6% compared with non-beneficiaries, and the participation rate of women was 4.3% higher than that of men (Oliveira et al., 2007). Colombia's *Juntos* has also increased female urban employment and male rural employment rates (Econometría, 2006, cited in Soares and Silva, 2010).

Asset programmes in Bangladesh found positive changes in women's livelihood strategies, moving away from dependence on daily wage labour (in agriculture or domestic service) towards self-employment (in livestock rearing) (Bandiera et al., 2009; Conroy et al., 2010; Das and Misha, 2010). Increased savings have also been reported (Bandiera et al., 2009; Conroy et al., 2010; Das and Misha, 2010).

Finally, greater financial independence is an important programme impact, particularly for older women. In Madhya Pradesh, India, where older widows lost their home and land after their husband's death, the pension had improved family relationships because it enabled them to contribute to the family income, despite the small amount offered. It also increased dignity, confidence and social status, and reduced anxieties about money (Help Age, 2009). In South Africa, evidence suggests that, among households with older people, the poverty headcount would be 2.8% higher if pension income was to be removed. Such pensions are likely to have a particularly beneficial impact on women, given their position in the labour market and their role as unpaid caregivers. They are also critical to poverty reduction in households affected by HIV/AIDS if directed to caregivers, most of whom are women and girls (International Labour Organization, 2010a).

Cash transfers linked to complementary services may also provide linkages to economic services. For instance, in Ghana's LEAP, access to informal credit from neighbours and family has increased, as participation in the programme is seen as a guarantee that loans will be repaid (Amuzu et al., 2010). Similar benefits have been found in Brazil's *Bolsa Família* (Suarez and Libardoni, 2008, cited in Soares and Silva, 2010).

Education and health

Financial incentives for girls can promote behaviour change and parents' willingness to send them to school. Numerous evaluations of Mexico's *Oportunidades* have found significant impacts in this respect. Primary school enrolment increased by between 0.74% and 1.07% for boys and between 0.96% and 1.45% for girls, and secondary school enrolment by between 7.2% and 9.3% for girls (recipients of an increased transfer) and between 3.5% and 5.8% for boys (Schultz, 2000). Once children are enrolled, the likelihood of being enrolled in the next period increases by 15% for boys, and is even higher in secondary school and for girls, while the likelihood of child labour declined by between 15% and 25% for boys, and 15% for girls (Kabeer, 2008).

In Malawi's Zomba cash transfer programme, re-enrolment rates among girls who had dropped out of school before the programme started increased by two and a half times, and the dropout rate at baseline fell from 11% to 6% within the first year. Higher transfers given directly to girl students were associated with considerably improved school attendance and progress when the transfer was conditional on their school attendance. There were also positive effects on beneficiaries' sexual behaviour, including declining rates of early marriage and adolescent pregnancy (Baird et al., 2009b).

With regard to health outcomes, in Turkey it was found that CCTs which encouraged attendance at pre-birth hostels for pregnant mothers and deliveries in public hospitals alongside investment in the supply side of services reduced the maternal mortality rate from 70 per 100,000 live births in 2000 to 19.8 per 100,000 by 2009 (Prata et al., 2010). In India, the *Janani Suraksha Yojana* CCT increased the number of assisted deliveries in the presence of a skilled attendant by around 36%, although final outcomes with regard to maternal mortality are not yet known (Lim et al. 2010, cited in World Bank, 2011b).

Skills and knowledge

Cash and asset transfer programmes that enhance women's knowledge and access to skills training have had positive outcomes. In Nicaragua, attending workshops increased women's awareness of their rights and gave them the opportunity to speak in public and share their experiences with other women (Adato and Roopnaraine, 2010). In Bangladesh, asset transfer programmes result in increased economic skills and increased knowledge on rights (Conroy et al., 2010; Das and Misha, 2010).

Challenges

The above discussion indicates some positive trends towards achieving greater gender equity through transfer programmes. However, many challenges remain. For instance, in many cash transfer programmes, enhancing women's empowerment has been instrumental in achieving the primary objective of better outcomes for the family – Molyneux's 'mothers at the service of the state' (Molyneux, 2006). Indeed, the 'empowerment' effect is perhaps the largest area of contention in the CCT debate on gender.

Another key criticism, of CCTs in particular, relates to human capital development. While some programmes have addressed a number of important risks facing girls and women (especially those related to reproductive health), others have largely ignored these. For instance, despite improvements in other gender-related health indicators, teenage pregnancy continues to be a major problem in many Latin American countries, and one that is more acute in rural areas and among poorer populations (Soares and Silva, 2010). This has enormous ramifications for life chances.

The lack of men's involvement in meeting CCT requirements and community awareness raising is another limitation (Molyneux and Thomson, 2011). If men were involved more systematically, it is likely there would be more positive outcomes in terms of gender equality within the household (e.g. egalitarian division of labour, reducing tensions and violence, and increasing women's role in decisionmaking).

Moreover, most programmes are not cognisant of women's dual roles as carers and productive workers, and do not consider the costs of having to collect transfers, including the time spent travelling, often at the expense of other income-generating activities. This is particularly relevant to women living in more isolated areas (Britto, 2007; Molyneux and Thomson, 2011).

Indeed, transfer programmes that fail to acknowledge – let alone promote – the productive capacity of women and their families reduce the opportunities for beneficiaries to graduate out of the programme and poverty. Key to this criticism, for instance, is that women are 'empowered' only as guardians of children and as channels for child-centred policies, rather than being the focus of interventions to promote women's strategic interests across the lifecycle (Jenson, 2009; Molyneux, 2007). Lack of attention to the tensions between women's care and work activities is also central to this debate. A number of actors advocate for CCTs to integrate a livelihoods or income-generating component (Molyneux and Thomson, 2011).

Finally, CCTs have been criticised for their paternalistic approach to poverty reduction. There is a tension between how programmes relate to beneficiaries (with women treated as 'girls') and the development of a rights-based approach that raises women's consciousness as full citizens (Faur, 2008; Jones et al., 2007; Vargas and Salazar, 2009). Referring to Mexico's *Oportunidades* programme, Molyneux sums up this tension as follows: 'its construction of need reveals that different logics operate in relation to daughters and mothers – the former are invested in as citizens, and their capabilities and life chances are expanded through education and health; the mothers, meanwhile, are treated as having responsibilities rather than needs and rights' (Molyneux, 2007:30).

Case studies: cash and asset transfers in Ghana, Peru and Bangladesh

Keeping both the key advances and challenges of cash and asset transfer programmes from a gender perspective in mind, we discuss three case studies

- cash transfer programmes in Ghana and Peru and an asset transfer initaitive in Bangladesh - in more detail so as to highlight not only the tensions and complexities involved but also some of the potential opportunities for more transformative programming. They are drawn from primary qualitative research (see Introduction for discussion of methodology) and were chosen because they were relatively under-researched, especially from a gender perspective. All three programmes also have unique characteristics for their genre. Ghana's LEAP is at the time of writing the largest cash transfer in West and Central Africa – the poorest and most vulnerable region in sub-Saharan Africa. Peru's *Juntos* started to be rolled out in areas most affected by civil war as part of national reconciliation efforts, and Bangladesh's CFPR emerged as one of the first asset transfer models, which is now being replicated in other national contexts. Moreover, all three programmes demonstrate interesting design features in terms of linkages to complementary services and programmes. Table 3.2 provides an overview of the key features of each programme.

Ghana[8]

Programme design

Ghana's LEAP is a 'quasi-conditional' cash transfer programme – that is, families are made aware of programme conditions, but are not penalised for not adhering to them. Launched in March 2008, it is financed mainly by donors and implemented through the Department of Social Welfare. In 2012, it reached 68,000 households in 100 districts, transferring approximately $8–15 a month to the family's caregiver. The programme employs complex targeting methods to reach the poorest, involving the selection of deprived districts and a mix of community-based selection and proxy means testing. The aim is to supplement the income of the poor and provide linkages to complementary services. There are both positive conditions (school enrolment and retention, registration at birth, registering with the National Health Insurance Scheme (NHIS), accessing postnatal care and immunisations for young children) and negative ones (ensuring children are neither trafficked nor engaged in the worst forms of child labour).

LEAP's design also outlines a broad array of potential linkages with other programmes through the development of a single registry, such as microfinance initiatives, supplementary feeding, agricultural inputs and skills training (Amuzu et al., 2010). This addresses, in theory, a key criticism of many other CCTs, namely that they do not promote sufficient opportunities for improving livelihoods or income generation.

The extent to which gender considerations have been embedded in LEAP is mixed. Of the six overall programme objectives, two are most relevant from a gender perspective. The first relates to targeted beneficiaries – women

Table 3.2 Cash and asset case study programme details

	Ghana	Peru	Bangladesh
Programme name	Ghana's Livelihood Empowerment Against Poverty (LEAP)	Programa de Apoyo a los Mas Pobres, *Juntos*	Challenging the Frontiers of Poverty Reduction (CFPR)
Year started	2008	2005	2002
Programme administration	Department of Social Welfare, Government of Ghana	Government of Peru	BRAC (non-governmental organisation) and funded by donor consortium
Programme objectives	To supplement the incomes of extreme-poor households through the provision of cash transfers and link them with complementary services and also promote community awareness; to secure birth registration for children	To provide beneficiary households with nutritional support, healthcare, education and identification documents to improve maternal and child health status; to decrease school dropouts; to promote registration and identification	To provide a comprehensive assistance package to increase income opportunities while reducing vulnerability and risk
Programme design	Quasi-conditional cash transfer. Monthly transfers from GH¢ 8 ($6.90) for one dependant up to a maximum of GH¢ 15 ($12.90) for four dependant. The programme is also meant to be time-bound in that beneficiaries are expected to 'graduate' within 3 years. Conditions include: (1) no engagement in harmful forms of child labour or human trafficking; (2) ensuring that children are in school; (3) ensuring that children's	CCT. Transfers of approximately $30 monthly grants conditional on attending health check-ups, school and registering personal identification	The programme extends the 'laddered strategic linkage' approach. Participants receive: (1) an income-generating asset transfer (Tk 3,000–9,000: $50–150); (2) income-generation skill training in poultry- and/or livestock-rearing, vegetable cultivation, shoe-making, etc.; (3) technical follow-up of enterprise operations; (4) provision of support inputs for the enterprise; (5) monthly stipends for subsistence of Tk 10 (about $0.17) per day for 12–15 months; (6) social development (e.g. social awareness and confidence building, legal awareness, social action on early marriage/dowry, etc.); (7)

Table 3.2 (continued)

	Ghana	Peru	Bangladesh
	births are registered; (4) taking newborns to postnatal check-ups and ensuring children are fully immunized		mobilisation of local elites for support (pro-poor advocacy through seminars, workshops and popular theatres); (8) access to health care
Gender design features	Two explicit gender-related objectives (out of six): • Women are targeted directly as caregivers of orphans and vulnerable children and/or as people with disabilities or people over 65 years themselves, and indirectly as recipients of complementary services insofar as they are caregivers for those with disabilities and the aged. Recognition of potential benefits of targeting women – increasing status within and outside the household • Special care is given to identify girls engaged in the worst forms of child labour	No explicit design to empower women/transform gender relations, but important implicit features are as follows: • Transfer is received by women • Positive discrimination towards girls' secondary education • Compliance with conditionalities is mainly women's responsibility • Some linkages to complementary programmes and services, including civic documentation, anti-violence, and productive activities. Women beneficiaries are elected as community facilitators, linking programme facilitators and beneficiaries	Explicit attention to gender inequality is embedded within programme objectives: • Women are targeted with an economic transfer, on the basis that income poverty is highest among females, often single women, even though they may be living in a joint family • By improving women's economic position, the programme aims to increase women's bargaining power within the household • The programme aims to increase women's social capital through their involvement in the specially created village poverty reduction committees, and increase mobility and communication in the public domain and knowledge and skills to reduce their vulnerability • It addresses social inequalities, such as violence against women, dowry and early marriage, through complementary social development

activities aimed at contributing to wider changes in equality between men and women, at the individual, household and community level

Targeting/eligibility	Targeted at the extreme-poor. The programme employs complex targeting methods, involving the selection of deprived districts and then a mix of community-based selection and proxy means testing	Poor rural households with children under 14 years of age. The programme combines geographical targeting, proxy means testing and community assessment to select beneficiaries	Targeted at the ultra-poor. Geographical targeting based on poverty maps to select the poorest areas, then selection of villages using BRAC's local knowledge, then participatory wealth-ranking exercises to identify locations in villages where the poorest live; households are then ranked on targeting indicators, later visually confirmed by BRAC staff. Targeting ensures identification of the poorest, but is also instrumental in developing partnerships with local communities
Coverage	68,000 households in 100 districts (2012)	492,000 households (2012)	412,700 households (2012)
Cost	Budget is 0.1% of GDP. Budgetary allocation was GH¢7.5 million in 2009	2006: $100 million, about 0.11% of GDP	Per household cost is $300

Source: Amuzu et al. (2010); Barrientos et al. (2010); Fiszbein and Schady (2009); Holmes et al. (2010).

Coverage in Ghana: www.ghana.gov.gh/index.php/news/features/11651—68000-households-benefit-from-leap.
Coverage in Peru:www.peruviantimes.com/11/report-finds-juntos-program-helps-decrease-malnutrition/14657/

receive the transfer as people living with disabilities or people over 65 years of age themselves, and indirectly through complementary services insofar as they are caregivers for orphans, people with disabilities and the aged. Of note here is that the government explicitly seeks a gender balance among aged beneficiaries. The objective is to not only improve men and women beneficiaries' consumption and health impacts but also to contribute to women's improved social status within and outside the household (e.g. by increasing their bargaining or decision-making power).

The second gender-related objective speaks explicitly to adopting a gender-sensitive approach to implementation, which is manifested in three ways: (1) ensuring 'a reasonable balance between men and women aged 65 years and above' in the payment of transfers; (2) providing the transfer to men if they are the main caregivers; and (3) giving 'special care … to identify girls engaged in the worst forms of child labour, such as hired domestic work' (Government of Ghana, 2007b).

Impacts[9]

Like many other cash transfer programmes, LEAP makes important contributions to consumption and investments in human capital development at the *individual level*. Beneficiaries often use their cash grants for payment of NHIS premiums, to purchase school supplies, and for essential food items (Jones et al., 2009b). These basic household expenses are typically seen as women's domain, although male and female respondents across the lifecycle recognised the value of this, as is highlighted by Bange's story (see Personal Narrative 3.1). However, the small size of the transfer means that the impact is limited, especially with regard to potential investment in productive activities. Other tangible benefits include improved access to loans from family and friends as a result of greater confidence in the ability of beneficiaries to repay loans, and increased ability to hire labour to work on farms (especially for female-headed households). However, the small value of the transfer is insufficient to serve as start-up capital for new businesses.

Moreover, although at the time of research the programme had not yet provided any formal capacity building or education, social welfare officers had made an effort to make recommendations about 'spending the transfer wisely', including buying nutritious food, spending it on the care of beneficiaries (especially in the case of the aged or disabled), and supporting children's schooling.

At the *family/intra-household level*, the transfer has not changed dynamics notably, as the testimonies from both women and men in the following extracts show:

Personal Narrative 3.1: Cash transfers can provide relief for the poorest – Bange's experience of living with illness in Ghana

Bange is a widow in her fifties. She has leprosy. Of her seven children, only one has survived. Her daughter, who is mentally ill, and her new baby live with her.

Despite her illness, Bange still farms. She has her own plot of land near her brothers' farm and lives in their compound. She was sent home to her family even before her husband died, as he did not want to care for her when she became seriously ill. After his death she was denied any inheritance, except for her children.

LEAP has made her life significantly better. It has improved the quality of her food, as she can now afford to buy what she wants, and it has allowed her to build a two-roomed house for herself. She wishes that she were not so stigmatised for her illness; she also longs for treatment for her daughter. After watching her other six children die, she feels that her daughter is her hope for the future.

Source: Amuzu et al. (2010).

I make the decisions about how to use the LEAP money – my two wives do not disagree with me.

(Married man, Gushiegu, cited by Amuzu et al., 2010:32)

When my husband was alive he consulted me about decisions. I now receive LEAP money and give it to my son who decides how to use it. He gives me some of it back.

(Elderly widow, Gushiegu, cited by Amuzu et al., 2010:32)

Possible reasons for this include the newness of the programme (it had only been operating for 18 months when the research took place), low transfer amounts, limited public awareness raising about the value of transfers going to women (perhaps reducing the attention given to women's caregiving role and related time burden), and the absence of a specific education component, such as those in Latin American programmes. Moreover, Latin America's relatively vibrant civil society has highlighted gender inequality issues, but this sector is much thinner in Ghana, especially outside Accra. As such, there are fewer reinforcing messages and initiatives in communities to take advantage of LEAP's gender sensitisation potential.

At the *community level*, the programme demonstrates some important impacts, although these too have had limited effects on gender relations. LEAP has generally been positive in terms of social capital development. Non-beneficiaries and beneficiaries alike pointed out that beneficiaries share food for all to enjoy from their LEAP transfer, help to cover neighbours' health costs in the case of persistent illness, support neighbours to pay school fees, and provide loans to non-beneficiaries. There was also a general consensus that LEAP enhances beneficiaries' ability to contribute to community projects. Some respondents noted that LEAP had contributed to increased social cohesion and social networking through more regular discussions about community issues and enhanced confidence in the government.

In terms of programme governance, although women have been invited to programme-related village meetings, this has not yet translated into effective voice. As one widow from Chereponi explained, 'women are invited to meetings but they have nothing to say, so they don't really participate' (Amuzu et al., 2010:34). Moreover, women's representation in community LEAP implementation committees (CLICs) is also minimal partly because there is no mechanism to ensure equal participation in such community fora.[10] Future consideration could be given to ensuring equal participation of women in LEAP local governance structures, including CLICs and beneficiary fora.

Key drivers of programme outcomes

A number of political, institutional and socio-cultural drivers have contributed to the mixed implementation record of the gender dimensions of LEAP. Partisan politics, underinvestment in capacity building for programme implementers, inadequate coordination mechanisms, and weak political support for the project among district authorities emerged as key constraints on realising the gender-related goals of the LEAP design document.

Local political actors generally concurred that, because LEAP beneficiaries were recruited around election time, a great deal of confusion was generated about the programme objectives, and that this politicisation has unfortunately been perpetuated even postelection in the identification of beneficiaries. District welfare officers also reported problems of elite capture of the CLICs and inaction in the face of irregularities.

Moreover, although social protection, and especially LEAP, is growing in profile in national circles in Ghana, investment in ensuring effective implementation at district and community levels has been quite limited in general, especially with regard to gender-related design commitments. Social welfare officers lamented the high workload that the programme had generated, and an inability to effectively monitor its implementation and outcomes. In particular, data collection and analysis capacity in the Department of Social Welfare is very limited, particularly from a gender perspective. As experience with cash transfers in other countries has shown (Mexico's *Oportunidades* stands out in this respect), improvements in these technical capacities have been shown to be important to a programme's long-term political and financial viability, as well as being a valuable data resource for the country.

Concerns about limited training in programme delivery (including gender-sensitive features) for implementers were also widespread. Training had been only cursory, with people not involved in the programme included in some cases, and those on the frontlines, including district LEAP implementing committees (DLICs) and CLICs, excluded in others. This is particularly problematic given the important role that social welfare officers play in defining the criteria employed locally for targeting beneficiaries. Efforts to provide training for new appointees have also been poor. Moreover, while a considerable degree of the potential of LEAP relates to the opportunity to discuss programme conditionalities with communities and other relevant issues linked to the well-being of vulnerable groups, social welfare officers have received no specific guidance on what to talk to communities about.

Challenges regarding decentralisation are also apparent. The programme is seen as driven by the central government, and as such district authorities have minimal involvement and ownership. This is reflected in the limited role played by DLICs, and the fact that many district officers are unaware of the programme's details, especially its gender-related features.

Meanwhile, although the programme design has provisions for a district coordinating body – the DLIC – these have not become functional, due to a lack of funds. Importantly, too, the gender desk officer had not played any role to date in LEAP. Government officers responsible for promoting gender equality are generally absent from implementation committees, effectively limiting the potential for implementing gender-sensitive design elements.

For LEAP to realise its potential, an emphasis on linkages to complementary services facilitated by a single registry system will be crucial. However, little progress appears to have been made in working towards such synergies. National-level protocols on complementary services have not been signed or rolled out, nor have regional-level LEAP implementation committees been set up to involve key actors such as the regional Department of Women's Welfare. Although the Ministry of Women and Children's Affairs is involved in tackling a number of key age- and gender-related economic and social vulnerabilities, linkages with LEAP are weak. Like district social welfare officers, gender desk officers are seriously under-funded (the post is unsalaried and reliant on the volunteer labour of officials with other full-time posts). Coordinated efforts to maximise scarce financial and human resources earmarked for gender mainstreaming at district level could help to address some of the underlying vulnerabilities that cash transfers alone will fail to resolve.

Peru

Programme design

In Peru, the government-led *Programa de Apoyo a los Mas Pobres, Juntos*, was launched in April 2005, inspired by similar CCTs in Mexico and Brazil. In 2012, *Juntos* reached just over 490,000 households in 14 regions. It has achieved an efficient geographical focus on the poorest (quintiles 1 and 2), and targets households with children under 14 years of age or pregnant women. In 2010, *Juntos* transferred approximately $70 every 2 months to the poorest rural households (regardless of the number of children), equivalent of around 13% of total monthly household consumption. This is relatively modest compared with other programmes in the region (Porter with Dornan, 2010).

Juntos promotes access to basic health, education and nutrition to break the intergenerational transmission of poverty through investments in human capital. The cash transfer is conditional on families meeting the following commitments: obtaining civic identification documents for women and children, attendance of children at primary school, health and nutritional check-ups (which include vaccination, growth and development controls, and nutritional complements for children, as well as antenatal and postnatal check-ups), delivery in a health facility, and capacity building in sexual and reproductive health (primarily family planning) and nutrition. If these conditionalities are not met, sanctions are applied.

Juntos beneficiaries receive the transfer for an initial 4-year period, which can be extended for a further 4 years. The transfer is given to mothers on the assumption that they are likely to be more accountable for their children's well-being. However, like many other CCTs in Latin America, *Juntos* was not explicitly designed as a mechanism for empowering women or transforming gender relations (Molyneux and Thomson, 2011; Vargas, 2010).

Nevertheless, a number of programme features have potential implications for promoting gender equity, as we discuss in the section on programme impacts below. These include the conditions on civic registration, participation in training and information sessions facilitated by programme implementers, attendance at health talks on nutrition and family planning, links made with public services for protection against violence and abuse, and a mechanism for representing the views of beneficiaries through elected women community leaders.

Programme impacts[11]

A number of important impacts at the individual, intra-household and community level emerge from *Juntos* in relation to gender equity and women's empowerment.

In terms of *individual* impacts, *Juntos* has reduced the depth of income poverty (Perova and Vakis, 2009). The additional household income is of particular value for single-parent households (especially single mothers, who represent up to 40% of beneficiaries in some areas), given the greater vulnerabilities they face (Vargas, 2010).

Juntos has also improved access to basic services (Perova and Vakis, 2009). Immunisations of children under 1 year of age increased by 30% within 1 year of implementation, antenatal and postnatal visits to health clinics increased by approximately 65%, and there was a reduction in home births (Jones et al., 2007). Although actual *outcomes* are not clear, these results are seen as a significant improvement, given the high levels of maternal mortality in poor rural areas (Jones et al., 2007).

Positive changes in accessing education are also reported, especially for girls, given their household responsibilities (Perova and Vakis, 2009, cited in Molyneux and Thomson, 2011). *Juntos* has resulted in greater parental involvement in children's education. Women report increased interaction with teachers about their children's progress (Perova and Vakis, 2009, cited in Molyneux and Thomson, 2011). Evidence also suggests improvements in literacy. Women beneficiaries have learned to sign their names and can now recognise their civic identification number and name on *Juntos* registers. These aspects are highly valued and diminish their sense of social exclusion (Vargas, 2010).

Improvements in food security have also been reported (Perova and Vakis, 2009), especially with regard to children's quality of diet, resulting from a combination of programme factors and complementary programme linkages motivated by concerns about high chronic malnutrition rates. These include the cultivation of domestic vegetable gardens, increasing women's knowledge about nutrition through greater access to public services and messages from *Juntos* staff, and greater emphasis on nutrition in health facilities, through practical nutritional sessions and follow-ups. However, the latter are often oversubscribed, which has prompted a redesign in *Juntos* 2 to include a more structured information and education component (Molyneux and Thomson, 2011; Vargas, 2010).

Another important impact is on women's mobility. *Juntos* is promoting significant changes in women's daily routines, as they attend meetings and training sessions and travel to the bank. Although many men were initially opposed to women's involvement in frequent meetings – accusing them of 'losing time' and neglecting domestic and productive responsibilities – there is now greater space for negotiation (Vargas, 2010).

However, two critical concerns arise with regard to the individual impacts of *Juntos*. The first relates to limited livelihoods options. *Juntos* promotes some financial autonomy for women (see below), as they administer money not previously available to them, and they can utilise part of the money for income-generating activities (e.g. buying small livestock, developing kitchen gardens, weaving). However, linkages with rural livelihoods programmes, such as *Mi Chacra Productiva* and *Agro Rural*, which seek to promote the uptake of validated low-cost technologies (e.g. watering, crops, livestock, etc.) and improve productivity and profitability in rural areas by fostering family and community businesses, were not considered in the initial programme design. These initiatives are still nascent or non-existent in some districts, but they are of increasing importance as a result of growing concerns about sustainability (Vargas, 2010).

The second constraint relates to women's time poverty. *Juntos* promotes women's role as the caregiver in the family, but local authorities and some beneficiaries (particularly women) are concerned that it increases women's time poverty. Women have to fulfil programme conditionalities and participate in complementary activities, and are frequently told that the transfer will be taken away if they fail to comply with such requests (Molyneux and Thomson, 2011; Vargas, 2010).

At the *intra-household* level, *Juntos* has had several unexpected impacts. These include changes in gender roles with regard to responsibilities in the household, decision making and attitudes towards violence. Beneficiaries revealed a gradual move away from traditional caring roles towards greater equity in the distribution of care responsibilities, particularly for younger couples (Vargas, 2010). Men mentioned greater participation in tasks such as looking after children and performing domestic chores (Alcázar, 2008), particularly when women need to attend meetings, although older children and particularly girls continue to have an important role in this regard. Men also said that this had resulted in a learning process that enabled them to be more involved with children, as they were now less concerned about being stigmatised for taking on 'women's tasks':

> *Before, I would come home and grumble when dinner wasn't ready, I would tell her 'What do you do all day, you should at least have a meal ready for when I get home.' Now I don't say that to her since I've experienced her responsibilities; I cook, wash the dishes, do the children's laundry, wash them, clean the house and when she suddenly gets home, the food is not ready yet [laughter].*
>
> (Male, Arizona, cited in Jones et al., 2007:11)

The impact on women's empowerment and decision making in the household is mixed. On the one hand, *Juntos* has contributed towards women having greater decision-making power and gaining more respect from men. It is mainly women who decide what to do with the transfer, and this puts them in a better position to confront situations of devaluation, and also gives them a sense of being less dependent on men (Vargas, 2010):

> I don't have to wait for my husband to give me money from his pocket. … For some women who don't work, the man tells you 'You don't work, you don't know how to bring money [to the household].' Only now I bring money. … When you earn money, you can defend yourself.
>
> (Female, Liriopata, cited in Vargas, 2010:35)

However, this does not necessarily equate to greater negotiation or decision-making power in other spheres. According to Molyneux and Thomson (2011), several women indicated that men still made the important decisions (on major investments, buying expensive goods, etc.) in the family. Moreover, men's frequent opposition to the use of contraception is problematic, and women argued that the programme had had no impact in terms of questioning gender patterns that give greater power and decision-making capacity to men:

> It's always the same; the man always decides what to do: in the field, in the home, even little things, and when he goes to work I stay with the children.
>
> (H. woman, Acomayo, cited in Molyneux and Thomson, 2011:36)

Evidence suggests that there are positive trends with regard to reducing violence. Women now refer to legislation that protects victims of violence, as a result of interventions by several public and private institutions (including the Municipal Ombudsperson for Children and Adolescents, the Women's Emergency Centre and non-governmental organisations) and health facilities and also *Juntos* facilitators raising awareness of these issues, usually through local initiatives rather than as part of the overall programme strategy (Jones et al., 2007; Molyneux and Thomson, 2011). Indeed, Vargas (2010) found that a strong history of past interventions promoting women's rights had led to greater awareness of domestic violence.

At the *community level*, a number of mixed impacts emerge. The promotion of women as elected community facilitators (as a link between programme facilitators and beneficiaries[12]) offers opportunities for participation and strengthening women's leadership. Women report that it increases their self-confidence and self-esteem and helps to overcome traditional barriers such as perceived lack of skills and fear of speaking in public (Vargas, 2010). However, some studies point to complaints about such women behaving in an authoritarian manner (Molyneux and Thomson, 2011). Moreover, apart from as facilitators the programme does not include beneficiaries in design, implementation or evaluation (Molyneux and Thomson, 2011). In addition, some beneficiaries reported being subject to negative perceptions by the rest of the community for receiving *Juntos* 'handouts.' Nevertheless, *Juntos* has also had a positive influence on women from the most marginal communities, as they have more opportunities to be in public spaces and to interact with people with whom they previously had little contact, such as teachers (Molyneux and Thomson, 2011).

Finally, there is also tension with regard to women's demand for their rights. One of the longer-term aims of *Juntos* is 'to change the paternalistic relationship between the citizenry and state-funded social programmes, and to present accessing basic services for children as a joint responsibility of both parents and the state' (Jones et al., 2007:17). Central to this is the idea that, in order to ensure service providers are accountable for the provision of quality services, citizens must demonstrate their demand for access to these (Jones et al., 2007). However, Molyneux and Thomson (2011) indicate that the relationships between local *Juntos* staff and beneficiaries have not increased awareness of rights or led to greater demand from citizens.

Key drivers of programme outcomes

Juntos demonstrates important progress towards gender-equitable outcomes for both girls and women. Importantly, targeting women with the transfer only partly explains these gains. Maximising its benefits has required leveraging additional complementary services and programmes and utilising social welfare staff to provide training and awareness raising. As such, beneficiaries gain much more than just income.

However, like many other CCTs, addressing gender inequality has been used as an instrumental approach to achieving programme objectives and, as such, benefits have been largely unintended. Indeed, despite advances in promoting gender equity, state interventions remain characterised by a welfare and anti-poverty approach, in which women are conceptualised mainly as groups needing assistance. Molyneux and Thomson (2011) argue that one of the key reasons why *Juntos* has reinforced women's traditional mothering and caring roles, rather than addressing their wider strategic gender concerns (e.g. relating to strengthening and building women's skills or fostering their participation in programme design and in the community), is the limited strategic connections between the Social Protection Department and women's equality mechanisms or units within the government that might enhance women's social position. *Juntos* does have contact with different state programmes, but these linkages have been limited to food distribution, nutrition and access to identity documents, rather than mainstreaming the equal opportunities policy or integrating women's rights into *Juntos* (Molyneux and Thomson, 2011). In addition, the Ministry for Women and Social Development has limited power to promote gender mainstreaming in different government agencies with responsibilities touching on different aspects of poverty and vulnerability. Overall, gender focal points in public offices tend to be largely tokenistic, with little or no involvement in mainstream policy and programming processes (Roeder et al., 2008).

Moreover, where there has been progress beyond explicit programme design features, these have been a result of the role undertaken by *Juntos* community facilitators, who explicitly transmit messages about gender equity, particularly the importance of shared responsibilities within the household, women's leadership and political participation at community level and, to a lesser extent, violence against women. These have had positive results where there is a history of public and non-governmental collaboration interventions regarding women's rights, leading to greater awareness (Molyneux and Thomson, 2011; Vargas, 2010).

The role that *Juntos* facilitators play in promoting gender-equitable outcomes could be more effectively institutionalised and strengthened. Facilitators have received training in areas such as leadership, participatory methodologies and organisation, but these initiatives are often viewed as insufficient, as are corresponding educational materials. Limitations also include difficulties with regard to follow-up of households, especially because of high levels of geographical dispersion and limited numbers of staff. In particular, guidelines and training on addressing gender issues are lacking, and skills for raising awareness of women's rights need strengthening.

Finally, the gendered impacts of *Juntos* are still not strategically monitored. Although gender-sensitive indicators have been developed, at the time of writing (2012) they have not yet been incorporated into the programme (Molyneux and Thomson, 2011),[13] hampering the potential to strengthen an evidence-based gender-sensitive approach to design and implementation.

Bangladesh

Programme design

Bangladesh's CFPR, implemented by the non-governmental organisation Building Resources Across Communities (BRAC), aims to enhance the economic and social capabilities of ultra-poor households, primarily through transfers of productive assets (e.g. livestock). It takes a two-pronged approach, explicitly recognising the need to address economic and social vulnerabilities to achieve poverty reduction, to develop livelihood options and to simultaneously remove wider socio-political constraints on development (Building Resources Across Communities, 2009). Gender equality is central to the design, recognising that poverty reduction can be effective only if women's 'ability to make decisions in the household is increased, if they are more able to move and communicate in the public domain and have increased knowledge and skills to reduce their vulnerability' (Building Resources Across Communities, 2009:145). Indeed, as one BRAC staff member noted, 'households who do the best out of CFPR are those where families work together – these are the "over-achievers." The strugglers are the ones where women don't take any decisions' (Holmes et al., 2010:20).

The CFPR targets women with the transfer on the basis that income poverty is highest among females, and also seeks to reach single women even when they are living in a joint family. By increasing women's economic position, the programme aims to increase women's bargaining power within the household. The transfer is coupled with skills training, an 18-month cash stipend, 2 years' free access to health services and awareness raising on women's rights, including violence against women, dowry and early marriage, and nutrition.

The programme also seeks to increase women's social capital through the formation of village poverty reduction committees – an innovative (but often controversial[14]) approach that involves the community 'elite' to coordinate and focus existing local charitable efforts for the ultra-poor and help to promote local awareness of the problems they face (Building Resources Across Communities, 2009).

The CFPR is divided into two components – the Specially Targeted Ultra Poor (STUP) and the Other Targeted Ultra Poor (OTUP).[15] Geographical targeting based on poverty maps is used to select the poorest areas, villages are selected using BRAC's local knowledge, participatory wealth-ranking exercises identify locations in villages where the poorest live, and then households are ranked on targeting indicators, which are later visually confirmed by BRAC staff.

Programme impacts[16]

At the *individual level*, the CFPR (STUP) has had important economic benefits for recipient households. A first-phase evaluation of beneficiaries found significant improvements on five asset indicators (physical, financial, human, natural and social), with the greatest gain found in financial assets, and the least in human assets (Rabbani et al., 2006). Indeed, when income generation from the asset is reliable, women are able to start reducing their reliance on daily wage labour and to spend more time on self-employment activities (Das and Misha, 2010) (see Asma's story in Personal Narrative 3.2).

However, household income does not automatically increase as assets are transferred, but depends on the income generated from the asset (e.g. selling of milk, eggs, goat kids and calves), household labour capacity, and choices as to how this income is spent.

Personal Narrative 3.2: Asma's experience of integrated social protection in Bangladesh.

Asma is 55 years old and has participated in the CFPR for 3 years. Her situation was good until 10 years ago when her husband left her and she had to return to her parents' home. She had to start work to look after her two children and to send her daughter to school.

She still finds it difficult to eat properly and to clothe her children and give them a good education. She works as a housemaid to buy food, for which she receives Tk 100 a month.

She received a cow and a goat from BRAC. The cow is pregnant, she has two goat kids and one mother goat, and she previously sold two goat kids (for Tk 2,000). She spent the money on tin for the house and on food. She intends to keep the calf until she needs it to pay for her daughter's wedding in the future. Only after this will she use her money to buy land.

Source: Holmes et al. (2010).

Households spend their money on food, children's education, health treatment, improving the house and small savings. Many households reinvest their income where possible. A number of respondents had received loans from BRAC, which also supported this reinvestment.

Only God knows how much I am happy after getting the support. For instance, if I face health problems, I could sell one of my cattle and could use the money for my treatment. If I had the cattle before, I wouldn't have had to borrow money from others. [How many goats and cows do you have right now?] One cow and eight goats. [How many goats would you sell?] Six. [What would you do with the money?] I want to buy land. … I told you, my hopes are big,

(Elderly woman, Narail, cited in Holmes et al., 2010:21)

At the *intra-household level*, households as a unit take responsibility for the asset because it is seen as beneficial for the whole household, and awareness of male household members about the benefits of women's participation is raised before the programme starts. Although women in particular spend time at home tending to the livestock – an additional workload on top of their existing domestic and income-generating responsibilities – women respondents did not see this as a burden. Time and support from other family members are seen as critical to programme success, and in many households other family members (often women) help to look after the assets when the beneficiaries are working elsewhere. Women also rely on male relatives in the household to look after the animals, as well as receiving their financial support (e.g. to ensure that food is available for the cows).

Turning to other social impacts, women beneficiaries reported that they had more confidence and knowledge as a result of asset ownership and economic and social development training. Through the economic training and the ownership of assets, women's confidence had increased, and they reported being well equipped with improved skills to support their household to move out of poverty. They also stated that they felt a greater sense of dignity, received more respect from family members since becoming beneficiaries, and had more control over the money they earned as part of the programme and contributed to small-scale household purchases and, in some cases, larger investments.

However, women did not feel that this had translated into significantly more decision-making power in the household (see also Building Resources Across Communities, 2009). Nevertheless, progress is being made and should be recognised. Both women and men reported that men increasingly heard wives' opinions, and men were supportive of women working outside and increasing their mobility (e.g. to attend the BRAC office) because of the benefits that this brought to the household.

A key concern, however, is that women participants remain dependent on men to make a living from the asset. A BRAC evaluation (Building Resources Across Communities, 2009) found that although it is not yet completely acceptable for women to be present in rural marketplaces, women from STUP II households are more likely to have visited the market compared with non-beneficiaries. Even so, beneficiaries noted that they remain dependent on men to go to the market and to negotiate prices for assets and produce:

> [*You told us that if you need to sell something, your husband goes to market. Have you ever wanted to go to the market to sell things?*] *Why should I go? I have a husband, a son.*
>
> (Married woman, Magura, cited in Holmes et al., 2010:24)

Like many transfer programmes, at the *community level* another important social impact is women's increased social capital. Beneficiaries reported better social networks among themselves, their neighbours, BRAC staff and members of the village poverty reduction committee. Women and their family members felt that they received more respect from other community members, and were invited to different community occasions, as a result of participating in the programme. Although the village poverty reduction committee is controversial, women felt that they benefited from participating and speaking in meetings.

Despite increased participation in community meetings, findings suggest that the programme has not enhanced women's access to, or demand for, government services (see also Building Resources Across Communities, 2009):

> *If I go to them [government officials] and say, 'sirs are distributing cards [government safety net programme cards] but we are not getting them' … they would say we don't need that, whatever we have is enough. We are not going to get the cards anyway.*
> (Single elderly woman, Narail, cited in Holmes et al., 2010:25)

Moreover, despite clear broader processes of change towards gender equality in Bangladesh, such as reducing child marriage and dowry practices, changing practices as a result of the social awareness training has proved difficult. Beneficiaries can relate to the social development issues that they learn about, but are unable to put these into practice, often because of persistent customary and traditional norms:

> *For instance, my daughter is married now, if she is facing violence in her family, if we the women go to the police station together, then the police will help us; these kinds of issues they have taught us; they also suggested to us where to go if we have problems like this. If we are all together nobody causes harm to us. However, the truth is we hardly do whatever we have learnt.*
> (Single elderly woman, Narail, cited in Holmes et al., 2010:25)

Key drivers of programme outcomes

The outcomes of the CFPR are influenced by BRAC's unique capacity as an implementing organisation, and therefore the replicability of this complex model to different contexts or by different actors needs to be treated with caution. That said, important lessons can be learned, which are already being translated into other programmes across the developing world.

The current design and delivery of the CFPR are a consequence of innovative and iterative applied learning processes within BRAC, resulting in a design that addresses the multiple dimensions of poverty facing the ultra-poor in comparison with other poor groups (Matin, 2002).

BRAC launched the CFPR in 2002, partly because its existing micro-finance programme rarely reached the poorest women, and partly because at least 30% of female beneficiaries of a BRAC/World Food Programme scheme did not progress to microfinance as intended (Hulme and Moore, 2007). These women were more likely to live in female-headed households that did not have a working adult male and/or to suffer from chronic illness (Hashemi, 2006, cited in Matin et al., 2008). In particular, shortcomings of previous programmes targeted at the poorest households pointed to the need for a cyclical and more complex perspective of the process to graduate out of poverty, rather than a linear one based on a single economic approach. The CFPR was designed to enable households to benefit from carefully sequenced 'protective' mechanisms (such as the stipend and health services) and 'promotional' mechanisms (asset grants and skills training), and to address socio-political constraints through 'transformative' measures (linking separate initiatives to provide social development inputs to address gender inequalities and the mobilisation of local elites for support, thereby building women's social capital). This would enable beneficiaries to have both the material (e.g. poultry, cages, veterinary support) and non-material (e.g. technical skills, social standing) resources to engage with the economy (Hulme and Moore, 2007).

In terms of implementation, a number of key features stand out as contributing to the programme's effectiveness, such as implementation efficiency, investment in the capacity of staff with regard to gender, coordination between economic and social components, and impressive gender-sensitive monitoring and evaluation indicators.

BRAC is one of the world's largest service delivery non-governmental organisations (Hulme and Moore, 2007). It 'has a capacity to manage operations across Bangladesh that rivals the business sector and often outperforms the government; has substantial experience in programme experimentation and learning; and its economic programmes are heavily loan driven and envision poor people as micro-entrepreneurs' (Hulme and Moore, 2007:2). The CFPR is designed, implemented and monitored solely by BRAC, with donor funding. By reducing the number of partners involved and thus the administration that this entails, BRAC has been able to focus on issues that make graduation more likely, such as quality of training, building confidence and cohesion among beneficiaries, follow-up, and supervision and mentoring (Matin et al., 2008),

Indeed BRAC invests in its staff, and the CFPR's objectives and strategy, including the gender-sensitive features, are clearly understood and followed. There are clear organisational structures and lines of responsibility, and BRAC rewards good individual performances (Hulme and Moore, 2007). The CFPR is highly labour-intensive, with BRAC staff mediating strategically at household and community level, generating buy-in from husbands and community leaders to allow women to participate (Holmes et al., 2010). Staff are responsible for supporting beneficiaries to make appropriate judgements on the asset transfer they receive, taking into consideration a number of factors, including family circumstances.

Beneficiaries are supported, at least for the first year to 18 months, by regular engagement and follow-up with staff. This facilitates both the economic aspects (e.g. helping households to decide when to sell the offspring from livestock and ensuring a fair price) and the social aspects (where mentoring and empowering instil confidence in women to overcome ultra-poverty). The weekly meetings to disburse the cash stipend are also used as a forum for members to discuss problems related to enterprise, health and social care.

The impact of the social development meetings in particular has been mixed. Women can recollect the training components but do not put the learning into practice, in part because practices such as dowry and early marriage are deeply embedded in the culture, and economics, of communities. Aware of the challenge in changing embedded cultural norms, BRAC's approach is to raise awareness among men and women of discriminatory and unequal practices, seeing this as part of a broader and longer-term social change process to which it can contribute. There are different expectations for the different components of this training, and expectations of how women – and communities – will use it are realistic.

Meanwhile, staff capacity is still identified as one of the key challenges to enhancing the integration of gender into the CFPR, although BRAC staff do receive training, including that on gender, specifically in relation to livelihood activities as well as communicating the social development skills training. BRAC staff are trained by the BRAC gender team, which usually includes just a half-day orientation workshop. This has been identified as a concern by the gender team, which recommends that it should be much more focused, and in particular go beyond assumptions about gender being only about women, to integrate the bigger issue of how to include men and address unequal gendered and social relations.

Finally, monitoring and evaluation have been a critical factor in programme success. Undertaken by BRAC's Research and Evaluation Department, monitoring and evaluation includes the maintenance of a panel dataset that tracks key indicators for a sample of selected ultra-poor households that have participated in the programme since 2002 and non-selected ultra-poor households, and regular subjective assessments of beneficiaries and control groups in terms of poverty and welfare indicators and change. The monitoring framework incorporates the collection of data disaggregated by gender and also age (i.e. children, adults), and in addition a number of specific indicators of women's economic, social and political empowerment, such as decision making in the household, mobility, financial autonomy, interaction in the public sphere, political and legal awareness, and attitudes towards violence against women.

Conclusions

The evidence base on the gendered effects of cash and asset transfers is considerably more robust than that on other social protection instruments. There is a clear consensus emerging that CCTs in particular have advanced human capital development among girls and boys, and higher financial incentives to send girls to school have broken down both financial and traditional attitudinal barriers to girls' education.

However, a key question relates to whether targeting women has only reinforced their traditional roles as mothers or carers, or whether it has provided an opportunity to tackle gender inequality in a more transformational way. Overwhelmingly, the evidence suggests that transferring CCT income to mothers has supported women in carrying out their caring and domestic roles, and enhanced their status within the household. In some cases, transfers have also had deeper impacts, enhancing women's status within the family, reducing family tensions, and increasing community mobility and participation. However, programme conditions have also exacerbated women's time poverty, and many have not strategically promoted opportunities to support women's livelihood activities (with the exception of asset transfers). In addition, although women have sometimes gained household status and respect, this change has not yet significantly altered the division of labour and power within the household.

Part of the reason for this is that few programmes set out explicitly to transform gender relations beyond targeting women as transfer recipients, with the exception of a few CCFs and a number of asset transfer programmes. However, even implicit gender-sensitive features of programme design have shown positive trends towards gender-equitable outcomes, suggesting that, if these were made explicit and embedded more strategically within implementation processes, we might see larger-scale impacts on gender vulnerabilities and gender inequity. Indeed our analysis highlights the fact that cash and asset transfers are not a silver bullet – programme design requires gender-sensitive features to maximise the benefits for women, men, girls and boys. Transfers need to be combined with interventions that support women's economic independence as well as those that tackle social risks, such as promoting women's empowerment, reducing gender-based violence, promoting equal gender relations in the household and community, and supporting citizenship rights. Where such linkages to complementary programmes and services are in place, small-scale progress towards more positive outcomes can often be seen.

Links with training programmes increase women's confidence and knowledge (e.g. in nutrition, healthcare and education) and provide income-generating opportunities (in the case of Bangladesh's asset transfer programme). Furthermore, support to secure civic registration results in increased documented citizenship, linkages with gender-focused programmes help to break down barriers and traditions relating to gender-based violence and support changes in the household division of labour, and electing beneficiaries as community facilitators raises awareness about women's participation and leadership.

Even so, gender-sensitive design does not always translate into gender-equitable impacts. Programmes have seen much less progress in areas such as women leveraging their reproductive health rights and exercising their citizenship rights, and there have been some concerns over the creation of power imbalances through the role of local programme leadership. Overcoming these challenges will necessitate increased political commitment (at national and local level), investment in institutionalising coordination between transfer programmes and gender-focused institutions. Complementary programmes to tackle economic and social vulnerabilities, as well as training of social welfare staff and programme facilitators to implement gender-sensitive features and promote gender equality through awareness-raising mechanisms, and, importantly, strengthening mechanisms whereby beneficiaries can know and exercise their rights and demands. Finally, as we discuss in more detail in the concluding chapter, such changes need to be informed by the generation and analysis of relevant gender-disaggregated data.

FOUR

Working one's way out of poverty: public works through a gender lens

Introduction

In many countries, women's economic participation is significantly lower, more poorly remunerated and more precarious than that of men. As discussed in Chapter 2, poor rural women in particular often have few income-generating opportunities, and are hampered by limited assets and/ or control over household assets, low skills and low literacy levels (see Personal Narrative 4.1). They also face disproportionate domestic and care work responsibilities, alongside discriminatory socio-cultural norms with regard to appropriate forms of work. In short, and as Table 4.1 illustrates, women remain over-represented in vulnerable employment,[1] including that in own-account, unpaid family and low-skilled casual wage labour, often receiving lower wages than men in the same jobs.[2] This chapter examines the extent to which public works programmes (PWPs) as a social protection measure can help to address such gendered vulnerabilities.

Although PWPs have a long history,[3] and are increasingly implemented in developing countries (see Annex 1), most of them do not guarantee

Table 4.1 Gender differences in labour force participation

	Women	*Men*
Population over 15 years of age (global)	2.5 billion	2.5 billion
Labour force participation rate (global)	51.60%	77.70%
Middle East	25.40%	75.30%
North Africa	27.40%	76.40%
South Asia	34.90%	81.60%
Sector of employment		
Services (global)	46.90%	40.40%
Industry (global)	16.10%	26.40%
Agriculture (global)	37.10%	33.10%
South Asia	69.90%	44.30%
Sub-Saharan Africa	61.10%	61.80%
South-East Asia and Pacific	44.50%	44.50%
Share in vulnerable employment (global)	51.20%	48.20%
South Asia	84%	73.10%
Sub-Saharan Africa	83.50%	69.60%

Source: International Labour Organization (2010b)

Personal Narrative 4.1: PWPs as a lifeline for the extreme poor – Tamenu in Ethiopia

Tamenu is an Ethiopian single mother in her forties who has four children, including 7-year-old twins. She was married as a young adolescent, her firstborn son died in infancy and her second-born is epileptic. She also has an older, married daughter, and a grandchild. The fathers of her children have never helped to support them, and she is too poor to marry again – she believes nobody will marry a woman without cattle. Lacking assets and education, and facing very limited income-generating opportunities in her rural surroundings, she has long struggled to find a sustainable livelihood source.

None of Tamenu's children have been to school: fees and materials have always been expensive, and this is compounded by the fact that Tamenu is now too ill to work. Her 7-year-old son lives with another family and herds their cattle, while his twin sister works around the home. Her older daughter works in a mill and provides the family with some flour.

However, the family's main means of support is provided by Tamenu's 20-year-old epileptic son through his work for the PSNP. Even though his seizures are often severe, Tamenu feels she has no option but to send him to work. The 70 kg of grain that the family receives each month for his labour are all that stands between them and hunger.

Tamenu is very grateful to the PSNP. She sees her life as being constrained by never-ending poverty, but would like her children to have better lives. In particular, although she knows that her son's epilepsy is not curable, she would like to be able to afford medication for him.

Source: Jones et al. (2010b).

---

employment. Instead they are designed to provide temporary or irregular access to income, usually to tide over the most vulnerable groups during sudden-onset economic crises and natural disasters (Hagen-Zanker et al., 2011; McCord, 2008). However, entitlement programmes that guarantee the right to a job have considerable potential. In conditions of structural unemployment, they can – with other interventions – function as 'engines' of economic development, poverty alleviation and social inclusion (Antonopoulos, 2007). Although the country-specific reasons for unemployment and underemployment are varied and complex, employment guarantee programmes can generate income, increase food security, contribute to environmental regeneration and water conservation, create necessary infrastructure, empower local communities, reduce the unpaid care burden of women, and contribute to the achievement of the Millennium Development Goals (Antonopoulos, 2007).

In order to explore the gendered dimensions of employment guarantee programmes, we first review the secondary literature on the history of women's involvement in PWPs and the gendered dimension of programme design, implementation and impacts. The second half of the chapter draws on primary research evidence from Ethiopia's Productive Safety Net Programme (PSNP) and India's Mahatma Gandhi National Rural Employment Guarantee Scheme (MGNREGS) – large-scale programmes that actively promote women's participation, but with mixed impact. We explore the strengths and weaknesses of the PSNP and MGNREGS through a gender lens, identifying the key drivers that shape programme outcomes for women, men and children.

The aims of public works programmes

PWPs are labour-intensive infrastructure initiatives that aim to provide payment (in cash or food) for target populations, often during 'hungry' periods.[4] They are often politically attractive, requiring that beneficiaries 'help themselves'[5] (Bloom, 2009). PWPs address shortages of infrastructure (e.g. roads, irrigation, water harvesting, tree plantations, schools, health clinics), and are typically self-targeting, given the low level of the benefit and the heavy physical labour requirements (Subbarao, 2003). As such, targeting costs[6] are lower than those of many other social protection interventions (although overall administration costs are much higher, given the costs of recruitment, supervision of work, etc.) (McCord, 2008). Where communities are involved in the selection of projects, there is a greater sense of ownership of assets and a greater likelihood of their maintenance (Devereux and Solomon, 2006; World Bank, 2009).

Applying a gender lens to public works programmes

Programme design

PWPs must contend with a number of intersecting gendered labour-market inequalities. Women typically have fewer formal-sector employment options (for the reasons discussed in Chapter 2), and are disproportionately represented in the informal sector, where social security benefits are rare.[7] They often receive only a fraction of the wages of their male counterparts,[8] or are given payment in kind (usually food).[9] Women's employment opportunities also tend to be more insecure because of culturally specific gendered work norms that determine not only whether they work, but also what types of work they do (Food and Agriculture Organization of the United Nations, 2011). For instance, in Ethiopia and Northern Ghana, women can only perform a narrow range of agricultural tasks, excluding, for example, ploughing. In Indonesia, even in dry land areas, rubber extraction is deemed to be men's work and rice cultivation women's work. These differences are often exacerbated by the constraints that women face in balancing income-generating opportunities outside the home with childcare and other domestic demands.

In order to address these labour-market inequalities, PWPs have – to varying degrees – sought to embed issues of gender equity in their design. Gender-sensitive features include the following:

- *Institutionalising quotas for women's participation to address women's historical exclusion from PWPs.* Examples include India's MGNREGS, which requires that at least one-third of beneficiaries are women (Ministry of Rural Development, 2008), South Africa's Expanded Public Works Programme (EPWP) (Devereux and Solomon, 2006) and Malawi's Social Action Fund (SAF), which have quotas of at least 40% for women participants.
- *Recognising that women have specific life-cycle needs, some programmes make provision to ensure that women are not penalised in PWP participation.* Botswana's Labour-Intensive Public Works Programme (LIPWP) allows lactating mothers rest periods in which to feed their children (Antonopoulos, 2007). Ethiopia's PSNP provides direct cash transfers, with no work requirement, for all women who are more than 6 months pregnant or nursing an infant younger than 10 months (Jones et al., 2010b). India's MGNREGS requires women to receive preferential work placements close to their homes, and stipulates that crèche facilities must be provided for young children (Holmes et al., 2010).
- *Offering women flexible working hours so that they can better balance their care work and income-generating work responsibilities.* For example, Ethiopia's PSNP allows women to structure their working hours around their family obligations, arriving late and leaving early if necessary (Jones et al., 2010b). South Africa's Zibambele Rural Roads Maintenance Programme (ZRRMP), in KwaZulu-Natal, allows multiple adults to work together to fulfil the household's monthly labour requirements, so families are not constrained by illness or death (McCord, 2004).
- *Targeting female-headed households, which are often labour-constrained and extremely vulnerable.* South Africa's ZRRMP is able to 'smooth' constraints on single mothers' time by promoting

labour sharing. Ethiopia's PSNP, which largely focuses on creating community infrastructure, also allows participants to work on the private landholdings of female-headed households.

- *Guaranteeing equal wages for men and women.* For example, Bangladesh's Rural Maintenance Programme (RMP) requires that women and men receive the same wages for comparable jobs (Kabeer, 2008).
- *Opening supervisory positions for women.* Bangladesh's RMP and Botswana's LIPWP (Dejardin, 1996) employ women as supervisors and provide relevant training. Sri Lanka's National Housing Development Authority also allows women to supervise construction projects (Antonopoulos, 2007).
- *Involving women in programme planning.* Ethiopia's PSNP and Zambia's Micro Projects Unit (MPU) (Kamanga, 1998) both call for women to have equal representation on committees, and Malawi's Social Action Fund (SAF) mandates women's participation (Kabeer, 2008).
- *Supporting women's access to savings and credit programmes.* Bangladesh's RMP[10] and Ethiopia's PSNP[11] are both linked to credit provision mechanisms to facilitate participants' graduation from PWPs. In addition, Nepal's Dhaulagiri Irrigation Development Project (Lokollo, 1999) has created women's savings groups, and India's MGNREGS offers women individual bank accounts.
- *Linking participants with complementary services.* Argentina's *Programa de Jefes y Jefas de Hogar Desocupados* provides women with literacy education, child tutoring, and family counselling for drug abuse and domestic violence (Kabeer, 2008). Senegal's *Agence d'Exécution des Travaux d'Intérêt Public* also provided women with adult literacy classes (van der Lugt and Kuby, 1997).
- *Supporting women's domestic roles by creating infrastructure that eases women's time constraints.* Zimbabwe's Rural Transport Study (Antonopoulos, 2007) and Zambia's MPU (Kamanga, 1998) are examples. Malawi's SAF has also used PWP labour to build maternity clinics (Kabeer, 2008), and South Africa's EPWP has provided training and work opportunities for carers of people living with HIV and orphans in home and community-based care, and early child development (McCord, 2004).

Programme impacts

Although women's involvement in PWPs can have many positive impacts – on individual women, their households and communities – the gendered design features described above are not extensively implemented. Women's participation in PWPs can have the following effects:

- *Improvement of household food security.* For example, women participants in Bangladesh's RMP were able to give their families three meals a day on average – something they had rarely achieved before the programme (Kabeer, 2008).
- *Offering a route out of poverty.* Argentina's *PWP* programme (see above) in which 69% of participants were female, led to a marked positive impact on rates of extreme poverty, keeping 10% of its participants from falling below the poverty line (Galasso and Ravillion, 2003, cited in Kabeer, 2008). More than 50% of the RMP graduates stayed out of poverty after graduation, for instance, with around 75% earning the same wages they had earned in the programme (Kabeer, 2008).
- *Improvement of women's empowerment and independence.*Botswana's LIPWP and Sri Lanka's NHDA both place women in supervisory roles within the programme and provide them with training, increasing their representation and decision-making power in the process. To this end, the emphasis of Zambia's MPU on gender equality in its committee representation also serves to encourage women's empowerment (Antonopolous, 2007; Dejardin, 1996; Kamanga, 1998).
- *Increased access to financial institutions.* Bangladesh's RMP has provided women participants with access to savings and credit groups – as well as formal financial institutions – to help them to manage their finances after graduation (Ahmed et al., 2007). Women's saving groups implemented in Nepal's Dhaulagiri Irrigation Development Project have likewise aided women in managing their incomes, while providing relevant training in income-generating activities and accounting (Lokollo, 1999).
- *Providing some protection from gender-based violence.* Khera and Nayak (2009a:54) highlight the fact that in India, for example, women's work for private landlords and contractors is 'often replete with an underlying threat or possibility of sexual abuse and exploitation', whereas work on government schemes provides greater 'dignity' and is 'safer.'
- *Creation of community assets that directly benefit women and their families.* For example, Zimbabwe's Rural Transport Study creates infrastructure to reduce the amount of time women spend collecting water (Antonopoulos, 2007). Zambia's Food for Work programme, which is almost entirely utilised by women (as men have typically refused to work for non-cash payments), builds pit latrines. These latrines, given the incidence of sexual violence, are in turn more beneficial for women than for men, as they help to reduce the

distance that women can be compelled to walk in their absence, and in turn their vulnerability to assault (Kabeer, 2008).

However, evidence suggests that few women actually see anything more than minimal, immediate benefits from their participation in PWPs. One reason for this is design flaws that ignore women's domestic duties (Antonopoulos, 2007), which limits their participation. Short-term PWPs that deliberately set wages at levels below the prevailing wage rates (and often below minimum wage rates)[12] effectively promote self-targeting, limiting involvement to only the most vulnerable and most desperate (Devereux, 2009; Song and Philip, 2010). Given women's limited labour-market participation, this may compel women to self-select in a way that men do not. Not only is this differential treatment inequitable a priori from a gender perspective, but also it means that significant numbers of women who would otherwise qualify for participation may not benefit. Furthermore, in many cases, programmes tend to exclusively target household heads, often men, thereby preventing women in male-headed households from exercising their right to participate and claiming their entitlement (Antonopoulos, 2007).

Wages in PWPs are often so low that men choose not to participate (Devereux and Solomon, 2006). As a result, food for work programmes in Malawi and Zambia, for example, mostly involve women (90% of participants in Zambia are female) (Kabeer, 2008). Enrolment differentials are not the result of women preferring payment in food, but rather of men considering food payments to be so stigmatising that they refuse to participate (Kabeer, 2008). Argentina's *Programa de Jefes y Jefas de Hogar Desocupados*, which saw women's participation reach 75%, found that cash alone (a low wage) was not sufficient to attract men (Antonopoulos, 2007). Some analysts therefore argue that PWPs are faced with a double-edged sword when it comes to meeting women's needs (Dejardin, 1996). On the one hand, they have to enrol women so that they can benefit. On the other hand, in order to drive up women's participation it seems that, at least in some cases, they have resorted to offering such low wages that they deter men from taking part. When PWP jobs become more desirable (e.g. in the context of job scarcity), as evidence from Burundi and Tanzania suggests, women may be pressured by men not to compete for places (ibid., 1996).

Even when the wages paid by PWPs are theoretically sufficient and gender-neutral, women can be disadvantaged. For example, there is often a distinction between 'heavy' and 'light' work, typically based on cultural norms. Women are assigned the former, which tends to be lower paid and to require fewer working days, as in the case of India's MGNREGS (see below) (Devereux and Solomon, 2006). Conversely, where women are paid the same rate for the same heavy physical labour – which many cannot undertake – there is evidence (from Zambia's MPU) that they may be forced to subcontract out to men in exchange for 50% of their wages (Kamanga, 1998). In the same vein, piecemeal rates may be gender biased, and where rates are based on male work norms, women end up being paid less (Antonopoulos, 2007).

Evidence suggests that PWPs have rarely increased women's broader empowerment and independence. Women's representation in decision-making structures is often inadequate to promote their voice, and is often constrained by socio-cultural barriers such as illiteracy that remain to be tackled (Dejardin, 1996).

Finally, and perhaps most importantly, PWPs have largely focused on the productive sphere of work. They have not sought to redistribute the costs of social reproduction, thereby reinforcing the existing gender-based division of labour (Antonopoulos, 2007). Thus far, minimal attention has been paid to projects that deliver social services or improve their efficiency (Antonopoulos and Fontana, 2006). Antonopoulos (2007) maintains that the unpaid household and care work that women undertake de facto subsidises under-resourced social services, and that this work must be acknowledged in the policy arena and compensated. One way to do this would be to expand PWPs to include social sector activities. Given that social services are, by their very nature, highly labour-intensive, such activities would be well suited to workfare schemes and also to 'unskilled' women workers. After all, many poor unskilled women are already undertaking this kind of work for no pay (for examples, see Box 4.1).

The remainder of this chapter focuses on the design and implementation of two of the world's largest PWPs which are seeking to address these gendered shortcomings to varying degrees. We assess how they are contributing to greater opportunities for women and simultaneously addressing unequal intra-household and community gender relations.

Box 4.1 Using public works labour in social sector activities

Initiatives using public works labour in social sector activities have largely taken place in middle-income countries, targeting urban areas. For instance, in Korea, following the 1997–1998 economic crisis, the government's emergency PWP included 'social service and charity organisations such as community centers and welfare institutions' (Lee, 2000:7, cited in Antonopoulos, 2007:39). In Argentina, the *Programa de Jefes y Jefas de Hogar Desocupados*, which was established to tackle soaring unemployment triggered by the 2001 financial crisis, provided cash transfers in exchange for 20 hours of community service per week. Women were often involved in care work – frequently for community projects in which participants were already engaged – and men were involved in construction-related activities (Faur, 2008). Ghana's National Youth Employment Programme also has a social services component – women and men under 35 years of age, irrespective of location, receive a stipend in exchange for work as community education teaching assistants or auxiliary health workers.[13]

However, the most advanced initiatives addressing care work challenges – and that include an explicit gender focus – are the Early Child Development (ECD) and Home/Community-Based Care (HCBC) components of South Africa's Expanded Public Works Programme (EPWP). In South Africa, 'the two care areas of ECD and … HCBC are critically interconnected. As a result of the high HIV/AIDS prevalence rates among those in the middle age ranges, older children and older women become the primary caretakers of orphans and children living in households with HIV patients' (Antonopoulos, 2009:6).

The ECD component aims to achieve multiple goals, namely reducing poverty, improving childcare, providing employment opportunities for women, and promoting the professional development of women working in childcare. It can also 'free parents and other adult carers to take up opportunities for education and employment' (Department of Social Development, 2006:12, cited in Lund, 2009b:33). The HCBC component aims to deliver home-based care, counselling and better nutrition to 20% of (the most vulnerable) households that have people living with HIV or AIDS (McCord, 2005). The demands placed on women's time for unpaid care work will therefore decrease (Antonopoulos, 2009).

The South African government provides training and employment opportunities in non-profit private-sector organisations – an interesting model of a private–public partnership in public works activities. Although there have been criticisms with regard to under-resourcing, slow rollout, favouring employment among younger rather than older women, and the availability of more facilities in urban than in rural areas (Budlender and Parenzee, 2007), the programme has nevertheless strengthened women's capacities and skills, as well as the delivery of social services (Lund, 2009b).

Ethiopia's Productive Safety Net Programme (PSNP): an antidote to emergency-focused development[14]

Ethiopia's PSNP is built on decades of experience in targeting aid and PWPs, but with a critical shift in focus towards longer-term solutions rather than emergency-based appeals (Pankhurst, 2009). Launched in 2005, the PSNP is one of two main components of the government's food security strategy. Reaching 7.75 million chronically food-insecure people in rural Ethiopia (see Box 4.2),[15] it aims to smooth consumption through the provision of food and cash transfers, to prevent the depletion of household assets, and to create community assets through public works in return for food and/or cash. Households who are unable to work receive transfers of cash and/or food. The second component, the Other Food Security Programme (OFSP), provides extension, fertiliser, credit and other services to enable households to graduate from the PSNP.

Box 4.2 Rural poverty and gender in Ethiopia

Since 2004, agricultural growth in Ethiopia has been strong, but an estimated 45.4% of the rural population remain below the national poverty line (Ministry of Finance and Economic Development, 2002). Households in food-insecure regions are particularly susceptible to shocks due to agro-climatic conditions, highly limited market access, poor infrastructure, remoteness, land degradation and a lack of formal insurance mechanisms (Dercon et al., 2007b).

Experiences of rural poverty and vulnerability are highly gendered. Female-headed households are more vulnerable than male-headed households (54% vs. 48%) to shocks (e.g. illness or death of a family member, drought, price hikes, loss of livestock), partly because they are more labour-poor and therefore have fewer coping mechanisms. Only 32% of male-headed households said they would struggle to raise 100 birr in a week to cope with a crisis, compared with 53% of female-headed households.

Although recent reforms have improved women's security of land tenure, implementation varies significantly across states. Overall, it is generally accepted that only the household head – who is typically male – can be a landowner. Women who are separated are likely to lose their house and property, and when a husband dies, other family members often claim the land from his widow (Social Institutions and Gender Index, 2009). Moreover, whereas female-headed households with land can access public loans, married women need to secure the permission of their husband first.

Gender and programme design

The design of the PSNP acknowledges gender-specific vulnerabilities resulting from family composition, socio-cultural roles and life-cycle factors, and includes numerous provisions to support women's 'practical gender needs' (Molyneux, 1985:232–3). Programme documents acknowledge that female-headed households are more labour-poor, women and men have different physical labour capacities, women face higher levels of time poverty, and women with small children need special provisions to enable them to work. There are also provisions (although no specific targets) to promote women's involvement in community decisions about the programme (Sharp et al., 2006), supported by representation of the government's Women's Bureau in committee structures at the state and district (*woreda*) levels. In addition, there is a gender-sensitive approach to the type of community assets created (e.g. creating water points and fuel wood sources to reduce girls' and women's time poverty, and using public works labour to support the cultivation of private land-holdings of female-headed households).

The design is weaker in terms of promoting women's 'strategic gender interests' (Molyneux, 1985: 232–3). First, it pays little attention to tackling unequal gender relations within different types of households and the community (see Haile's story in Personal Narrative 4.2). It does not address unequal decision-making power within male-headed households over the use of resources (income, labour and assets). Participation in the PSNP (and payment) is based on the household unit, irrespective of who does the work, even though men have absolute control over decisions and income management in many cases (Ministry of Finance and Economic Development, 2005). Moreover, the programme design assumes that households have adequate adult labour to participate, whereas in practice this is often not the case, especially in female-headed households (Sharp et al., 2006).[16]

The conceptualisation of 'community assets' embedded in the programme design also has important gender implications. There is a strong focus on building tangible infrastructure, but little consideration as to whether community assets meet women's and men's needs equally, or whether other assets (e.g. the construction of health clinics located closer to the community with a higher ratio of outreach workers) might increase people's ability to contribute to agricultural productivity and food security. Moreover, the community assets selected, involving heavy physical labour, do not present work opportunities that reflect the diverse capacities of women and men at different stages of the lifecycle. However, there is growing awareness of the value of diversifying the type of public assets created. Several pilots are underway, and the 2011–2015 phase of the

Personal Narrative 4.2: Family headship norms may disproportionately affect young men – Haile in Ethiopia

The gendered effects of PWPs can shape opportunities for boys and men, as well as for girls and women. Haile, an adolescent boy living in rural Ethiopia, has three younger siblings. His parents wanted him to stay in school, but after seeing four of his siblings die from malnutrition and illness, he felt compelled to shoulder the burden of feeding his family.

Haile has several jobs, and herds cattle and does weeding on the farm on his 'days off.' He considers his work for the PSNP to be his real job. This is always more regular – something he considers crucial. The PSNP sometimes pays cash, but he prefers to receive grain, as the amount he receives is always far higher than the amount he could buy with his salary.

Haile hopes to return to school one day. However, he plans on living at home for at least another decade, to see his younger siblings grow up and leave home. He wishes that the PSNP had a student exemption that would allow him to stay in school and study.

Source: Jones et al. (2010b).

programme is being expanded to include the construction of schools and clinics and the provision of community education on nutritional practices and dietary diversity, coupled with training in basic gardening and animal husbandry.[17]

Gendered impacts

Translating a programme design document into practice is an imperfect science, as programmes interact with existing socio-economic, institutional and cultural conditions and systems. Overall, the PSNP has had mixed impacts. It has been quite positive at the individual level for women, but weaker at the intra-household and community levels, as we explain.

At the *individual level*, in contrast with other PWPs, women's participation in the PSNP has been high, with a number of positive impacts (World Bank, 2008a). Participation has supported women's practical gender needs, including increased household food consumption and providing for children's needs such as clothing, schooling and healthcare. This particularly benefits female-headed households, which previously had fewer alternative income sources (e.g. Evers et al., 2008).

Individual households are also less likely to resort to negative coping mechanisms such as selling assets. For example, households now rely less on measures such as harvesting immature coffee berries (which reduces profits), renting out their land and trees to others and keeping *hara* cattle for others,[18] and the out-migration of family members to urban areas. Teenage girls and young women suggest the programme has reduced their need to work as domestic employees in nearby towns – a role that is often subject to low remuneration and abuse by employers. In other words, the PSNP is providing women with income-earning opportunities that are especially scarce in many parts of rural Ethiopia.[19]

That said, despite formal provisions for equal payment, men's labour remains more highly valued, both in remunerative terms and normatively. In sites close to towns with daily labouring work opportunities, the programme needs to offer significantly higher payments to men to persuade them to participate.

Direct support for pregnant and breastfeeding women has allowed some degree of income security, enabling beneficiaries to attend to their reproductive health and early infant care responsibilities. However, the duration of this support varies considerably across *woredas* (districts).

Gains in social capital have also emerged as an important unintended benefit. Both women and men highlight the fact that, as a result of greater livelihood security, they have more opportunities to become involved in social networks from which they were previously excluded. This is highly valued, and may be of particular significance for women, given their generally lower levels of participation in rural village life.

At the *intra-household level*, impacts have been more mixed. Overall, the programme has reinforced gendered notions of agricultural work, and has had a limited impact on unequal gender relations. However, some women reported being accorded more respect by their husbands as a result of their participation in PWPs, and valued this even if did not increase their role in decision making. Some men also acknowledged that their attitudes towards women's work capabilities had changed as a result of regular joint work on PWP sites.

However, implementation shortcomings mean that the programme has not addressed women's time-poverty constraints to any significant extent. Flexible working hours for women are not always offered, and few sites have the required childcare facilities (Evers et al., 2008). This is due to a combination of insufficient funds, programme implementers' lack of awareness (or de-prioritisation) of these gender-sensitive provisions, and limited demand from women participants, who may be concerned about leaving their children with strangers.

The PSNP's payment modality – to the head of household rather than directly to women – has further limited its impact in terms of changing unequal decision making within the household. A significant number of women noted that they prefer food to cash payments, as they have greater control over food than cash within the household.

At the *community level*, the PSNP's gender impacts have been minimal. In terms of programme governance, women's involvement in community decision making has, in practice, been limited. This is perhaps not surprising – participants are overwhelmingly illiterate or semi-literate, and previously had few opportunities to articulate their views. Without awareness-raising or mentoring support, expecting women to exercise voice and agency in PWP meetings would be overly optimistic. There have also been few attempts to link community discussions on PWPs with other social issues. Only in one region were examples found of links between PSNP rollout and community conversations about key social and gender-based vulnerabilities, including child marriage, gender-based violence and reproductive healthcare, as provided for in the Women's Development Package (an integrated approach to strengthening women's role in development).

More broadly, the lack of a rights-based discourse in Ethiopia (in sharp contrast with the Indian case, discussed below) hampers the potential to strengthen citizen demands for more effective government provision. The programme is widely regarded as a 'gift' from the government or God, which no one wants to jeopardise by criticising it.

Lastly, the recognition in the PSNP that women and men have differential capacities is often actualised in a way that reinforces traditional gender norms. Because of the narrow focus on physical infrastructure development, women's contributions and productivity levels are widely seen as inferior by communities and local officials alike. Moreover, men are seen as 'shouldering women's burden' by contributing more, even though women and men may have different contributions to make to community development.

Key drivers of programme outcomes

A number of key drivers – political, institutional and socio-cultural – underpin the mixed impacts described here. Overall, there has been limited political commitment from government and donors towards ensuring that the gender dimensions of the PSNP are implemented effectively. Considerable emphasis has been placed on ensuring that female-headed households are well represented and that women participate in PWP activities, including direct support during pregnancy and breastfeeding. However, efforts to address women's time poverty and provide equal access to agricultural extension services and resources have been much weaker.[20]

These weaknesses are reflected in the very limited investment in capacity building for programme implementers and communities. In rural Ethiopia, where gender roles are starkly differentiated, programmes are unlikely to contribute to meaningful change in the social norms that constrain women's economic engagement without a significant investment to ensure that beneficiaries and implementers alike are aware of the rationale for the gender-sensitive programme features. Such activities would not necessarily need to be undertaken by the Ministry of Agriculture and Rural Development, but could be delivered by other bodies with a gender remit.

In this regard, the PSNP has made some progress. The Women's Bureau is represented on the programme implementation committee – an important first step. However, it has proved inadequate to effectively mainstream gender into programme rollout. Links to gender focal points within key agencies and/or those offering complementary services would be valuable, but these have remained weak to date:

> *Men dominate leadership positions, and their opinions are more likely to be taken into account than those of women.*
>
> (Programme officer, World Food Programme, Ethiopia, 2009, cited in Jones et al., 2010b:36)

Failure to achieve potential synergies with other gender policy infrastructure, especially the Ethiopian Women's Development and Change Package and the National Action Plan for Gender Equality, and limited intersectoral coordination at the provincial and *woreda* levels, also appear to have precluded the realisation of such complementarities. This is partly due to insufficient investment in capacity building for staff employed in gender posts, and their integration into decision-making and planning processes as the following quotes from key informants highlight:[21]

> *Gender training and awareness-raising programmes are not intensive and are inadequate.*
>
> (Head of Women's Bureau, Ethiopia, 2009, cited in Jones et al., 2010b:35)

> *The activities are not gender-sensitive. There is no gender mainstreaming. The programme is theoretically well developed but practical application is flawed.*
>
> (Project manager, Wolayta, 2009, cited in Jones et al., 2010b:36)

This in turn translates into low awareness among communities about the programme's gender dimensions. For instance, provisions regarding the use of public works labour to construct water points and fuelwood sources, as well as to work on the land of female-headed households, are not widely known about and are therefore not prioritised in decision making about which community assets to focus on:

Although the programme implementation manual provides for training on gender to beneficiaries before or after the public works, it has not materialised. Women are prescribed work regardless of their specific challenges (health and personal problems owing to their role in the household). There is a lack of will by some implementers to make the work suitable to women.

(Programme officer and focal person for PSNP, World Food Programme, Ethiopia, 2009, cited in Jones et al., 2010b:35)

Women were not consulted during design, implementation and evaluation processes, which are just top-down.

(Project manager, Wolayta, 2009, cited in Jones et al., 2010b:36)

Finally, limited institutional resources and support mean that gender-sensitive monitoring and evaluation have also been minimal (for example, there are no records of the gender or age of those who turn up each day at the public works sites). This makes it difficult to assess the relative balance of investment in assets designed to reduce women's time burden and enhance their economic and community participation. Donors supported a gender audit undertaken in 2007–2008 by Evers et al. (2008), suggesting an interest in the programme's gendered dimensions. However, follow-up on its recommendations was only partially reflected in the Phase 3 (2011–2015) programme implementation document.

India's Mahatma Gandhi National Rural Employment Guarantee Scheme (MGNREGS): a transformative approach to tackling poverty[22]

India's National Rural Employment Guarantee Act was passed in 2005, linked with the vision in the country's Five-Year Plan to reduce rural vulnerabilities and increase employment and agricultural productivity (see Box 4.3).[23] Although India has a long history of PWPs and in particular the rights-based Maharashtra Employment Guarantee Scheme – seen as a precursor of the MGNREGS – the design of the latter represents a paradigm shift in a number of important ways. These include its backing by a parliamentary act, its national character, the household basis of offered employment, the one-third quota for women, and provisions for more multi-layered monitoring and accountability procedures, including a social audit process (UN Development Programme, 2010a).

Overall, the new design features suggest a transformative rights-based approach to poverty reduction. Under the MGNREGS, poor rural households are entitled to 100 days of employment every year – a citizen entitlement for which the government is held accountable. It is also the first PWP in India – organised and funded by the federal government but

---

Box 4.3 Agriculture, poverty reduction and gender in India

Poverty in India remains highly concentrated in rural areas (41.8%, compared to 25.7% in urban areas (Government of India Planning Commission, 2011 quoted in Nino-Zarazua and Toury Adison, 2012), and particularly among agricultural labourers. A key priority of India's Eleventh Five-Year Plan is employment generation in the rural economy and agricultural growth. The MGNREGS is seen to have an important role to play in transforming rural livelihoods and agricultural productivity. Within this, there is recognition that women face specific barriers to productive engagement. Most Scheduled Tribe (ST) and 40% of Scheduled Caste (SC) casual workers are poor, with landless casual workers being the poorest (Planning Commission, 2008). Women are more highly represented in such work and are adversely incorporated into the wage labour market, where the wage is 30% lower for women than for men and 20% lower for the same task (World Bank, 2007, 2009).

Women face particular discrimination in ownership of and access to productive resources. They constitute two-thirds of the agricultural workforce, but own less than 10% of the agricultural land (National Alliance of Women, 2008). Small farmers (particularly women) lack access to agricultural services. Lack of access to formal credit for economic activities, social events and health expenditures pushes farmers into indebtedness, often taking loans from moneylenders at high rates of interest.

Finally, women are the principal stakeholders in natural resource use and management but, even with quotas in place, are under-represented (making up less than 10% of the decision-making positions in participatory planning and development programmes) (Agarwal, 1997; Meinzen-Dick and Zwarteveen, 1997).

---

implemented at state level – that is national in coverage. The MGNREGS started in 2006 in 200 districts, and from 2008 it spread across all districts in India. Recent data show that almost 55 million households had accessed employment under the scheme by 2010–2011.[24]

The MGNREGS marks an important shift from allocated or supply-driven work to demand-based work. Workers apply for registration, obtain a job card, and then seek employment through a written application for the duration that they choose. There is also a legal guarantee that the requested work be given within 15 days; if it is not, the state must provide an unemployment allowance at a quarter of the wage for each day that employment is not given.

Gender and programme design

The MGNREGS has considerable potential to transform rural livelihoods through its rights-based approach to employment. Although women's participation has been only a secondary objective (Pankaj and Tankha, 2010), and the transformation of gender relations has not been an intended goal (Pellissery and Jalan, 2011), 'empowering rural women' is among its indirect objectives, and several provisions aim to tackle some of the barriers that hinder women's participation in the workforce and in decision-making structures.

First, there is a quota stipulating that at least one-third of all workers who have registered and requested work in each state are women. Crèche facilities should be provided when five or more children below the age of 6 years are brought to the worksite. Women (especially single women) are given preference to work on sites close to their homes if the worksite is 5 km or more away (Ministry of Rural Development, 2008).

Secondly, equal wages must be paid to women and men under the provisions of the Equal Remuneration Act 1976. When opening bank accounts for labourers, the bank or the local assembly (*panchayat*) should give a choice between individual and joint accounts. If joint accounts are used, husbands and wives should be co-signatories, and care should be taken to avoid crediting earnings to individual accounts held by the male household head. Separate individual accounts for women household members may be opened in the case of male-headed households, and single-member families are also considered to constitute a household.[25]

Thirdly, to supervise work and record attendance, 'mates' can be designated for each activity, with adequate representation of women. Mates must have been educated up to Class 5 or 8, depending on the task (Ministry of Rural Development, 2008). Women should also be adequately represented among worksite facilitators.

Lastly, women should be represented on local-level committees (*gram sabha*) and in the social audit process, as well as on state and central councils. Meetings should be held at convenient times.

However, the programme also has a number of design weaknesses. Despite the quota, there is limited attention to addressing the socio-cultural barriers (e.g. gender discrimination, time poverty, care work responsibilities) that prevent women's engagement in the labour market. Although there is strong evidence of a correlation between women's status/control over resources in the household and household well-being and productivity, these are not well articulated. Control over household resources and the financial inclusion of women represents an important mechanism for strengthening women's role in decision making and their economic empowerment, yet the opening of bank accounts in individual or joint names is left to the discretion of the *panchayat* or bank.

Furthermore, the programme design does not consider gendered life-cycle vulnerabilities. Unlike the PSNP in Ethiopia, there are no flexible hours for women to accommodate their care work responsibilities, and no exemptions or other special provisions for pregnant or breastfeeding women. Given that MGNREGS entitlement sits with the household, lack of emphasis on household demography and intra-household dynamics can mean that single women within households are unable to exercise their right to employment, especially if bank accounts are not in their name (Gupta, 2009; Kelkar, 2009).

Finally, a narrow conceptualisation of women's role in agricultural work has also limited consideration of the appropriateness of community assets for women and men. Although there is potential to support women's 'practical needs' through the creation of assets (e.g. by building water sources nearby), neither women's practical needs nor the potential to address their 'strategic interests' by improving their status and structured involvement in local area development have been adequately thought through (Gupta, 2009:332). The types of work that are undertaken to support women's agricultural productivity could be broadened to include healthcare and literacy/skills programmes, improving market access and infrastructure, and supporting investments and training in other agricultural activities.

Gendered impacts

Turning to programme implementation and impacts on women's wellbeing, at the *individual level*, the MGNREGS has had a number of positive impacts, increasing women's labour-market participation, improving access to credit, and paying equal wages. Recent data (from 2009–2010) indicate that 48% of all participants nationally are women (compared with 41% in 2006–2007 and 43% in 2007–2008). However, there are considerable variations across and within states.[26]

To account for regional variations, several sources note the stronger human and gender development indicators of the four southern Indian states compared with the northern states. Yet north – south differentials do not fully explain the variations in women's participation in the MGNREGS. For instance, Rajasthan, despite being a northern state with low human development and gender indicators, has one of the highest rates of women's participation (see Box 4.4).

Constraints at the individual level include disproportionate rates of illiteracy among poor women, and cultural norms in some areas which

Box 4.4 Accounting for variation in women's participation by state

High rates of women's MGNREGS participation in Kerala and Rajasthan have attracted considerable interest – not least in terms of trying to identify the key drivers. Sudarshan (2011) concludes that outcomes depend largely on programme implementers, levels of public awareness, local organisational structures and social networks, and the economic status of villagers.

In Kerala, a crucial factor in women's high participation rate was the involvement of the *Kudumbashree* (the state poverty eradication programme) in MGNREGS management. This programme, which started in 1998, created neighbourhood groups made up of several households living below the poverty line, each represented by a woman. These women's groups engaged in micro-enterprises to improve their families' situation.

In the first year of MGNREGS implementation in Kerala, the results were poor. The state has some of the best rural infrastructure in India, so demand for unskilled labour was limited and wages were below market levels. The state government could not mobilise the population to participate, so it transferred responsibility for its implementation to *Kudumbashree* groups (Williams et al., 2010). Women workers were mobilised into self-help groups, worksites were managed by women, and flexible working hours were offered. Women's previous experience of project management and working together further strengthened their position.

Women's participation has also been high in Rajasthan, partly due to its previous experience of large-scale PWPs known as the 'famine works' (providing drought relief), a tradition of paid work for women and men, a government committed to the programme, and active civil society organisations that engaged with the programme from its design phase. These social movements mobilised the population, and some participated in social audits to improve implementation. Yet, although the state government initially supported independent audits, it faced strong resistance from the *panchayats* and thus allowed each to create its own social audit forum. The government also undertook initiatives such as the revision of wage productivity norms to increase the real income of participants, regular training of mates, reducing the educational qualification required for women to increase their involvement as programme 'mates' (see above), and the creation of a committee to discuss implementation issues.

Source: Sudarshan, 2011

prevent women from working outside the home, or with men, thus denying them their right to access employment days (Samarthan Centre for Development Support, 2007). Entrenched ideas about the gender division of labour also affect the type of work that is viewed as acceptable for women to do. In Madhya Pradesh, for example, although women's representation overall is quite high (46%), in practice women receive fewer days because they do 'soft' work (e.g. throwing out the soil from digging wells). In some cases, even when women want to work, they have been excluded by the *panchayat* because of social norms relating to the type of work that is 'appropriate' for them (Khera and Nayak, 2009b).

The impact of the targeting mechanism (the household unit) on women's participation has generated considerable discussion (Bhatty, 2008). On the one hand, larger households (e.g. joint families with many adults) are better able to demand employment because of better labour availability. On the other, the benefits are diluted because of the large size of the household (only 100 days are given per household). Men in particular report that, in extended families, each brother's family should receive a job card. However, women would prefer that each adult receives a job card (see also Gupta, 2009). Indeed, many single women, especially in extended families, are unable to claim their entitlements independently.

Female-headed households (which account for at least 20% of rural households) with limited labour availability are generally less able to take up MGNREGS employment opportunities. This is partly because the type of work requires women and men to work together in teams (typically family-based couples), and partly because the provision of work often depends on contact with the *panchayat* – something that poor women tend not to have. In Andhra Pradesh, the Young Lives study (Young Lives, 2010) found that better-connected households with five or more powerful relatives were 10% more likely to register. Jha et al. (2009, cited in Porter and Dornan, 2010) reported that households with greater land ownership participated more.

Within male-headed households, the evidence about how decisions to participate in MGNREGS is somewhat mixed. Sudarshan (2011) finds that decision-making is shaped by practical calculations - in the case of two wage earners and higher market wages for men, women are often the ones who participate in MGNREGS (Sudarshan, 2011). By contrast, Panjak and Tankha's work in Bihar, Jharkhand, Rajasthan and Himachal Pradesh found that although 58% of women independently decide, 38% are requested to undertake public works activities by the household head (Pankaj and Tankha, 2010).

A second positive impact of the MGNREGS has been the provision of equal wages for women. This is particularly significant considering the widespread practice of discriminatory wages: in 2004-5 the all-India average daily wage of a casual rural worker was Rs 55.03 for males and Rs 34.94 for females (Pankaj and Tankha, 2010). Moreover, although women's MGNREGS wages have been less than the prescribed minimum, in practice in a number of states including Bihar, Jkarkhand and Rajasthan, they remain higher nevertheless than the average daily wage of a female causal rural worker (ibid), and have even resulted in Kerala in a broader upward movement of female market wages (Sudarshan, 2009).

However, women still face wage discrimination, most notably because of high productivity norms and piecework rates based on men's average output, which means that women often have to work longer for the same payment or else receive less. This affects single women in particular when wages are 'productivity-linked' and physical infrastructure building tasks depend on family-based couples working together (e.g. Gupta, 2009).[27]

A third positive outcome for some women has been the programme's impact on access to credit and loans, with some suggesting that MGNREGS income has helped some vulnerable families to obtain access to loans and meet repayments. However, for many households, MGNREGS income is simply not sufficient for anything other than meeting immediate consumption needs.

At the *intra-household level*, impacts have been more mixed, with limited changes in the unequal gendered division of labour (as with Ethiopia's PSNP). As discussed earlier, failure to address women's life-cycle vulnerabilities and dual responsibilities in domestic/care and productive activities restricts their ability to participate. For instance, although pregnant women are reportedly sometimes allocated different types of work on an ad hoc basis, in other cases they have been refused work by the *panchayat* (UN Children's Fund, 2007).

Moreover, although the scheme theoretically provides crèche facilities, the lack of actual provision (varying from 17% to just 1% in four states) (Jandu, 2008) is a serious weakness and reflects limited understanding of the extent of women's dual responsibilities. Khera and Nayak (2009a) confirmed a lack of facilities in all 98 MGNREGS worksites included in their study of six northern Indian states; in most cases, mothers left their children at home, often with older siblings (mainly daughters who had been taken out of school due to lack of alternative options) (e.g. Sudarshan, 2011). Other women brought their young children to the worksite, risking exposure to environmental hazards. This problem is part of what has been described as the 'gendered familialism of employment and wage policy' (Palriwala and Neetha, 2009:22) in India:

Gendered familialism reiterates that care work is the responsibility of women, thereby defining the pool of carers as well as women's possibilities to acquire the resources necessary to enable care in the best manner possible. Women remain embedded in family relations in employment and in the formulation of social protection policy. There is a refusal to accept women's double day or the issue of care responsibilities as a collective concern of the state.

(Palriwala and Neetha, 2009:22)

Indirect positive impacts on migration patterns have been noted. In Madhya Pradesh, for example, seasonal migration is an important livelihood strategy. Before the MGNREGS, whole households migrated, whereas now it is often only men who do so (Holmes et al., 2010). With fewer family members migrating, the strain of frequent migration is reduced, with important knock-on effects on household well-being and the continuity of children's education (Jandu, 2008).

There is also some limited evidence of improvements in women's situation in the household, with a recent UN Women study suggesting that women's income from the MGNREGS has led to a decrease in their experiences of domestic violence and harassment (UN Women, 2011). However, the analysis by Holmes et al. (2010) of Madhya Pradesh found that women's MGNREGS income had no effect on the level of domestic violence they faced.

Other studies cite improvements in women's status, including greater self-confidence and involvement in household decisionmaking. Khera and Nayak (2009a) found that 79% of women interviewed collected their own wages and kept them. Pankaj and Tankha (2010) found that 68% of women collected their wages themselves, and 55.6% retained up to a quarter of their wages (29% handed all their earnings to men). Women who retained their wages used them to buy food, cover health and education costs, visit relatives, participate in social ceremonies or meet personal needs. Positive changes have also been linked to women having their own bank accounts (Holmes et al., 2010; Khera and Nayak, 2009a), although, as already noted, the rollout of this provision has been uneven.

At the *community level*, the evidence base on gendered impacts (largely through the creation of community assets) remains limited, with mixed reports. Although watershed development in Madhya Pradesh, for example, has supported greater crop production (Holmes et al., 2010), there are concerns in other areas that assets have not always benefited the rural poor as intended (e.g. wells benefiting households with land). In this vein, proponents of women's empowerment and gender equality have called for a refocusing of the types of works offered under the MGNREGS, suggesting activities linked to healthcare, literacy/skills programmes, nutrition and sanitation as possible alternatives (see also Table 4.2). This would need to be coupled with efforts to address the lack of involvement of communities in general, and women in particular, in decision making on the types of assets to be created. Although this

Table 4.2 Unpaid work and its implications for community asset generation through PWPs

Type of unpaid work	Description of unpaid work activities	Implications for use of public works labour	Spillover effects on individual and community assets and wellbeing
1. Non-market economic activities: acquiring/collecting basic necessities	1. Fetching water	1. Construction of water-harvesting structures 2. Deepening tanks/improving traditional structures 3. Organising distribution of water supply and laying pipelines	1. Public provisioning of necessities
	2. Fetching fuelwood from common lands	1. Regeneration of common lands and plantation: social forestry 2. Regeneration of forest lands 3. Constructing smokeless/improved stoves 4. Constructing of biogas plants running on cow dung, biomass 5. Plantation of biofuel trees	1. Access to low-cost healthy energy 2. Promotion to income-generating activities 3. Improved environmental resources
	3. Walking long distances for relief	1. Construction of latrines 2. Construction of drainage	1. Improved health facilities
2. Non-market economic activities: collection of raw material for income generating	1. Collection of fodder from common lands	1. Regeneration of common lands for fodder crops or fodder farms	1. Improved income/productive employment
	2. Collection of wood/bamboo, etc. for crafts/manufacturing	1. Regeneration of common lands: social forestry 2. Regeneration of forest lands 3. Waste land (public) development	2. Improved environmental resources

Table 4.2 (continued)

Type of unpaid work	Description of unpaid work activities	Implications for use of public works labour	Spillover effects on individual and community assets and wellbeing
3. Unpaid domestic work: care-related activities	1. Childcare	1. Constructing childcare activities 2. Constructing child development centres for children under five 3. Constructing school rooms and facilities 4. Construction of midday meal kitchens	1. Improved child health 2. More time for women to rest or to work in productive employment 3. Improved education: more enrolment and less dropout
	2. Care of the sick, old and disabled in the household	1. Constructing of health centres/ dispensaries 2. Improving/repairing/expanding existing health facilities 3. Constructing facilities for public sanitation and hygiene	1. Improved health facilities
4. Unpaid domestic work: household repair in non-durable shelter	1. Repair and maintenance of house: floor, walls and ceiling	1. Construction of durable housing for the poor	1. Improved homes of people 2. More time available for rest/work
5. Unpaid work: travelling	1. Travelling for different reasons on foot	1. Construction of roads: approach roads, feeder roads, paving of internal roads	1. Less drudgery of walking 2. More time for rest/work

Source: Hirway et al. (2008).

problem is not specific to the MGNREGS, it does need to be taken into account by programme implementers and evaluators and, as we discuss in our concluding chapter, appropriate alliances need to be forged with other actors who are working to tackle entrenched gender inequalities.

Finally, evidence as to the impacts MGNREGS has had at the community level are also mixed. Holmes et al. (2001)'s work in Madhya Pradesh found that participation in the programme had contributed to increased social capital within communities, both for women and for men, albeit along existing caste lines. Social networks have been strengthened, leading to improved relationships; women and men are working together and even engage in small informal borrowing (Holmes et al., 2010). They found no real evidence, however, of women's participation in the social audit process, nor any spillover effects in terms of improvements in access to other government services such as extension, credit facilities or basic social services (Holmes et al., 2010).

Key drivers of programme outcomes

Given the complexities of India's decentralised governance system and the diverse political economy dynamics of each state, here we focus on the underlying political – institutional and socio-cultural drivers shaping the gendered outcomes of the MGNREGS in Madhya Pradesh, drawing on the primary research by Holmes et al. (2010). Existing evidence suggests that political commitment to promoting gender equitable outcomes in the roll-out of MGNREGS has been mixed. On the one hand, there has been strong commitment to ensuring that women are represented in employment at federal and state levels. On the other, there has been less commitment to promoting a broader understanding of the linkages between gender equality and improved agricultural productivity and poverty reduction. This includes addressing the socio-cultural barriers that women face when demanding and accessing PWPs, the extent of their domestic and caring responsibilities and life-cycle vulnerabilities, their lower levels of human capital, and their limited access to productive assets, agricultural inputs, markets and financial services.

As in the Ethiopian case, this weakness is manifested most clearly in the limited investment in capacitybuilding for programme implementers with regard to the gender-sensitive features of the MGNREGS. Where training is given, it mainly focuses on implementation and rural development issues, such as watershed management and irrigation. The case for promoting linkages to strengthen gender equality and improve impacts on rural development has not been made to programme staff.

Part of the problem is that MGNREGS funds have given the *panchayati raj* institutions more financial responsibilities and power than before.

Although this strengthens decentralisation, there is weak capacity at local level to implement gender-sensitive programmes. If the MGNREGS is to refocus its efforts to achieve more consistent impacts and promote a more institutionalised gender-sensitive approach, capacity building on gender issues at the *panchayat*, district and state levels is essential.

There is also an important accountability deficit in the way that the MGNREGS is implemented. As one male focus group discussant noted: 'Although people know about the MGNREGS provisions, they do not have a major say in deciding about the type of work to be done in the village, nor about the provision of crèche facilities' (cited in Holmes et al., 2010: 27).

This is linked in part to local-level political economy dynamics (see Chapter 7), and reflects the tensions between assigning responsibility for implementation to the lowest tier of government so as to enhance accountability, on the one hand, and the realities of deeply embedded power imbalances which illiterate poor lower-caste populations are ill equipped to challenge, on the other.

These shortcomings have been reinforced by a lack of inter-ministerial coordination, hindering opportunities for mainstreaming gender concerns across related poverty and vulnerability reduction fields and in budgeting processes. Instead, individual motivation rather than institutional structures appear to be driving policy and programming synergies, where they exist. Improvements could also be made in collecting, analysing and using sex-disaggregated data, which could include monitoring of the use of community assets and assessment of the appropriateness and benefits of these using a gender lens, as well as the extent to which women are participating in the various social audit processes at the community level. Only with such information will there be an adequate information base with which to develop more tailored and strategic interventions to advance gender equity.[28]

Conclusions

PWPs have emerged as an important strand of social protection, and have considerable potential to strengthen women's contribution to agricultural productivity and promote more gender-sensitive approaches to food security for the rural poor. Ethiopia's PSNP and India's MGNREGS have both made important advances in enhancing women's role in rural PWPs. However, our detailed gender analysis of their impacts at individual, intra-household and community levels reveals a number of important lessons that can be used to inform policy dialogues on public works initiatives in other contexts. We have highlighted some key areas of design and implementation that can support a more positive impact, in terms of both gender equality and programme effectiveness.

On the positive side, PWPs in Ethiopia and India promote women's participation by setting a quota for women's inclusion and guaranteeing equal wages, in theory at least. Moreover, the MGNREGS offers huge potential for the rural poor in India to exercise their right to employment and in turn strengthen state – citizen relations, with potential gains in terms of the political, social and economic empowerment of the poor through the Act. Both Ethiopia's PSNP and India's MGNREGS also include features such as childcare facilities to address tensions between women's productive and reproductive roles.

However, gender-sensitive design does not always translate into gender-equitable impacts. Serious bottlenecks include challenges on the demand side – that is, poor people's limited ability to exercise their rights (especially in the context of illiteracy, social exclusion and entrenched power relations), a dearth of funding to implement gender-sensitive features, and also significant gaps in knowledge, capacities and attitudes of programme implementers, and restrictive gender norms, which may result in fewer days' work for women or lower wages when based on male productivity norms. Moreover, a narrow conceptualisation of community assets and limited community consultation has resulted in the prioritisation of infrastructure at the expense of other assets, including human capital development.

However, there is cause for optimism, especially in India, where civil society is playing an important role in raising poor people's awareness of their legal entitlements, mobilising communities to demand employment from local governments, and setting up or supporting public hearings for grievances (Reddy et al., 2011). Although these have not had a particularly strong or systematic gender approach to date, they are vehicles through which awareness raising and capacity building on gender-equitable programme provisions and outcomes could be strengthened. They also mark an important contrast with the broader context in which Ethiopia's PSNP is being rolled out. Not only is the PSNP not rights-based, but also civil society voices have been suppressed in recent years, including through a controversial non-governmental organisation registration law in 2009. That said, the establishment of programme grievance mechanisms as well as community dialogues within the PSNP design does offer potentially important opportunities to articulate participants' voices and strengthen the responsiveness of the programme going forward.

FIVE

Insuring against shocks: the gendered dimensions of insurance

Introduction

Insurance – the pooling of resources among groups for protection against risk – is a risk management strategy to protect against shocks, and constitutes a key strand of social protection (Norton et al., 2001). Insurance programmes generally involve some form of upfront or regular contribution, and products may be designed and implemented by a range of providers, including the state, private companies, non-governmental organisations or, more informally, communities. For poor people, insurance can smooth household expenditure and thereby reduce the impact of shocks. It can also facilitate the retention of wealth and assets (Alderman and Haque, 2007).

Poor and vulnerable populations often rely on a mix of informal mechanisms to deal with shocks, including self-insurance (through savings and reduced spending), emergency credit and the liquidation of assets, as highlighted by Pho Ly's story in Personal Narrative 5.1. It is estimated that each year 100 million people fall into poverty because of the financial burden of healthcare (World Health Organization, 2010). Yet access to formal insurance can transform a shock or risk from a high-stress event, potentially leading to a long-term loss of productivity, to a low-stress one, perhaps resulting in short-term lifestyle changes and a reduction in unnecessary expenditures (Cohen and Sebstad, 2006). Insurance can also encourage investment in productive assets, higher-yielding crops and risk-taking behaviour, particularly in agriculture, and thus help to build more sustainable livelihoods (Mechler et al., 2006; Sabates-Wheeler et al., 2009). Accordingly, insurance for the poor is a growing area of importance and, although global reach remains relatively limited, innovative products and approaches are emerging and worthy of further attention, not least because estimates suggest that 350–400 million people in Asia, 45–50 million people in Latin America and 24 million people in sub-Saharan Africa have some form of micro-insurance (Churchill and McCord, 2012).

This chapter begins with a brief conceptual discussion of insurance and social protection, before presenting a general framework for discussing the gender dimensions of insurance design, implementation and impacts.

Personal Narrative 5.1: The ripple effects of health vulnerabilities – Pho Ly in Vietnam

Pho Ly is a single father raising a 5-year-old daughter in rural Vietnam. His wife died soon after delivery, even though he spent all his savings on medical care. He lost his farm when he was unable to repay the mortgage – and with it his stable income *'When my daughter and wife were ill – nothing was left.'* Now he works carrying stone, which is exhausting and poorly paid.

His daughter has been ill for most of her life. He makes sure she eats well, even if he must do without, but she still suffers from frequent coughs and fevers and is very small for her age. Pho Ly says that he cares for her as best he can, but his care is *'not as good as well-to-do families. Everything is lacking.'* He admits he is stretched too thin, and sometimes he is so tired and impatient that he smacks her for being disobedient.

Source: cited in Jones and Tran (2010).

It then reviews two broad categories of insurance mechanisms through a gender lens – informal and formal – dividing the latter into social insurance programmes and micro-insurance initiatives and their differential potential to promote greater resilience among poor women, men and children. The evidence base on gendered dimensions of insurance is generally thinner than that on social transfers and public works programmes, and therefore our conclusions in this chapter are more tenuous in nature.

Conceptualising insurance as social protection

The literature on insurance and social protection lacks a general consensus on what can and cannot be included under social protection-oriented insurance. As such, we begin with a brief review of the different approaches that analysts and policy actors take, and then present our own synthesis definition. Our starting point is that not all products qualify as social protection, but nor can we distinguish by type of provider alone. As Chapter 2 emphasised, we share the definition of social protection offered by Devereux and Sabates-Wheeler (2004:9), as 'all *public and private* initiatives … with the overall objective of reducing the economic and social vulnerability of poor, vulnerable and marginalised groups' (emphasis added). As the state in developing countries is often unable to provide social protection to sizeable proportions of the population living at or below the poverty line, it is important to consider a plurality of providers (Barrientos and Hulme, 2008a). So, for instance, the state may work through private for-profit providers, or private not-for-profit providers may provide micro-insurance products to poor and vulnerable populations under regulation by the state (Norton et al., 2001). Most market-based approaches consider poor populations too hard to reach for too little reward (Churchill, 2006), although, as we discuss below, demand is considerable[1] and large companies are beginning to offer products that target the poor, often in partnership with microfinance institutions.

Others, including Devereux and Sabates-Wheeler, emphasise the need to consider both formal and informal social insurance schemes. The former refer to 'formalised systems of pensions, health insurance, maternity benefits and unemployment benefits, often with tripartite financing between employers, employees and the state' (Devereux and Sabates-Wheeler, 2004:10).The latter include savings clubs and funeral societies, which, as we discuss further below, are often especially important among women (Ardener and Burman, 1995).

Generally speaking, however, when thinking about insurance and social protection, most people have social insurance in mind. Such programmes are state-led, with payments typically paid through wage-based mechanisms (rather than being tax-financed) (Barrientos, 2010). The risk-pooling mechanism is based on social solidarity rather than a commercial actuarial calculation of individual risk, thus allowing in principle for more equitable distribution of benefits (International Labour Organization, 2010a). However, this tends to limit coverage to employees in the formal sector (International Labour Organization, 2010a), who represent quite a small proportion of the population in developing countries.[2] Accordingly, we need to broaden our understanding of the role of the state vis-à-vis insurance to include not only direct provision but also 'facilitating and regulating provision in partnership with other actors' (Norton et al., 2001:57). Where private insurance markets are available and relatively effective, the state can either subsidise or underwrite insurance policies appropriate for the poor that private insurers would not otherwise offer.

There is also an often unclear distinction among analysts between the terms 'social insurance programmes' and 'social security.' For instance, Devereux and Sabates-Wheeler find that social protection is sometimes narrowed down and equated with social security, interpreted as meaning 'the specific public programmes of assistance, insurance and benefits that people can draw upon in order to maintain a minimum level of income' (Devereux and Sabates-Wheeler, 2004:12). Part of this conceptual blurring appears to be shaped by the International Labour Organization's preference for the term 'social security' (International

Labour Organization, 2010a), which encompasses both tax-financed social assistance and social insurance instruments, and thus it is important not to use the term interchangeably with social insurance premised on a contributory model – even if contributions are often waived or are made by the state on behalf of poor people. A social security approach places a strong emphasis on its collective character. It is a public responsibility and public institutions are typically the providers, through compulsory membership rather than voluntary individual agreements (International Labour Organization, 2010a). Moreover, inclusion is typically secured through a person's contribution record, with contribution and benefit rates often related to earnings. Although this is clearly valuable from an equity perspective, high levels of informality and the challenges of reaching such populations in developing countries mean that a more flexible view of potential providers is critical.

Indeed, given low coverage of statutory social security schemes, especially in Asia and Africa, micro-insurance schemes – 'the protection of low-income people against specific perils in exchange for regular premium payments proportionate to the likelihood and cost of the risk involved' (Churchill, 2006:12) – are important for the poor. They 'constitute a complementary and valuable strategy for extending social security to all' (International Labour Organization, 2007b:1). Churchill (2006) argues that micro-insurance would be even more effective if it were supplemented by government schemes to facilitate a redistributive effect. Approaches are characterised by low premiums and limited benefits, but products cover a range of risks that arguably speak more to the needs of the poor outside the formal labour force, including health, life, funeral expenses and asset and crop loss, than do employment-based approaches, which tend to focus primarily on income security and availability of medical care.

In summary, then, we define social protection-oriented insurance as contribution-based instruments that aim to mitigate risk for all social groups, including the poor, by pooling group resources either community- or society-wide. Formal programmes are led by the state or not-for-profit private/non-governmental organisations, with a number of possible providers – state, private for-profit and/or non-profit – at the ground level. Informal schemes are locally run and involve pooling contributions from members to help cushion the experience of sudden-onset shocks and/or stresses.

Integrating a gender lens into insurance

All forms of insurance need to consider the nature of the risk (including the potential for moral hazard, adverse selection and covariate risk) at hand,[5] as well as the impact of the local regulatory environment and transaction and marketing costs (Dercon et al., 2007a). As we discussed in Chapter 2, women and men face different types of risks (from unequal health burdens to differential life-cycle risks), and the coping options at their disposal are unequal (as a result of, for example, gendered labour markets and cultural norms). Product design, implementation and evaluation need to embed such differences in order to make it possible to effectively tackle the vulnerability of both women and men to economic and social risks. Here we discuss gender considerations relating to programme design, implementation and impacts on well-being.

Programme design

Given their distinct experience of risk and vulnerability, design must consider women's and men's differential position in the household, community and labour force. The work of MacDonald (1998; see also Chapter 1) on gender and social security uses feminist economics to identify the importance of the following key gender dimensions of programme design:

1. *Factoring in intra-household inequalities.* Typically, programming is informed by a breadwinner model that treats the family as a unit, with implicit assumptions about income sharing within the family. Moreover, programmes target women as wives or mothers rather than as individuals, yet individual entitlement to social insurance is very important. By assuming that all members of the family are equal and share the benefits provided, programmes risk reinforcing women's disadvantageous position. Indeed benefits are not always used to support all family members. Evidence suggests, for example, that women may not benefit from unemployment insurance (e.g. Sabates-Wheeler and Kabeer, 2003), while women undertaking unpaid family work in agriculture are unlikely to benefit directly from insurance, given that intra-household relationships are likely to mediate impacts (Farrington, 2005).[4]

2. *Recognising the existing gender division of labour and women's greater reproductive responsibilities, including unpaid family and care work.* Programmes based on the male breadwinner model and traditional gender division of labour in the household often fail to adequately consider women's responsibilities, and provide only minimal compensation for their reproductive labour. Cross-country comparisons, for instance, reveal that poverty alleviation is more effective and work incentives are better in western European countries with well-developed programmes supporting children's costs than in countries that use more means-tested social programmes (e.g. Kamerman, 1984). This is particularly problematic where single

mothers are prompted to work but support for their reproductive responsibilities is either limited or absent. Maternity leave exists in the majority of countries, but tends to be offered only to workers in the formal economy. Without the provision of paternity leave, it also reinforces the traditional gender division of labour, with spill-over effects on women's income, length of employment and pension coverage.

In a similar vein, given women's role as 'household risk and resource managers' (Banthia et al., 2009:v), it is also critical to examine whether schemes support them to deal with urgent household shocks, such as in their increased care burden in the wake of natural disasters, or ensuring their children's future well-being in the event of their own death.

3. *Taking into account distinct gendered labour-market experiences.* When programmes use male work patterns, such as continuous and full-time employment, as the norm for establishing eligibility, women's access to social insurance benefits is likely to be restricted. In the case of agricultural insurance, for instance, it is necessary to assess whether emerging index-based approaches are addressing women's specific vulnerabilities as primarily subsistence-oriented smallholders with limited land ownership and restricted access to financial services and credit (Bird and Espey, 2010).[5] Moreover, in many cultural contexts, women's poorer access to labour and financial markets generally renders them more risk-averse.[6] Although this should render schemes more attractive, in reality this is not the case, in part because of lower literacy and awareness. Accordingly, greater effort is required to promote product uptake among women. As we shall discuss shortly, it is here where micro-insurance providers have been especially innovative (Banthia et al., 2009).

4. *Allowing for a plurality of family arrangements.* Male breadwinner-type social insurance has often ended up reinforcing a particular (patriarchal) family model informed by the idea of a male family wage, the economic dependence of women and the economic authority of men (Folbre, 1994, cited in MacDonald, 1998). Accordingly, some social insurance policies differentiate between female and male survivors and provide benefits exclusively to the former, but only up until remarriage, thereby reinforcing the male breadwinner model, providing protection to women within the family but not female autonomy (Arza, 2012). Given that women on average have a longer lifespan, the specificities of widowhood also need to be taken into account.

Implementation

In terms of programme implementation, there are also a number of important gender dimensions. First, access to and processing of information on insurance provisions and claims procedures typically pose a more serious barrier to poor women than to poor men. Lower literacy and self-confidence levels, combined with greater time poverty, make insurance uptake more challenging. Providers need to ensure that information is accessible and easy to process (Cohen and Sebstad, 2006), and support clients who need assistance, especially with the documentation for processing claims (e.g. negotiating with officials) (Ahmed and Ramm, 2006).

Affordability is a second key axis of gender-sensitive insurance. Low-income women are predominantly casual and seasonal workers, who find it difficult to meet regular monthly premium payments, especially as they often have limited household bargaining power over expenditures. Annual payments may also be challenging, so flexible payments (including grace periods of several months) are often most appropriate (Mathauer et al., 2008). There are, of course, important implications for the financial viability of microfinance institutions. Ahmed and Ramm (2006) suggest that micro-insurance should be offered at various price points. Charging poor people lower premiums could help to include poor women,[7] as could using price to create incentives for certain behaviours, such as enrolling whole families or promoting small family size. Meanwhile, commissions for renewals are typically much lower than for new policies, but experience shows that illiterate people – mainly women – tend not to remember expiry dates and therefore do not renew. Measures are thus needed to discourage agents from prioritising new policies at the expense of following up on renewals (Ahmed and Ramm, 2006).

A range of governance and institutional factors, although they are not specific to gender-sensitive insurance products, are also important. At a macro level, evidence suggests that it is necessary to forge complementarities with existing social protection mechanisms, especially social security and state-funded social assistance. Governments (perhaps with donor support) need to ensure that regulatory frameworks are in place with regard to insurance provision and related consumer protection (Trommershäuser et al., 2006), while simultaneous efforts to improve service access and quality are critical for meeting increased demand, including that among poor populations (Latortue, 2006).

At a meso level, capacity building and technical assistance to support grass-roots organisations in particular in providing appropriate, good-quality and affordable services to the low-income market emerge as a key area for improvement (Latortue, 2006). This is likely to be even more pressing in promoting more gender-equitable insurance (Ahmed and Ramm, 2006). Information clearinghouses could help formal insurers and government agencies to access better information on the low-income market and the risks that its members face, including gender-specific risks, and benchmarking micro-insurers' performance across peer groups could help managers to improve performance (Latortue, 2006). Finally, strengthening information and education on insurance and its potential as a risk management strategy for poor people is important not only for increasing programme reach but also for improving governance and demand for social protection from civil society groups (Ahmed and Ramm, 2006).

Impacts

We still know relatively little about the impacts of insurance uptake and implementation on women's empowerment, overall household welfare, control of resources, and poverty and vulnerability levels (Ahmed and Ramm, 2006; Dercon et al., 2007a). Furthermore, our understanding of the relative merits of social insurance versus micro-insurance compared with traditional mechanisms of risk management remains limited (Magnoni and Zimmerman, 2011), especially with regard to gendered experiences (Banthia et al., 2009). It has been suggested that male members are more likely to submit claims (Ranson et al., 2006; Sinha et al., 2007a),[8] but most analysts focus on product design and features that encourage women to take out a policy (Ahmed and Ramm, 2006; Cohen and Sebstad, 2006; Sinha et al., 2007a). Part of the problem is that few evaluations collect or analyse disaggregated data.[9] The remaining sections of this chapter synthesise the existing gender-sensitive evidence, but with the caveat that this is a field where the available evidence base remains very thin.

Informal insurance mechanisms

Informal insurance mechanisms, defined as 'arrangements between individuals and communities rather than through publicly managed programs or market-provided insurance schemes'(Morduch, 1999:187), can help the poor to reduce risk and mitigate the impact of shocks (Dercon et al., 2006). Examples include drawing down savings, reciprocal gift exchange, selling physical assets and diversifying income-generating activities (Morduch, 1999). Poor women in particular rely on self-help groups, such as rotating savings and credit associations (ROSCAs), accumulating savings and credit associations (ASCRAs) and burial societies (Anderson and Baland, 2002; Kongolo, 2007; Teshome et al., 2012; Tsai, 2000). Whereas formal insurance can be rigid in terms of information demands and entry and exit, informal insurance is built on mutual trust and may allow members to maintain their 'self-respect' (Aredo, 1993). Such networks have attracted considerable attention, and they may have a potential role vis-à-vis more formal institutions (Anderson et al., 2003; Clarke and Dercon, 2009;

Heemskerk et al., 2004). However, as we discuss below, although these mechanisms can be effective in the case of idiosyncratic shocks, overall the evidence suggests that they are relatively weak.[10]

Rotating Savings and Credit Associations (ROSCAs)[11]

ROSCAs, which are found across the developing world, are small groups (typically with 12 to 20 members) that meet voluntarily on a regular basis and contribute a set sum of money to a common 'pot', which is then distributed to a single member on a rotating basis (Ambec and Treich, 2007; Bouman, 1994; Kwon and Skipper, 2007). Most are geared towards saving for assets to enhance productivity or income-generating opportunities (e.g. small livestock, sewing machines), or for major life-cycle events, especially weddings. A member who has not yet received their payment and experiences an idiosyncratic shock may be able to borrow ahead of others (Satkunasingam and Shanmugam, 2006). In Eritrea, for example, about 25% of respondents reported that their *ekub* provided credit to cover illness costs (Habtom and Ruys, 2007).

Bidding pot or auction ROSCAs serve more explicit insurance purposes (Donoso, 2011). In the case of Malaysia:

> *The role of a ROSCA as insurance against events is clearer in a bidding or auction ROSCA where a participant who wants the funds will outbid others and obtain the funds when the need is great. However, this is only possible where that participant has not yet received the funds.*
> (Satkunasingam and Shanmugam, 2006:105)

However, ROSCAs do not provide insurance against general income loss, as participation depends on contributions from an independent source. Nor can they insure against broader community-wide aggregate shocks, such as agricultural losses or natural disasters, as most of the participants will be affected in a similar manner (Donoso et al., 2011).

Gender relations play an important role in ROSCA dynamics and outcomes. Women's and men's need for and use of savings tend to differ significantly, and this shapes the generally more effective dynamics of women-only ROSCAs (Johnson, 2004b; Mayoux and Anand, 1995). First, for many women, having a safe place to save to meet household and family needs can be important (Anderson and Baland, 2002), especially because many women have limited knowledge of and/or access to formal insurance and financial services.

Secondly, expenditure patterns and income streams tend to have distinct gender patterns. Men are typically responsible for expenditures which are 'relatively large and lumpy and their income streams are often also uneven', whereas women are more likely to have more small regular streams of income that allow them to purchase food and other household necessities on an ongoing basis (Johnson, 2004b:1366). For example, Malaysian women use ROSCAs to save for family emergencies and consumer goods that their husbands do not prioritise, although men typically know and approve of their participation (Satkunasingam and Shanmugam, 2006). Kenyan women, on the other hand, find ROSCAs ideal specifically because the money is then inaccessible to their husbands (Anderson and Baland, 2002; see also Ardener and Burman, 1995). In short, women need to convert their smaller and regular amounts to savings for larger household items, whereas men's lumps of income (e.g. from season-dependent cash crop payments or salaried employment) but higher overall expenditure levels are less conducive to ROSCA operations (Johnson, 2004b).

Thirdly, given the greater amount of time spent by poor women on household and care work tasks, as well as the socio-cultural mobility restrictions that they face in some countries, ROSCAs tend to fulfil an especially important social networking function (Anderson and Baland, 2002; Ardener, 1995). Indeed social relationships are key to making ROSCAs work (Bouman, 1995; Etang et al., 2010; Varadharajan, 2004). Close social ties, small group size and regular face-to-face interaction reduce the free rider problem (Bouman, 1994; Kwon and Skipper, 2007; Varadharajan, 2004). ROSCAs comprising only women tend to do best in terms of stability and growth, which may explain why women dominate membership (Anderson and Baland, 2002; Anderson et al., 2003; Dagnelie and LeMay-Boucher, 2008; Varadharajan, 2004).[12] This is related to the more effective use of informal sanctions among women vis-à-vis non-compliance (Johnson, 2004b).

In addition to ROSCAs, the literature identifies three other types of informal insurance associations, all of which are more oriented towards covering sudden-onset shocks, which we now review.

ASCRAs

ASCRAs are non-rotating funds with much larger membership (up to several hundred). Members make regular 'deposits', which are left to accumulate so as to pay for expected expenses such as school fees (Bouman, 1995). Funds are also available for short-term loans, albeit with higher interest rates, with emergencies typically a priority (Anggraeni, 2009). Low-income members can avail themselves of these funds (Bouman, 1994; Thieme, 2003), although in general ASCRAs tend to attract better-off members. However, there are very few data on the gender composition of such groups. Only Thieme (2003), reflecting on Nepalese migrants in Delhi, notes that men typically dominate these networks, partly because there are more male than female migrants. Migrant women have started to establish their own ASCRAs, in part because they want to form women-only social spaces:

> We did not want men in our society, because we do not want to witness how our husbands sit together and drink. And many wives are too shy in the presence of their husbands.

(ASCRA member, cited in Thieme, 2003:29)

Informal insurance groups

Other approaches are more informal in nature and involve groups offering insurance against shocks. In Benin, informal groups have been created specifically as a response to living in a risky environment and the prohibitive costs of formal insurance (LeMay-Boucher, 2007). Groups have clear rules as to what constitutes a reimbursable shock and how many indemnities a member may claim in a given cycle (LeMay-Boucher, 2007, 2009). Gender is not a significant variable in shaping participation. Analogous types of informal non-kin-based associations exist in Eritrea and Ethiopia. Members make periodic contributions and benefits are paid out in money or in kind in the event of job loss, accident, illness or death (Mequanent, 1998). Again, information on gender dynamics is very limited.[13] In Ethiopia, women undertake food preparation at gatherings and are generally excluded from leadership roles, but it is unclear whether this spills over onto the financial dimensions of these networks (Mequanent, 1998).

Burial societies

Burial societies are focused predominantly on covering funeral costs (Teshome et al., 2012), although they sometimes cover additional non-covariate risks, such as fire, house, harvest or livestock destruction, hospitalisation and weddings (Dercon et al., 2006). They are particularly common in East Africa, and meetings are regular and discipline tight; some are restricted to women only (Dercon et al., 2006; Molefe, 1989; Thomson and Posel, 2002; Warnecke, 1994). Societies charge membership fees and require regular dues. In the event of death, funeral expenses and often logistics are partially covered. In Ethiopia and Tanzania, where membership rates are as high as 95%, the average pay-out represents 40–60% of average monthly income (Dercon et al., 2006). Many individuals join multiple risk pools, maintaining membership in several societies (Dercon et al., 2006).

However, there are some important limitations, especially in terms of groups' inability to handle covariate risks facing multiple members (Dercon et al., 2006). It is unclear, for example, what impact HIV/AIDS incidence will have on their financial solvency (Pankhurst and Mariam, 2004; Thomson and Posel, 2002). Given that in Ethiopia the poor already have 25% less coverage than the non-poor, rising fees may shut out more families precisely when more need to be included (Dercon et al., 2006).

Gender analyses of burial society participation and benefits are limited, with the partial exception of Ethiopia. Kloos et al. (2003) note that there is strong participation by women in the case of *equbs* (ROSCAs), but Dercon et al. (2008) note that being a female-headed household does not have any statistically significant impact on the likelihood of joining an *iddir* (burial society). However, in their survey of women's *iddirs*, Teshome et al. (2012) note broader empowerment effects. Over half of women reported greater connection to their community, and over a third reported improved self-confidence. Indeed such social support emerged as much more important than the financial aspects of group membership, at 51.7% and 4.1% of responses, respectively (Teshome et al., 2012). This is not surprising, as women's *iddirs* tend to be financially weak; 25% of 87 surveyed *iddirs* reported zero balance (Teshome et al., 2012).

Informal – formal insurance complementarities

In summary, informal insurance mechanisms offer important insights about differential gender dynamics relating to expenditure patterns, income flows and associated demand for financial services which can both inform the design of formal insurance schemes as well as opportunities for synergies between informal and informal insurance mechanisms (Clarke and Dercon, 2009). Tight social networks reduce moral hazard and monitoring costs and, given high rates of coverage, offer a reasonably inclusive way of delivering a product (Dercon et al., 2006). In some contexts, including China and Malaysia, ROSCAs and formal insurance coexist happily, each contributing to risk reduction and economic security (Fang and Ke, 2006; Satkunasingam and Shanmugam, 2006).

However, such groups have important limitations, including a low capital base, low revenue mobilisation, a small risk pool and limited managerial capacities (Habtom and Ruys, 2007). Moreover, they are particularly weak when it comes to supporting individuals and communities in the face of aggregate shocks – and it is here where formal insurance can arguably play a vital role.

Formal insurance

Formal insurance approaches can be subdivided into social or state-led initiatives and private but pro-poor-oriented micro-insurance programmes.

Social insurance

Formal social insurance mobilises funds, pools risks and redistributes income between different wealth and social groups in order to facilitate financial access to social services for the poor and vulnerable (Hsiao and Shaw, 2007). Membership is compulsory and based on employer and/or employee contributions, and often coexists with other forms of insurance and benefits. It typically encompasses unemployment, sickness/disability and maternity coverage as well as healthcare. We shall briefly discuss the gendered evidence on each of these subtypes, but note that most analyses are focused on design rather than implementation and impact issues.

Employment-based social insurance

Employment-based social insurance provides coverage against unemployment, illness, disability and old age, and often maternity benefits. However, most workers in developing countries are not employed in the formal sector with regular wages, so the premiums are often too high (Sabates-Wheeler and Kabeer, 2003). Globally women's share in vulnerable employment (including own account and unpaid family work) is 51.2%, compared with 48.2% of men (International Labour Organization, 2010b). Significantly higher gender gaps are found however in the Middle East, North Africa, South Asian and sub-Saharan Africa.[14]

The largest share in vulnerable employment in six out of nine regions is unpaid family work, taking up nearly 25% of women, who thus lack both pay and employment insurance (International Labour Organization, 2010b). Even where women have access to the paid workforce, including that in export-oriented industries, access to social insurance remains limited. Chinese women, for instance, who comprise almost 80% of the semi-skilled workforce in special economic zone factories, are typically rural migrants with temporary status in their workplace and no access to social protection measures (Davin, 2004).

The most significant factor explaining women's exclusion from social insurance is thus their over-representation in the informal economy (Sabates-Wheeler and Kabeer, 2003). Worldwide, nearly 40% of the working-age population are legally covered by contributory old-age pension schemes, yet in Africa this proportion is less than one-third (International Labour Organization, 2010a). In terms of effective coverage, the percentages are much lower – 37% in Latin America and the Caribbean, 10% in North Africa, 18% in Asia and the Pacific, and only 5% in sub-Saharan Africa (International Labour Organization, 2010a). The percentages for women are much lower again (Osei-Boateg, 2011) (see also Box 5.1 on domestic workers).[15]

Box 5.1 Domestic workers and social insurance access

Most domestic workers worldwide are women, many from disadvantaged ethnic groups, facing long working hours, low payment and limited autonomy in their employer's home. In a growing number of countries, however, alliances between domestic workers' organisations and labour, feminist and indigenous advocates have lobbied governments to pass laws that provide them with basic rights, such as a minimum wage and health and unemployment insurance. Argentina, Chile and South Africa have passed such legislation, although implementation needs close monitoring and sustained pressure.

In South Africa, domestic workers are covered by the Unemployment Insurance Fund. Employers must register domestic workers and pay a monthly contribution to a fund; workers also have to make a contribution. Legal changes have also introduced minimum wages, written contracts, paid leave, severance pay and dismissal notes. Although enforcement is not easy, overall results have been encouraging. Minimum wages raised hourly earnings by over 20% within a year, and the proportion of domestic workers with a written contract increased from 7% in 2002 to 36% in 2007, and the share reporting unemployment deductions increased from 3% to 32%.

In at least 54 countries, domestic workers are now covered by maternity leave legislation. In Mauritius, casual and part-time workers are included in maternity protection legislation. In Vietnam, domestic workers and apprentices are explicitly covered, and in South Africa, domestic workers are legally entitled to at least 4 consecutive months of maternity leave, and to cash benefits.

Sources: International Labour Organization (2010c);
Lund (2006); Razavi et al. (2012).

In terms of a gendered evidence base, there is most information available about women's access to contributory pensions. When women have social insurance and receive a pension they tend to receive it on the same basis as men – that is, according to contributory years and earnings, and with the same vesting period (Arza, 2012). This is gender biased, as women are mainly employed in jobs with lower earnings and often have interrupted employment histories, given their reproductive and caring responsibilities (International Labour Organization, 2010a). Moreover, elderly women are frequently covered much less than elderly men (Arza, 2012).

Equally important from a gender perspective are indexation mechanisms. Women often live longer, and if pensions are not indexed to follow inflation rates and wage growth, their levels may not allow for a decent living standard (Arza, 2012). For example, following the 2001 economic crisis in Argentina, pensions needed to be adjusted to reflect price changes, which were particularly problematic for women, as many of them were receiving minimum benefit levels. The 2008 reforms introduced automatic indexation of benefits twice a year, a move of particular importance for women given that, on average, Argentinian women spend 19.1 years in retirement, compared with 6.6 years for men (Arza, 2012).

Meanwhile, women typically retire earlier than men, yet in defined-contribution systems this means that they access more limited benefits, as they have a shorter working period in which to save up and a longer retirement period over which to distribute savings. The impact is more pronounced when mortality tables are used in benefit calculation. For example, in Chile, prior to recent pension reforms, single women received a pension around 30% lower than that of single men on account of their longer life expectancy (Yañez, cited in Arza, 2012) (see also Box 5.2).

In systems based on the breadwinner model, women who do not work and whose husbands contribute to social insurance schemes have some entitlements, although in divorce cases there is generally no splitting of claims between husband and wife. In many cases, women, low-skilled workers and people from ethnic minorities in particular have an incomplete work history and inadequate contributions, thus limiting their pension entitlements (International Labour Organization, 2010a).

However, the contributory pension landscape is not all bleak in terms of gender equity. Over the past decade, a number of Latin American countries have undertaken a range of innovative gender-sensitive reforms, as discussed in Box 5.2.

Box 5.2 Gender-sensitive pension reforms in Latin America

There have been a number of innovative gender-sensitive pension reforms in Latin America in recent years. Chile's 2008 pension reform introduced a package of gender-sensitive reforms which included allowing the splitting of pension accumulation on divorce (as women's domestic responsibilities allow men to work and have pension rights), enabling women working in the household to pay voluntary contributions to an individual account and access benefits, establishing that the minimum wage for domestic workers cannot be below that for a full-time employee, abolishing fixed administrative fees discounted from individual accounts, providing a widower's pension to the husband or the father of women's children, and creating a solidarity pillar to provide basic social protection to all Chileans aged 65 years or over in households in the three lowest income quintiles, regardless of contributory history. The pillar also tops up benefits of workers with limited contributions and thus low benefits from the contributory system. In addition, the reform established the *Bono por Hijo* child credit for women, equivalent to 18 months' contribution on a minimum wage, for every child born alive, to increase their pension entitlement.

Bolivia's 2010 pension reform also introduced a number of important gender-sensitive features, underpinned by the explicit inclusion of gender equality as a principle of the new social security system. The semi-contributory pillar is the most important innovation, as it provides better benefit guarantees for workers with low earnings and poor contributory records, most of whom are women. Workers with at least 10 years of contributions and aged 58 years or over are now entitled to an old-age solidarity benefit. Although it is too early to assess its impacts, this system is expected to improve the pensions of low-income workers with short contributory histories and low savings – including women. The second important change is the introduction of child credits for women with children, equivalent to 1 year of contributions per child up to a maximum of 3 years. Given women's very low contributions, these can be used to help women in the contributory system to reach the 10-year minimum record for an old-age pension or increase the benefits to which they are entitled. A third important innovation is the establishment of single mortality tables for the calculation of benefits for women and men, to reduce the gender effect of differential life expectancy. Single tables avoid penalising women for their typically longer life expectancy. With equal accumulation and retirement age, women and men will receive an equal monthly benefit from their individual accounts.

Reforms in Costa Rica and Venezuela recognise non-marital cohabitation or dependency as part of pension eligibility, enabling women who are not legally married to qualify for a survivor's pension if their partner dies. This is important given the relatively high levels of cohabitation rather than marriage in the region, especially among younger women.

Sources. Arza (2012); International Labour Organization (2011).

Besides contributory pensions, there are a number of other employment-related social insurance benefits, including those for unemployment and injury. Gender-disaggregated data are not available for employment injury; they are in the case of unemployment insurance, but this has very limited coverage in developing countries, and there are no cross-country gender-disaggregated data.

Unemployment benefits provide income support to those facing temporary unemployment; the amount is either related to previous earnings or paid at a flat rate. However, in countries with high poverty rates, underemployment is more prevalent than unemployment (because everyone needs to do something to survive). Moreover, 58% of countries do not have statutory unemployment schemes, and not even workers in the formal economy are entitled to such benefits; only 8% of low-income countries have such schemes (whether social insurance or social assistance based). In total, just 33 million out of 212 million people who were unemployed in 2009 received unemployment benefits, representing approximately 15% of the unemployed (International Labour Organization, 2011).

Most countries offer some injury coverage for work-related accidents; a few also include occupational-related diseases. Again, however, coverage is limited to those in the formal economy, and even then effective coverage is rather low. Meanwhile, only in Central and Eastern Europe do social insurance schemes cover employment injury. In all other regions, employer liability schemes complement social insurance ones. Coverage in Africa and Asia is only around 20%. Migrants in the informal economy are particularly vulnerable to work injuries and diseases, but are often excluded. Women workers in private households are also without protection (International Labour Organization, 2010a).

Maternity benefits are in principle a key part of employment-based social insurance, but are relatively limited in coverage in much of the developing world.[16] Only 30% of member states comply with the ILO Convention, providing for at least 14 weeks of leave at a rate of at least two-thirds of previous earnings, paid by social insurance or public funds and not solely by the employer. Not surprisingly, regions with the lowest compliance rates are Asia and the Pacific and the Middle East (International Labour Organization, 2010c). Clearly, pregnancy and the early postpartum/lactation period impose constraints on women and their daily workload, yet the majority of poor women cannot afford not to work, with often significant risks to both maternal and fetal or infant health (Sabates-Wheeler and Kabeer, 2003).[17] The challenges involved in extending maternal health coverage to poor and vulnerable women are discussed in more detail below.

Social health insurance

Social protection for health is limited in many developing countries (Cohen and Sebstad, 2006; Holmes et al., 2007; Lund, 2009a), even though health shocks are one of the key factors pushing households into or further into poverty,[18] and demand is high for health insurance products where they exist.[19] Social health insurance entails public or publicly organised and mandated private insurance against social distress and economic loss caused by ill-health-related reductions in productivity or earnings, and/or the costs of necessary treatment (International Labour Organization, 2008). It provides an alternative financing mechanism to health service user fees, which can act as a serious deterrent to health-seeking behaviour (Walsh and Jones, 2009). Successful schemes require long-term political will and commitment, but have been identified as affordable (International Labour Organization, 2010a; see also Table 5.1).

Women and men face a range of distinct health risks, as a result of both biological and social factors (Sen et al., 2007).[20] As we discussed in Chapter 2, reproductive health vulnerabilities are a major area of difference, but so too are risks of infectious diseases such as HIV, different types of violence and related health effects, mental illhealth and substance abuse. There are also intra-household sources of vulnerability. Not only are women generally responsible for household health-seeking behaviour (Blackden and Wodon, 2006), but also their assets are more likely to be depleted in order to cope with catastrophic health costs (Quisumbing et al., 2011).

It is critical to assess not only which mechanisms can support poor households in coping with general and gender-specific disease burdens and health shocks, but also whether such programmes help to break down male resistance to women's and family health service use. Liu et al. (2009) found that women were more likely to participate in China's New Rural Cooperative Medical Scheme, and that this was probably because, although participation is voluntary, it is contingent on registration of the whole household. This is positive for women's health service uptake, given women's worse health status, higher incidence of chronic health problems and lifetime need for reproductive and related services. Accordingly, households with more women are likely to participate, which is significant in a cultural context characterised by strong son preference, especially in rural areas (Jones et al., 2011).

In terms of affordability, free premiums through universal access or policies at a subsidised rate (possibly with a more limited range of benefits if resource constraints are large) can significantly increase women's access, including those in the informal sector, to health insurance. In China, annual premiums are low at 10 yuan per capita, and this has contributed to increased health service utilisation by rural women, including institutionalised deliveries (Liu et al., 2009). In Ghana, efforts have been made to facilitate access through low and free premiums, although lack of

Table 5.1 Social health insurance examples from developing countries

Country	Programme	Implementation
China	New Rural Cooperative Medical Scheme, created in 2003	Household-based voluntary scheme with low annual premiums per person (approximately $1.50) but high co-payments. Sub-national governments have to contribute locally according to the number of participants; the poorest are subsidised. By 2009 it was the largest state subsidized and linked micro-insurance system in the world covering 833 million people – 94% of the target population up from 10% health insurance coverage of the rural population in 2002.
Ghana	National Health Insurance Scheme, launched in 2004	Financed from several sources, including formal employees' contributions and premium payments. The basic package covers most diseases, including maternity care with an emphasis on female reproductive health. Pregnant women and children under 18 are exempted from paying a premium to register. By 2007, there were 8.2 million members, almost 38% of the population, including informal sector workers; the number of registered people continues to increase along with increased use of formal health facilities.
India	Rashtriya Swasthya Bima Yojana (RSBY), launched in 2008	A national health insurance scheme, launched by Indian Ministry of Labour and Employment to provide in-patient health care cover to those living below the poverty line (BPL). Beneficiaries pay Rs.30 (less than one US$) as a registration fee used for administrative costs. The RSBY benefits package also includes maternity and newborn care, and includes a transport allowance up to Rs.1,000 (around US$20) per year.
		At the time of enrolment each beneficiary household is issued a Smart Card with biometric data; apart from identification purposes Smart Cards contain all data regarding household enrolment and use of the scheme.
		Central and state governments pay per-family premiums to the insurer selected by the state government according to a competitive bidding process, incentivising the insurer to enrol as many BPL households as possible. Hospitals also have the incentive to treat RSBY beneficiaries as they are paid by the insurer per beneficiary treated. The scheme includes both private and public health providers to foster competition and enhanced service quality. The scheme also involves NGOs and MFIs as intermediaries that reach out to and assist BPL beneficiaries to use the services after enrolment.

		By 2012 32.5 million households were enrolled covering 110 million individuals across 26 states. Although not gender-sensitive in design, the scheme has improved healthcare access for female beneficiaries, with evaluation evidence suggesting that in nine districts 53% of all those who used the RSBY cards were women. There is still a gender gap in enrolment rates but this is narrowing.
Kenya	National Hospital Insurance Fund, first launched in 1966 and restructured in 1998	Aims to be the main provider of health insurance in the country and to provide quality and affordable health services to all Kenyans. Membership is mandatory for all adults, with no distinction between formal and informal workers. All salaried employees make monthly premium contributions according to their income;; the self-employed and informal workers pay a fixed premium. The fund covers certain dependants such as spouses, children, students and disabled dependants. It covers an estimated 2.7 million people and has increased utilisation rates of health care and out-of-pocket expenditure.
Mexico	*Seguro Popular*, launched in 2004	Offers voluntary social insurance and covers health care, maternity and drugs. Some 54.2% of registered participants are women, and by 2010 it reached 43.5 million people. The programme has reduced catastrophic health expenditure and benefited female-headed households particularly.
Nigeria	National Health Insurance System, launched in 1999 but redesigned according to the 2006 National Health Policy	Includes three main programmes to provide health care to all socioeconomic groups, and is funded primarily by members' contributions. The Formal Sector Social Health Insurance Programme covers those in the formal sector and dependants, with employers contributing 10% and employees 5% of the basic salary. The Informal Sector Programme covers the self-employed and rural community dwellers, who make monthly contributions according to the benefits package they choose. The Vulnerable Groups Programme is a subsidy programme covering pregnant women, children under five, the unemployed, orphans and the disabled. Maternity care for up to four live births for every insured contributor is offered along with preventative care and family planning services. The scheme overall covers 5 million people; although it has extended coverage, it is largely used by formal workers, with use of services lower among low-income groups and young people.

Table 5.1 Continued

Country	Programme	Implementation
The Philippines	Philippine Health Corporation, created in 1995 but reformed in 2005	Aims to achieve universal coverage. Enrolment is mandatory for the formal sector and members pay a premium of up to 3% of their monthly income for them and their dependants. Informal workers are enrolled voluntarily. A government subsidy is offered for the enrolment of the poor. The benefits package is nearly comprehensive and includes deliveries and catastrophic coverage. Coverage is 78.39 million people as of 2011 or 82% of the population, but reaching the informal sector and the poor remains a challenge.
Thailand	Universal Coverage Scheme (UCS), launched 2002.	UCS is a tax-financed national health insurance scheme that provides health care services free of charge to 75% of the Thai population; initially, a small co-payment of 30 Baht per visit or admission was enforced (and thus the scheme was initially known as the 30 Baht Scheme), but this was terminated in 2006. The UCS enrols those not covered by the two other insurance schemes, the Civil Servant Medical Benefit Scheme (CSBMS) which covers government employees, retirees and dependents, and the contributory Social Security Scheme (SSS) which covers private sector employees.

The benefits package is comprehensive including includes preventive, promotive, curative and rehabilitative services; it also includes obstetric care only for the first two deliveries, ARVs for HIV, renal replacement therapy, and a wide range of sexual and reproductive health services; yet safe abortion service is only covered for rape victims and for those whose health is at risk. In 2011 an independent assessment of its first ten years found that the UCS improved access to necessary health services, improved equity of service utilization, and prevented medical impoverishment.

In addition UCS has also decreased poverty as according to a UNDP study 88,000 households in 2008 were prevented from falling below the poverty line. Thai women in the low income quintiles have also benefited; a study covering 40,000 women in 2005–2006 found that there were almost no rich–poor gaps in access to maternal health care and contraceptive services. However, minority and migrant women (and men), as well as homeworkers continue to face difficulty in accessing health care services. |

Vietnam	National Health Insurance System, reformed through 2008 Law on Health Insurance	Compulsory Health Insurance was introduced in 1992 and covers formal sector workers. Contributions are low, at 4.5% of the salary, with 3% paid by the employer. Voluntary Health Insurance, also introduced in 1992, covers those not eligible in the other two programmes, such as farmers, informal workers and students. Payments are on a flat rate, and the current cost is 4.5% of the minimum wage. Financial incentives are offered to the near poor. Social Health Insurance now incorporates the Health Care Fund for the Poor. It provides free or subsidised health insurance to specific groups such as children under six, the poor, pensioners and veterans. Overall, 36.5 million people are covered. Yet in 2008 Contributory Health Insurance covered only 10% of those with health insurance, and Voluntary Health Insurance coverage was limited. Social Health Insurance has been able to increase access to health care, but 41% of people aged over 60, 24% of ethnic minorities and 31% of the poorest are not covered, and the fund was in debt.

Source: Apoya and Marriott (2011); Arun and Steiner (2008); ILO, nd; King et al. (2009); Liu et al. (2009); McManus (2012); Ravindran (2012); RSBY (2011); Swarup (2012); UNDP (2011); UN ESCAP (2011); http://jointlearningnetwork.org/countries; www.seguro-popular.gob.mx

finance is still the most cited obstacle to joining for 90% of non-participants (Mensah et al., 2010).

Mexico's voluntary *Seguro Popular* provides premium exemptions for people in the five lowest income deciles.[21] The scheme has a focus on female-specific health problems, maternal mortality, HIV/AIDS, cervical and breast cancer, and gender-based violence.[22] National statistics suggest that 94% of women now have at least one antenatal appointment, and 93% have a skilled attendant present at birth.[23] Moreover, *Seguro Popular* reduced catastrophic health expenditure by 23% from the baseline, with the highest overall effect in poorer households and a positive effect in female-headed households (King et al., 2009).

Ensuring provision for women's reproductive health is an area of increasing interest, given the important potential dividends in terms of maternal and neonatal health outcomes. In Ghana, where pregnant women have received free healthcare since 2008, women enrolled in the National Health Insurance Scheme are far more likely than the uninsured to give birth in hospital (81% of those who are insured deliver in a hospital, compared with 57% of those who are uninsured), have their birth attended by trained health professionals (81% vs. 59%) and receive antenatal care (94% vs. 76%), and they experience fewer infant deaths (twice as many uninsured women reported the death of a child under 5 years of age).[24] India's *Rastriya Swasthya Bima Yojana*, through the provision of free premiums and low registration for people below the poverty line, has extended coverage to poor families in the informal economy (International Labour Organization, 2011). This is already reaching 110 million individuals, which makes it an example worthy of further investigation.

In other cases, however, affordability remains a significant challenge. For example, despite ensuring near universal (96%) coverage, including among low-income workers, Chile's National Public Health Fund (*Fonasa*) remains gender inequitable. Women are subject to significantly higher premiums than men of the same age, given the high cost of maternal care. Indeed one private insurer's plan was closed to women aged 18 to 45 years following the withdrawal of a government maternal subsidy in 2002 (Mesa-Lago, 2008). Moreover, costs for normal childbirth are highly inequitable among women (German Agency for International Cooperation, 2004). Women who are relying on private health insurance and a monthly income of $400 pay more than five times as much from their own pockets as those with statutory insurance. Those with a high income and private insurance pay on average only half the amount paid by statutory scheme members.

Similarly, while Colombia's 1993 health reform benefited women, as they paid the same contributions despite their higher risks due to reproductive needs, there were also some limitations in terms of gender equity (Ewig and Bello, 2009). On the one hand, the state compensatory fund paid insurers additional sums according to predetermined risk factors, and thus risks were pooled and not individualised. Moreover, women paid a percentage of their salary and not a predetermined contribution. As their earnings are usually lower than men's, this offered some compensation for labour-market inequalities. On the other hand, however, subsidised beneficiaries, including groups with increased vulnerability such as pregnant women and female household heads, received inferior-quality healthcare. In particular, between 1998–2006, the rate of maternal mortality in the subsidised sector was on average twice that in the contributory sector, and women in the subsidised system did not receive salary coverage for maternity leave and sick pay as women in the contributory system did.

Micro-insurance programmes

Micro-insurance comprises contributory schemes that meet the basic social protection needs of people excluded from formal social security, especially workers in the informal economy and their families. Unlike most social insurance, membership is not compulsory. Schemes can be run by already established civil society organisations (e.g. microfinance institutions, non-governmental organisations, or trade unions), community-based organisations (e.g. mutual benefit associations), or commercial insurers (which work with organisations through partner – agent agreements). The state, international agencies and even state-owned insurance companies may provide subsidies. Various risks are covered, but the most frequent ones relate to life, health, disability, property, assets and crops.

Micro-insurance helps to compensate for the failure of financial markets in low-income contexts by protecting the poor in exchange for regular monetary payments 'proportionate to the likelihood and cost of the risk involved' (Churchill, 2006:12). Schemes benefit from insurance companies' expertise in developing and pricing policies, as well as access to reinsurance markets to ensure sustainable products. Insurance companies benefit from the reach and reputation of microfinance institutions to access the client base.

Demand for this type of product is quite high (Mendoza, 2011), with an estimated 40 million people in China covered, arguably even more in India (although accurate figures are difficult to obtain), and a further 14.7 million across 32 African countries (Churchill and McCord, 2012). Furthermore, given that women make up the majority of micro-credit customers, coverage among women is also high, especially as many microfinance institutions in Africa, Asia and Latin America lend exclusively to women (World Bank, 2011b).[25] In 2004, micro-insurance health schemes were the most popular in Africa and the Philippines, whereas life insurance was the most popular in South Asia (Jacquier et al., 2006). We shall focus on both of these subtypes, and also discuss emerging programmes focused on disaster micro-insurance.

Analysts generally agree that micro-insurance can make a positive contribution in the extension of social protection, especially in the context of limited governmental financial and institutional capacity, where programmes may increase finance and human resources (e.g. Ahmed and Ramm, 2006). Schemes can also enhance the participation of civil society and empower specific population groups, such as women, given their ability to reach those excluded from statutory social insurance (e.g. rural workers, workers in the informal economy), their lower transaction costs (as schemes are often operated by civil society, relying on voluntary self-management), their capacity to respond better to local needs and financial realities (as benefits are often designed in consultation with the target population), and their lower risks of abuse and fraud compared with more centralised systems (resulting from social ties and informal community 'policing') (Jacquier et al., 2006).

However, key concerns include the fact that, despite their proliferation, coverage is only an estimated 3% of the poor who need such insurance (Qureshi and Reinhard, 2012), they have limited viability and sustainability, members are often able to pay only a very low premium and thus access only limited benefits, they have minimal redistributive potential (as contributions are often based on a flat rate), legislative and regulatory frameworks are often not conducive to their replication and expansion, and, as schemes are usually self-governing, interests diverge from the government's broader social protection strategies, and, to maintain their autonomy, insurers do not want to become part of national social protection systems (Jacquier et al., 2006). In short, the role of micro-insurance is supplementary only, and it cannot realistically replace the state's role in protecting vulnerable groups comprehensively, especially against covariate risks such as epidemics or natural disasters (Ahmed and Ramm, 2006). This is where the role of social insurance, as discussed above, as well as other forms of social assistance, as discussed in Chapters 3, 4 and 6, plays a critical role, especially for poor women and men.

Life and funeral insurance

Death of a family member, especially a breadwinner, can constitute a major source of vulnerability for poor households (Dercon et al., 2004) (see Personal Narrative 5.2). Micro-life insurance policies are gaining in coverage in developing countries, offering benefits to surviving family members on the death of the policy holder, either as a lump sum or through regular payments over a certain period of time, with the aim of maximising the utility of the benefit for household well-being (Cohen and Sebstad, 2006).

Personal Narrative 5.2: Without life insurance, surviving family members often face long-term vulnerabilities – Osman Mohammed in Ghana

Osman Mohammed is a 19-year-old northern Ghanaian boy. He had to stop school in Grade 6, when his father died, to take care of his blind mother and his siblings. His friends farm and buy motor-bikes, and make fun of him since he must spend his money on food. He is sad because nobody has 'advised' him since his father died. Last year his brother was bitten by a snake and had to go to hospital. It was especially difficult because his father did not leave anything for them to rely on. *'If my father were alive, I would be fine.'*

Source: Amuzu et al. (2010).

This vulnerability has important gendered economic and socio-emotional impacts, on two broad fronts. First, the likelihood of a woman being widowed is quite high, because of the longer average lifespan of women and also because in some cultures women marry men who are many years older than them. Widows often have to survive independently, with opportunities to remarry rare (Banthia et al., 2009), and they frequently lack a formal title to property and land and risk eviction from their own home, especially if they have no children. In addition, the HIV/AIDS epidemic has led to an increased number of evictions of women widowed by the disease, particularly if they themselves are also infected (Joint UN Programme on HIV/AIDS, 2008).

Secondly, as primary household caregivers, many women are concerned about the fate of their children, especially their daughters, in the event of their own death. Women worry about being able to repay outstanding debts and provide adequate financial benefits to children, and fear that any pay-out from a life insurance policy will go only to their spouse or on unintended purposes, rather than towards broader household well-being (Banthia et al., 2009).

The design of life insurance policies is central to their gender impact. In the event of widowhood, well-defined policies could increase women's security by covering ongoing costs, including repayment of spousal loans, loss of income and funeral expenses (Roth et al., 2005), which may also enable women to maintain land and property rights. Meanwhile, loan-linked coverage typically includes only women, leaving them unprotected in the event of their husband's death. In the Philippines, the Center for Agriculture and Rural Development Mutual Benefit Association now includes spouses in loan portfolios, in recognition of the fact that the death of a spouse can affect the ability of a woman to repay (Banthia et al., 2009). In India, the Self-Employed Women's Association (SEWA) offers spouse coverage as part of its family insurance, which also covers hospitalisation and asset loss (Ahmed and Ramm, 2006).

Recognition of the demand for more flexible life insurance approaches is also increasing. Although many schemes assume that husbands will benefit from wives' life insurance claims, many women want the freedom to choose another beneficiary (such as friends, relatives or adult children) so as to better protect children in the event of their death. Cohen and Sebstad (2006) found in Kenya, Tanzania and Uganda that women were increasingly designating their friends as beneficiaries and instructing them to use the money for children's school fees and other necessities, rather than naming their husbands. Policies can also ensure that insurance money is spent wisely and on items that are traditionally women's responsibility. *La Equidad* in Colombia provides a policy whereby ongoing payments are made for education as well as a one-off funeral payment (Banthia et al., 2009). Delta Life in Bangladesh has a savings scheme to benefit the policy holder's daughter when she reaches 18 years of age. This is marketed as a marriage product, but it could be used for education or other purposes.

A key ingredient of gender-sensitive insurance involves ensuring that women can access information and communication easily. In many cases, however, dealing with claims or problems may necessitate a trip to a distant city, which poor people and especially women can ill afford (Roth, 1999). To address this need, increasingly innovative delivery channels are being piloted, including funeral parlours offering funeral insurance in South Africa, and Internet kiosks selling life insurance in India (Lloyds 360 Risk Insight, 2009).

Evidence suggests that micro-life insurance premiums have become affordable for many poor people, in part because mandatory programmes are common. Many microfinance institutions value the protection that they offer in their loan portfolios, and some are motivated by the revenue potential from commissions and may not want or have the capacity to invest in convincing clients to buy products voluntarily. Although this approach effectively negates client choice, it does mean that premiums tend to be significantly lower than those for voluntary programmes, as administration costs and risks to insurers are kept low. Even so, successful and profitable voluntary schemes, including SEWA in India and *BancoSol* in Bolivia, have found that poor women will pay for micro-insurance if they are aware of the advantages, and value the opportunity to select from a range of benefits customised to their needs (Banthia et al., 2009).

There is a dearth of gender-aware monitoring and evaluation of life insurance products. Sinha et al. (2007b) found for VimoSEWA's bundled insurance scheme that claim submission rates were relatively higher for life than for asset or health insurance among the poorest members in both rural and urban areas. Although this clearly reflects lower life expectancy among the poor and an upper age limit of 60 years for this particular life insurance policy, it does also indicate the relative importance of life insurance cover for poor women.

Box 5.3 Self-Employed Women's Association (SEWA) – micro-insurance good practice

Formed in 1972, SEWA is a registered trade union of women working in the informal sector in Gujarat, India, which started offering insurance through its sister organisation, VimoSEWA,[26] in 1992, open to both women and men, and non-members. By 2010, around 120,000 people were insured, of whom 62,060 were women. To promote the inclusion of female children, the scheme offers lower premiums to women members who enrol their whole family, which simultaneously encourages broader transformative gender attitudes.

The product has changed a number of times, in response to members' demands and emerging evidence on distributional impacts. The current voluntary product includes life, health and asset coverage, and allows the policy holder to add their spouse and children for an additional premium. It is 'bundled' – that is, members must buy all three types of coverage as a single contract. The product is sold by community agents, who also collect annual renewal payments, and evidence suggests that women value regular face-to-face interactions highly, especially the opportunity to ask questions and discuss household risk. SEWA also relies on both small and large client meetings to provide non-threatening women-only forums on how women can best protect their families from risks by using micro-insurance.

Sources: Ahmed and Ramm (2006); Banthia et al. (2009); Churchill (2006); Devadasan et al. (2007); Sinha et al. (2007a).

Micro-health insurance

Micro-health insurance approaches have been found to reduce out-of-pocket health expenditure and increase use of healthcare services in Africa and Asia (Radermacher et al., 2012), and are increasingly filling gaps in affordable healthcare financing among low-income populations in the developing world (Leatherman et al., 2012). As with micro-life insurance, although gender-disaggregated findings are limited, existing evidence suggests that such programmes, if well designed, may have positive gender effects, especially in terms of programme access and reductions in catastrophic health expenditure. Microfinance institutions that offer insurance often have close links to women through microcredit groups, which can help to overcome problems of trust and confidence for those with no experience of such products (Division for the Advancement of Women, 2009). In VimoSEWA (see Box 5.3), members' catastrophic expenditure on hospitalisation halved, which is significant, especially as many members come from seriously socio-economically disadvantaged households (Ranson et al., 2006). That said, the poorest members are often disadvantaged with regard to hospitalisation benefits, primarily because of different rates of claim submission (Sinha et al., 2007b). This may be due to the scarcity of hospitals and to poor transportation systems, as well as to weaker capacity to obtain documentation from medical personnel and liaise with those who provide links between members and scheme administrators to submit claims (Sinha et al., 2007b).

Flexible payment and renewal modalities as well as coverage of extra-hospitalisation costs constitute key gender-sensitive design features. In VimoSEWA, clients can pay an annual lump sum, with the interest accrued going towards paying the premium (Sinha et al., 2007a). However, lack of face-to-face contact still emerged as the primary (57%) self-reported reason for dropout among more than 17,000 women in Ahmedabad, India (Sinha et al., 2007a). Women with stronger links to SEWA are more likely to renew, and improved awareness-raising campaigns during the annual renewal period are reported to have raised the renewal rate.

Ensuring accessibility in documentation requirements is another important dimension of gender-responsive micro-health insurance. SEWA has adopted several innovative approaches to help members make claims, including the use of extension agents as well as a barcode scanner system which allows illiterate or semi-literate members to make a claim by attaching a sticker to a prepaid envelope and sending it to the micro-insurer, who in turn sends a fieldworker to provide support and also encourage policy renewal (Botero et al., 2006). These also help to overcome power differentials between often poorly educated, lower-caste, low-income women and the doctors required to support insurance claims, as well as issues of time poverty in travelling to local SEWA offices to submit reimbursement paperwork. Such approaches are clearly needed, as although the majority of members of VimoSEWA are women, male members are significantly more likely to submit claims (Ranson et al., 2006).

Distance to healthcare facilities and related transport expenses and opportunity costs of travel can serve as additional barriers for women. To address such challenges, in addition to working with government to encourage improved health services, several micro-insurance companies now provide their own health services. In Latin America, *Pro Mujer* operates a direct partnership with providers and has its own clinics (UN Population Fund, 2010).[27] In other cases, policies explicitly cover costs of treatment and related transport. In Jordan, all customers of the Microfund for Women, 97% of whom are women, are enrolled in the Care Giver Policy and receive expenses to cover the costs of medical facilities and related transport.[28]

Despite their often explicit targeting of women, a number of micro-health insurance schemes do not offer maternity benefits, partly because pregnancy is viewed as a risk that women can control and so cannot be pooled like illness or accidents (Ahmed and Ramm, 2006). When the Indian non-governmental health insurance programme Shepherd was negotiating its policy with the state-owned United India Insurance Company,[29] it was informed that the price would double if it included child delivery, and would include a 9-month waiting period to exclude women who were already pregnant. Members thus ultimately decided not to include maternity care. Instead, a soft loan scheme helps them with the cost of childbirth (Berkhout and Oostingh, 2008). Some analysts suggest that savings and access to emergency loans may be a better way of mitigating 'predictable events', including pregnancy-related risks (Roth et al., 2005). That said, Bolivia's *BancoSol*, which provides full maternity coverage, offers a rare case study of good practice. The initiative has a 7-month waiting period, giving women a valuable 2-month window in which to purchase insurance prior to childbirth (Banthia et al., 2009).

However, not all women are interested in maternity care coverage. In Guatemala, for example, women with an average age of 42 years were not interested in the inclusion of maternity benefits in health insurance products, were not more concerned about their children's health than their own, and did not want to insure their children, as they relied on free clinics (Qureshi and Reinhard, 2012). This challenges a number of common assumptions about gendered interests.

Finally, the evidence on programme impacts on the health of poor women and men is very thin, and what there is appears to be mixed. In India's *Yeshasvini*, no significant impact on maternal healthcare is found, yet in Mali's Equity Initiative, members are twice as likely to make four or even more antenatal visits compared with pregnant women in the overall population (Churchill and Matul, 2012).

Disaster insurance

Disaster insurance is an important emerging field, given the devastating effects that natural disasters can have on the lives of poor and vulnerable populations. Between 1980 and 2004, over 95% of natural disaster-related deaths occurred in developing countries, with direct economic losses alone averaging $54 billion a year (Munich Re Foundation, 2005). In 2010, a total of 373 natural disasters killed over 296,000 people, affected nearly 208 million others and cost nearly $110 billion (UN Office for Disaster Risk Reduction, 2011). Moreover, in the context of climate change, there is growing evidence that natural disasters are increasing with the worst effects on poor agricultural communities (Pierro and Desai, 2008). Climate change also has implications for the urban poor and for rural-urban change. Most informal urban settlements are built illegally and without formal planning, and are typically characterised by limited availability of water, high child and infant mortality rates and a very high disease burden (Davies et al., 2008). As a result, analysts are emphasising the importance of adaptive social protection, including approaches such as index-based insurance, to promote more climate-resilient livelihoods, but as we discuss below current approaches are rarely gender-sensitive and often struggle to reach the poorest and most marginalised population groups (ibid).

Natural disasters have multiple gendered impacts, shaped by both biological and social factors. Women generally do not have the same physical capacities as men, and when this is compounded by cultural factors, such as restricted mobility and caring responsibilities for children, the sick and aged, they may be more vulnerable to sudden-onset disasters because they are less able to escape. Neumayer and Plümper (2007) using data from 141 countries over the period 1981 to 2002, found that natural disasters lower the life expectancy of women more than that of men, and that the effect is stronger, the more severe the disaster. There is also a strong correlation with socio-economic status – the higher a woman's socio-economic status, the weaker the effect on the gender gap in life expectancy. Similarly, Peterson (2007 quoted in UNDP, 2010) found that women, boys and girls are more than 14 times more likely than men to die during a disaster.

Women's caring responsibilities can also intensify during the recovery phase. For instance, droughts and floods may have an impact on women and girls, as an increased amount of time is required for water collection, or they may face higher workloads as men resort to out-migration in response to extreme events (UNDP, 2009). Finally, the informal coping mechanisms that are used by women as a buffer during 'normal' shocks are likely to break down as the same event affects large numbers of people. Of course, disaster does not solely affect women. Men are for example far more vulnerable during the rescue phase of disaster recovery, as they may undertake risky activities while trying to save lives and salvage property (Delaney and Shrader, 2000; Guha-Sapir et al., 2006). Furthermore, men's gender roles may be disrupted more easily in post-disaster environments (Dimitrijevics, 2007), due to loss of their anchors when fields and jobs are gone.

Despite limited experience, the argument that insurance can encourage mitigation through investments in disaster prevention and rewards for risk-reducing behaviour is strong, especially as disaster-related risks can cause multiple and simultaneous losses. Insurance has the potential to increase security and facilitate recovery and reconstruction through interventions such as index-based insurance (whereby financial protection is provided vis-à-vis a physical trigger – such as rainfall measured at a regional weather station – so that payment is provided if the index falls below a certain trigger regardless of actual individual losses), catastrophe bonds (risk-linked securities developed in the mid-1990s following Hurricane Andrew where a specified set of risks are transferred to investors rather than insurers in order to spread the risk) and complementary micro-insurance which can provide incidental support through life and asset insurance products (O'Donnell, 2009) .

Weather-index insurance has been developed in the context of micro-insurance since the beginning of the 21st century. The first known example was introduced in Mexico in 2001 to provide drought cover for farmers, and subsequent examples have included rain-based index insurance in India in 2003, livestock insurance in Mongolia in 2006 and drought insurance in Malawi and Ethiopia in the mid-2000s.

Increasingly insurance is also being organised at the meso- or macro-levels to protect broader target groups. For instance, index-based meso-solutions have been piloted in West Africa, India and Peru covering the portfolios of members of agricultural or small producer cooperatives. The pay out is not related to the individual loss adjustment but depends on defined thresholds for the weather event, and is then used by the cooperatives to make favourable emergency loans available to affected borrowers (Loster and Reinhard, 2012). Macro-level index insurance involving millions of people typically involves insurance coverage for a national government (e.g. Mexico's AGROASEMEX weather insurance programme) or governments (the Caribbean Catastrophe Risk Insurance Facility) which is then used to support the poor during the relief and recovery process, although in general there is little public awareness of these mechanisms as they are generally viewed simply as disaster relief (ibid).

While index-based insurance mechanisms are gaining in popularity there are also considerable challenges including targeting the most vulnerable with payouts, very high costs of premiums for local governments, the demands of complex cost-benefit analyses and the risk that attention is diverted from arguably more critical disaster risk reduction approaches

(Pierro, 2010). Davies et al. (2008) also point out that gender differentials are typically not considered. An important exception is that of SEWA's rainfall index insurance - which covers excesses or deficits of rainfall to rural members in three districts. The policy is based on an index reading of aggregated rainfall during the cover phases. In 2009 there were 1441 policies linked to 780 clients with a 50/50 male female ratio (Sharma et al., 2011).

Several indemnity-based insurance approaches (i.e. where claim pay-outs are based on actual losses) targeting women have also been piloted in India and Nepal. These disaster micro-insurance schemes follow two basic models –an extension of microcredit and micro-savings programmes and stand alone programmes for disaster micro-insurance– both of which may be bundled or voluntary schemes, and variously target urban and rural poor.

Nepal's NGO Centre for Self-Help Development, a micro-credit and micro-insurance provider for women, is an example of the first model. It offers disaster micro-insurance voluntarily to its 15,000 female members in the event of death of the women or collapsed dwellings. A similar model is followed by the southern Indian Working Women's Forum which includes insurance against damages due to natural disasters as part of the property component of its bundled micro-insurance scheme. The WWF's primary focus is micro-credit and it offers health, life, accident and property micro-insurance to its 570,000 women members who are organised into neighbourhood groups of 8 to 10 people (Mechler et al., 2006).

The second type of micro-insurance schemes targeting women is specifically designed to provide financial protection for disaster impacts and mostly has a specific disaster risks management focus. Afat Vimo in Gujarat India is a good example, providing disaster insurance to an estimated 6,000 men and women microenterprise owners vulnerable to earthquakes, floods and fires through the All India Disaster Mitigation Institute. Premiums are on average only 0.5% of clients' annual income, thanks to public insurer involvement, donor support and limited cover, although they have been criticised as being insufficient to provide the capital that the poor need to restore their livelihoods after a disaster. Overall, however, the programme seems to be affordable and effective, and is thus expanding. It targets existing microfinance groups, thereby generating a platform for awareness raising and trust building to ensure that communities understand the value of insurance and its potential positive impact (Sadhu and Pandya, 2005; Microinsurance Network, 2010). The Andhra Pradesh Disaster Preparedness Programme provides micro-insurance embedded within a broader disaster preparedness initiative (which includes support for housing, health awareness, water and sanitation and capacity building), with technical and financial support from Oxfam in partnership with the Oriental Insurance Company. It targets groups of women in the 10-75 age group providing coverage for natural disasters to more than 1000 families (Mechler et al., 2006).

Conclusions

This chapter has defined social protection-oriented insurance as contribution-based instruments that aim to mitigate risk for all social groups, including the poor, by pooling group resources either community- or society-wide. We have argued that it is important to recognise a diversity of approaches, including locally run informal schemes that involve pooling contributions to help to cushion the experience of sudden-onset shocks and/or stresses, as well as formal programmes led by the state or not-for-profit private/non-governmental organisations, with a number of possible providers at the ground level.

The chapter began by reviewing informal insurance approaches, and identified rotating savings and loans groups, non-rotating accumulated savings associations, more informal groups to protect against sudden-onset shocks, and burial societies. Such groups often support individuals when they experience idiosyncratic shocks, but are much more limited in the face of covariate shocks. In terms of their gender dynamics, the evidence base is somewhat limited, except for ROSCAs, which tend to be dominated by women and also are more effective when they are composed solely of women, because of differential gendered income and expenditure patterns and the relative weight of social sanctions in ensuring compliance. Given the important complementary role that informal insurance mechanisms can play alongside formal programmes, more in-depth gendered analysis of such groups is urgently needed.

The second half of the chapter reviewed formal insurance. Social insurance is state led and aims to mobilise funds, pool risks and redistribute income between different wealth and social groups, in order to facilitate financial access to social services for the poor and vulnerable. Membership is compulsory and contribution based, and often coexists with other forms of insurance and different benefit packages. We focused on three broad types of social insurance, namely unemployment-based insurance, social health insurance and maternal health coverage, and whether gender differentials are taken into account in design, implementation and impact evaluations. Overall, we found that schemes in the developing world do not reflect gender differences well, including women's care work responsibilities and more limited employment service, their predominance in informal employment, their longer life expectancy and their different reproductive health needs. There are some partial good-practice examples in Latin America.

The final section of the chapter focused on life, health and disaster micro-insurance, highlighting the growing demand for such products, including demand by women. Products need to be designed and implemented in a gender-sensitive manner in order to help to mitigate general and gender-specific risks. Ensuring that policies are accessible, easy to use and renew, and thoroughly understood by poor and often illiterate populations, including women, is vital. This may require tailored outreach and support mechanisms that take into account women's greater time poverty, mobility constraints and more limited capacity to negotiate with service providers and programme officials. Addressing affordability concerns through flexible payments and building the capacity of insurance providers, especially grass-roots organisations, to work effectively with low-income populations, including women, are also key issues. Integrated packages of insurance types could be the most beneficial approach, to respond to multiple vulnerabilities and minimise transaction costs. Such approaches are still quite rare, but VimoSEWA in India is a good model from which to draw lessons.

SIX

Ensuring access to state provision: towards more gender-sensitive subsidy schemes

Introduction

In many countries, subsidy programmes are considered an important component of social protection policy, as they reduce the financial barriers that poor people often face in accessing basic goods and services. Indeed, inequalities in accessing goods and services remain a serious challenge across and within developing countries, often exacerbated by gender inequalities. As we discussed in Chapter 2, for instance, although significant progress has been made in recent decades in reducing disparities in accessing education and healthcare, particularly for girls and women,[1] progress has been slowest for the poor, and in many countries this is compounded by gender inequality and discrimination. Moreover, women face specific constraints and inequalities within the productive sectors, too. Poor rural households remain highly dependent on agriculture for their livelihoods, yet have limited access to agricultural inputs or financial services, keeping them trapped in low-return activities. The problem is particularly acute for women, due to lower levels of education, mobility constraints, domestic responsibilities and institutional bias.

Subsidy programmes cover a wide range of social and economic objectives, including improving consumers' real purchasing power, addressing calorie and nutrient deficiencies, increasing uptake of social services to develop human capital, augmenting agricultural productivity, and supporting labour-market participation. In this chapter we provide an overview of subsidy programmes through a gender lens, examining five types – food, agriculture, basic services (health and education), childcare and integrated services – using primary and secondary research evidence from Latin America, Africa and Asia. We assess their potential to promote greater access to goods and services among poor households through a gender-sensitive approach.

Subsidy programmes: an overview

Certain types of subsidy programmes are politically popular, favoured by national governments as relatively straightforward to implement. For instance, agricultural inputs, fuel or food subsidies are particularly politically attractive, given their high visibility and ability to meet a range of economic, social and political objectives through one instrument[2] (Wiggins and Brooks, 2010). Moreover, many subsidy programmes have been able to overcome the political, financial and capacity constraints to deliver at a scale that other social protection programmes still cannot (Ellis et al., 2009).

Despite their political attractiveness, subsidy programmes have not always received support. They can be costly, inefficient and subject to high levels of corruption. For instance, an estimated 71% of public spending on food subsidies in India and the Philippines is wasted through poor targeting, fraud and excess costs (Jha and Ramaswami, 2010). High leakage to the non-poor is often also reported (as high as 83% in Egypt's large-scale food subsidy, for instance) (Marcus and Pereznieto, 2011). Moreover, subsidies often disproportionately benefit the non-poor, who have the financial capacity to pay for goods and services which the poor may not be able to access, even at subsidised rates. Many subsidies are also characterised by late and unpredictable delivery and poor quality of goods and services (Hastuti, 2008; Pasha et al., 2000; Saxena, 2001). Subsidies can also be difficult to sustain without cutting expenditure on other public goods; they are an inefficient and often inequitable mechanism through which to transfer resources (Wiggins and Brook, 2010). In some countries, these inefficiencies have led to subsidies being integrated into other types of social protection. In Brazil, for instance, the *Bolsa Família*, a conditional cash transfer, developed out of absorbing other cash transfers as well as gas and food subsidies in the early 2000s (Barrientos et al., 2010).

Food subsidies date back to the 1960s (e.g. rice in Sri Lanka, wheat in Egypt, and maize in Tanzania) (Ellis et al., 2009). A popular subsidy, delivered primarily by national governments, they often combine goals of improving food security for the poor and price stability for farmers, and usually offer a proportion of staple food at below the market rate.

Agricultural subsidies for fertiliser or other inputs are frequently seen as part of broader development policy, but those that explicitly target smallholder farmers or are specifically designed to overcome food insecurity and/or reduce poverty are arguably part of social protection (Ellis et al., 2009). Like food subsidies, they often have strong support from politicians, who view farmers as an important constituency. They typically have multiple objectives, which include supporting cash-constrained smallholders to access inputs and improve land and labour productivity (for food and cash crops), promoting economic growth, and reducing food insecurity, hunger and poverty by tightening labour markets and raising real wages.

Health and education subsidies are relatively popular policy responses to persistently low levels of human capital development by removing the financial barriers to accessing health and education services, particularly for subgroups of the poor. In particular, girls benefit from subsidised education, and under-fives and women benefit from increased access to health services, especially for reproductive health.

Childcare subsidies are increasingly recognised as an important component of social protection policy, especially in Latin America. Their key objectives are often twofold – to promote child development, and to enable the participation of parents (particularly women and single fathers) in the workforce. This is in recognition of women's childcare responsibilities and the constraints these put on women's integration into the labour market.

Finally, *integrated subsidy programmes* aim to address the range of interconnected social and economic deprivations and vulnerabilities experienced by poor people. They include access to credit and basic services, linked with human capital development programmes such as school fee exemptions, vocational training, loans for tertiary education, and investments in health and sanitation.

Gender dimensions of subsidy design, implementation and impact

Looking across the range of subsidy instruments from a gender perspective, a number of cross-cutting themes emerge. Here we group these in terms of subsidy design, programme implementation and impacts.

Subsidy design

Despite the problems associated with subsidy programmes, if they are well designed and targeted towards the poor, they can make an important contribution to reducing poverty and promoting social equity by channelling resources to disadvantaged areas and groups, and expanding their access to services (UN Children's Fund, 2010; Wiggins and Brooks, 2010).

Some types of subsidy programmes – mostly basic service and childcare subsidies – have applied a gender lens to programme design, addressing (to some extent) life-cycle and gender-specific vulnerabilities (see Chapter 2). These include health subsidies targeting pregnant women and children under five, education subsidies targeting girls, and childcare subsidies designed to enhance children's well-being and increase women's labour-market participation. Food, agricultural and integrated subsidies, on the other hand, have largely relegated gender concerns to secondary objectives, or ignored them altogether. With few exceptions, food subsidies have not tackled key life-cycle nutritional vulnerabilities, such as those facing pregnant women and young children, and agricultural input subsidies have not strategically considered women's role in agriculture and the challenges that women farmers face as a result of persistent inequalities in access to and ownership of productive resources.

Implementation

A number of key gender dimensions emerge as important considerations in the implementation of subsidies. First, although subsidies can reduce the financial barriers to accessing goods and services, associated costs often remain a challenge for poor households, especially women. For instance, women are over-represented in lower-paid, casual work and subsistence farming, and are less likely to have control over household income, even though they are often responsible for managing the household's food security and their children's well-being.

Secondly, other barriers, such as social barriers resulting from gender inequalities embedded in social and cultural norms, can restrict women's uptake of subsidy programmes. These include restrictions on women's movement outside the household or community, the low value placed on girls' education, women's lack of access to and ownership of productive assets and financial services, and lower literacy rates. Gendered roles and responsibilities also create barriers for men and boys. In many contexts, boys' paid and unpaid work makes them vulnerable to being taken out of school (see also Faisal's story in Personal Narrative 6.1).

Personal Narrative 6.1: Boys are also vulnerable to being taken out of school – Faisal's experience, Indonesia

Faisal lives with his wife and four children. He was born into a relatively rich family, but when he was in the last grade of elementary school his father was injured and his family was forced to sell their house. Things got worse when his father died. As the oldest boy, Faisal worked hard to help his mother support their family, and was not able to go to secondary school. He feels that his father's death, and the responsibilities that it placed on him, significantly influenced his current life in poverty.

Like many other men in the village, Faisal's main concern is finding work. In the rainy season this is difficult. He often finds work for only two days a week. He rents a neighbour's land, but has little money to buy seeds. He cannot afford pesticides, and even though fertiliser is subsidised, he cannot afford it because of other household spending priorities.

Source: Arif et al. (2010a).

Thirdly, although subsidies aim to increase demand for goods and services, the quality of those goods and services is often poor. Improving the quality, governance and accountability of services is particularly seen as important in order to respond to women's and men's differential priorities and demands (Brody, 2009). Health and education subsidies often go hand in hand with broader supply-side interventions, such as investing in female teachers, and a number of subsidy programmes encourage women's participation in programme governance structures, including community targeting mechanisms. However, across the board few subsidy programmes have been influenced by citizen participation or civil society groups shaping or advocating for improved gender-sensitive subsidy schemes.

Impacts

Evidence on the gendered impacts of subsidies, compared with other forms of social protection such as cash transfers, is limited and fragmented. Monitoring and evaluation are rarely integrated into programme design. However, a number of important findings have emerged, which we discuss in more detail in the case studies that follow. On a positive note, these findings include improved access to health and education services (especially for women and girls), enhanced opportunities in the labour market for women, and increased wages. However, findings also suggest that subsidy programmes often reinforce traditional gender roles and have little effect in terms of tackling the gendered patterns of poverty, which could lead to improved programme effectiveness.

We shall now discuss each subsidy programme type in more detail, from a gender perspective.

Food subsidies[3]

Many food subsidy programmes reach a larger proportion of the population than other social protection mechanisms (although they do not always reach the poorest). For instance, Egypt's Baladi bread programme reaches approximately 80% of all households (World Food Programme, 2010), India's Targeted Public Distribution System reaches 80 million poor households (Planning Commission, 2008) and Indonesia's Raskin rice subsidy programme reaches 18.5 million households (Arif et al., 2010a). They are often implemented to address chronic food insecurity and malnutrition, or in response to economic shocks.

Food security and gender inequality

Gender inequality is strongly correlated with food insecurity and malnutrition. As we discussed in Chapter 2, women's responsibility for managing the household's food, whether through purchase or production, means that their access to income and their household decision-making power are particularly critical. Child under-nutrition is in turn strongly correlated with maternal educational levels – the greater the degree of control that women exercise over family income, the greater the proportion of income spent on food (e.g. Engle, 1989; Haddad, 1992; Hopkins et al., 1994; Smith and Haddad, 2000).

Although it is often assumed that subsidising food can increase consumption by the most vulnerable household members, this ignores unequal intra-household dynamics, which can skew consumption patterns (Quisumbing and McClafferty, 2006). As discussed in Chapter 2 women often become 'shock absorbers of household food security', reducing their own consumption to allow more food for others (Quisumbing et al., 2008:1). In India, for instance, women and girls usually eat last and least (Chorghade et al., 2009; Sinha, 2006). During Indonesia's financial crisis in 1997, mothers' body mass index (BMI) declined as they buffered the impact of the crisis on their children and husbands. However, evidence also showed that a year after the crisis, both mothers' and adolescent boys' BMI was lower (De Pee et al., 2000). In the 2008 food price crisis, research in Indonesia found that children or men were put first, and in no communities were women, including pregnant women, reported to be offered the most nutritious foods (Hossain et al., 2009). However, women face particular life-cycle events, such as pregnancy, which present specific nutritional needs. Turning again to examples from Indonesia, 40% of pregnant women suffer from iron-deficiency anaemia, which alone is responsible for 25% of maternal deaths nationally (Asian Development Bank, 2009). Food security programmes must therefore consider individual needs and intra-household dynamics if they are to be effective.

Integrating a gender lens into food subsidy design, implementation and impacts[4]

Despite the importance of gender-specific food security vulnerabilities, few food subsidy programmes have incorporated these into programme design. Programmes in Mozambique, Egypt and Bangladesh are exceptions. Mozambique's Food Subsidy Programme recognises the nutritional vulnerabilities of pregnant and breastfeeding women, and specifically includes malnourished pregnant women in its eligibility criteria (Taimo and Waterhouse, 2007), as does Egypt's Baladi bread subsidy (World Food Programme, 2008). In Bangladesh, responses to the food-price crisis in 2007–2008 recognised women's disadvantages in the urban labour market and included a price subsidy on cereal grains for women garment and tea workers as part of the larger response to rising food prices (Köhler et al., 2009).

However, most food subsidy programmes simply target the household as a unit. In the case of Indonesia,[5] an umbrella safety-net package was introduced in 1998 to mitigate the impacts of the Asian financial crisis, and the Raskin rice subsidy programme constituted an important component. This is designed to provide 10 kg of subsidised rice to poor rural households at below market price, and by 2010 it had reached more than 18 million households. But, the programme has no gender-related goals or objectives, despite the evidence on the gendered dimensions of food insecurity mentioned earlier.

The distribution of the subsidised Raskin rice is however influenced by intra-household dynamics. Research suggests that children are given priority, followed by men, and finally women (Arif et al., 2010a). Moreover, women report that although the Raskin rice subsidy does not always increase rice consumption directly, it frees up income to buy nutritious foods or meet other expenses, such as education and debt repayment.

If there is Raskin we can save money, and the money can be used to buy fish. If there is no Raskin we cannot buy fish, only vegetables, so we don't get to taste fish.

(Female focus group discussion, Indonesia, 2009, cited in Arif et al., 2010a:34)

If when Raskin comes we are behind on our children's school fees, we pay the school fees. Sometimes if it rains we cannot tap [the rubber trees], and we go into debt. Then after the harvest we pay.

(Female focus group discussion, Indonesia, 2009, cited in Arif et al., 2010a:34)

However, implementation problems constrain the effectiveness and delivery of the programme. Although not specific to Raskin, numerous studies on food subsidies highlight high rates of corruption, dilution of benefits because of targeting errors and leakages, late and unpredictable delivery, and poor-quality food (Hastuti, 2008; Pasha et al., 2000; Saxena, 2001). Raskin has sought to improve accountability through community participation in the identification and selection of beneficiaries. However, there are no efforts to ensure that women have a say in community meetings, which involve (usually male) village heads and administration staff (Arif et al., 2010a). Moreover, lack of attention to gender dimensions in the design phase affects its implementation. Attention to the differential needs of women (as female-headed households or widows) is given on a personal basis, rather than as part of a systemic effort to make Raskin gender-sensitive.

More generally, despite the highly political nature of Indonesia's food subsidy programme, there has been little involvement of gender equality activists in regional or national policy debates. This is also the case in other countries (and in other social protection programmes, too: see Chapter 7 on political economy dynamics). In India, for instance, despite evidence of the gendered inequalities in nutrition (International Institute for Population Sciences and Macro International, 2007) and a strong civil society input on food security issues, which includes organisations promoting women's rights, the Public Distribution System lacks a gender-sensitive approach.

In summary, food subsidy programmes rarely consider the gender dimensions of food insecurity. Given the significant public resources invested in them and their scale (especially relative to other social protection programmes), this is a key concern. Overlooking life-cycle nutrition needs may reduce the effectiveness of such programmes, and food subsidies targeted at the household may fail to fulfil their objectives if they do not address intra-household inequalities.

Agricultural input subsidies

Three out of every four poor people in developing countries live in rural areas, and most of them depend directly or indirectly on agriculture for their livelihoods (World Bank, 2007). Agricultural input subsidies, like food subsidies, were common in the 1960s and 1970s but declined in the 1980s and 1990s, re-emerging on the policy agenda of many countries in the 2000s (World Bank, 2007).[6] They were originally introduced to promote the adoption of new technologies by cash-constrained smallholders, and thus increase productivity (Ellis, 1992). Subsidies have also been implemented as part of policies to support agricultural development in more remote areas, coupled with credit and extension services to encourage optimal use of inputs through practical application and increased learning (Dorward et al., 2008). Since the 2000s, some subsidies have taken on a social protection focus, aiming to reduce food insecurity, hunger and poverty by tightening labour markets and raising real wages.

Gender inequalities in the agriculture sector

Evidence from around the world demonstrates that gender inequalities and failure to address them limit agricultural productivity and efficiency (Food and Agriculture Organization of the United Nations, 2011). Failure to recognise the different roles that women and men perform in agricultural production results in forgone output and incomes, and higher levels of poverty (Peterman et al., 2010; World Bank, 2007, 2009).

As Chapter 2 discussed, women's role in agriculture varies significantly across the world. Women work as both market-oriented smallholders and subsistence farmers. Although female-headed households are more often subsistence farmers, in Ghana and Nigeria they are more likely to be market-oriented (World Bank, 2007). Although many factors influence market orientation, within the same household women are more likely to be engaged in subsistence farming, whereas men are more likely to be cultivating cash crops (World Bank, 2007).

However, women's participation in market-oriented activities and their potential to increase subsistence production are constrained by gender-related vulnerabilities and discrimination, such as institutional bias, mobility constraints and low literacy, poor access to financial services (including credit), limited access to extension services and training, and limited voice and representation in leadership of rural organisations (World Bank, 2009).

Integrating a gender lens into fertiliser subsidy design, implementation and impacts

The design and implementation of agricultural subsidies largely assume that all farmers are men, ignoring the gender-specific constraints that are apparent in the sector. There are few impact evaluations that disaggregate findings by gender. Here, we look at available evidence from Ghana and Malawi.

There is some research indicating that women's uptake of subsidies is more limited. In Ghana, women's uptake of a fertiliser subsidy was significantly lower (39%) than uptake by men (59%) (World Bank, 2009); this was also the case in Malawi's Agricultural Input Subsidy Programme, where male-headed households benefited more from the distribution of fertiliser and seed coupons (Dorward et al., 2008).

Even when inputs subsidies are gender-blind we find important implications for gender in terms of programme design, implementation and impacts. Drawing on Dorward et al.'s (2008) study in Malawi, the design of the targeting criteria unintentionally skewed the distribution of coupons towards men. It prioritised farmers with access to land and the capacity to adopt new technology. This excluded many women, who were more likely to grow crops for home consumption, less likely to use fertiliser, and less likely to obtain extension services. Women also found it more difficult to raise the payment to redeem their coupon for fertiliser. Mobility constraints and reproductive responsibilities meant that women were less likely to travel long distances to collect the fertiliser. Finally, despite women's representation on the programme committee, their voice was found to be limited, and their views have been largely overridden (Dorward et al., 2008).

However, Malawi's fertiliser subsidy has had some important gender-specific impacts (Dorward et al., 2008). Women have been able to command higher wages for short-term rural employment (although not as high as those of men). Agricultural extension officers have encouraged people to form fertiliser savings groups, and have sought to include women. The existence of these groups has fostered innovation and greater uptake of technology, including that by women. The impacts on agricultural production are varied, with the income either being spent by women on children's education or being invested back into productive assets (Dorward et al., 2008). Both investments demonstrate a strategy for translating immediate benefits into longer-term gains.

Education and health subsidies

Education and health subsidies aim to prevent the intergenerational transmission of poverty by facilitating poor households' access to the critical basic services necessary for human capital development. Health subsidies also aim to reduce the impact of catastrophic health expenditures (for a discussion of health insurance, see also Chapter 5).

Gender inequality in accessing education

The costs of education are an important barrier to girls' and boys' education, and socio-cultural and institutional factors often perpetuate a gender bias (see also Chapter 2). Girls are less likely to participate in school because their work within the home is more time-intensive than the work that boys may undertake in wage activities. Early marriage is also a key constraint (Chitrakar, 2009; UN Children's Fund, 2001). Teachers' attitudes, the nature of the curriculum, harassment, concerns about safety, and the quality of school infrastructure may all keep girls out of school (Subrahmanian, 2005).

Meanwhile, boys' schooling is often more highly valued for future income-earning opportunities, although boys are also often taken out of school to contribute to household income and tasks[7] (see Faisal's life story in Personal Narrative 6.1). Such household decisions about children's schooling are very context-specific. In South Africa, for instance, at secondary level, Hunter and May (2002) found that households were more likely to protect girls' education than that of boys. This possibly reflected greater opportunities for boys as casual labourers, the importance of completing high school as a prerequisite for female-dominated careers such as nursing and teaching, and the fact that young men were more likely to migrate and thus contribute less to their natal households in the longer term (Marcus and Gavrilovic, 2010).

Integrating a gender lens into education subsidy design, implementation and impacts

Subsidising education costs can be implemented either through transferring cash directly to households conditional on school attendance (see also Chapter 3 on cash transfers) or by reducing or waiving fees or other associated costs. Despite many countries abolishing school fees for primary education, direct school user fees continue to be common and represent a percentage of all primary education costs ranging from 8% in Indonesia to 80% in Cambodia (Bentaouet-Kattan and Burnett, 2004).

It is widely recognised that although tackling the financial barriers to girls' access to school (especially secondary schooling) is an important first step, it is insufficient to equalise the bias in educational outcomes, for reasons discussed in the section above. Some education subsidy programmes have simultaneously addressed these additional barriers to girls' education. Guaranteeing a safe learning environment for girls, for instance, is a key gender-sensitive programme design feature. This could entail, for example, providing training in child protection issues and pastoral care, with an emphasis on girls' safety (e.g. the Southwest Basic Education Project (SBEP) in China, cited in Cambridge Education, 2010). Ensuring school rules and regulations are non-discriminatory are another key gender-sensitive feature. This might, for instance, include re-entry policies for pregnant girls or providing guidance and counselling services for girls in schools (e.g. the Secondary Education Development Programme (SEDP) in Tanzania cited in the Ministry of Education and Vocational Training, 2010). Generating reforms in the delivery of education services has also been identified as a critical feature for promoting girls' education, for instance, increasing the number of female teachers and female students through scholarships/incentives, and investing in the institutional capacity of the implementing institution by developing training packages and conducting training inclusive of equity and gender awareness (e.g. Nepal's Secondary Education Support Programme cited in Danida, 2009).

As is the case across many social protection programmes however, translating gender-sensitive programme design into positive impacts on gender equity is often hindered by weak implementation. Taking the Secondary Education Development Programme in Tanzania as an example, an early evaluation of the first phase of the programme suggested that girls' enrolment had increased from 86.0% in 2004 to 87.9% in 2007 (World Bank, 2008a). However, a report by the African Development Fund (2007) identified considerable regional disparities in gender equity, and a World Bank evaluation noted that dropout rates were higher for girls than for boys, and girls' performance continued to be lower than that of boys, especially in co-educational schools (World Bank, 2008c). The same evaluation identified lack of training for programme staff about its gender focus as an important weakness (World Bank, 2008c). Similar findings were reported in the evaluation of Nepal's Secondary Education Support Programme, which identified a lack of evidence on the inclusiveness of institutional capacity-building activities and the extent to which they attempted to address equity-related issues (UNICEF, 2007).

Gender inequalities in accessing health services

Health subsidies often target pregnant women and children under 5 years of age, recognising specific life-cycle vulnerabilities and high rates of child and maternal deaths globally. Indeed, as we discussed in Chapters 2 and 5, women's and men's disease burdens and associated health service needs differ considerably.

Although financial barriers are the greatest obstacle to poor people accessing health services, women face non-financial barriers, too. Because of their disadvantaged position in the labour market they are more likely to be cash-constrained than men. Moreover, women's assets are generally sold first to pay for healthcare. Women's limited status and bargaining power within the household are also a key constraint on accessing healthcare. In addition, time poverty and mobility constraints are key factors, especially if clinics are far away and childcare is unavailable (Blackden and Wodon, 2006; Jones and Baker, 2008).

User fees, which are the most regressive form of health financing (Walsh and Jones, 2009), disproportionately affect women. It is estimated that worldwide, 178 million people each year, particularly women who face low incomes and financial insecurity (Emmet, 2006), are unable to pay for the services they need to restore their health (World Health Organization, cited in Walsh and Jones, 2009). The removal of user fees in 20 African countries could prevent 233,000 deaths of children under five a year (Walsh and Jones, 2009).

Integrating a gender lens into health subsidy design, implementation and impacts

Health subsidies can be delivered through various mechanisms – for instance, subsidising health costs at the point of delivery, or vouchers entitling the holder to free or subsidised care. Health equity funds are an umbrella mechanism; they take various forms, but are generally implemented under guidelines provided by the Ministry of Health, with donor support and some government funding. Most health equity funds are implemented through local and international non-governmental organisations as third-party schemes purchasing health services from district health facilities and national hospitals on behalf of the poor.

Targeting pregnant women and young children is an important recognition of the unequal health burdens they face. In addition to aiming to improve women's access to reproductive healthcare services through targeting subsidised or free healthcare directly to women, simultaneous efforts to improve the supply-side of health services are often implemented too. In some cases, programmes have also broadened the array of services which women can access at a subsidised rate, including, for example, safe maternal and family planning services and services for gender violence recovery (see for instance the Reproductive Health Output-Based Aid Voucher Programme in Kenya cited in Arur et al. (2009) and Bellows and Hamilton (2009).

Some health subsidy programmes also recognise the importance of integrating a gender-perspective into the implementation of programmes. In Bangladesh, the Urban Primary Health Care Programme, for instance, included provision for equal participation of women in programme governance, with at least 30% of the national project steering committee, project management unit and project implementation unit to be women, and women were to comprise at least 50% of health providers. In addition, monitoring and evaluation indicators were disaggregated by socio-economic status and gender.

Evidence suggests that schemes that provide vouchers for antenatal and postnatal care and institutional deliveries have demonstrated positive progress in terms of institutional capacity to deliver health services (Witter, 2011) and positive outcomes in terms of increasing women's utilisation of healthcare as a result of subsidising or waiving health care costs can be seen. For example, results from one study in Bangladesh found that institutional deliveries increased from 2% to 18%, and utilisation of antenatal and postnatal care by trained providers rose from 42% to 89% and from 10% to 60%, respectively (Ubaidur et al., 2010). The health equity fund in Cambodia found that approximately half of the targeted women benefited and would not have attended facilities otherwise; for about one-third of these, access to a facility was life-saving (Annear, 2010).

However, fragmented implementation of such schemes and the combination of supply-side interventions and management strengthening activities affect the reliability of findings on impacts (Annear, 2010). Moreover, not all programmes can demonstrate the capacity to deliver quality healthcare, with poor quality of care and poor governance and accountability mechanisms being cited as a key barrier to women's access to health services (Mamdani and Bangscr, 2004). In Tanzania, for example, the health subsidy programme resulted in unequal access as a consequence of social discrimination in healthcare centres against clients who were unable to pay, especially women under 20 years of age and less well-educated women (Mamdani and Bangser, 2004; Smithson, 2005, cited in Burns and Mantel, 2006). Institutional bias in the implementation of healthcare suggests the need to inform beneficiaries about their rights and agency to claim them, highlighting the importance of continuous advocacy and practical training at all levels of the health service.

Another key concern is the challenge of reaching the poorest through such interventions (see for instance, Gardener and Subrahmanian, 2006). Indeed, reaching the poor remains a key challenge for programmes that reduce rather than eliminate user costs, as indirect costs can also make accessing health care prohibitive for the poor. In Tanzania, for instance, a health fee exemption scheme targeted at children under five and pregnant women was constrained by long distances to facilities and inadequate and unaffordable transport systems (Mamdani and Bangser, 2004).

Non-income barriers can also be just as important in creating barriers to access. In Kenya, for instance, despite increases in access to the Safe Motherhood Programme, there was limited use of gender-based violence recovery services, most likely as a result of the stigma associated with gender-based violence and the limitations on the ability of the health system to respond to it (Bellows and Hamilton, 2009).

Subsidised childcare services[8]

Childcare subsidies as a social protection instrument bring the gendered care/work divide sharply into focus. The key objectives are often twofold – to promote child development, and to enable participation (particularly of women and single fathers) in the workforce. Subsidised childcare services are a rapidly evolving social protection mechanism, particularly in Latin America. In Mexico, for instance, the *Estancias Infantiles para Apoyar a Madres Trabajadoras* (Child Crèches to Support Working Mothers) programme created more than 9,500 day care centres, reaching more than 200,000 children in 2012. Within 2 years of operation, the programme had outnumbered the capacity of the Mexican Institute of Social Security's centres developed over 30 years. By 2008, it was the major provider of childcare for children under 4 years of age, running 84% of all centres and covering 56% of enrolled children (Staab and Gerhard, 2010). Similarly, in Chile, the number of public crèches has increased significantly, from around 700 in 2006 to more than 4,000 in 2009 (Ortiz, 2009).

Gender inequalities in childcare: the care/work divide

Providing better access to childcare services recognises not only the importance of early education for children from poor households, but also the labour-market challenges facing single parents (particularly women), carers and working parents. Mexico's *Estancias* programme, for instance, explicitly aims to address labour-market inequalities resulting from women's reproductive roles and responsibilities. It supports eligible mothers and single fathers so that they can have time to access the labour market or continue studying (Pereznieto and Campos, 2010). It subsidises home-based services rather than expanding the role of public care institutions, creating a 'quasi-market' for home-based day care services (Staab and Gerhard, 2010). It also forms part of a larger national strategy to reduce poverty and inequality, in which women's role as earners is seen as crucial (Staab and Gerhard, 2010).

Similarly, the *Hogares Comunitarios Programme* (Community Homes Programme), established in Guatemala City in 1991, provides subsidised childcare through home-based services. Its key objective is to reduce poverty in urban areas by relieving the main constraint facing working parents, namely the need for alternative childcare (International Food Policy Research Institute, 2008). A group of parents selects a woman from the locality and designates her as the 'caretaker mother', who then cares for up to ten children under 7 years of age. The programme provides basic equipment, training for the caretakers, and menus to guide the preparation of meals, as well as monthly payments for food, donations from the World Food Programme (WFP) and an 'incentive' of $3.33 per child per month. Parents are expected to complement this with a $5 contribution per child per month (International Food Policy Research Institute, 2008).

The *Chile Crece Contigo* (Chile Grows With You) programme in Chile has a stronger educational focus, promoting child development and equal opportunities for children from low-income or vulnerable families, with women's employment being a secondary objective. Children (rather than women) are the main beneficiaries, having the right to a crèche and kindergarten place (Staab and Gerhard, 2010). The programme targets all children, supporting their development up to entry into the school system at pre-kindergarten level. Components include a child health programme covering prenatal development, personalised attention during birthing, and comprehensive care for hospitalised children (Staab and Gerhard, 2010).

Integrating a gender lens into childcare subsidy design, implementation and impacts

Childcare subsidy programmes vary in the extent to which gender is embedded as a programme goal. In Chile, the main objective of the *Crece Contigo* programme is to guarantee children from disadvantaged households a 'fair start', rather than focusing on gender inequalities. The programme is designed to have strategic linkages with other social protection programmes, addressing the multiple vulnerabilities that poor children and households face. Healthcare in particular is seen as a critical link to improve the efficiency of childcare programmes[9] (Staab and Gerhard, 2010).

However, gender equality is a central component in the design of Mexico's *Estancias* programme. Its objectives include the elimination of any type of gender-based discrimination, guaranteeing equal opportunities for women and men to develop and exercise their rights, and facilitating women's access to labour markets through the expansion of the Network of Child Care Centres to Support Working Mothers (*Diario Oficial*, 2009, cited in Pereznieto and Campos, 2010). Pereznieto and Campos (2010)[10] note that the programme has had a positive effect on women's participation in the labour force, in terms of either being able to work for the first time or, more frequently, getting a more stable job (Santibañez and Valdes, 2008, cited in Pereznieto and Campos, 2010). It has also had positive effects on single mothers, in particular through access to a dependable and stable form of childcare. Nevertheless, the types of jobs that women are able to obtain have not changed significantly. To continue benefiting from the programme, women need to have a low income, so beneficiaries are by definition working in low-paid employment. Moreover, most women have jobs in the informal sector (with no contracts or social security benefits) or are self-employed. Nevertheless, *Estancias* helps women to cope better with the challenge of raising a child on their own while needing to earn an income. It has also had a positive impact on early childhood development, for children who would not typically have access to such a service.

At the intra-household level, *Estancias* has contributed to women's greater autonomy over decision making with regard to their own income, and there is some initial evidence of men being more cooperative at home to support their wives in their new roles as earners (see Box 6.1). This last finding is not widespread, but it demonstrates that a slow transformation of gendered domestic roles is possible. However, it should be noted that many women needed to negotiate participation with their husbands first. Other potential beneficiaries have been unable to access it because of an ingrained belief that women should remain in the home and care for children. Although evidence suggests that these patterns are changing, some men whose wives were working said they only 'allowed' them to do so because the money was needed, and if the household's economic situation improved, they would prefer their wives to stay at home. Pereznieto and Campos (2010) conclude that, although *Estancias* supports women's increased economic autonomy, and in some cases has influenced their capacity to negotiate some domestic activities with spouses, there is

Box 6.1 Estancias and intra-household dynamics

Interviews with parents using *Estancias* highlighted women's greater autonomy over decision making about their own income, and there were indications that men are being more cooperative at home in support of their wives as income earners:

When I wasn't working, my husband would never help me. But now that I work, he does help me around the house, he helps me dress the children before I leave. So it has helped me.
(Female focus group discussion, La Esperanza)

Sometimes women don't want to leave their husbands because they don't know how they would manage. But with this help you become more autonomous, you can work and generate your own income. Now, if I want to buy shoes I don't have to tell him, I just buy them.
(Female focus group discussion, La Esperanza)

If she decides to work it's fine. I can't ask her to be locked up the whole time. She also has a right to work if she wants to.
(Married father, Chapulhuacanito)

He really supports the programme. In fact, he is the one that goes drop [the children] off and picks them up because I am working.
(Female focus group discussion, Chapulhuacanito)
Source: Pereznieto and Campos (2010:39).

not enough evidence of it triggering a deeper transformation of gender roles and women's empowerment.

The same is also true at community level. The programme design was informed by a principle of community co-responsibility, but there are no mechanisms in place to foster networks among beneficiaries. In practice, support is provided by some proactive heads of *Estancias*, who assume their de facto role as community focal points for women, mobilise community members (mainly families) around the programme, and communicate important information to beneficiaries. However, this depends on the individual's personality and level of commitment, rather than being an explicit part of the programme's implementation. Indeed, Pereznieto and Campos (2010) highlight the fact that there is no evidence of women beneficiaries being more active in community decision making or trying to find better jobs for themselves as a result of the programme.

In addition, an important outcome of childcare subsidies noted across all three programmes (in Chile, Guatemala and Mexico) is the role of women as micro–entrepreneurs in the care sector. However, the 'commodification of care' through subsidised services has not changed the fact that childcare is still largely regarded as 'women's work' and accorded low value (Staab and Gerhard, 2010). The quality of the jobs in care is questionable, since care workers and their assistants are self-employed and thus lack social security benefits. Moreover, women working as child carers are not connected in any meaningful way to allow them to organise around their entitlements and working conditions (Staab and Gerhard, 2010).

Another obstacle to a more profound change in gender relations is the absence of men from policy debates relating to child care. Staab and Gerhard (2010) note that there has been little improvement in public policies aimed at a more equal intra-household division of caring labour – at least formally, by including fathers among those eligible for childcare services or parental leave. Maternity leave remains short and is still restricted to mothers. As a result, although expansion of services such as *Estancias* 'contributes to reducing women's burdens of unpaid childcare, it does not in and of itself resolve gender inequalities' (Staab and Gerhard, 2010:25).

Integrated subsidies[11]

Finally, we look at Vietnam's National Targeted Programme for Poverty Reduction (NTPPR), to illustrate the potential opportunities and challenges that an integrated subsidy programme can offer. The NTPPR is the government of Vietnam's flagship poverty reduction programme. It reached up to 6 million people from households living below the poverty line in 2009, and seeks to address a range of deprivations experienced by poor households and communities and to improve their productive capacities. It couples access to credit and basic services such as infrastructure, agricultural extension services, landholding and legal aid with human capital development programmes, such as school fee exemptions, vocational training, loans for tertiary education, and investments in health and sanitation (see Box 6.2).

Integrating a gender lens into integrated subsidy design, implementation and impacts

In recent years, there has been considerable progress in advancing gender equality in Vietnam. Women are more economically active than in most other countries in the region, and the gender pay gap is comparatively low (UNDP, 2006). Furthermore, girls' and boys' school enrolment

---

Box 6.2 Social protection in Vietnam

In Vietnam over the past 5 years there has been growing policy momentum around social protection issues, motivated by a concern to reduce poverty and vulnerability, emphasised in the country's first- and second-phase national development plans, the Socio-Economic Development Plans 2001–2005 and 2006–2010. Vietnam now has an array of social protection programmes, including *social assistance programmes* such as the NTPPR, *social insurance schemes* (including health insurance for all children under six as well as all households below the poverty line), *social welfare services* (including programmes targeted at child protection and domestic violence) and *social equity measures* (such as the 2007 Gender Equality Law and the 2007 Gender Violence Law). In 2009, a consultation process around the draft National Social Protection Strategy was also initiated.

---

rates are comparable, and maternal and child mortality rates have fallen dramatically. On the other hand, women and girls, especially those from ethnic-minority groups, are considerably disadvantaged. For example, women are over-represented in economic sectors that are particularly vulnerable in times of economic downturn, including the informal sector. They lack equal rights to land and equal access to agricultural credit and technologies, which means that they bear the brunt of the negative impacts of trade liberalisation and have seen few of the benefits (World Bank, 2011). Finally, although progress towards educational equity has been laudable, ethnic-minority girls remain significantly disadvantaged compared with ethnic-minority boys (ibid.).

Despite broader progress towards gender equality and attention to gender in national policy documents (for example, the 2006–2010 Socio-Economic Development Plan incorporated gender-specific indicators in agriculture, employment, the environment, health and education), the design and implementation of the NTPPR pays little attention to the gendered nature of poverty and vulnerability. In fact, apart from the targeting of female-headed households and a general mention of the need for gender-sensitive programming, it contains no gender-specific targets or measurable outcomes.

Notwithstanding these weaknesses, Jones and Tran (2010) found positive effects in terms of serving the basic needs of poor women and their children, as is illustrated by the life story of Mi Lenh in Personal Narrative 6.2. In particular, participants consider the health insurance card to be valuable, as it enables them to conserve scarce resources and take less time off work to tend ill children. It has also enabled women to access contraceptives without the agreement of their husbands.

The school fee exemption policy, which includes free notebooks and textbooks, was also particularly valued by respondents, who agreed that more children were going to school for longer (especially Grades 5 to 9), including girls, and were therefore able to learn the Kinh (majority) language, making it easier for them to engage in trade and business. However, the poorest respondents still felt that there were barriers to education, particularly costs such as clothing, transportation and the loss of the child's labour. Fathers still discourage school attendance by girls, because they see little gain from their investment, given that girls marry into other families rather than supporting their parents over the life course.

Access to credit emerged as another key impact of the NTPPR on women, facilitating investment in productive assets such as livestock. This is especially important for women, as they often take charge of the purchase of livestock. It makes a useful contribution towards the household economy and allows women more control over household resources.

Programme beneficiaries also noted intangible gains, especially in terms of more harmonious intra-household relations. By relieving pressure on overstretched household resources, the programme reportedly led to some couples being less likely to quarrel. The availability of loans has also facilitated more discussion among husbands and wives about the use of household resources. In households where women have taken out loans to engage in petty trade and/or participated in vocational training, women reported greater respect and less violence from their husbands as a result of their economic contribution and new knowledge.

At the community level, NTPPR policies and programmes that target poor communities have considerable potential to generate positive impacts, especially through infrastructure investments, increased community participation and enhanced social inclusion. Women reported that they are now attending community and women's association meetings more often, partly because of their greater access to credit and increased economic participation. However, some beneficiaries said that poor women rarely expressed their ideas at meetings as they were afraid to do so, and that women were participating more mainly because meetings were being held during the day when men were out at work. If the meetings were held in the evening, men attended instead. Language issues, cultural gender roles, and gendered education and literacy gaps can also mean that women are less likely to attend or contribute to community discussions.

The NTPPR has thus achieved mixed impacts. Its comprehensive approach is a double-edged sword. Growing awareness of the multi-dimensionality of poverty calls for a multi-faceted policy response (Jones

Personal Narrative 6.2: Integrated subsidy programmes help serve basic needs – Mi Lenh in Vietnam

Mi Lenh is an adolescent Hmong boy living in Vietnam. He is one of four children, and his father died when he was very young. He recently passed the entrance exams required for boarding school; he is now in Grade 9. Last year he was sick and had to take a term off school, but he was able to study hard and catch up with his classmates.

Mi Lenh's family has little land. His older brother left school in Grade 6 so that he could help to support the family. His 15-year-old sister has never been to school, as she was needed to help around the house. His 12-year-old sister is still in school. His mother needs all the help she can get on the farm. Some days, Mi Lenh walks home from boarding school after classes – a two-hour journey – to do chores. Other days he stays at home and walks to school in the morning – again a two-hour journey.

Government subsidies have been key to improving Mi Lenh's life. He is able to attend school at very low cost; he pays in kind, only 25 kg of rice per year, which also covers his meals and school supplies. The government has also loaned the family money to rebuild their house and to buy a harvester, which helps with rice production. Healthcare is also now free for Mi Lenh's family.

Mi Lenh would like to finish secondary school and then return home to farm. Although some of his classmates dream of careers in business or teaching, Mi Lenh wants to go home, marry, and farm with his mother and brother.

Source: Jones and Tran (2010).

et al., 2009), but striking a balance between comprehensiveness and undue complexity has remained elusive. Indeed, general coordination challenges highlight the difficulties in implementing a multisectoral programme. The programme is housed under the Ministry of Labor, Invalids and Social Affairs (MOLISA), but the inclusion of sectoral benefits requires close involvement of other line ministries. However, officials from line ministries are largely unfamiliar with NTPPR objectives and provisions. This perhaps reflects the fact that the NTPPR is not a programme per se, but rather a collection of diverse instruments and mechanisms, which has potentially undermined its effectiveness and certainly hindered the evaluation process (ibid.). Mechanisms to overcome this challenge are being sought, including the establishment of a steering committee to be led by the deputy prime minister (MOLISA/UNDP, 2009). However, it is recognised that coordination is always time-consuming, that in reality there are still few models of good practice that can be replicated, and that knowledge translation efforts need to be accelerated (Jones and Tran, 2010).

These institutional weaknesses are exacerbated by problems in the mainstreaming of gender into the NTPPR. For instance, there is limited routine collection and analysis of gender-disaggregated data. In addition, although gender training for programme implementers has been provided, key informants reported concerns about quality, relating to limited budget, language barriers for ethnic-minority populations and insufficient practical guidance vis-à-vis programme goals and implementation approaches. Language is a particular issue for ethnic-minority women, who often cannot access agricultural extension services and training because sessions are taught in the majority Kinh language. Another institutional shortcoming is the inadequacy of the gender focal point system at national, provincial, district and community levels. Focal points are usually untrained and relatively junior, with little decision-making power and no dedicated budget (Jones and Tran, 2010).

Conclusion

The extent to which gender has been considered in the design and implementation of subsidy programmes varies widely. On the one hand, subsidies that promote access to services such as health, education and childcare have largely recognised the disadvantages that girls and women face, and some have been accompanied by investments in supply-side improvements. Some childcare subsidies have also taken a strategic gendered approach by providing financial support for childcare, in some cases explicitly recognising that this is vital for promoting women's labour-market participation. By contrast, the food, agricultural and integrated subsidy programmes discussed here have paid little attention to gender inequalities at the intra-household and community levels, despite evidence that failing to tackle them can impede programme outcomes.

Key gaps in food subsidy programme design include the unequal distribution of food at the intra-household level, and the need to recognise women's life-cycle vulnerabilities (e.g. nutritional needs during pregnancy). Likewise, if agricultural input subsidies are to benefit women farmers and enhance their productivity, more attention needs to be paid to addressing gender inequality in agriculture. Even in the case of Vietnam's NTPPR, which takes an integrated approach to addressing the multiple vulnerabilities facing poor households, evidence suggests that, in practice, little has been done to address the constraints facing women, particularly ethnic-minority women. That said, the examples discussed in this chapter indicate some progress towards gender-equitable outcomes, including increased wages for women (in the case of Malawi's agricultural subsidy) and positive impacts on women's role in decision making and community participation (in the case of Vietnam).

In summary, subsidy programmes need to consider integrating core gender-sensitive features in programme design and implementation and/or institutionalising strategic linkages to other services and programmes if they are to adopt a gender-sensitive approach to tackling poverty. This could entail measures to increase girls' and women's empowerment (which would translate improved household access to food into improved nutritional benefits for all the family), to promote intra-household equality (to remove the social as well as financial and other barriers to girls and women accessing health and education), and to overcome mobility constraints and the unequal division of labour in the household.

SEVEN

Why politics matters: a gendered political economy approach to social protection

Decision making is very challenging as government officials are predominantly male. Getting women's perspectives heard in political struggles is a continuous struggle. ... There is lots of mischief by men [including] deliberately excluding women from committees.

(Director of Women's Association, Ethiopia, 2009,
cited in Jones et al., 2010b:39)

Even when we request local government officials to collect data on men and women, they don't respond – so there simply aren't any [gendered] beneficiary data at the national level.

(Head of Department of Labour, Cultural and Social Affairs,
Ministry of Planning and Investment, Vietnam, 2009,
cited in Jones and Tran, 2010:36)

Yes, I know that the government has provision [for crèches at public works sites] but this is not provided. ... No one listens to poor people. After the elections, no one hears, be this sarpanch [village head] or ministers.

(Married Scheduled Tribe Woman, India, 2009,
cited in Holmes et al., 2010b:27)

Introduction

Effectively mainstreaming gender into social protection policy and programming requires careful consideration of the politics that underpin choices about strategies and programmes. The steps involved are relatively straightforward, as discussed in Chapters 3 to 6, but gender mainstreaming in any policy sector is as much a political issue as it is a technical one, as the quotes at the beginning of this chapter illustrate. Discussions on social safety nets remain underpinned by often highly polarised views on gender roles and responsibilities the world over (Folbre, 2008).

There is a growing body of work looking at the politics of social protection, including how programme choices are shaped in response to elite and public buy-in, as well as the reasons underlying variable implementation practices at grass-roots level (e.g. de Britto, 2008; Hickey, 2007; Zucco, 2008). However, interest in the gender dynamics of social protection in general (see previous chapters) and in political economy dimensions in particular remains embryonic, with the important exceptions of the work of Sarah Bradshaw and Maxine Molyneux on Latin America, as discussed below (Bradshaw, 2008; Molyneux, 2007). Accordingly, this chapter proposes a framework that bridges political economy and new institutionalism literature with gendered political economy analysis to explore how gender relations shape the institutions, interests and ideas behind social protection policy and programming in developing countries.

Defining political economy

The concept of 'political economy' has had different meanings over time and across disciplines, but generally entails the interdisciplinary study of how the state and the market, or political and economic institutions, interact with and shape each other. Analysts are interested in how 'the public authority and public goods required for development arise through domestic political processes and contestation between interest groups.'[1] Development policy and programme outcomes are therefore viewed as involving a process of bargaining between state and society actors and interactions between formal and informal institutions (Helmke and Levitsky, 2004), rather than the external imposition of normative ideals about 'good governance' (Booth, 2011; Grindle, 2011). While political economists typically focus on institutional dynamics and competing interests or power relations between different economic, political and social actors in a given policy arena, we also draw on insights from historical institutionalism, which focuses on the interplay between institutions and ideas in shaping policy and programming outcomes. As Steinmo et al. (1992:23) have noted, 'rather than bracketing the realm of ideas, or treating ideas and material interests as separate and unrelated variables (or as competing explanatory factors), they explore how the two interact within specified institutional contexts to produce policy change.' Accordingly, this chapter is concerned with what Rosendorff (2005) has dubbed the 'three I's' of political economy, and their role in shaping social protection policies and programmes:

1. *Institutions* or institutional arenas (e.g. elections and party politics, the legislature, the judiciary, informal politics) and the opportunities or constraints that they present in the negotiation of social protection policy and programme development.
2. *Interests* of key actors who are likely to gain or lose from policy shifts (e.g. political elites, bureaucratic agencies, donors, civil society champions) and the relative balance of power between them (e.g. power imbalances between ministries of finance/

economics and of social welfare, which are often among the weakest).

3. *Ideas* held by elites and the public regarding poverty and its causes, the social contract between state and citizens, and the merits of particular forms of state support. This may include notions of the 'deserving poor', concerns about 'dependency', and attitudes towards inequality and social fragmentation (Hickey, 2009).

Conceptualising gendered political economy[2]

Integrating a gender lens into this framework adds an additional layer of complexity. To interrogate the assumed gender neutrality of political economy analysis (Roberts and Waylen, 1998:184), a gendered political economy approach explores how 'households, markets and states as gendered institutions are created and regulated in part by socially constructed norms at local, national and international levels.' In this regard, instead of thinking of social policy as an afterthought, we need to accept 'that all macroeconomic policies are enacted within a certain set of distributive relations and institutional structures; and that all macroeconomic policies entail a variety of social outcomes which need to be made explicit' (Elson and Cagatay, 2000:1347–8).

Pomares (2011) argues that a gendered political economy approach entails three distinct but overlapping levels – *micro* (an individual's socially constructed preferences), *meso* (household and community microeconomics) and *macro* (state and international gender orders whereby gender relations underpin state formation, maintenance and reproduction).

Micro level

In recent decades, understandings of human behaviour have moved away from notions of 'rational economic man' (Tickner, 1992) towards a recognition that actors hold asymmetric and imperfect knowledge, with individual decisions shaped by formal and informal rules and norms. In this context, Folbre (1994) advances the notion of 'purposeful choice', whereby individual choice is meaningful but understood to take place within interlocking structures of constraint (economic, political and socio-cultural). This has important implications for understanding women's participation in the formal economy and public sphere, as it highlights the need to complement efforts to promote women's individual human capital development by addressing women's care and domestic work roles and responsibilities, and the effects that these have on, for instance, their time, capacity-strengthening opportunities and self-identity.

Meso level

At the meso level, feminist economists have called into question the neoclassical economic conceptualisation of the family and household as lying outside the realm of economics (e.g. Waylen, 1997). Shedding light on the invisibility of women's work has required a re-conceptualisation of the divide between the public and the private, and a revaluing and incorporation of four types of work borne disproportionately by women (i.e. informal employment, subsistence production, domestic work, and reproduction and care work) into official statistics and economic accounts. The inclusion of the domestic sector is critical, as 'it plays a foundational role in the production of people who possess not only the capacity to work but also to acquire other more intangible social assets – a sense of ethical behaviour, a sense of citizenship, a sense of what it is to communicate – all of which permit the forming and sustaining of social norms' (Elson, 1998:197).

Macro level

Finally, the macro level reflects the centrality of the question of power in feminist thinking. An important development in this realm has been the introduction of the concepts of *gender regime* and *gender order* by Connell (1987).The former is the 'state of play in gender relations in a given institution' (e.g. school, state) and the latter characterises more broadly the gender patterns in a society at a specific point in history (Connell, 1987:119). These concepts have been applied widely to gender analyses of institutions and to understandings of nation-building projects and state modernisation. For example, Besse (1996) examines how, in Brazil's Vargas era (1914–1930), industrialisation and intensification of mercantile relations created new opportunities for middle-class and elite women to gain an education, have a career and postpone marriage. Worried that this shift was challenging the foundations of Brazilian society, policymakers and the Catholic Church attempted to influence the situation through policies to provide the 'modern' Brazilian woman with a sense of fulfilment and at the same time bolster the family, promoting 'scientific' forms of child-rearing and tailored women's education. However, although gender roles were modernised, the changes were not transformative – they simply restructured male domination.

Similarly, the work of Hossain (2007) on Bangladesh highlights the fact that the state has been strongly supportive of social programmes to help poor women on account of a deeply embedded ideology of 'political motherhood' which views destitute mothers as the 'deserv-ing poor', particularly given the history of rape of tens of thousands of women during the liberation war. In other words, gender relations often constitute a key pillar of governance interventions, and understanding these dynamics as well as the key historical junctures that underpin them can be critical in addressing bottlenecks in policy and programming.

This macro to micro gendered political economy approach mirrors the individual, household and community levels in our vulnerability and social protection analysis (see Chapters 1 and 2), while contextualising these dynamics within broader country and international gender structures. In the remainder of this chapter we seek to apply these insights to our discussion of gendered institutions (formal and informal), interests (of programme architects, implementers and beneficiaries) and ideas (of political and civil society actors) that influence the parameters and patterning of social protection in a given national or sub-national context.

Political economy opportunities and challenges for gender-sensitive social protection

We begin with an exploration of the institutional filters that shape social protection discourse and action in a particular country context, and the extent to which these are gendered.

Institutions

Institutions – the fora in which negotiations take place over policy issues – play a key role in shaping the parameters of social protection policy and programming choices. We briefly consider five broad fora, namely the electoral, legislative and judicial arenas, informal politics and social protection systems (comprising coordinating bodies, monitoring and evaluation, and capacity-building mechanisms).

The electoral arena

In a number of developing countries, electoral politics have had an important influence on social protection policy and programming decisions (Zucco, 2008, 2009), and to a lesser extent their gender dimensions.[3] A relatively positive example (however, see also Box 7.3) is that of Mexico's subsidised crèche programme, *Estancias*, which was initiated by President Calderon in 2007 to promote women's incorporation into the labour market. Since its launch in the same year, the scheme has resulted in greatly expanded childcare options for poor families (Pereznieto and Campos, 2010) (see Chapter 6). However, as Molyneux (2007) argues of the *Comedores* (popular soup kitchen) programme in Peru of the 1980s and 1990s, there is often also a risk that women will be mobilised and manipulated by party elites through support to social assistance programmes in order to shore up electoral support:

After the imposition of a harsh adjustment package known as the
Fuji-shock, a social emergency plan was built on the basis of the women's
organizations ... [including the Comedores, which were charged with]
overseeing food distribution for poverty alleviation. ... In this process,
the Comedores gained in importance and in public profile, but they also
lost their autonomy, becoming increasingly identified with the president
[Fujimori], turning out in force at rallies and duly delivering votes from the
communities they served.

(Molyneux, 2007:34)

Electoral politics have also proved problematic in the rollout of ostensibly gender-sensitive cash transfer programmes in Ghana and Pakistan. In Ghana, the launch of the Livelihood Empowerment Against Poverty (LEAP) cash transfer (discussed in Chapter 3) in the impoverished north coincided with presidential elections in late 2008 and thus became politicised, resulting in uneven implementation (Amuzu et al., 2010). Supporters of the opposition party in some locales refused to be included, and then found they were too late to register once the elections were over (Amuzu et al., 2010). Confusion and suspicion about the programme's aims also had negative spillover effects on implementation. In particular, although the design was intended primarily to benefit women, given their disproportionate caring responsibilities, in a number of cases 'caregivers' were conflated with 'household heads', resulting in the inclusion of a significant number of male household heads (Amuzu et al., 2010).

In Pakistan, the Benazir Income Support Programme (BISP) was launched in 2008 by the Pakistan People's Party government as a safety-net response to the financial, fuel and food crisis. However, naming the programme after the party's deceased leader suggested broader underlying political motivations, and was criticised as an attempt to gain political support for the next parliamentary elections. From a gender perspective this was unfortunate, as it shifted attention away from some of the programme's more transformative design features (see Box 7.1).

The legislative arena

In most developing countries, the legislative arena has not played a very significant role in shaping social protection policies and programmes. Important exceptions include South Africa, where the right to social security is enshrined in the Constitution and underpins its 2004 Social Assistance Act, and India, which we focus on here, given our discussion of the Mahatma Gandhi National Rural Employment Guarantee Scheme (MGNREGS) public works programme in Chapter 4.[4] The MGNREGS is part of a broader set of rights-based laws, including the Right to

---

Box 7.1 The gendered political economy of cash transfers in Pakistan

Political motivations have fuelled the two largest cash transfer programmes in Pakistan, with mixed effects on gender-related design features.

The *Zakat* programme was initiated in 1980 to support deserving needy Muslims (including widows and poor women). In accordance with *zakat*, the obligation on all Muslims to give a portion of their wealth (around 2.5% or more) each year to the poor, the programme was for many years financed through a 2.5% wealth tax imposed on specified financial assets of individual Muslims (e.g. bank deposits worth more than a certain amount). In 1999, however, the Supreme Court ruled that payments should be voluntary; this resulted in a considerable reduction in the programme's funding.

The overall impact of the programme has been limited. Critics suggest that it was originally motivated by the Zia-ul-Haq government's desire to shore up its Islamic credentials, rather than by any specific economic or social objective. Moreover, although the programme targeted Muslim widows, a sizeable vulnerable group in the Pakistani context, given its charitable rather than transformative motivations it – not surprisingly – did little to reshape gender relations.

Almost three decades later, the BISP was launched. From a gender perspective, it reflects a stronger government commitment to tackling gendered experiences of poverty and vulnerability, with the family defined as a unit headed by a woman who is married, divorced or widowed. In addition, participation requires that women obtain computerised national identification cards, with the aim of supporting their attainment of full citizenship rights, including access to public services. As the BISP is being introduced by a relatively weak elected government without a strong political culture of citizenship rights (as in India, for example), it will be important to monitor how these developments affect gendered experiences of citizenship in the coming years.

Sources: Khan and Qutub (2010); Sinha (personal communication, 2012).

Information Act 2005, the Forest Rights Act 2009 and the Right to Education Act 2009, that mark the shift from 'development as a welfare activity ... to a policy that recognises basic development needs as rights of the citizens' (UN Development Programme, 2010a:6).

In the context of drought and rural distress in Rajasthan in the late 1990s and early 2000s, civil society networks called for an end to passive beneficiary-oriented employment programmes in favour of a demand-based approach. In 2001, Congress Party leaders, including Party President Sonia Gandhi, included the issue in their 2004 national manifesto. Following the party's surprising electoral success and its formation of a majority government, a National Advisory Council, including influential intellectuals closely associated with the MGNREGS lobby (Jean Drèze and Aruna Roy), drew up a draft National Rural Employment Guarantee Act. After a nationwide campaign and Gandhi's direct intervention, the guarantee of 100 days of unskilled work per household per year on public works programmes was enacted.

A central pillar of the MGNREGS, as discussed in Chapter 4, is that all workers – women and men alike – receive equal wages, and one-third of all workers should be women, supported by crèche facilities and the scheduling of social audit initiatives at times that do not disadvantage women and other marginalised groups (Sudarshan, 2009). This level of gender sensitivity was secured in part because of the composition of the activists (including organisations mandated to promote women's empowerment), but also because of a strong commitment to improving gender equality among members of the National Advisory Council.[5]

The judicial arena

The role of the judiciary in influencing social protection policy has been less significant, but courts in developing countries have engaged with social protection issues indirectly by dealing with cases of social and economic rights, although explicit attention to gender dimensions remains absent. Gaunt and Kabeer (2009:3) argue that a significant number of national constitutions include commitments to the right to social security, but also emphasise that the judiciary 'is essentially reactive [acting only as] the final arbiter on whether violations have occurred.' In a few cases, citizens have availed themselves of regional judicial bodies, as for example in the case brought before the Inter-American Commission on Human Rights by a group of Argentinean pensioners on the grounds of their right to social security.

An important exception here too comes from India where the Supreme Court's judicial activism has redefined economic and social rights as fundamental and legally enforceable. India's Constitution distinguishes between Fundamental Rights (such as the right to equality and to freedom) and Directive Principles (the rights to work, education, public assistance, and a living wage for workers, and the duty of the state to raise levels of nutrition, standards of living and public health), with the latter temporarily non-enforceable. However, Supreme Court judgements have rendered some Directive Principles related to social welfare justiciable, thus upgrading them to Fundamental Rights. For example, a 1993 Supreme Court ruling stimulated an act for the provision of free and compulsory education to all children aged 6 to 14 years, as this 'is implicit in and flows from the right to life guaranteed under Article 21' (Corbridge et al., 2012). Likewise in 2001 the Supreme Court established a constitutional right to food - also based on Article 21 interpreted as the right to life with dignity rather than mere survival. (It is important to note that the National Food Security Bill which would provide more detail as to what this constitutional right to food entails has not yet been passed as an Act and remains highly contested). This was in response to a public litigation case brought by the People's Union for Civil Liberties against the Indian government when, despite the fact that the Food Corporation of India had extensive food grain stocks, some areas of Rajasthan were experiencing famine (Birchfield and Corsi, 2010; FAO, 2011).

Informal institutions

Informal institutions refer to the 'socially shared rules, usually unwritten, that are created, communicated, and enforced outside of officially sanctioned channels' (Helmke and Levitsky, 2004:727). Some social protection programmes have been designed specifically to correct historical tendencies towards clientelism in the social sector, and to establish more transparent and accountable modalities of programming. For example, Peru's *Juntos* was designed to address problems of political colonisation that had plagued the *Vaso de Leche* and *Comedores* programmes (Jones et al., 2008). However, informal institutions often continue to shape implementation practices significantly. In the old-age pension scheme in Maharashtra, local elites and officials have a negative effect on the welfare rights of the poor, as they are often at critical state – society interaction points, and the nexus of wealth and power makes them crucial actors in the market provision of social security (including their role as gatekeepers to claims) (Pellissery, 2008).

Informal politics of this nature may particularly disadvantage women, given what we know about local power hierarchies and gender discrimination (Kabeer, 2010; Miraftab, 2010). The work of Tripp (2001:101) on post-colonial Africa highlights how women's movements have been subject to 'enormous pressures for cooptation', with leaders seeking to promote women's leadership to serve their own ends. The challenge from a gender perspective is that clientelistic ways of working are typically overlaid with patriarchal ways of relating. Although mainstream research on clientelism tends to assume that women and men are similarly affected, Iraola and Gruenberg (2008:4) emphasise that 'the use of violence (physical, psychological, emotional, sexual) under clientelistic arrangements unveils the dual matrix of domination (patriarch and clientelism) that women living in poverty face in their search to secure a living and solve their basic survival needs.' Evidence suggests that even programme participants in the MGNREGS, which was implemented amid heightened debate about the rights of poor and vulnerable people, have limited ability to claim entitlements, and many – especially women – fear the reactions of local village leaders:

> *[Do you know that everybody has the right to demand 100 days of work?] If they fight with the sarpanch [elected head of panchayat/local government] there will be no work. They know that they should have the work.*
> (Married woman (Scheduled Tribe), India, 2009, cited in Holmes et al., 2010b:27)

Social protection systems

The fifth institutional forum we consider is social protection systems themselves, which encompass institutional arrangements for programming and policies and capacities of key actors, coordination mechanisms, monitoring and evaluation, and participation mechanisms.

Institutional arrangements and capacities

One of the key challenges facing efforts to promote more inclusive and gender-sensitive policies and programmes is the weakness of social protection institutional arrangements in many low-income countries. This is compounded by decentralised and poorly coordinated implementation and limited resources at local level. Meanwhile, not only is expenditure on social protection often low, but also administration costs are frequently very high. Human capacity constraints are a significant concern, especially in terms of integrating and implementing gender objectives into programming. Staff at local level in particular have limited technical capacities in general and even weaker gender mainstreaming proficiency, and lack relevant guidelines and training opportunities. Technical assistance to strengthen local gender machineries, including gender-sensitive budgeting capacities, is often still in a fledgling state (Holmes and Jones, 2010c).

Even in Mexico, which has a robust social protection system, understanding of gender dimensions among responsible agencies is quite weak, as are links with government agencies and strategic frameworks mandated to address gender equality. Although there has been progress at national level in integrating a gender perspective into the legislative and policy arenas, there is still inadequate use of existing knowledge and evidence on gender in implementation (Pereznieto and Campos, 2010), especially given the considerable heterogeneity in the rollout of federal gender-related legislation and policies to the state level. In *Estancias* (discussed in Chapter 6), this is exacerbated by the fact that earmarked federal funding does not go through state governments but rather directly to the implementing agency. Moreover, in states where the ruling party is different from that at federal level, motivation is lower, as programme success largely reflects well on its federal-level architects. The limited involvement of state authorities in some cases has reduced the potential for synergies with other state-supported gender initiatives, such as those designed to promote job opportunities and skills training and reduce gender-based violence, which are typically implemented by state and not federal authorities (Pereznieto and Campos, 2010).

Similar problems have emerged in the rollout of the MGNREGS. Although India has a long tradition of implementing public works programmes, there has been very limited capacity-strengthening support to ensure maximum dividends from the programme's gender-specific provisions and broader objectives to enhance livelihood security, reduce poverty and create assets for rural development (Holmes et al., 2010b). Moreover, a number of initiatives undertaken by the Indian government to support women's empowerment have not been matched by budget resources. Although the government introduced gender budget statements into the Union budget from 2005–2006, and created the Ministry of Women and Child Development in 2006, there is little evidence that extra resources are directed to the latter and, in the 2009–2010 Union budget, allocations for women's programmes under the ministry actually declined by 42% (Mishra and Jhamb, 2009, cited in Corbridge et al., 2012).

In low-income countries such as Ethiopia and Ghana, international agencies have helped to integrate gender dimensions into programme design, but there has been little or no investment in gender-related capacity building in major social protection programmes. National through to village officials in Ethiopia attribute the gap between the gender-sensitive design of the Productive Safety Net Programme (PSNP) and its implementation to an underinvestment in capacity strengthening on gender issues:

> *Government officials have training on gender equality, gender rights and generally gender issues, but no specific training on the gender dimensions of the PSNP. Women are consulted but their participation is low.*
>
> (Kushet, (village) leader, Ethiopia, 2009, cited in Jones et al., 2010b:35)

> *Sensitisation activities for implementers on gender are not adequate (not formal or intensive). There is also no formal communication channel to involve women representatives in decision-making processes. The unfair selection*

process and shortage of quotas at the village level have been a great obstacle to women's enrolment.

(Chair of Women's Association, Ethiopia, 2009,
cited in Jones et al., 2010b:36)

People in charge of implementing the PSNP have knowledge on gender, but there's no gender sensitisation specifically for the PSNP. The PSNP implementation does not consider gender vulnerabilities. … The fact that women undertake household chores and take care of their children is not considered in job allocations – women are usually told not to say any activity is 'difficult' or 'impossible.'

(Women's Association, Ethiopia, 2009, cited in Jones et al.,
2010b:33)

The problem with the PSNP is not simply that inadequate attention to persistent gendered beliefs and attitudes translates into poor mainstreaming of gender-related objectives. Rather, in a context of resource constraints and limited institutional gender sensitivity, gender issues are frequently considered unrealistic or burdensome additions (Jones et al., 2010b). Without tailored capacity-building initiatives, the majority of institutional actors fail to realise that addressing gender inequality is likely to increase general effectiveness.

In Ghana's LEAP, the challenge is arguably more taxing still in the light of the limited institutional experience of the lead agency – the Department of Social Welfare (Government of Ghana, 2007). District social welfare officers emphasised their heavy workload and their inability to monitor implementation, with only untrained National Youth Employment Programme volunteers and inadequate transport services (Amuzu et al., 2010). In this context, despite LEAP's gender-related design provisions, their implementation has faced weak political support, especially at district and community levels. Many district officers reported being unaware of the details of the programme, and viewed it as being driven by central government. At the community level, a number of problems related to elite capture were reported (Amuzu et al., 2010).

In Bangladesh, despite the wide reach of social protection interventions, the lack of a coherent social protection framework, implementation deficits, poor capacity and targeting, low coverage (currently estimated to be only 10% of the poor) and corruption have all compromised their success (Köhler et al., 2009; World Bank, 2006). Moreover, although gender seems to be relatively well integrated at national policy level, government officers continue to have a rather poor understanding of gender and, with limited resources at their disposal, implementation of gender policies usually suffers (Holmes et al., 2010a).

A partial exception is the Challenging the Frontiers of Poverty Reduction Programme (CFPR) in Bangladesh, implemented by the non-governmental organisation BRAC.[6] As discussed in Chapter 3, this programme aims explicitly to promote women's economic empowerment and subsequently their social status. Yet even here gender training has been inadequate. BRAC staff have a weak understanding of gender and how to promote gender issues in practice. They undergo some training on gender in relation to livelihood activities and on social development skills. However, key informants suggested that training needs to address conceptual issues more clearly, such as the assumption that gender means women, and to integrate men effectively into interventions. Staff, especially those who interact with beneficiaries directly and regularly, noted that they would benefit from more training opportunities (Holmes et al., 2010a).

Coordination mechanisms

Although coordination mechanisms are in part a reflection of broader governance capacities, they are also indicative of political commitment to addressing multiple vulnerabilities, including gendered vulnerabilities.

To begin with examples of good practice, Brazil's Zero Hunger Strategy, which was initiated in 2003 in tandem with the *Bolsa Família* conditional cash transfer, aimed to promote cross-sectoral coordination among programmes designed to tackle food insecurity and extreme poverty by addressing previous problems of duplication of resources and missed opportunities for programme synergies.[7] Subsequent evaluations have attributed the success of *Bolsa Família* to the shared management model used. This facilitates the consolidation of the much needed Single Registry, which tracks all services and programmes with which an individual citizen interacts. The inclusion of specific questions on women and other population groups with particular needs or vulnerabilities can help to identify and target these groups. The registry can also identify demand for specific social policies through information on housing, sanitation and water, health and education, and highlight self-perceptions of poverty and attitudes towards cultural and gender issues (such as HIV/AIDS and domestic violence), which are usually inadequately understood by officials (Mostafa and da Silva, 2007).

By contrast, in social protection programmes in more resource-poor settings, which are frequently also beset with poor governance, coordination challenges can significantly hamper opportunities for effective programme rollout, including the integration of gender provisions. In Ethiopia, limited inter-sectoral coordination at state and district levels in the rollout of the PSNP hindered the potential for synergies with other key gender policy initiatives, particularly the 2008 Ethiopian Women's Package for

Development and Change and the 2006–2010 National Action Plan for Gender Equality (Evers et al., 2008). Lack of power and resources have prevented the Women's Bureau from playing a significant coordinating role in the public works programme implementation committee. The other government agencies represented do not necessarily have the necessary knowledge about gender and its incorporation in their own programmes to promote any synergies.

Similar problems were reported for Ghana's LEAP. In one district in Northern Ghana a local legislator emphasised that gender-sensitive implementation could not be realised without addressing coordination challenges (Amuzu et al, 2010:36):

> There is no coordination between social sector actors. There are education and health officers in the district but the assembly doesn't coordinate with them and, although there should be a position of gender desk officer, we don't even have one in Chereponi.
>
> (Assemblywoman, Chereponi, 2009)

In Vietnam, although some attention was given in the conceptualisation of the National Targeted Programme for Poverty Reduction (NTPPR) (discussed in Chapter 6) to addressing multidimensional poverty, the relative weakness of the coordinating ministry – the Ministry of Labor, Invalids and Social Affairs (MOLISA) – has meant that the programme has essentially been operationalised as a collection of diverse instruments and mechanisms. This has resulted in considerable fragmentation and implementation overlap (Ministry of Labour, Invalids and Social Affairs and UN Development Programme, 2009), as has also been recognised at the sub-national level (Jones and Tran, 2010:35):

> There is not enough coordination between DOLISA [the Department of Labor, Invalids and Social Affairs] and the Departments of Finance and Planning. The needs of the poor, from literacy to agricultural technology, are vast – it is hard to coordinate. It's really hard to get the results if each policy is to be implemented on its own, separately.
>
> (Head of Social Protection Unit, DOLISA, Ha Giang, 2009)

> There are too many groups taking care of the same things – the state cannot keep track of it all – women's groups, farmer groups, etc. We also have a lot of social security programmes, poverty reduction programmes, as well as other policies, but they are not focusing enough. The less focus the greater the overlap.
>
> (DOLISA official, An Giang, 2009)

In this case, senior leadership (such as that of the deputy prime minister) was seen as the means necessary to address these coordination challenges (Jones and Tran, 2010).

Monitoring and evaluation mechanisms

Monitoring and evaluation mechanisms are a critical part of any social protection system, and can also reflect political commitment to effective programming. Here we see a marked divide between Latin American programmes, which are increasingly underpinned by state-of-the-art mechanisms, and those in more resource-deprived contexts, especially sub-Saharan Africa, but also in parts of Asia (India's MGNREGS is a partial exception; see Box 7.2). In the latter cases, monitoring and evaluation are weak, particularly in the case of gender-disaggregated indicators.

Evaluations of Brazil's *Bolsa Família* have encompassed quasi-experimental techniques, with data from large independent surveys or national household surveys and administrative sources. Gendered indicators have been used to evaluate impacts on female and male labour participation and household bargaining power. Evaluations of *Chile Solidario* and Colombia's *Familias*

Box 7.2 MGNREGS's social audit approach

Through their core principles – transparency, participation and accountability – MGNREGS social audits are a tool for bottom-up accountability to strengthen citizens' voices.[7] They can enable reflection on the programme's local progress and ensure that it improves to better meet local needs, including gender-specific concerns. They include some gender-specific questions related to the programme's gender provisions – whether registration is refused to single women or female-headed households, the average proportion of women employed in a village, and whether there are different female and male tasks.

However, there are no questions on the use of the community assets created and their gender benefits, women's participation in decision-making structures, or budget allocations for capacity building on gender-specific programme features. Moreover, despite strong civil society pressure for the programme's effective corruption-free implementation, civil society 'has not been attentive toward the prevailing norms of gender inequality in control rights to productive assets and to the token presence of women in local institutions and structures of monitoring of schemes, including social audits' (Kelkar, 2009:16).

en Acción have also included attention to gender issues such as women's confidence in perceiving themselves as individuals and not only as wives or mothers, their increased mobility in public spaces, and their self-image as protagonists who are able to change their lives (Larrañaga et al., 2009). However, there is no indicator to assess women's time poverty or changes in husbands' attitudes towards domestic chores.

That said, gender evaluations of Latin American conditional cash transfer programmes have generally not revealed which programme components are the most significant, in part because they focus on conventional gender indicators rather than mechanisms responsible for women's empowerment and ways to measure gendered time poverty (Soares and Silva, 2010). In addition, little attention has been paid to the effects of interaction between gender-specific design measures (Soares and Silva, 2010). In other words, there is still more to learn about which measures work in isolation and which are synergistic.

By contrast, programmes in other contexts have largely neglected to tackle the gendered dimensions of poverty and vulnerability. For instance, Vietnam's NTPPR contains no gender-specific targets or measurable outcomes, and consequently its mid-term evaluation was rather weak on these points, with no differentiated figures for women, men, girls and boys (Ministry of Labour, Invalids and Social Affairs and UN Development Programme, 2009). It also overlooked the language barriers and social discrimination facing ethnic-minority girls and women in particular in accessing human capital and income-generation opportunities. Moreover, there are issues in terms of data quality, adequacy and timeliness. General Statistics Office data are not necessarily reliable, and it is thus difficult to discern impacts on female and male participants. In addition, survey data are often released too late and are thus excluded from annual development plans, and significant data on informal employment, migrant workers and time poverty are not available, although women are particularly vulnerable in all three of these areas (Jones and Tran, 2010).

In Indonesia, the subsidised food security programme, Raskin, does not consider households' differential nutrition needs, which are of particular concern for children under five and pregnant and nursing women. Central Bureau of Statistics uses National Economic Survey data for official statistics on poverty incidence, but these use the household as their unit of measurement (Suryahadi et al., 2010). There are also concerns over data accuracy and local administrations' limited capacity and the weak prioritisation that they give to collecting gender-disaggregated data. This issue is also political, linked to power relations among state and non-state actors involved in programme implementation (Suryahadi et al., 2010).

For Ethiopia's PSNP, there is some information on the participation of female-headed households, but worksite daily attendance records are not disaggregated by gender. In addition, there is no clear record of how long women are exempted from public work activities as a result of pregnancy and birth. The absence of a gender lens in the monitoring of the community assets created prevents further assessment of the balance of investment in assets aimed at reducing women's time poverty.

Explanations of this widespread under-prioritisation of gender dimensions include an institutional disconnect between the growing body of evidence on the gendered nature of poverty and vulnerability and policy and programme design, in part because of weak linkages between governmental gender focal points and policy and programme designers (Holmes and Jones, 2010a), and a largely technocratic approach to gender mainstreaming which does not support tailored and operational approaches to the systematic integration of gender (Daly, 2005). These are exacerbated by an underinvestment in capacity building for programme implementers, especially regarding the gendered rationale for provisions, and a general absence of gender-sensitive indicators in monitoring, evaluation and learning systems.

Interests of key actors

The constellation of actors involved in social protection policy and programming is diverse, and includes political elites, government bureaucrats (typically spanning a range of ministries), social welfare, women and children's affairs, health, food security and rural development, civil society actors and bilateral donors and multi-lateral agencies. Although increasingly there are good-practice examples of cross-agency cooperation,[8] not surprisingly these actors have a range of different interests in promoting social protection, and differing degrees of influence and capacities in particular contexts. A careful mapping of this complex landscape at the national level, including recognition that these different categories of actors are themselves not homogeneous, is critical when assessing both the opportunities for and potential obstacles to the integration of gender into the social protection agenda.

Political elites

Political elites often initiate social protection programmes to further their own institutional aims – for example, to demonstrate a commitment to a strengthened social contract between the state and the citizenry (as with India's MGNREGS), and to promote social cohesion, especially in times of political flux. Examples include redressing a legacy of political violence among impoverished communities in Peru's *Juntos*, responding to macroeconomic crises in Indonesia's *Raskin*, harnessing public works labour to promote environmental rehabilitation in Ethiopia's PSNP, showing a commitment to poverty reduction in the run-up to elections in Ghana's LEAP. Developing a reputation as a new international leader, can be another source of motivation. Lula's Workers' Party government in Brazil, which has strengthened its stature as an emerging global power through its leading role in South–South learning on 'social technologies' on the basis of its now famous *Bolsa Família* programme is a case in point.[9]

However, as we discussed in previous chapters, only in a very few cases does tackling gender inequality feature as a primary programme objective, and even then resourcing may be a challenge, as is highlighted by Box 7.3. That said, even though gender equality concerns are frequently secondary to overall programme aims, governments have at times been happy to claim responsibility for progressive gender outcomes – for example, for increased participation of women in Ethiopia and India as a result of public works programmes, the enhanced capacities of female caregivers to support their children's development in Latin American cash transfers, and the smoothing of women's role in ensuring adequate food consumption in Indonesia's *Raskin* (Jones and Holmes, 2010).

Box 7.3 A mismatch between government commitment to women's economic empowerment and resourcing

Mexico's subsidised crèche scheme, *Estancias*, has seen its budget steadily increase since its inception in 2007, allowing it to become the single most important childcare provider for children under four, and creating jobs for over 38,000 women (Staab and Gerhard, 2010). However, evaluation evidence suggests that this expansion is occurring at least in part at the cost of decent employment for women. *Estancia* assistants are hired at low salaries without being registered as formal employees with access to social security, because *Estancia* heads often struggle to make a profit; if they were to pay the employer's contribution, this would make the centres' chances of financial viability even more challenging. In other words, despite *Estancias'* flagship role in the government's policy repertoire, in practice government subsidies are too low to cover the real costs. Gains in some dimensions of social protection for women still need to be matched in other areas, including labour-market regulations.

Source: Pereznieto and Campos (2010).

Bureaucratic agencies

The lead agency for social protection strategies often plays a key role in shaping the relative priorities accorded to different goals. Where ministries of social welfare, women and children lead, there is potentially more scope for attention to gender inequalities, although these agencies typically face capacity constraints in coordinating with other more powerful government agencies. For instance, Ghana's LEAP is housed within the Ministry of Employment and Social Welfare, but tensions with the Ministry of Women and Children have hampered linkages with complementary services and broader empowerment synergies. Not only have protocols on certain services not been signed, but also programme implementation committees have not promoted collaboration with actors such as regional Departments of Women's Welfare. In Northern Ghana, gender desk officers have only a vague idea about LEAP, and are not actively promoting synergies with already existing programmes targeting women and girls, although most beneficiaries in the district are women (Amuzu et al., 2010).

Similarly, Vietnam's NTPPR comes under MOLISA, which suffers from significant capacity constraints. Although MOLISA's mandate offers good opportunities for cross-fertilisation of ideas, in practice representatives from the Department of Gender Equality have participated only minimally in consultations on social protection, and this is reflected in the relatively weak integration of gender considerations into the new national social protection strategy (Jones and Tran, 2010). Few officials know how to adequately incorporate gender dimensions into programming, despite attendance at gender mainstreaming workshops, as the latter fail to provide practical and specific guidance:

> It is critical to have detailed guidelines for each ministry – not just generic gender training, which we have again and again.
>> (Head of Department of Labour, Cultural and Social Affairs, Ministry of Planning and Investment, Vietnam, 2009, cited in Jones and Tran, 2010:37)

> Currently they [bureaucrats in other ministries] don't respond, so they need to be forced to [consider gender dimensions] if we want real change.
>> (Head of Department of Labour, Cultural and Social Affairs, MPI, Vietnam, 2009, cited in Jones and Tran, 2010:37)

Where ministries of rural development lead on national social protection strategies, gender dynamics tend to be accorded low priority, and are usually poorly integrated into ways of working, as reflected in significantly lower uptake of agricultural extension services by women than by men (Meinzen-Dick et al., 2010). This is compounded by weak linkages with gender focal points, and a general dearth of funding for capacity building for implementers around gender issues. India's MGNREGS, implemented by the Department for Rural Development, has yet to effectively integrate gender equality objectives into, for example, the creation of gender-sensitive assets and initiatives to reduce women's time poverty, mitigate their life-cycle vulnerabilities and provide skills training (Holmes et al., 2010b). Although Ethiopia's PSNP, implemented by the Ministry of Rural Development, is arguably more gender-sensitive in design, the Ministry's low prioritisation of gender dynamics is manifested in programme implementation and evaluation practices (Jones et al., 2010b; see also Chapter 4).

Civil society

The third key group of actors that we need to consider is civil society. In developed countries, organised women's groups have sometimes played a key role in shaping the contours of the welfare state and the content of social protection programmes (see Box 7.4). However, in developing countries the role of the women's movement in shaping social protection discourse has been weak to date (Holmes and Jones, 2010c).

In Africa and Asia, international non-governmental organisations have played an important role in influencing social protection discourse, but the focus on gender equality has not been as strong as might be expected, in large part because of the primary focus on age-based (e.g. Save the Children, Help Age) and spatial (e.g. Oxfam's work on pastoral communities) exclusion and vulnerability. In Latin America and South Asia, domestic civil society actors have been relatively more influential, especially in Bangladesh, where BRAC has undertaken path-breaking work in social protection programming aimed at supporting women's productive and social capital. However, again while some gender equality champions (e.g. in Bangladesh, India and Peru) have helped to ensure, for instance, equal wages for women, sensitivity to women's time poverty, and linkages with complementary programmes that tackle socio-cultural forms of gender discrimination,[10] gender equality activists have been much less prominent than in other areas of public debate, such as political participation, and human and labour rights.

This is perhaps because women's movements have not been sufficiently adept at moving towards strategically influencing new programme areas such as social protection. Possible reasons include a general tendency for gender equality movements to pay relatively less attention to issues affecting the poorest,[11] the often narrow income and consumption focus of social protection programmes, and suspicion on the part of women activists of what they may view as welfarism rather than the advancement of women's rights or empowerment. Funding pressures, which have kept women's organisations siloed rather than facilitating their capacity to engage effectively with cross-sectoral issues such as social protection, are another likely contributing factor (Holmes and Jones, 2010c). Increasingly tense relations between national governments and civil society organisations in

---

Box 7.4 The pivotal role of women's voluntary organisations in constructing early-twentieth-century social welfare policy in the USA

In the first decades of the twentieth century, the USA did not develop the type of paternalistic welfare state that is seen in western Europe, where male bureaucrats administer regulations and social insurance for the good of male breadwinner workers. Rather it approximated a maternalistic welfare state, including measures such as mothers' pensions (paid to widows), the development of the Children's Bureau, clinics that dealt with maternal and child health, and labour regulations that limited women's working hours. The women's movement at this time was particularly influential and brought together women from diverse backgrounds with a rhetoric that 'honoured' motherhood. Although women were effectively excluded from political life at the time, they were highly educated and well prepared to participate in community life underpinned by notions of 'municipal housekeeping.' Women's voluntary associations could build networks across states and work simultaneously across multiple levels of politics. Not only did no other type of civil society group have this level of reach at the time, but also their activism corresponded to a period when judges and legislators were willing to pass legislation that protected women but not male-dominated worker unions, thereby elevating their relative influence.

Source: Skocpol (1992).

---

some contexts, such as Ethiopia and Vietnam, further restrict the voices of gender equality champions in social protection policy debates.[12]

Donors

Finally, donors have become critical actors in the social protection arena, especially in sub-Saharan Africa, and have been able to exert influence with regard to the inclusion of measures to address social exclusion, including gender inequalities. In Ethiopia, for instance, although the PSNP is without doubt a nationally owned programme, donors have played a significant role in shaping related policy debates. A consortium of donors commissioned a gender audit in 2007–2008 to assess the programme's performance vis-à-vis promoting gender, and to feed into the revised Programme Implementation Manual. Moreover, the Canadian International Development Agency has been particularly proactive in supporting gender-sensitive social protection efforts, funding social development advisor positions in regional Food Security Bureaus to strengthen attention to the gender dimensions of the PSNP and linkages between gender, food security and social protection. The World Bank has also engaged actively with gender-related concerns as they have emerged in Ethiopia, and supported the integration of measures to address them in subsequent programme governance documents.

More generally, however, the focus in the development community has remained on helping the poor and vulnerable to harness the benefits of economic growth.[13] There have been efforts to highlight the importance of equity and social inclusion but, with the exception of UN Women, which remains a very small player in the field, gender dynamics have not received much attention to date among agencies working on social protection. This reflects a general weakness in gender mainstreaming outside a few key sectors in the donor community. Although this is gradually changing, especially with regard to exploring the potential of social protection instruments to enhance girls' educational achievement and girls' and women's reproductive health in the context of the broader Millennium Development Goal (MDG) agenda, gender mainstreaming has yet to receive the resourcing that a more systematic approach would demand.

Ideas matter

Political economy analysts emphasise the centrality of ideas (e.g. Hickey and Bracking, 2005) and the ways in which scholarly and public policy discussions shape policy and programming parameters. This is certainly the case with social protection, where the divergent contours of national systems reflect a wide range of ideas about poverty and vulnerability and their underlying causes, as well as the purpose of social protection and the role of the state (see Chapter 1). Hickey (2008) argues that the absence of a social contract between the state and citizens constitutes a significant barrier to the development of social protection, especially where this is replaced with clientelism. For example, attempts to deal with chronic poverty in the Northern Region of Uganda, where notions of a social contract are absent, are characterised by piecemeal social funds and diluted by patronage (Hickey, 2008).

When gender relations are added to the mix, ideas often play a particularly powerful role, as they are embedded in complex socio-cultural norms surrounding understandings of family, care and social reproduction (Folbre, 2009). In Bangladesh, discourses on poverty have been elevated to a moral level above party politics, and destitute mothers are universally considered to be the 'deserving poor' in decision making about social assistance interventions (Hossain, 2007). Our discussion that now follows, as to why ideas matter to gender-sensitive social protection, focuses predominantly on social assistance and subsidy programmes that have embraced the notion of what Molyneux terms 'good motherhood' (2006:438). Pension and unemployment insurance programmes would probably reveal a different set of discursive strategies, given that they have been designed primarily with a male breadwinner model in mind.[14]

Ideas about poverty, vulnerability and gender

Gendered understandings of poverty and vulnerability have been mainstreamed relatively recently, and only to a limited degree (see Chapter 1). In Indonesia, the 1997–1998 crisis focused policy attention on poverty and vulnerability, but the resulting discourse largely neglected social risks and especially the role of gender relations in trapping people in poverty (Arif et al., 2010b). In Vietnam, national strategy documents are concerned primarily with economic development and growth dynamics (Schech and Vas Dev, 2007). Meanwhile, gender relations are often seen as the purview of individual families and/or groups, and therefore not an area in which the state should intervene. In Ethiopia's PSNP, for instance, gender training has at times met with resistance from local government administrators (Jones et al., 2010b).

However, change is apparent in some contexts. Mexico has an explicit social policy strategy, *Vivir Mejor*, aimed at meeting the needs of particularly vulnerable groups, which include women victims of violence and abuse. Similarly, India's Eleventh Five-year Plan (2007–2012) acknowledges that economic and social inequalities prevent the poor from taking up productive opportunities, and that this situation has negative impacts on the growth potential of the economy. And Ghana's National Social Protection Strategy explicitly includes a 'gender-sensitive approach' as one of its six pillars, providing a detailed account of gender vulnerabilities, which influenced the design of LEAP.

Discourses surrounding MDG achievement have also played a valuable role in promoting more gender-sensitive social protection programming. Peru's *Juntos* is based on the MDGs, as is Colombia's *Familias en Acción* and the Indonesian *Program Keluarga Harapan* (2007–2015). The Filipino *Pantawid, Pamilyang Pilipino Program* also includes the MDGs in its objectives.[15]

However, even when programmes reflect recognition of gender differences, they may still conceptualise women in their traditional roles as caregivers and reinforce a gendered division of labour in the name of 'political motherhood.' In Mexico's *Progresa/Oportunidades* and Peru's *Comedores Populares*, women are often rewarded with state help for being good mothers. This entails 'dependency on a subsidy which confirms mothering as women's primary social role, one which may enhance their social status and self-respect, but nonetheless, in doing little to secure sustainable livelihoods, puts them at risk of remaining in poverty for the rest of their lives' (Molyneux, 2006:440).

In the same vein, the 'social investment perspective' on which the majority of conditional cash transfers in Latin America are based is in reality built on a set of child-centred policies, with women's role conceptualised in instrumental terms and their own well-being accorded less visibility (Jenson, 2009). In *Bolsa Família, Familias en Acción* and *Chile Solidario*, women have increased their bargaining power in the household and improved their social status, but none of these programmes has addressed women's needs more comprehensively, with their main objective being children's well-being (Soares and Silva, 2010) (see also Box 7.5). Even in the case of maternal health provisions – still ostensibly linked to infant

---

Box 7.5 Transformative opportunities only partially realised

Opportunities for transforming gender roles remain only partially tapped in a number of social protection programmes. On the one hand, Mexico's *Estancias* acknowledges that care functions have an economic value and women can improve their labour participation if they can access supporting mechanisms that relieve them of their domestic and caretaking responsibilities. On the other hand, the programme's full name, 'Crèches to Support Working Mothers', tends to emphasise that such responsibilities belong to women alone, and that mothers rather than couples are those in need of support. In the same vein, single fathers are recognised as carers in need of support. A more transformative outcome would be promoted if there was some indication of the importance of men contributing to domestic responsibilities in order to reduce women's time burden.

In Bangladesh, it is widely (both publicly and politically) acceptable for social protection interventions to target women.[16] Accordingly, the CFPR focuses on women, providing them with training and support in asset management to increase their economic position and relative power within the household. However, as the programme recognises that economic transfers are insufficient to address poverty in a sustainable way, it also tries to increase women's social capital through their involvement in village poverty reduction committees. Complementary social development activities to acknowledge and address issues such as violence against women, early marriage and dowry are also included. That said, if gendered understandings of vulnerability in this context are deconstructed, the limits to their transformative potential emerge:

> *The argument that is given for constructing this category [widows, abandoned mothers, young mothers] is that, being husband-abandoned and young and with small children, these women after returning to their natal home cannot (or is it should not?) work outside the home. … The operative notions here are two – young and mother – and both raise general 'sympathy' arising out of deep patriarchal values.*
>
> (Matin, 2002:15)

In other words, the CFPR is 'operating largely within the realm of socio-cultural acceptance' (Holmes et al., 2010a:29), and so has not been able to challenge existing gender inequalities. To obtain the transfer, women participate in weekly meetings, which are also forums for discussing the problems they face and receiving information about their entitlements and training. However, in practice many women struggle to set aside long-standing traditions and put their learning into action (Holmes et al., 2010a).

well-being – the resources dedicated to evaluating impact have been far fewer than those related to child health, nutrition and educational outcomes (Jones et al., 2011).

Ideas about social protection, citizenship and social inclusion

Conceptualisations of citizenship and social inclusion also have important implications for social protection. On the positive side, a number of programmes are underpinned by rights-based understandings of citizenship, with positive spill-over effects on gender equality. Peru's *Juntos* supports the 'right to identity' as a key measure to enable women's full citizenship and access to public services and resources (Molyneux and Thomson, 2011). Moreover, rather than employing a discourse of conditionality, *Juntos* promotes the concept of co-responsibility for uptake between the state and citizens. Women and the state are seen as jointly charged with maximising the available resources for their children.[17]

India's MGNREGS is another example of official recognition of all citizens' rights to state-guaranteed social protection, but legal rights are but a first step in a much longer citizenship-building process. Awareness-raising activities are critical to ensure that all participants benefit, yet progress to date in this area has been patchy at best (Reddy et al., 2010). Any initiatives have generally been led by civil society, as in Rajasthan and with women's self-help groups in Andhra Pradesh, rather than the state itself (Reddy et al., 2010).

By contrast, the absence of a rights-based approach to social protection in Ethiopia and the dominance of the ruling party in rural areas mean that many participants view interventions as a 'gift' from the government or from God, which means that nobody wants to jeopardise their inclusion in the programme by pushing for the fulfilment of social inclusion provisions, including those related to gender relations (Jones et al., 2010b). This attitude is reinforced by very high illiteracy rates among participants and particularly among women, who often have very little exposure beyond their village, and few opportunities to formulate let alone voice concerns for programme improvements.

In Vietnam's NTPPR, for some highland ethnic-minority groups the state is seen as belonging to 'the other', so people tend to look within the community first (Jones and Tran, 2010). Accordingly, implementers need to build up communities' understanding of the state and of citizenship rights. Staff need support in developing the appropriate 'soft skills' for such a role, especially for women. Often language and cultural diversity are not factored adequately into programme design, which means that women in ethnic-minority communities in particular are often unaware of programme provisions. This problem can be compounded by cultural gender roles and gendered education and literacy gaps, so women are less likely to contribute to community discussions and/or are prevented from attending meetings on account of time poverty (Jones and Tran, 2010).

Conclusions

The links between gender, economic growth and development sustainability are increasingly well recognised by mainstream development actors, but these insights have yet to gain real traction within social protection debates, policy and practice. Key constraints relate to the gendered politics of social protection (at macro, meso and micro levels), and in particular a general tendency for gender dynamics to be integrated into institutions, actor interests and ideas in only a partial and subordinate way.

Key political economy factors to consider at the institutional level include the incorporation of gender equality goals as only secondary programme objectives, weak coordination between governmental gender focal points and implementing agencies, the limited role of legislative and judicial bodies in championing the integration of gender equality into poverty reduction and social protection policies and programmes, and the inclusion of at best narrow gender-related indicators in monitoring and evaluation systems.

In terms of ideas, entrenched socio-cultural norms with regard to the appropriate role of the state vis-à-vis intra-household relations, and an underinvestment in tailored awareness raising for programme staff and participants on the rationale for gender-related provisions, both continue to present major impediments to transformative change.

Lastly, the constellation of actors involved in social protection, and their respective interests, matters. Gender equality activists have played a part in ensuring the inclusion of gender-sensitive programme components (e.g. equal wages for women, links to complementary services that tackle socio-cultural forms of gender discrimination) in some contexts, but overall activists have been notably less prominent than in other areas of public debate.

EIGHT
Conclusions and recommendations: advancing gender-sensitive social protection

Introduction

This book has sought to demonstrate not only the importance of applying a gender lens to social protection policy and programming, but also that this can be achieved with relatively simple design changes, coupled with more strategic implementation practices. We have argued that, if social protection strategies, policies and programmes integrate a more trans-formative agenda to promote gender equity and women's empowerment, the objectives of social protection – reducing vulnerability and poverty and promoting social justice – will be achieved more effectively.

A critical component of designing appropriate interventions lies in understanding the drivers of context-specific experiences of poverty and vulnerability. Social protection agendas to date have focused pre-dominantly on the *economic* risks and vulnerabilities that households face. However, as we have highlighted, *social* risks and vulnerabilities at the individual, household and community levels are just as important, and often inseparable from economic risks and vulnerabilities. Consider, for instance, the personal narratives of Tamenu in Ethiopia, Bange in Ghana, Mi Lenh in Vietnam and Faisal in Indonesia, which we have drawn upon to illustrate the inter-linkages and multiple vulnerabilities of individuals at the intra-household and community levels.

Social protection programmes can address vulnerability in a more strategic way, and as we highlight in Annex 2, 'Summary of gendered impacts of key social protection instruments', a number of them have achieved impressive progress in promoting more gender-equitable impacts at the individual, intra-household and community levels. However, many initiatives have fallen short of this potential. As Annex 2 also shows, some programme designs have simply assumed that the household is a homogenous unit, and overlooked important gender and intergenerational inequalities within it. Social protection policy and implementation processes have also tended to underestimate inequalities at the community level, and largely ignored the importance of agency, voice and participation in reducing poverty and vulnerability and promoting resilience.

As the programme case studies in this book have shown, social protec-tion programming, with only a few good practice exceptions, has largely served to reinforce women's traditional roles and responsibilities. Many programmes play an important role in meeting women's practical needs (even where this was not an explicit intention of the programme design), but few have advanced the transformative potential of social protection.

Moreover, only a very limited number of programmes address social risks and vulnerabilities and their linkages to economic risks to effectively tackle poverty, reduce vulnerability and increase resilience and social justice by supporting what Molyneux (1985) has famously dubbed women's and girls' 'strategic gender interests.' However, where programmes are cognisant of unequal gender relations and have sought to redress these through programme design and/or complementary programme linkages, the outcomes for women and men, and for girls and boys, are increasingly progressive.

One important question remains. *Why*, despite the evidence and advocacy around the developmental importance of gender equality, women's rights and women's empowerment over the past few decades, has social protection – an increasingly important policy approach in national and international development – failed to sufficiently incorporate a gender lens? The answer is complex and shaped by many factors. These include an underinvestment in the institutions and structures that promote gender mainstreaming, and an institutional disconnect between these and social protection institutions. These are compounded by differential stakeholder interests and influence in promoting social protection, and diverse ideologies underpinning understandings of poverty and its causes, the purpose of social protection and the role of the state in shaping gender relations. Indeed, support for a more comprehensive approach to tackling gender-specific vulnerabilities has not been very forthcoming among a range of actors, as gender relations are often seen as the purview of individual families and/or cultural or religious groups, and therefore not an area in which the state should intervene. These constraints are reinforced in some contexts by a strong pro-government orientation and/or the absence of a rights-based approach to programme implementation.

Recognising the complexities inherent in social protection policy and programme development, we now summarise six key cross-cutting conclusions that have emerged aceross the book, briefly synthesising the state of the evidence base, recapping on the innovative features of good practice examples in Tables 8.1 to 8.5, and presenting our analysis of policy and practice implications.

Policy and programme design

The transformative potential of social protection depends on its ability to tackle underlying structural causes of poverty and vulnerability, either through core programme design or by strategically linking beneficiaries to a range of complementary programmes and services.

State of the evidence base

Poverty and vulnerability assessments are increasingly being undertaken to inform national development plans and social protection strategies, but too often the gender dimensions of vulnerability are at best reflected weakly in programme design, treated superficially or even overlooked altogether. This is problematic, because there is a strong body of evidence showing the distinct ways in which poor women, men, girls and boys experience poverty – and their differential capacities to deal with risks and vulnerability. Simple assumptions cannot be made about these differences, as the gendered patterning of poverty and vulnerability differs significantly within and across countries, as was highlighted in Chapter 2.

The extent to which gender has been considered in social protection policy and programme design varies widely (see Table 8.1. for good

Table 8.1 Examples of good practice in policy and programme design

Innovative feature	Examples in practice
Addressing gender gaps in education and health	• Promoting girls' education through higher financial incentives in CCTs or reducing costs of accessing education (subsidies): – *Oportunidades CCT, Mexico* – *Social Risk Mitigation Project CCT, Turkey* – *Secondary Education Development Programme (subsidy), Tanzania* • Targeting boys in CCT programmes where their enrolment is lower than girls: – *CCTs in Bangladesh, Cambodia and Jamaica* • Encouraging pregnant women to attend antenatal and/or postnatal visits and health and/or nutrition seminars: – *Bolsa Família, Brazil* – *Health Equity Fund, Cambodia*
Tackling gendered economic and social risks through an integrated approach	• Actively strengthening women's economic capacities and at the same time promoting women's bargaining power, access to health services, and raising awareness on social inequalities: – *BRAC's Challenging the Frontiers of Poverty Reduction, Bangladesh* – *Chars Livelihoods Programme, Bangladesh*
Recognising women's role in the care economy	• Childcare subsidies established to promote women's participation in the labour force: – *Estancias subsidised crèche scheme, Mexico* • Provision of flexible working hours and childcare facilities to facilitate women's participation in public works programmes: – *Productive Safety Net Programme, Ethiopia*

practice examples). Most explicitly, many programmes (especially transfers and subsidies) have targeted women and girls to enhance their access to healthcare and education based on evidence that they face barriers to school attendance and reproductive health service access. Such programmes have had positive impacts on improving access to these services and, in some cases, human capital outcomes.

To a lesser extent, the design of a number of programmes has been informed by an appreciation of (and in turn a desire to tackle) the existing discriminatory socio-cultural environment, which hinders poverty reduction and poor households' potential to exit poverty. These programmes have coupled economic activities with opportunities to enhance women's bargaining power and position in the household as well as the wider community. They have also recognised the importance of supporting women's care work so as to facilitate their increased participation in the labour force.

Policy and practice implications

Designing gender-sensitive social protection programmes and policies needs to go beyond simply targeting women and girls. Although their inclusion is an important first step, this is insufficient to increase their voice, social status and agency, and to address deeply entrenched unequal power relations within and outside the household – all of which are needed for effective poverty reduction. As such, a clear analysis of economic and social vulnerabilities across an individual's lifecycle is needed to inform policy and programme design (see, for instance, Holmes and Jones (2010c) for guidance on designing and implementing gender-sensitive social protection). Programmes should therefore:

- ascertain that the type of benefit being delivered (e.g. cash, assets, food, employment, fee waivers, insurance products) is known to be of value and use to women, men, girls and boys
- promote mechanisms to address women's strategic interests as well as practical needs
- ensure that the way in which the benefit is delivered considers gender-specific constraints (e.g. women's and girls' greater time poverty and socio-culturally derived mobility restrictions), and that conditions do not exacerbate gender-specific vulnerabilities, such as time poverty and inequalities in labour-market participation
- institutionalise adequate linkages to complementary services, programmes, information provision and awareness-raising initiatives in order to tackle gender-specific vulnerabilities
- promote equal participation of women and men in programme decision making
- embed monitoring and evaluation systems that require age and gender-disaggregated data and indicators as integral elements.

Implementation capacity and fiscal space

Designing gender-sensitive social protection programmes and policies is a necessary first step, but to maximise their positive impacts, effective implementation and delivery are vital. Investing in building institutional capacity and allocating financial resources to gender-sensitive programme features are necessary where capacity is weak.

State of the evidence base

Institutional capacity varies significantly between the regions and countries discussed in this book. In Latin America, for instance, institutional capacity is much stronger than in other regions, partly because decades of experience in implementing social policy programmes have facilitated the rollout of social protection programmes. However, as we have seen, a number of African countries are delivering social protection at scale (e.g. the Productive Safety Net Programme (PSNP) in Ethiopia), and institutions in South-East Asia are increasingly delivering more comprehensive systems (e.g. Vietnam's integrated subsidy, the National Targeted Programme for Poverty Reduction (NTPPR)). However, institutional capacity remains a key challenge to the rollout of gender-sensitive social protection.

With relatively few exceptions (see Table 8.2), the implementation

Table 8.2 Examples of good practice in terms of implementation capacity

Innovative feature	Examples in practice
Investing in gender-sensitive implementation capacity	• Staff receive gender training and have a clear understanding of programme objectives and strategy, including its gender-sensitive features • There are clear organisational structures with lines of responsibility, rewards for good individual performance, and considerable interface time between staff and beneficiaries through follow-up, supervision and mentoring of beneficiaries: – *BRAC's CFPR, Bangladesh*
Designing systems and support to reduce barriers to women's participation	• Scheme actively seeks to overcome barriers (e.g. low literacy and power differentials) to reach poor female beneficiaries (with insurance products) by using extension agents to support members in making claims and developing systems to support illiterate or semi-literate members to make a claim: – *SEWA, India*
Promoting women's skills and capacities	• Programme invests in training and employment opportunities for women working in childcare and delivering programme components: – *EPWP, South Africa*

of gender-related aims has been identified as a significant weakness in many programmes discussed in this book, even where broader institutional capacity is comparatively strong. This serves to undermine the potential of gender-sensitive programme design. These institutional weaknesses are due partly to the largely technocratic approach to gender mainstreaming in many developing countries. A lack of tailored, operational approaches to the systematic integration of gender into policies and programmes is reflected in a general underinvestment in capacity building for programme implementers (such as gender-related training and tailored background materials), especially on the rationale behind gender-sensitive provisions at local level. This is highlighted in Ethiopia's PSNP where, despite significant progress in terms of the gender-sensitive design of the public works programme, implementer knowledge of these features (and especially their underlying rationale) is relatively weak. In Peru's *Juntos* conditional cash transfer (CCT), implementers have supported the realisation of gender-related outcomes, including encouraging a more egalitarian division of household labour and reducing violence. However, these impacts are highly dependent on individual motivation, rather than being the result of strategic gender-sensitive training, and outcomes have therefore been highly varied and site-specific.

These weaknesses are exacerbated by the limited capacity of government gender focal points (for instance, as a result of their marginalised status in mainstream agencies, lack of skills and high staff turnover) responsible for supporting gender mainstreaming through programmes at the local level. Furthermore, limited mechanisms for beneficiaries to hold programme implementers accountable for these features mean that they are often ignored or left to be interpreted at will, and are therefore at risk of reinforcing existing discriminatory practices.

Although affordability and financing debates also have important implications for the design and implementation of gender-sensitive social protection programmes, there has so far been little gender analysis of these. Gender budgeting tools which track and monitor the level of resources allocated to the implementation of gender-related programme provisions have been applied to sectors such as health and education, but this knowledge has not been transferred to the social protection sector.

Policy and practice implications

To improve the institutional capacity of institutions delivering gender-sensitive programmes, investment is needed to strengthen implementers' knowledge and capacity with regard to gender and women's empowerment. Attention to accountability mechanisms and ensuring that programme participants know their rights and can claim these are also of critical importance. This requires the development of tailored and ongoing capacity building for programme implementers and participants (men and women alike) on gender-related programme objectives, including equal participation in programme governance, and ensuring that monitoring and evaluation indicators and methods are gender-sensitive (as we shall discuss in more detail below).

Gender budgeting could also be an important tool in future budget analyses and affordability discussions. Key questions that need to be asked include the following. Are funds available for gender-sensitive provisions such as childcare facilities or direct cash support for expectant mothers? Are funds available for training of all programme implementers on gender-related programme aims and features? Are funds available for community awareness-raising programmes on gender-sensitive schemes?

Cost-benefit analyses of social protection programmes also need to be gender-sensitive. Generating evidence on the efficiency of mainstreaming gender into programmes has proved to be an important advocacy tool for gender-sensitive design and implementation in other sectors, such as health, education and agriculture, and this urgently needs to be applied to social protection.

Institutional coordination and linkages

If social protection policies and programmes are to go beyond 'welfarism' and become transformative, the forging of strong and well-coordinated institutional linkages with complementary programmes and services is critical. Most people's experiences of vulnerability are complex – that is, different sources of vulnerability tend to overlap and reinforce one another. Accordingly, our analysis suggests that integrated services within programme design or strategic linkages to complementary services and programmes can be valuable and reinforce programme gains.

State of the evidence base

In line with our analysis of the specific vulnerabilities facing individuals across their lifecycle, complementary programmes need to address not only vulnerabilities facing women in their reproductive years, but also those facing girls (e.g. risk of exclusion from secondary education) and older women (e.g. widowhood and accompanying social stigma, loss of land and property) (see Table 8.3 for good practice examples). Cash transfers have demonstrated strong potential to link beneficiaries to additional social services, most notably health and education, with positive outcomes on women's access to antenatal and postnatal services and girls' access to education. Moreover, women's exposure to health education sessions and improved knowledge about nutrition has contributed to improved children's nutrition.

In a similar vein, health and education subsidies have been linked to broader objectives, in some cases focusing more strategically on improving

Table 8.3 Examples of good practice in institutional coordination and linkages

Innovative feature	Examples in practice

Single registry to link beneficiaries to multiple programmes and services	• Strong institutional linkages can help to tackle the multidimensional vulnerabilities that often trap households in chronic poverty, including linkages between providers of health and reproductive health services, social housing services, judicial services, credit access and skills/employment training, school allowances and elderly benefits:
	
	  – *Solidario, Chile*
	  – *Bolsa Família, Brazil*

Linkages to complementary programmes and services	• Efforts to link beneficiaries to initiatives such as consciousness raising on women's rights (BRAC's CFPR) and violence against women (Peru's *Juntos*) can seek to address gender equality and empowerment, especially when in-house resources and gender expertise are limited:
	
	  – *CFPR, Bangladesh*
	  – *Juntos, Peru*

Investing in supply-side constraints	• Improvements in service quality have been addressed in recognition of the supply-side constraints acting as a barrier to access, such as creating a safe school environment for girls: – *Southwest Basic Education Project (SBEP), education subsidy, China*

the supply and quality of services with a particular emphasis on gender-sensitive issues, such as encouraging the recruitment of female teachers and ensuring a safe school environment for girls. Social protection programmes with linkages promoting economic opportunities have been fewer to date. The asset transfer model overcomes this by creating synergies between economic components such as encouraging savings and access to credit, as do certain public works programmes that enhance beneficiaries' access to loans and other agricultural services.

However, a key concern that repeatedly arises, irrespective of the type of instrument, is the relative weakness of line ministries for gender equality and women's empowerment. Such ministries frequently struggle to command a meaningful cross-agency coordinating role with other more powerful ministries that typically accord gender equality a lower priority.

Policy and practice implications

Recognition of the many dimensions of vulnerability can prompt a more strategic approach to institutionalising linkages with other key services, and consideration of both economic and social services should be explored. A single registry database system can facilitate such linkages. This could cover, for example, health, education, protection from violence and neglect, access to agricultural extension programmes, rural financial services, credit services, skills training and legal aid (e.g. for land titling).

It is also important to provide opportunities to sensitise participants about social development issues such as the importance of avoiding early marriage, contraceptive access and the risks of human trafficking (see the following section on 'Community–programme interface'). Linkages with economic infrastructure and services could, for example, consider creating safe spaces for women in markets by constructing and/ or improving common public facilities in 'growth centre markets' and including an exclusive area for women vendors in markets (World Bank, 2009).

Strengthening the provision of gender-sensitive basic quality services will be critical to overcoming non-financial barriers to improving women's and girls' access to healthcare and education. This could include, for instance, addressing women's mobility constraints through mobile clinics with female personnel, challenging discriminatory cultural attitudes through campaigns (e.g. to discredit nutritional taboos during pregnancy), and promoting women's right to quality reproductive health services and their right to have a greater say in family planning decisions. To ensure these linkages, programme designers need to foster strong political commitment and strategic coordination, and provide institutional incentives across implementing agencies and service providers.

Moreover, in order to address institutional disconnects between government gender focal points and programme designers at national and local levels, it is critical to forge better linkages between implementing agencies and women's government agencies. This should be twinned with support for the latter's informed engagement in social protection design and implementation dialogues.

Community–programme interface

State of the evidence base

Given that a transformative social protection approach aims to go beyond achieving changes in individual lives and promote more structural and sustainable socio-cultural and political change, it is critical to understand the dynamics of the interface between communities and implementing agencies and staff. To effectively tackle the social dimensions of risk and vulnerability at community level – especially gender-based discrimination and social exclusion – our analysis has highlighted the fact that, where

Table 8.4 Examples of good practice at the community–programme interface

Innovative feature	Examples in practice
Raising awareness on gendered social concerns	• Draws attention to social concerns such as dowry practices, and develops social networks, not only among participants but also among neighbours and village elites, to facilitate collective action: – *CFPR, Bangladesh*
Encouraging voice and agency	• Community dialogues are initiated by community facilitators (local women with intimate local knowledge), who serve as a bridge between vulnerable women and programme officials: – *Juntos, Peru*

Institutionalising accountability mechanisms	• Village/ *kebele* appeals committees have been established to monitor programme selection processes. To ensure women's participation, the involvement of health extension workers – who tend to be female – has been mandated, while links to local government women's machinery are being strengthened:
	
	   – *PSNP, Ethiopia*
	
	 • The right to social protection is enshrined in national constitutions or laws, promoting a rights-based approach to social protection and strong underpinnings for citizens' demands for equitable and accountable programme implementation:
	
	   – *India*
	   – *South Africa*

programmes have such goals embedded in their design, they are more likely to be given due attention during implementation (see Table 8.4 for good practice examples). In such cases, programme staff are typically involved in behavioural change communication activities with communities, and the programme is seen as more than just a transfer or hand-out. It is important to note, however, that this type of social change approach, where it exists, is more likely to be included within social transfer programmes (cash, assets, cash/food-for-work) rather than subsidy or insurance programmes. In informal insurance mechanisms, it is possible that such community conversations are already happening organically, although there is very little evidence in this area.

A second key dimension of the community-programme interface relates to participants' involvement in programme governance and decision making. Promoting women's ability to articulate their views in a meaningful way (voice) and to become the agents of their own empowerment (agency) is critical to effectively reducing poverty in general and supporting progress towards women's empowerment. Women and girls often have limited opportunities to exercise meaningful voice and agency at the household and community levels, and this is typically compounded where gender-based exclusion intersects with other forms of social exclusion – for example, of minority groups, marginalised castes or displaced populations. A number of social protection programmes have explicitly aimed to increase women's representation through quotas in programme governance structures such as targeting or implementation committees, or community programme feedback meetings. This has given women a forum in which to speak about programme-related issues.

However, participation does not automatically result in women actively articulating and sharing their views. Evidence suggests that, even where women are aware of their formal rights, they often feel unable to demand them, as little has been done to address deeply entrenched local power dynamics. That said, our findings suggest that, where there is more frequent and regular engagement between implementers and participants (again, these tend to be social transfer schemes, often with daily contact for certain periods of time on public works schemes or monthly or bimonthly contact in the case of cash transfers), and where targeting processes are more systematic, notions of accountability and demand for grievance mechanisms are likely to be stronger. It must be noted, however, that this tends to be from a very low base, and that positive impacts in terms of promoting rights and citizenship have, overall, been limited. Accordingly, good-practice examples indicate that it is critical for programmes to invest in awareness raising and mentoring support for women so that they can, over time, be supported to make substantive inputs into community discussions and programme governance. Even so, evidence highlights the fact that barriers remain in translating women's knowledge of their rights into actual claims, suggesting that the role of social protection programmes needs to be part of a wider process to enhance voice and agency.

Policy and practice implications

The importance of the interface between programmes and participating communities cannot be underestimated. Where there are regular interactions, considerably more could be done to take advantage of opportunities to initiate community dialogue on collective ways to address gender inequalities and vulnerabilities. Community conversations could be promoted on gender-sensitive provisions, which are often innovative but poorly understood and implemented. Similar conversations could be initiated by implementers (especially if they are trained social workers) on issues related to gender-based violence, early marriage, the costs of child labour (especially in terms of stunting, and girls' and boys' human capital development), the intra-household division of labour and decisions relating to reproductive health. At the same time, raising community awareness (i.e. involving men and boys alongside women and girls) about programme potential to address these issues (or that of related complementary services, programmes and legal rights/entitlements) could enhance understanding of and demand for gender-sensitive social protection programme provisions. Given the deeply entrenched socio-cultural norms about women's auxiliary roles in relation to men in many developing country contexts, it is vital that community dialogue initiatives are accompanied by capacity strengthening and mentoring support for local women, to enable them to increase their voice and agency.

Monitoring, evaluation and lesson learning

State of the evidence base

The collection, analysis and dissemination of gender- and age-disaggregated data are essential to ensure that programme impacts are assessed through a gender lens. Are the differential risks and vulnerabilities experienced by women, men, girls and boys being addressed adequately, or are more tailored approaches and appropriate resource allocations required? Our analysis has highlighted the fact that gender-sensitive monitoring and evaluation of existing initiatives are relatively weak, especially in the case of subsidy and pro-poor insurance programmes. Some programmes are starting to make headway in developing more gender-sensitive monitoring tools, as evidenced by recent gender audits (see Table 8.5 for good practice examples). However, the gendered impacts of these interventions are not routinely reported or analysed, nor are they embedded within mainstream monitoring and evaluation systems.

As a result, we still know very little about, for instance, the effects of different forms of social assistance on intra-household gender relations, decision-making power and resource distribution (including time use implications), the impact of different interventions on women's and men's social capital formation, interaction effects between gender-specific design measures (i.e. which measures work in isolation and which are synergistic), and the relative importance of complementary programme linkages for women, men, girls and boys. These deficits in turn undermine the ability of citizens, and especially organised civil society groups with a gender equality mandate, to hold governments accountable for meeting the rights of all citizens – irrespective of their gender – to basic social protection.

Given the disconnect between the increasingly robust evidence base

Table 8.5 Examples of good practice in terms of monitoring, evaluation and lesson learning

Innovative feature	Examples in practice
Designing innovative monitoring and evaluation systems to capture gender-disaggregated impacts	• The establishment of a panel dataset tracks key indicators disaggregated by gender and age for a sample of selected ultra-poor households that have participated since 2002, as well as non-selected ultra-poor households • Regular subjective assessments of beneficiaries and control groups are carried out on poverty and well-being indicators and change over time. Key indicators include measures of women's economic, social and political empowerment (e.g. intra-household decisionmaking, mobility, financial autonomy/control over own income, interaction in the public sphere, political and legal awareness, attitudes to violence against women): – *CFPR, Bangladesh*
Establishing a social audit process to provide citizen input into processes	• A social audit process is embedded in programme design and aims to encourage ordinary citizens to speak out about programme abuses, including gender discrimination, in regular bi-annual public hearings. – *MGNREGS, public works, India*
Promoting transparency of monitoring and evaluation findings and related lesson learning	• Mandatory dissemination of evaluation findings of social programmes on government websites to promote transparency, knowledge exchange and lesson learning (Jones et al., 2009a): – *National Council for Evaluation of Social Development Policy (CONEVAL, Mexico)*

on the gendered dimensions of vulnerability, risk and resilience, and the extent to which social protection programmes reflect a recognition of gender differences in their design and implementation approach, there is a pressing need to promote learning (from good practice examples as well as from less successful ones) of gender-sensitive programming. Although international efforts to share lessons on social protection in general are increasing (such as the International Poverty Centre's online South–South collaborative web-based platform and the Africa Platform for Social Protection),[1] as is child-sensitive social protection programming by a range of international and academic agencies,[2] initiatives to promote cross-regional and cross-agency learning on gender and social protection are more incipient.[3] However, there is considerable scope to promote linkages, knowledge exchange and lesson learning between programmes implemented by government and national and international organisations in-country as well as regionally and globally.

Policy and practice implications

With increasing international attention on results-based programming, it is vital that those designing national social protection strategies are supported to source evidence creatively on how women, men, boys and girls experience poverty and vulnerability in different ways, so that programme designers can position gender equality as central to objectives. To this end, it is essential to institutionalise gender-sensitive monitoring and evaluation indicators that draw on mixed methods (quantitative, qualitative and participatory research) approaches. Too often, however, gender-disaggregated indicators become reduced to 'sex of programme participants.' Accordingly, designers need more support to develop context-sensitive indicators that speak to the multiple levels of impact which we have discussed throughout this book – that is, individual, intra-household, intra-community and programme governance (for detailed example indicators, see Box 8.1).

Box 8.1 Monitoring and evaluation indicators for gender-sensitive social protection

Programme participation

- What percentage of programme participants are men, women, boys and girls?
- If there are gender and age differences, what explains them?
- If programmes target households, what percentage of these are female-headed and male-headed?
- Are there provisions for women living in other types of households, such as polygamous households or extended family households?

Receipt and use of programme benefits

- How many men, women, boys and girls access subsidised goods and services? If there are gender differences, what are the key reasons? Domestic/care work responsibilities? Time poverty? Socio-cultural attitudes? Lack of interest? Lack of confidence?
- In the case of cash transfers, do women get to control the use of the income?
- In the case of asset transfers, can women sell the assets and produce and keep the profits?
- In the case of pro-poor insurance, have women's differential life-cycle characteristics been reflected in how benefit levels

---

are calculated (e.g. length of employment contribution, life expectancy, etc.)?

- To what extent has involvement helped women to meet their household food provision responsibilities? (Not at all, somewhat, significantly) Healthcare uptake? Care work responsibilities?
- Have gains in children's human capital development (school enrolment and achievement, nutritional status, health status, birth registration) been equal or have there been differential gender impacts? If so, were these differences intended as part of programme affirmative action (e.g. increased transfers to promote girls' secondary education) or unintended?
- To what extent have gender-sensitive programme components been implemented (e.g. the development of time-saving community assets in public works programmes, provision of crèches, construction of health clinics rather than roads, etc.)?

Intra-household impacts

- How has participation changed gender relations, if at all? More respectful relationships? More egalitarian division of labour? More egalitarian control of assets? More egalitarian control of income? More joint decision making about and care for children? More or less intra-household tensions? Physical violence?
- Have men's and boys' attitudes about the gender division of labour changed? In what ways? Are they doing more household labour?
- How many hours do men, women, boys and girls spend – before and after participation in the programme – on domestic and care work tasks, productive tasks and community meetings?
- If there has been an increase or decrease, what explains this? Greater decision-making power within the household due to economic independence? Awareness-raising programme component?

Community-level impacts

- Has participation resulted in greater attendance of women at community meetings (e.g. to discuss the choice of community assets to be invested in) and do their voices influence decision making?
- Has participation resulted in greater interaction by women with local authorities as part of increased citizenship?
- Has participation resulted in an increase in collective action by women?

Initiatives such as those currently being promoted by the Department for International Development (DFID), the Australian Agency for International Development and the International Initiative for Impact Evaluations for undertaking systematic reviews of social protection evidence (among other sectors) could also be adapted to promote synthetic analyses of gender-relevant evidence and, in turn, to identify opportunities to strengthen gender-sensitive social protection programming.

In terms of disseminating evaluation evidence and lesson learning, the South–South Learning Platform of the UN Development Programme International Policy Centre for Inclusive Growth (IPC-IG), the Labour and Social Protection database of the World Bank[4] and the DFID-funded Chronic Poverty Research Centre/Brooks World Poverty Institute Social Assistance in Developing Countries database are all important initiatives for consolidating resources on social protection evaluation evidence. Although none of these focuses explicitly on gender dimensions, this is an initiative that UN Women, for example, in its work with the International Labour Organization Social Protection Floor initiative, could usefully support. At the national level, governments, donors and non-governmental organisations (NGOs) also need to be incentivised to share and discuss evaluation evidence among implementing partners, as well as the broader public. This could, for example, be embedded in the design of technical support packages for programme designers and implementers.[5]

Political economy dynamics

State of the evidence base

The links between gender, economic growth and development sustainability have become increasingly well recognised by mainstream development actors, but these insights have yet to gain real traction within social protection debates, policy and practice. Key constraints relate to the gendered politics of social protection, and in particular a general tendency for gender dynamics to be integrated into the so-called '3 Is' – institutions, interests and ideas – in only a partial and subordinate way. We now discuss each of these in turn.

Institutional arenas such as elections, the legislature, the judiciary and informal politics, along with social protection systems (comprising institutional arrangements and capacities, coordination mechanisms, and monitoring and evaluation systems) together shape the parameters of negotiations on the development of social protection policies and programmes. Electoral politics have played a key role in shaping social protection developments in a number of contexts, but the legislature and judiciary have been markedly less influential (with the important exceptions of India and South Africa). At the same time, the role of informal politics should not be overlooked, especially as clientelistic ways of working often overlap with local patriarchal structures and practices, reinforcing women's vulnerability. The specifics of social protection systems are also important, given that a well-designed institutional architecture can help to overcome broader governance deficits.

Actor *interests* are also a vital component of political economy dynamics. Our analysis suggests that political elites often initiate programmes to further their own institutional aims – for example, to demonstrate a commitment to a strengthened social contract between the state and the citizenry, or to promote social cohesion, especially in times of political flux – rather than to tackle gendered risks and vulnerabilities per se. Although bureaucratic implementing agencies such as ministries of social welfare often have some commitment to addressing gender inequalities, they are typically hampered by capacity and resource deficits. Donors have played a major role in shaping social protection trajectories in Africa, but have seen greater expansion of programmes where there has been strong buy-in and commitment from national governments, and to a lesser extent in Asia and Latin America. By contrast, in South Asia and Latin America, civil society has played a meaningful role in shaping social protection debates and especially a focus on citizen entitlements, but civil society efforts have been less visible – especially in terms of advocating for gender-sensitive social protection – in other parts of Asia and Africa. In the field of pro-poor insurance in particular, it is essential to recognise the influential role that the private sector is playing in expanding access to health, life and disaster insurance for marginalised social groups, including women, and the potential for increased synergies with NGO and government partners going forward. Similarly, informal insurance groups, including support from religious institutions, remain quite important for addressing idiosyncratic shocks in much of the developing world, and such actors should also be included to promote complementarities.

Finally, the divergent contours of national social protection systems reflect a wide range of *ideas* about poverty and its causes, and the purpose of social protection and state–citizen relations. In terms of the state's role in shaping gender relations, in social assistance initiatives there is widespread buy-in to supporting women in their role as mothers and as those primarily responsible for children's welfare. Generally, however, support for a more comprehensive approach to tackling gender-specific vulnerabilities has not been forthcoming, as gender relations – especially intra-household power dynamics – are often seen as a domain in which the state should not intervene. In other cases, although prevailing ideas about gender relations do not conflict with the implementation of innovations per se, a proactive approach to support a transformation of the status quo is nevertheless missing.

Policy and practice implications

Given that work on the political economy dynamics of social protection is still relatively new, and especially scarce when it comes to understanding the intersection with gender relations, it is not surprising that we have been unable to identify good practice examples where policy or programme design and implementation have been informed by a clear understanding of gendered political economy dynamics. It is, however, clearly an area worthy of much greater attention if gender-sensitive programmes are to be effectively institutionalised and sustainable beyond the pilot phase. Such efforts require that political scientists and/or political economists are included in programme design and implementation teams to help planners to think more strategically about institutional power dynamics, potential blockages and solutions. They could also help with proposing synergistic alliances among diverse actors (state, NGO, private sector, groups providing more informal social protection, religious institutions) and perhaps especially contribute to framing programme aims and approaches using context-sensitive and resonant concepts and language (so, for example, helping to dispel concerns about 'creating dependency' and instead focusing on supporting 'graduation out of poverty' and 'helping everyone contribute to the national economy'). It would entail investing in documentation not only of the technical aspects of programme design and implementation, but also of the underlying politics and negotiation processes that underpin the choice of social protection instrument, and particular implementation processes, timescales, coverage, etc. These dynamics could be explored by drawing on, for instance, key informant interviews, media content analysis and discourse analyses of programme documentation.

Moving forward

Having read our book, we hope you are now as convinced as we are that integrating a gender lens into social protection policy and programming is vital if investments are to be maximised and the resilience of women, men, girls and boys alike is to be strengthened. We hope, too, that we have made a convincing case that relatively simple and cost-effective measures can be taken to ensure social protection instruments are gender-sensitive. Given this, we are optimistic that, in ten years' time, gender will no longer be a novel aspect of social protection debates and practices.

Instead, gender-sensitive vulnerability analyses, policy and programme design, implementing processes and monitoring and evaluation tools will routinely include gender dimensions, and we will, as a result, be much wiser about the relative merits of different instruments in addressing gendered economic and social risks and vulnerabilities in low- and middle-income country contexts.

In this regard, we believe an important research agenda going forward will involve action research around initiatives to address not only human capital development and food security, but also areas such as reproductive health deficits and social vulnerabilities, including time poverty, gender-based violence, and unequal intra-household relations. This could be through direct initiatives or through programmes with complementary linkages to ensure that overlapping and reinforcing economic and social risks are tackled synergistically. Of equal importance will be more empirical investigations of the political economy drivers of and barriers to gender-sensitive social protection. Whereas the technical dimensions of gender-sensitive social protection programming are relatively straightforward, as we have highlighted, the political economy dynamics are complex and highly context-specific. They will require nuanced thinking, institutionalised cross-agency partnerships and adequately funded capacity-strengthening initiatives by policy designers, programme implementers and participants alike.

ANNEX I

Public works programmes and their gender dimensions[1]

Afghanistan

Programme: Labour-Intensive Works Programme
Operational years: 2002–2003
Government or non-government organisation: Government, CARE and local NGO (Johnson, 2004a)
Main objective: Upgrade and rehabilitate rural infrastructure in 12 provinces with high unemployment and high poppy-growing density to reduce the number of labourers working in poppy fields and out-migration and to improve rural livelihoods (Johnson, 2004a)
Rural or agricultural target: Rural, mainly agricultural (Johnson, 2004a)
Female participation: Women a stated beneficiary group, yet there is no evidence that any women were hired, and men interviewed said it was inappropriate for women to work on such schemes (Johnson, 2004a)
Nature of gender focus: No gender design features or request for gender-disaggregated data in monitoring process (Johnson, 2004a)
Key findings regarding gendered impacts: Women did not benefit directly as they did not participate, yet it is suggested they clearly benefit from the schools built as part of the programme (Johnson, 2004a)

Argentina

Programme: Programa de Jefes y Jefas de Hogar Desocupados
Operational years: Launched in 2002 and scaled back in 2006
Government or non-government organisation: Government
Main objective: The main government programme for dealing with the impact of the 2001 economic crisis by paying half of the poverty-line income for 20 hours' work in community projects
Female participation: Female participation rate was high, and increased from 60% in the beginning to almost 75% in 2005 as an unintended result of the programme design and the low wages offered
Nature of gender focus: Employment offered in close proximity to women's homes and included activities not traditionally undertaken by women, such as building and carpentry. Participants also received free childcare, adult literacy classes, child tutoring and family counselling for drug abuse and domestic violence problems. One component aimed to create employment for vulnerable women, particularly household heads
Key findings regarding gendered impacts: Targeted household heads with children, but the average participant was female, not heading a household, married and with 8 years of schooling. Women's high participation rate was attributed to the type of work offered, such as work in community kitchens, and to the fact that women were allowed to participate while their husbands tried to find private-sector employment. The programme also changed the meaning of work by remunerating family care and community participation (Devereux and Solomon, 2006)

Bangladesh

Programme: Food for Work

Government or non-government organisation: Government with donor support

Main objective: Creation and maintenance of rural infrastructure and provision of employment to the rural poor

Rural or agricultural target: Rural, not necessarily agricultural

Female participation: Limited female participation

Key findings regarding gendered impacts: Although the poor accounted for 74% of participants, poor women were not able to benefit much, and were found to be confined to rural roadside projects, probably because these were the most accessible (Kabeer, 2008)

Programme: Rural Maintenance Programme

Operational years: Introduced in 1986; in 2006, CARE handed it over to the government

Government or non-government organisation: CARE Bangladesh and the Local Government Engineering Department

Main objective: Infrastructure maintenance and income provision for the poor through cash payments

Rural or agricultural target: Two components: construction (for both men and women) and tree plantation and maintenance (for women only)

Female participation: An average of 60,000 destitute women participated per year. A 1986 evaluation found that 89% of participants were divorced, deserted or widowed and supported on average 3.5 dependants; most suffered from food deficits (Kabeer, 2008)

Nature of gender focus: Targeted destitute rural women to work on maintenance of rural earthen roads for 4 years. The work was physically demanding, so age criteria were adopted (18–35 years) (Kabeer, 2008). Women could be supervisors and received equal pay for comparable work; those employed in maintenance and tree plantation were offered training and social development inputs on income generation. Over time, new components were added to offer women more skills and turn them into micro-entrepreneurs able to survive after the end of the programme (Kabeer, 2008)

Key findings regarding gendered impacts: Introduced bank accounts for poor female participants, facilitated their savings behaviour and enabled them to access formal financial institutions. Also offered them the opportunity to negotiate and manage activities (Devereux and Solomon, 2006). The programme improved women's self-perception and promoted their independence and social inclusion. Around 60% of graduates did not return to poverty, 75% of graduates were earning the same wages that they had on the project, and 57% became involved in other associations and local government activities; most were also able to offer three meals a day to their families (Kabeer, 2008)

Benin

Programme: *Agence de Financement des Intitiativesde Base* programme of the Benin Social Fund

Government or non-government organisation: Numerous NGOs involved

Nature of gender focus: 15 components in five regions, both infrastructure and microcredit. Infrastructure projects had management committees with five to seven members, of whom one had to be female. Only two of the components were headed by women; in the rest, women usually had the role of the treasurer (Kabeer, 2008)

Key findings regarding gendered impacts: Female participation in the committees was limited, as women's poor literacy was an obstacle, along with the lack of any training option; moreover, women were a minority in the committees and, even when they did speak, they were not usually heard (Kabeer, 2008)

Bolivia

Programme: Emergency Social Fund
Operational years: Started in 1986
Government or non-government organisation: Government and NGO
Main objective: Aimed to employ industry workers and create large infrastructure
Female participation: A focus on heavy construction resulted in a very low female participation rate
Key findings regarding gendered impacts: Extensive use of subcontractors; proposals chosen created jobs in male-dominated heavy construction sector, and thus women accounted for only 1% of beneficiaries (Kabeer, 2008)

Botswana

Programme: Labour-Based Relief Programme and Labour-Intensive Rural Public Works Programme
Operational years: Mid-1980s and 1990s
Government or non-government organisation: Government
Main objective: To provide employment after the 1980s droughts
Rural or agricultural target: Rural, not necessarily agricultural
Female participation: Female participation rate was high, between 60% and 70% of total employment
Nature of gender focus: Women were allowed time off for breast-feeding without pay cuts. Women could be programme supervisors

Burkina Faso

Programme: Special Public Works Programme
Operational years: Started in 1981
Main objective: Creation of employment opportunities and construction of infrastructure; increase in employment opportunities of workers as a result of their acquired skills (Dejardin, 1996)
Female participation: Female participation rate varied considerably between villages at the beginning, with female construction workers being largely under 30 years old and unmarried – that is, with fewer responsibilities (Dejardin, 1996)
Key findings regarding gendered impacts: Women from larger households were more likely to work in infrastructure projects, as they either had other female members to take care of household tasks or used part of their earnings to pay someone else to do so. Women were engaged mainly in the collection and transport of sand and gravel, and in soil compaction, yet training sessions enabled some of them to engage in making cement blocks, a traditionally male job. High female participation rate was largely the result of small women's associations engaged in income-generating activities prior to the programme; when the programme started, infrastructure work was incorporated in the group activities. These associations enabled women to take interest in and benefit from most of the employment opportunities offered. In addition, women contributed part of their earnings to funds for a common purpose (Dejardin, 1996)

Burundi
Programme: Special Public Works Programme
Operational years: Started in 1979
Main objective: Employment creation and income generation to tackle rural unemployment and poverty; also creation and maintenance of rural infrastructure to improve living conditions and reduce environmental degradation (Dejardin, 1996)
Rural or agricultural target: Rural, focusing on physical, and agricultural social infrastructure (Dejardin, 1996)
Female participation: Women's participation rate increased over time, and between 1989 and 1991 reached an average of 57.5% in the afforestation component of the programme (Dejardin, 1996)
Key findings regarding gendered impacts: Young and unmarried women who did not participate were more likely to be interested in doing so than married women because they had fewer care responsibilities. In Ruyigi province, with high unemployment, men exerted pressure on women not to compete for jobs (Dejardin, 1996)

Chile
Programme: Programa de Empleo Mínimo
Operational years: Started in 1975 and remained in operation for over a decade (1975–1987)
Government or non-government organisation: Government
Main objective: Used as a subsidy for the unemployed (30% in 1982), and offered part-time work at rates lower than the minimum wage; in the course of time, the real value of wages declined, although working hours increased (Kabeer, 2008)
Female participation: Female participation rate increased from 35.6% in 1980 to 52.3% in 1982 and 72.6% in 1987; a high percentage of these women were not previously economically active, and within the programme were employed largely in cleaning services in government schools and hospitals (Kabeer, 2008)
Key findings regarding gendered impacts: Large numbers of women were able to work for the first time, and it is likely that many stayed in the workforce after the end of the programme. Yet the jobs offered had little value, and stigmatised the participants (Kabeer, 2008)

Programme: Programa de Ocupación para Jefes de Hogar
Operational years: Started in 1982
Government or non-government organisation: Government
Main objective: Increased female participation in the Programa de Empleo Minimo did not meet with governmental approval due to traditional attitudes that women would be better off staying at home and looking after their children. Thus this second programme was developed with the aim to reduce unemployment and eliminate the former programme's 'deficiencies with regard to the target population' as it offered employment on infrastructure projects only to household heads with good work experience as it was expected that predominantly men would be able to comply with such a condition (Kabeer 2008).
Female participation: Only 28% of participants were women; many were household heads. Interviews with local authorities suggested that 80–85% of them were single mothers (Kabeer, 2008)
Key findings regarding gendered impacts: The programme helped to break the poverty cycle among single mothers with children, as it provided them with

enough money to address food and subsistence needs without relying on a partner. In fact both programmes embodied the gender ideology of the Chilean conservative military regime of the time, and no effort was made to address the gender pay gap; the first programme also segregated women as inferior labourers (Kabeer, 2008)

El Salvador

Programme: Fondo de Inversión Social
Operational years: Started in 1989
Government or non-government organisation: Government and NGOs
Female participation: Women were explicitly targeted
Nature of gender focus: Main focus was mothers and women in poor areas affected by the civil war, so there was close collaboration with community-based groups and NGOs working with women

Ethiopia

Programme: Productive Safety Net Programme
Operational years: Launched in 2005
Government or non-government organisation: Government
Main objective: To smooth consumption, prevent household assets' depletion and create community assets through public works in return for food and cash transfers (Jones et al., 2010b)
Rural or agricultural target: Rural, with a focus on agriculture and food security (Jones et al., 2010b)
Female participation: Around 40% of participants are women, but there are regional variations (Jones et al., 2010b)
Nature of gender focus: Design recognises that women and men have different physical capacities, women have a greater work burden, women with small children need special provisions in order to work, and female-headed households are more labour-poor. Thus there are provisions for equal wages for men and women, direct support for pregnant and lactating women, childcare facilities at worksites, flexible working hours, women's equal representation on committees, and the use of public works to create assets that reduce women's time poverty and to cultivate female-headed households' land (Jones et al., 2010b)
Key findings regarding gendered impacts: Has increased female participation in the formal economy; offered women access to better remunerated and potentially less exploitative and abusive types of work, enabled women to contribute to household needs and improve the nutrition, health and education of members, increased women's sense of security and their social capital, and enabled them to access credit and loans and retain their assets. Yet payment is low, flexible working hours and childcare facilities have been offered in very few cases, women's representation on committees has varied and not been well enforced, and there are problems with gender capacity building and monitoring (Jones et al., 2010b)

Programme: Programme of the Ethiopian Social Rehabilitation and Development Fund
Operational years: 1990s
Government or non-government organisation: Government
Main objective: To provide poor rural communities with the necessary assets and services to improve their lives (Kabeer, 2008)
Rural or agricultural target: Rural

Key findings regarding gendered impacts: Women were included on the staff from the start, women's groups were supported to submit proposals, gender-disaggregated data were collected, the impact of projects on women was facilitated through a checklist given to project managers, and gender assessments were encouraged (Kabeer, 2008)

Ghana
Programme: Programme of Action to Mitigate the Social Costs of Adjustment
Operational years: Started in 1988
Government or non-government organisation: Government
Main objective: To tackle poverty as a result of adjustment measures
Nature of gender focus: Designed to target women and other vulnerable groups specifically, but donor pressures and urban lobbying meant that this was not realised

Honduras
Programme: Fondo Hondureño de Inversión Social
Operational years: 1990–1993
Female participation: Limited female participation
Nature of gender focus: In its second phase, also offered a special project of training and employment for women to promote their presence in traditionally male construction work. It also included capacity building of men to make them accept female involvement (Kabeer, 2008)
Key findings regarding gendered impacts: Around 75% of 137,000 jobs went to men. An evaluation found that, despite efforts, women were paid less for the same work in almost half of the projects, and in some cases were not even paid the minimum wage (Kabeer, 2008)

India
Programme: Mahatma Gandhi National Rural Employment Guarantee Scheme
Operational years: Started in 2006
Government or non-government organisation: Government
Main objective: To guarantee 100 days of unskilled manual work to all poor rural households to increase employment, improve agricultural productivity, enhance livelihood security and reduce poverty (Holmes et al., 2010)
Rural or agricultural target: Rural
Female participation: In 2009–2010, over 48% of all participants were women, but there are considerable state and regional variations (Sudarshan, 2011)
Nature of gender focus: Programme design has gender features: at least 33% of employment to be offered to women, equal wages for both men and women, work to be provided within 5 km of the participant's residence, if more than five children below the age of 6 years are present at the worksite then childcare facilities to be provided, the option for individual bank accounts for women, female worksite facilitators, and inclusion of female representatives in the *gram sabha*, social audits and councils (Holmes et al., 2010)
Key findings regarding gendered impacts: Women have received equal wages and increased their household contribution, and thus improved their status and even their decision-making power in a few cases; they have also increased their social capital. Yet women have often received fewer than 100 days and have not been involved in all types of work because of gendered stereotypes

of appropriate work, single women have often been excluded, childcare facilities are not offered in most cases and thus many women with young children have been unable to participate or had to leave them with older daughters or in-laws, and women have been less likely to participate in local committees and social audits (Holmes et al., 2010)

Programme: Maharashtra Employment Guarantee Scheme
Operational years: Started in 1972/3
Government or non-government organisation: Government
Main objective: To guarantee unskilled manual work in the state of Maharashtra in response to drought
Rural or agricultural target: Rural, primarily agricultural works
Female participation: Female participation increased over time, from 41% in 1979 to reach 53% in 1987; other estimations raise it to 64% (Devereux and Solomon, 2006)
Nature of gender focus: Employment provided within 8 miles of participants' villages, childcare facilities to be provided at worksites, and men and women to be paid at the same piece rate (Kabeer, 2008)
Key findings regarding gendered impacts: Gender targeting positively assessed as large numbers of participants were young female agricultural workers who were poorly educated, were household heads and came from poor households. Yet they constituted only 9% of the female wage labour force. Women from lower castes were more likely to participate; female household heads were also more likely to participate compared with male household heads, but inadequate provision of childcare facilities made it less likely for mothers with young children to benefit. However, the overall impact was regarded as positive as women's self-confidence increased and their status within the family was enhanced (Devereux and Solomon, 2006). Although there was no official wage discrimination, in practice women were often assigned different tasks and thus earned less (Kabeer, 2008)

Programme: *Jawahar Rozgar Yojana*, restructured and renamed *Jawahar Gram Samridhi Yojana*
Operational years: Started in 1989
Government or non-government organisation: Government
Main objective: To guarantee rural work throughout India and, from 1993, particularly in backward districts
Rural or agricultural target: Rural, primarily community agricultural works
Female participation: Female participation rate was only 20% (Devereux and Solomon, 2006)
Nature of gender focus: There was a provision for 30% of employment opportunities to be offered to women, and for no gender wage discrimination
Key findings regarding gendered impacts: Despite provisions, female participation was low, and in some states there was some discrimination in the average daily wages paid to male and female workers (Devereux and Solomon, 2006)

Indonesia
Programme: *Padat Karya*
Operational years: Launched in 1998
Government or non-government organisation: Government
Main objective: Consisted of a series of emergency job creation projects to build infrastructure as a response to the financial crisis

Rural or agricultural target: Labour-intensive small-scale village-based infrastructure and public works in over 300 districts

Female participation: Low female participation rate (19%)

Nature of gender focus: Heavy physical labour demanded in most projects discouraged women's participation; moreover, household heads were targeted, which by definition in Indonesia excluded women

Key findings regarding gendered impacts: A 1998 assessment found six main weaknesses: failure to reach women was one of them (Devereux and Solomon, 2006)

Malawi

Programme: Work for Food

Operational years: Late 1990s

Government or non-government organisation: Implemented by World Food Programme

Female participation: Very high female participation rate due to male preference for Malawi Social Action Fund cash wages

Key findings regarding gendered impacts: High female participation rate was not the result of women's preference for food payments, enabling them to better feed their families, but largely because men considered such payments socially stigmatising and monopolised cash for work opportunities (Devereux and Solomon, 2006)

Programme: Malawi Social Action Fund

Female participation: Female participation rate varied from 42% in road rehabilitation contracts to only 27% in bridge work contracts

Nature of gender focus: Minimum 40% gender target for employment projects. Women also had to participate in project management committees, representing at least 30% of their members; as members, they received training in leadership, book-keeping, accounting and other skills (Kabeer, 2008)

Key findings regarding gendered impacts: Women were well represented in water committees and maternity clinics but less so in education (26%) and roads committees (20%). Only a few headed committees, and many faced problems such as domestic responsibilities, lack of experience in public forums, lack of authority and resistance from husbands, which undermined their participation (Kabeer, 2008)

Programme: A two-year pilot road maintenance programme in two districts

Operational years: 1999–2002

Government or non-government organisation: CARE

Main objective: Promotion of rural growth by maintaining feeder roads and promotion of household security, especially among extremely poor women (Kabeer, 2008)

Rural or agricultural target: Rural

Nature of gender focus: Two components: eight small-scale community contractors were established for complex road maintenance activities, and 1,600 contract associations made up of 10 women were created to undertake maintenance of feeder roads. One woman was chosen and provided with training and support to establish a group economic activity. A minimum wage was offered, and one-third of it was retained as part of a compulsory savings scheme (Kabeer, 2008)

Key findings regarding gendered impacts: Women whose husbands became involved in road maintenance had to take over their work on the farm, and their households overall did not benefit much. Yet women who were involved in contract associations reported increased food security, investment in productive assets, improvements in their economic situation and greater involvement in community affairs; however, some also faced increased domestic violence and community jealousy. An evaluation 3 years after completion found that half of the participants continued to save and thus were able to cope better with droughts and other emergencies (Kabeer, 2008)

Nepal
Programme: Dhaulagiri Irrigation Development Project
Operational years: Started in 1989
Government or non-government organisation: Government with funding from International Labour Organization, World Food Programme and UN Development Programme (Lokollo, 1999)
Main objective: To provide reliable irrigation water to small-scale farmers and thus increase food production and tackle poverty
Rural or agricultural target: Agricultural
Female participation: Around 3,000 women trained by 1999 (Lokollo, 1999). Women participants largely from landless ethnic groups, occupational castes and families living on marginal lands (Dejardin, 1996)
Nature of gender focus: Women's savings groups were created and provided with training (Lokollo, 1999)
Key findings regarding gendered impacts: Use of piece work ensured women were paid at the same rates as men. By 1999, there were 90 female savings groups and they proved successful in improving living standards and making families self-reliant and less vulnerable (Lokollo, 1999)

Peru
Programme: Programade Apoyo de Ingreso Temporal
Operational years: 1985–1990
Main objective: Implemented in Lima's shanty towns to enable people to cope with the economic crisis, offered work on a 3-month basis to both men and women aged 16–55 years with or without documents, underemployed and unemployed and living in marginal urban or rural neighbourhoods; only one member per family was allowed to apply, and families had to live close to the workplace (Kabeer, 2008)
Rural or agricultural target: Urban and rural
Female participation: Women constituted 76% of the 25,000 monthly participants in 1985 and 84% of 60,000 participants in 1986 (Kabeer, 2008)
Nature of gender focus: Explicitly aimed to provide at least 30% of jobs to women. Moreover, as it was designed and promoted as a community development programme, implemented by local organisations, it targeted women who were unpaid or volunteer workers in community development activities, and gave them the opportunity to substitute their unpaid work with paid work. In addition, it did not require any training, had flexible working hours, was located close to their homes and allowed them to bring their children to work. Childcare facilities were organised in community centres (Kabeer, 2008)
Key findings regarding gendered impacts: Jobs were originally designed for men, so women had to carry very heavy workloads or engage in tasks such as burning rubbish with their babies on their backs. Changes took place over time, and women undertook different types of work to men. Wages were very low,

and this is one reason why more women than men were attracted, not paying so much attention to the low wages and the stigma attached to a poverty programme. These women were also poorer and less well educated than men. Thus 75–80% of women aged 20–40 years benefited, with 33% of them economically inactive before the programme; 57% of these women were heads of families, and this percentage increased to 73% in 1986. Many found the programme important as it offered regular paid work, was located near home, had childcare facilities, and improved their income and family nutrition (Kabeer, 2008)

Rwanda

Programme: Special Public Works Programme

Operational years: Started in 1980

Main objective: Employment creation and income generation along with creation and maintenance of rural infrastructure

Rural or agricultural target: Rural with three main components: agricultural infrastructure to reduce degradation of the environment, infrastructure such as roads, and training of artisans in brick making and installation of better ovens (Dejardin, 1996)

Female participation: Female participation varied, and women were employed largely in afforestation and tree nurseries (Dejardin, 1996)

Key findings regarding gendered impacts: Over 75% of women interviewed were interested in taking part, regardless of age (excluding women aged over 60 years), marital status and children, but only 20% considered working throughout the year or for several days a week. Indeed, the majority of those employed were less than 30 years old and unmarried. In some cases, there were efforts to make recruitment more gender-sensitive. The normal procedure of recruitment relied on local authorities who preferred to employ men, taxpayers and members of the ruling party; thus women were excluded. However, intensive information campaigns, a clear message that women were welcome and involvement of communities increased women's turnout and recruitment (Dejardin, 1996)

Senegal

Programme: Agenced' Exécution des Travauxd' Intérêt Public

Operational years: Launched in 1989

Government or non-government organisation: Government

Main objective: Construction of labour-intensive infrastructure projects in response to previous civil unrest to adjustment measures (Kabeer, 2008)

Rural or agricultural target: Largely urban. Expanded into rural areas in the mid-1990s (van der Lugt and Kuby, 1997)

Female participation: Limited female participation, as jobs were given largely to unskilled young men (Kabeer, 2008)

Nature of gender focus: In the mid-1990s began managing programmes for female literacy (van der Lugt and Kuby, 1997)

Key findings regarding gendered impacts: Women were unable to benefit much. A study argued that the focus on municipal governments and failure to work with NGOs with links with the poor resulted in a failure to reach the poor and women who in rural areas had little or no contact with the political system, were less literate and did not have access to adequate information (Kabeer, 2008)

South Africa
Programme: Expanded Public Works Programme
Operational years: Started in 2004
Government or non-government organisation: Government
Main objective: A nationwide programme aimed to create temporary employment and tackle high poverty and unemployment rates, to develop the skills of the unemployed through training and increase their employability, and to provide basic social services and infrastructure to poor communities (Devereux and Solomon, 2006)
Rural or agricultural target: Rural
Female participation: In the first year, women benefited from 38% of employment opportunities (Devereux and Solomon, 2006)
Nature of gender focus: The guidelines initially included a specific target of 60% female participation, but this was later amended to at least 40%. Lack of a formal selection process with standard criteria led to variations between areas (Devereux and Solomon, 2006)

Programme: Gundo Lashu Programme in Limpopo
Operational years: Started in 2000
Government or non-government organisation: Government
Main objective: To improve the rural livelihoods through labour-intensive employment and transferring skills (McCord, 2004)
Rural or agricultural target: Rural
Female participation: Gender-balanced, with the majority of workers young, less 'poor' and better educated than in KwaZulu-Natal (McCord, 2004)
Nature of gender focus: Offered employment for from less than 1 to 4 months in road construction, and had a specific quota for 60% female participation (McCord, 2004)

Programme: Zibambele Programme in KwaZulu-Natal
Operational years: Started in 2000
Government or non-government organisation: Government
Main objective: Creation of sustainable job opportunities for the rural poor through maintenance of rural roads (McCord, 2004)
Rural or agricultural target: Rural
Female participation: The vast majority of participants were women, older, poorer, less well educated and more likely to be members of female-headed households (McCord, 2004)
Nature of gender focus: Offered flexible part-time employment (60 hours a month) on 12-month, annually renewable contracts. Targeted the poorest and membership of female-headed households was used as a secondary criterion. Contracts were offered to households, not individuals, allowing work to be shared (McCord, 2004)
Key findings regarding gendered impacts: Women were able to participate due to flexible working hours, allowing them to combine their participation with household and other responsibilities. Household expenditures on food and education increased, women's social capital grew, and activities such as begging for food or wearing ragged clothes declined (McCord, 2004)

Sri Lanka
Programme: National Housing Development Authority
Government or non-government organisation: Government

Main objective: Part of government's urban housing policy for building houses
and amenities such as wells and roads in low-income settlements through
engaging the whole community
Key findings regarding gendered impacts: Through community development councils, women were able to organise and supervise construction work

Sudan
Programme: Special Public Works Programme
Operational years: Started in 1988
Government or non-government organisation: Government with support from UN
Development Programme, US Agency for International Development and Italy
(Dejardin, 1996)
Main objective: Creation of employment opportunities and rural infrastructure
to improve living standards and also local capacities to plan and manage such a
programme (Dejardin, 1996)
Rural or agricultural target: Rural
Female participation: Married women constituted a major number of female
construction workers. Yet wage work for women was a low-status activity
in North Kordofan, and construction there was considered to be a male job
(Dejardin, 1996)
Key findings regarding gendered impacts: Participation of women in the programme
in North Kordofan occurred gradually, as manual wage labour and participation
in public meetings for women were socially unacceptable, especially among
the better-off to which village leaders belonged, and as women's participation
was believed to slow down the work and increase costs. Project staff allowed
sufficient time and used a step-by-step approach by involving women gradually
in construction of a school, rainwater basins and wells. A gender differentiation
(light and heavy) and allocation of tasks was introduced, and the need for gender collaboration was emphasised and demonstrated. Finally, women in need of
paid work were involved and were also represented in village sub-committees
(Dejardin, 1996)

Tanzania
Programme: Several public works programmes
Female participation: In two public works programmes between 20% and 25% of
unmarried participants were single mothers (Kabeer, 2008)
Key findings regarding gendered impacts: The reason put forward by non-partici-
pating women, although they wanted to be able to participate, was time poverty. Based on other studies, in the area of Ruvuma, low agricultural incomes
and scarce employment opportunities resulted in 'total non-participation' of
women in road construction projects, due to high male demand. Studies in
other regions showed that, when women had alternative sources of work, they
were less likely to participate in rural road maintenance projects or only did so
for short periods of time to cover specific needs; when such alternatives did not
exist, especially for poor divorced women with children and elderly parents,
jobs were seen as low status but their only source of income (Kabeer, 2008)

Uganda
Programme: Various rural public works programmes in Western Region
Rural or agricultural target: Rural, not necessarily agricultural

Female participation: Limited women's representation and participation in decision making and project selection

Zambia

Programme: Micro-Project Unity
Operational years: Started in 1991
Government or non-government organisation: Government
Main objective: To provide jobs for the poor by renovating existing infrastructure
Rural or agricultural target: Rural, with nearly half of all projects in remote areas, but they mainly included school, clinic and road rehabilitation (Kamanga, 1998)
Nature of gender focus: Tasks were categorised as light, moderate and heavy; men and women worked together in groups, but men were allocated the heavier tasks and women the lighter ones. Women usually participated in the unskilled work of the project cycle, but found it difficult to get as involved as men in the decision making. The programme later required women to represent 50% of committee members (Kamanga, 1998)
Key findings regarding gendered impacts: Women took the lighter tasks such as head loading baskets of rocks from the quarry to the roadside, while men performed heavier tasks such as breaking stones. Yet women still had to subcontract men for some tasks in exchange for 50% of their wage. Construction and rehabilitation of roads reduced travel distances, which benefited women in particular (Kamanga, 1998)

Programme: Food for Work
Main objective: Creation of domestic infrastructure in poor urban areas and employment generation for local residents (Kabeer, 2008)
Female participation: Around 90% of workers were women living close to the worksites, as men refused to work for food (Kabeer, 2008)
Key findings regarding gendered impacts: Supported vulnerable female-headed households and provided them with food supplements, while also creating much-needed infrastructure, such as pit latrines (Kabeer, 2008)

Zimbabwe

Programme: Rural Transport Study
Operational years: Started in 1997
Government or non-government organisation: Government
Main objective: To reduce burdens associated with travel and transport costs, particularly for women in two districts
Rural or agricultural target: Rural, with a focus on water collection
Nature of gender focus: Women participated in the selection of specific interventions, such as footbridges, footpaths and bore hole construction, given their particular travel needs
Key findings regarding gendered impacts: The interventions selected had direct positive results for women by enhancing their access and reducing their travelling time for collecting water

Source: All data used, except where noted otherwise, are from Antonopoulos (2007).

ANNEX 2

Examples of gendered impacts of key social protection instruments at individual, intra-household and community levels

Cash transfers (CTs)

Evidence of impact at the individual level:

Increased girls' school attendance:

- Impact evaluations of Mexico's *Oportunidades* show increases in girls' school enrolment rates of 0.96% to 1.45% for primary school, and 7.2% to 9.3% for secondary school (Schultz, 2000)
- Concurrently, the likelihood of female child labour decreased by 15%, as girls reduced their domestic activities to focus on their schooling (Kabeer, 2008)
- Although universal school access has yet to be realised in Peru, the *Juntos* conditional cash transfer (CCT) scheme has had positive impacts in terms of school enrolment and the transition from primary to secondary school, particularly among girls, alongside broader improvements in literacy (Alcázar, 2008)
- In Malawi, an evaluation of the World Bank's Zomba CT programme found that within the first year, re-enrolment of girls who had dropped out increased by two and a half times, while dropout rates among those in school fell from 11% to 6%. Higher amounts paid directly to girls but with conditions attached resulted in considerably improved school attendance and progress: for each $1 transferred, the likelihood of dropping out was reduced by 1.3 percentage points (Baird et al., 2009a)
- Additional cash incentives provided by Turkey's Social Risk Mitigation Project (SRMP) to households sending girls to secondary school increased the total enrolment rate by 10.7% (Ahmed et al., 2007)

Increased women's participation in labour markets:

- Among *Bolsa Familia* adult beneficiaries in Brazil, overall labour market participation increased by 2.6% compared with non-beneficiaries, and women's participation was 4.3% higher than that of their male counterparts (Soares and Silva, 2010)
- Colombia's CT programme also saw an increase in female urban employment (Econometria, 2006, cited in Soares and Silva, 2010)

Women's empowerment and knowledge:

- Qualitative reviews of Chile's *Solidario* programme show that 60% of women feel more empowered as a result of its family support component. Participants reported increased confidence in themselves as individuals, not only as wives or mothers, to leave the domestic sphere and move into public spaces, changing their life circumstances (Larrañaga et al., 2009, cited in Soares and Silva, 2010)

- Women beneficiaries also reported increased knowledge of basic nutrition as a result of messaging from *Juntos* promoters. This has in turn contributed to greater food consumption and higher nutritional-value caloric consumption among beneficiary households (Perova and Vakis, 2009)

Greater decision-making power for women:

- In Peru, women are the primary decision makers when it comes to spending the *Juntos* transfers. Training sessions provided by the scheme cover family planning, giving women a greater say in decisions about their reproductive health (Vargas, 2010).
- Similar results have been observed in Ecuador's *Bono de Desarrollo Humano* (BDH) programme, where beneficiary women reported increased ability to contribute to family expenses, in turn improving their relationship with their husband, and increasing their self-confidence (Molyneux and Thomson, 2011)
- Women beneficiaries of the *Red de Protección Social* in Nicaragua, and the Bourse Maman CCT in Mali, reported a new-found authority in their family as a result of controlling how to spend the transfer (Adato and Roopnaraine, 2010; Pereznieto and Diallo, 2009). However, such gains are not universal. Evidence from Indonesia's CCT shows little increase in women's household bargaining power (Bloom, 2009b; Sederlof, 2008)

Greater physical mobility of women:

- In Peru, changes in women's daily routines introduced by the *Juntos* programme are helping to overcome traditional barriers to free movement within and outside their community. Attending *Juntos* meetings and training sessions, and withdrawing transfers from the National Bank, has given many women their first opportunity to travel to an urban area (Vargas, 2010)

Increased access to maternal and child health services:

- In Peru, *Juntos* beneficiaries increased their demand for preventive health services for children under five and women and girls of childbearing age (Perova and Vakis, 2009). In the first year, child immunisation (0–12 months) increased by 30%, antenatal and postnatal consultations rose by 65% and home births declined (Jones et al., 2008)
- In Turkey, the SRMP programme encouraged pregnant women to attend pre-birth hostels and promoted hospital deliveries. This, along with broader investment in health service quality, contributed to reducing maternal mortality rates from 70 per 100,000 live births in 2000 to 19.8 per 100,000 in 2009 (Prata et al., 2010)
- India's *Janani Suraksha Yojana,* a CCT scheme, increased the number of assisted deliveries in the presence of a skilled attendant by 36% (Lim et al., 2010, cited in World Bank, 2011b)

Awareness of rights:

- CT programme workshops and training sessions have also empowered women.

Positive impact on women's decision-making power through ROSCAs:

- Participation in ROSCAs offers women the chance to increase their decision-making power and economic independence within the household. Kenyan women, for example, cite the importance of ROSCAs as a saving mechanism, as this allows them to prevent their husbands from accessing the money (Anderson and Baland, 2002; Ardener and Burman, 1995)
- In Malaysia, women similarly reported that ROSCAs allow them to prioritise savings for family emergencies and consumer goods, albeit with their husbands' knowledge and approval (Satkunasingam and Shanmuga, 2006)

Positive impacts of micro-health insurance in reducing women's catastrophic health expenditures:

- In Eritrea, 25% of ekub members note that these informal social security groups provide contingency funds in times of crisis to cover major health-care costs (Habtom and Ruys, 2007)

Evidence of impact at the household and intra-household level:

Reduced household poverty and exposure to risk:

- In Ghana and Brazil, beneficiary families of the LEAP and *Bolsa Familia* programmes are often viewed by community members as newly 'reliable consumers' who can be counted on to repay loans and help boost local markets (Amuzu et al., 2010; Suarez and Libardoni, 2008, cited in Soaresand Silva, 2010)
- In Peru, *Juntos* transfers represent up to 10% of women's daily wages. Beneficiaries report that this helps to cushion them against agricultural vulnerabilities resulting from climate change – shocks which disproportionally affect single-parent households (whether male- or female-headed).
- Beneficiaries of Ghana's Livelihood Empowerment Against Poverty (LEAP) programme reported similar increases in household security. The cash transfers have given them some protection from shocks such as price rises and crop destruction. Recipients have used the grants to pay into the National Health Insurance scheme, and to buy school supplies and essential food, although the small size of the grant has limited their ability to invest in these areas. LEAP social welfare officers encourage recipients to use the cash to buy nutritional foods and pay for schooling and healthcare (Amuzu et al., 2010; Department for International Development, 2011; Fiszbein and Schady, 2009)

Mixed impacts on intra-household violence:

- Some schemes have been linked with unintended increases in household violence. In Mexico, for instance, receipt of cash transfers led to short-term increases in domestic violence between partners (World Bank, 2011a). However, recognising this danger, other programmes were proactive in designing mechanisms to discourage domestic violence, such as those in Brazil, Colombia, Peru and Chile (World Bank, 2011a)
- Interventions by *Juntos* facilitators in Peru have helped to reduce violence in Los Morochucos and Chiara by addressing the issue in meetings. Public and private institutions, such as the Municipal Ombuds person for Children and Adolescents and the Women's Emergency Centre, and several local NGOs,

also use *Juntos* meetings to address issues relating to domestic violence (Vargas, 2010)

Changes in gender division of labour:

*   *Juntos* beneficiaries in Peru reported greater equity in the division of care responsibilities between younger couples, with men reporting more involvement in childcare and domestic chores while women attended programme meetings (Alcázar, 2009). Men also reported less shame in taking on 'women's tasks', although overall, male participation in the programme remains limited (Vargas, 2010)

Evidence of impact at the community level:

Participation in public meetings and community activities:

*   In Nicaragua, women reported that attending CT workshops enabled them to share experiences and voices with other women in public. In Peru, women attending *Juntos* meetings are encouraged to participate and lead at the community level, and have improved their ability to speak in public (Vargas, 2010)

Social capital development:

*   Qualitative data suggest that Ghana's LEAP programme has enhanced beneficiaries' capacity to contribute to community projects, potentially increased social cohesion and networking via regular community meetings, and enhanced confidence in the government to help individual communities. LEAP also encourages equal participation of women in local governance structures. Although women's participation in these structures has remained modest, they nonetheless reflect new opportunities for women's representation in and ownership of the programme (Amuzu et al., 2010)
*   Peru's *Juntos* programme also gives beneficiary women opportunities to engage with each other and with institutions and local authorities (Vargas, 2010)

Asset transfers

Evidence of impact at the individual level:

Gains in women's empowerment:

*   Women beneficiaries of Bangladesh's Challenging the Frontier of Poverty Reduction (CFPR) asset programme reported greater confidence and knowledge after attending training sessions. Women reported that asset ownership increased their general confidence, while economic training improved the skills they needed to lift their households out of poverty. They also reported greater respect from their family members since they had become beneficiaries, and a new-found ability to contribute to small (and sometimes larger) household purchases or investments (Building Resources Across Communities, 2009)

Evidence of impact at the household level:

Reduced household poverty and exposure to risk:

*   First-phase evaluations of beneficiary households in Bangladesh's CFPR programme show significant improvements to physical, financial, human,

natural and social indicators, with the greatest gains in financial assets. Income generation from assets has proved a reliable base from which households have been able to begin diversifying their livelihood strategies (Rabbani et al., 2006). The programme has also helped to smooth household income during seasonal shocks. Households spent their new-found income generated from the assets on immediate consumption needs, health and education, child nutrition, home improvements and small savings. Many households also reinvest their income – a strategy aided by BRAC loans to CFPR beneficiaries (Holmes et al., 2010)

Evidence of impact at the community level:

Enhanced social capital development for women:

- In Bangladesh, the CFPR asset transfer programme has encouraged new social networks among women, their neighbours, BRAC staff, and members of the village reduction committee. Women and their families report receiving greater respect from community members, greater inclusion in community occasions, and more opportunities to participate and speak in public meetings as a result of their participation in the programme. Poorer households, however, remain marginalised in general community meetings, and women's inclusion in community events remains limited as a whole (Holmes et al., 2010)

Public works

Evidence of impact at the individual level:

Mixed impact on improving wage equity:

- In Ethiopia, men's labour remains more highly valued in terms of wages and perceptions of productivity. Some work sites are forced to offer higher payments to men to secure their participation. In some areas, such as Seedama in Tigray, men occasionally receive 4 days' payment for 1 day's work to entice them to take part in PWPs (Jones et al., 2010b)
- India's (Mahatma Gandhi National Rural Employment Guarantee Scheme) MGNREGS has improved overall wage equity, but results by state remain highly variable. Emerging evidence also shows that wage differentials have actually risen in several states (Shah et al., 2010, cited in Pellissery and Jalan, 2011)

  Wage discrimination is still common; women (particularly single women involved in PWPs otherwise dependent on family-based couples working together) are often forced to work longer hours for less pay or the minimum wage (Gupta, 2009). Moreover, barriers related to high rates of illiteracy among poor women and entrenched norms regarding the gender division of labour continue to limit women's access to workdays under the scheme (Khera and Nayak, 2009b; Samarthan Centre for Development Support, 2007)

Limited impact on improving women's participation in decision making:

- Evidence from Ethiopia's PSNP shows that modest improvements have been reported by some respondents in terms of the respect husbands show to their wives, and men's perceptions of women's work capabilities (Jones et al., 2010b). However, the programme has failed to address women's unequal decision-making power within male-headed households, and may even have reinforced gendered notions of work regarding food security and agriculture (Jones et al, 2010b).

- In India, although positive changes have been linked to women's access to MGNREGS income through their own bank accounts, the large number of bank accounts opened in men's names only or in joint names suggests otherwise

Limited impact on reducing women's time poverty:

- The PW component of Ethiopia's PSNP, irregular implementation of childcare facilities, and allowances for flexible arrival and departure hours at work sites have done little to support women's schedules. Limiting factors here include insufficient funds, lack of awareness among programme implementers, and women's reluctance to leave children with strangers (Jones et al, 2010b)

Reduction in women's labour exploitation:

- Women participants in Ethiopia's Southern Nations, Nationalities and People's Regional State (SNPPRS) noted that while payment levels remain low, the implementation of a minimum benefit (either cash or food) range is an important step in reducing their overall vulnerability to labour exploitation, and has provided new income-earning opportunities. Teenage girls and young women reported that the programme has reduced pressures on them to work as domestic employees – positions vulnerable to low remuneration and potential abuse (Jones et al., 2010b)

Evidence of impact at the household and intra-household level:

Mixed impact on intra-household and household labour opportunities:

- The PSNP also assumes that households have adequate adult labour to participate in PWPs, which is often not the case in female-headed households with young children and/or other family members who are sick or disabled (Sharp et al., 2006). Unlike CTprogrammes in other countries, the PSNP payment modality does not target women, and many women complain that they are unable to stop men wasting the payments on alcohol and food outside the home (Jones et al., 2010b)
- In India, larger households have been able to take advantage of increased labour opportunities through the MGNREGS programme. However, as only 100 working days are allotted per household, large households accrue fewer benefits (Bhatty, 2008; Gupta, 2009). Gender issues relating to labour opportunities remain: female-headed households with limited labour availability (due to fewer adults, especially males, or seasonal migration) are often unable to take full advantage of MGNREGS or other employment opportunities. These households are routinely excluded from work that requires men and women to pool their efforts as a family-based couple. Provision of work also depends on contact with the *panchayat* (local government), which poor women rarely have (Young Lives, 2010; Jha et al., 2009, cited in Porter and Dornan, 2010)

Improved household food consumption and children's material well-being:

- Evidence from Ethiopia's PSNP, shows a positive impact on household food consumption and children's health, both of which represent practical gender needs for women. To this end, the PSNP has contributed to increased food consumption through grain payments to participants. It has also enabled households to meet child-related costs such as those of clothing, school and healthcare, as well as opening up new income opportunities. The greatest impact has been felt in female-headed households, which had fewer alternatives for such support before the programme (Evers et al., 2008). Increased food consumption has also reduced the need for distress sales of assets, including low-profit coping strategies such as harvesting immature coffee berries, renting out land and keeping *hara* (loaned) cattle for others, or out-migration of family members to urban areas

Better access to informal sources of credit for households:

- Ethiopia's PSNP shows that participating households have better access to informal sources of credit, as community members now have greater faith in their ability to repay (Sharp et al., 2006)
- In India, tentative findings suggest that some households taking part in MGNREGS have been able to access loans as a result of their earnings through the scheme (Holmes et al., 2010)

Poor impacts on improving household childcare:

- India's MGNREGS has routinely failed to provide crèche facilities at work sites. In several states, the percentage of worksites that provided childcare facilities was just 17% , while in other states the figure was as low as 1%.In Tamil Nadu, almost 70% of women participants reported that there were no childcare facilities (Jandu, 2008; Narayanan, 2008).
- Khera and Nayak (2009a) have identified a similar lack of childcare facilities in 98 MGNREGS worksites in six northern Indian states. This means that mothers have to leave their children at home, transferring the childcare burden to older siblings, mainly daughters, who are kept out of school as a result (Sudarshan, 2011). Other parents choose to bring their children to worksites, risking exposure to environmental hazards (Palriwala and Neetha, 2009; Sudarshan, 2011)

Evidence of impact at the community level:

Mixed impact on women's empowerment and participation at the community level:

- Evidence from Ethiopia's Productive Safety Net Programme (PSNP) shows that it has encouraged women's participation in public works, and their contributions to family income and food generation are regarded as important contributions to community welfare. However, within these same communities, and in the view of local officials, women's productive capabilities are still traditionally perceived as inferior to those of men. Moreover, there is often little acknowledgment of the barriers that illiterate or semi-literate women face in gaining greater empowerment and the confidence to express their views on PWPs in public, particularly in lieu of ongoing awareness-raising activities (Jones et al., 2010)

Gains in social capital for both men and women:

- In Ethiopia, both women and men reported that greater livelihood security as a result of their participation in the PSNP has opened up new opportunities to become involved in community networks from which they were previously excluded. For women in particular, these social capital gains have had an added impact on their levels of participation and mobility in rural village life (Jones et al., 2010)

Pro-poor insurance (informal insurance impacts)

Evidence of impact at the household level:

Positive impact on household abilities to cope with risks and shocks:

- Informal insurance mechanisms such as reciprocal gift giving, sales of physical assets, drawing down savings, and diversification of income-generating activities have contributed to reducing risk and the impact of shocks among poor households (Bramoullé and Kranton, 2007; Dercon et al., 2006; Morduch, 1999; Skoufias; 2003)
- Poorer women, who typically lack access to formal insurance and credit, are particularly reliant on informal insurance groups such as rotating savings and credit associations (ROSCAs), accumulated savings and credit associations (ASCRAs) and burial societies to mitigate risk and manage shocks (Anderson and Baland, 2002; Kongolo, 2007; Teshome et al., 2012; Tsai, 2000)

Evidence of impact at the community level:

Positive impact on social networking and empowerment opportunities for women in their communities:

- Participation in ROSCA groups in particular often provides a critical social networking function for poor women, who are otherwise constrained due to time spent on household work and caring for the family (Anderson and Baland, 2002; Ardener, 1995)
- Preliminary findings also suggest that burial societies such as women's *iddirs* in Ethiopia have broader empowerment impacts. More than half of the participating women report that *iddir* membership helped to improve their connection to the local community – a connection further aided by the fact that *iddirs* incorporate voluntary self-management, designed in consultation with target populations, and rely on collaborative participation in community 'policing' to discourage abuse and fraud (Jacquier et al., 2006; Teshome et al., 2012)

Pro-poor insurance (formal insurance impacts)

Evidence of impact at the individual level:

Mixed impacts of health insurance schemes in increasing women's and girls' access to healthcare:

- Mexico's voluntary *Seguro Popular* programme has incorporated a specific focus on women's health needs, and has achieved some success in improving women's access to healthcare through its coverage. At the national level, for instance, 84% of participating women have attended at least one antenatal appointment and 93% had a skilled attendant present at the birth (King et al., 2009)

- In Ghana, pregnant women have received free healthcare since 2008, and 81% of women enrolled in the National Health Insurance Scheme have given birth in hospitals, compared with 57% of uninsured women. These women are also more likely to receive antenatal care (94%vs. 76%), and experience half the number of infant deaths compared with their uninsured counterparts (Mensah et al., 2010)
- India's *Rastriya Swasthya Bima Yojana* also covers maternity healthcare costs, and has provided free premiums and a low registration fee for women living below the poverty line, thus extending its coverage to the large numbers of women in the informal economy (International Labour Organization, 2011)

Limited coverage of maternity benefits:

- Globally, only 30% of International Labour Organization (ILO) member states' social insurance programmes or public funds payment schemes comply with the ILO Convention's requirement on minimum maternity provisions, with the lowest regional compliance in Asia and the Pacific and the Middle East (International Labour Organization, 2010a, 2010c). This gap in maternity benefits has a negative impact on women's income and health. Pregnancy and the early postpartum/lactation period impose serious constraints on women and their daily workload, which are in turn linked to a significant decline in female labour force participation in most countries following the birth of the first child. As most poor women cannot afford to stop working during pregnancy or after the birth, they and their infants face added health risks (Sabates-Wheeler and Kabeer, 2003)

Gendered disparities in contributory pension payments:

- Pension payment systems have, in practice, reflected gendered disparities. Women who pay into pension schemes tend to receive pensions on the same basis as men, based on contributory years and earnings (Arza, 2012). However, given that these same women are primarily employed in low-earning jobs, and face reproductive and caring responsibilities that often interrupt their employment, their payments tend to be lower than those of their male counterparts (International Labour Organization, 2010a). Women also typically retire earlier than men and live longer, thus reducing their length of working time in which to accrue savings (Arza, 2012)
- In Chile, prior to pension reforms, single women received a pension 30% lower than that of single men as a result of this higher life expectancy (Yañez, cited in Arza, 2012)
- Pension coverage for older women tends to be far less than that for older men, with male coverage almost twice that of female coverage in the Dominican Republic, El Salvador, Mexico and Paraguay, and three times higher in Bolivia (Arza, 2012). This factor compounds the already low rate of effective old age pension coverage in general across the developing world (as low as 5% in sub-Saharan Africa), which in each case remains even lower for women (International Labour Organization, 2010a; Osei-Boateg, 2011, Sabates-Wheeler and Kabeer, 2003)

Evidence of impact at the intra-household level:

Mixed impacts of social insurance programmes on household gender equity and women's decision making:

- In Latin America, social insurance systems have long promoted the concept of women's economic dependence on male family wages, emphasised men's economic authority, and favoured male urban salaried employees. Similarly, life insurance schemes have restricted women's decision-making power by assuming the husband to be the primary beneficiary of their wife's insurance claims, even when women wish to leave these funds to friends, relatives or adult children (Banthia et al., 2009; Cohen and Sebstad, 2006)
- However, some innovative programmes have sought to address this issue. In Colombia, *La Equidad* offers a life insurance policy that allows ongoing payments to be made for education; while in Sri Lanka and Bangladesh, mutual insurance organisations ALMAO and Delta Life deliver payments directly to children (or to savings accounts upon the death of a parent) (Banthia et al., 2009)

Pro-poor insurance (micro-insurance impacts)

Evidence of impact at the individual level:

Mixed impacts of micro-health insurance schemes on increasing women's and girls' access to healthcare:

- Although gender-disaggregated impact findings are limited, evidence suggests that micro-health insurance programmes have also led to increases in women's and girls' access to healthcare. In Jordan, for instance, the Microfund for Women's Caregiver Policy covers the costs of customers' medical facilities and related transport. Close links between microfinance institutions offering such insurance schemes, and micro-credit groups that work directly with women, have further improved women's trust in the schemes and increased their buy-in (Division for the Advancement of Women, 2009)
- However, inclusion and retention of women in health insurance schemes has often proved challenging. Although it has achieved near-universal coverage, for instance, Chile's *Fonasa* (National Health Fund) fails to provide gender-equitable cover, as women pay higher premiums than men of the same age due to the high costs of maternal care (Mesa-Lago, 2008). Costs for normal childbirth are also highly inequitable among women (German Agency for International Cooperation, 2004). Women also experience difficulties in enrolment and claims submission procedures
- In India, catastrophic hospitalisation expenditure of Vimo SEWA members was halved – a significant impact given that a sizeable percentage of members are from poor households, and the majority are women (Ranson et al., 2006). However, due to the scarcity of hospitals and poor transportation in rural India, the scheme's poorest members also had a lower rate of claim submissions, and women – in part due to lower levels of literacy – were less likely to submit claims (Sinha et al., 2007b)
- In Mexico, the *Seguro Popular,* which reaches 34.5 million people (54% of them women), has reduced catastrophic health expenditure by 23%, particularly among poor, female-headed households (King et al., 2009)

Subsidy programmes (food subsidies)

Evidence of impact at the individual level:

Mixed impacts addressing individual nutritional needs:

- Food subsidies are commonly assumed to increase consumption by the most vulnerable members of a household, but often ignore the effects of gender inequality on intra-household dynamics; in certain circumstances, they can even reinforce and perpetuate unequal power relations (Quisumbing and McClafferty, 2006)
- In Indonesia, the distribution of subsidised rice through the *Raskin* programme gave priority to children first, followed by men, and finally women. Nowhere in beneficiary communities were women offered the most nutritious foods, not even pregnant women (Arif et al., 2010a; Hossain et al., 2009). This reflects larger global trends in women functioning as household food security 'shock absorbers' who forgo their own consumption in favour of other household members (Quisumbing et al., 2008:1)

Subsidy programmes (agricultural subsidies)

Evidence of impact at the individual level:

Mixed impact on uptake of agricultural input subsidies among women:

- Emerging research indicates that the uptake of agricultural subsidies is often more limited for women than for men. In Ghana, fertiliser subsidy uptake was found to be significantly lower among women (39%) than men (59%) (World Bank, 2009)
- In Malawi's Agricultural Input Subsidy programme, male-headed households disproportionately benefited from the distribution of fertiliser and seed coupons as a direct result of gender inequalities. These include targeting criteria which skewed coupon distribution towards men, and women's comparative difficulty in raising payments to redeem their fertiliser coupons. Moreover, women are also more likely to grow crops for home consumption and thus less likely to use fertiliser. Mobility constraints and reproductive responsibilities also mean that women are less likely to travel long distances to collect the fertiliser. (Dorward et al., 2008)

Positive impacts of agricultural subsidies on women's labour force participation:

- Evaluations of various agricultural subsidy programmes reveal positive impacts on women's access to the labour market. In Malawi, women who received fertiliser subsidies were able to command higher wages for their short-term rural employment, albeit with lower rates of success than for men (Doward et al., 2008)

Positive impacts on increased autonomy over decision making and women's empowerment:

- In Malawi, fertiliser savings groups have provided women with opportunities to use their profits to invest in productive assets or children's education (Dorward et al., 2008)

Subsidy programmes (health and education subsidies)

Evidence of impact at the individual level:

Positive gains in girls' education:

- Scholarships play an important role in increasing girls' enrolment and quality of education (Danish International Development Agency, 2009). In India, for instance, the Feminist Dalit Organization (FEDO) reported that scholarship provision has served as a major inducement to attend school and improve school performance among children, particularly girls (Institute for Integrated Development Studies, 2004, cited in Danish International Development Agency, 2009)
- In Tanzania, under the Secondary Education Development Programme (SEDP), girls' enrolment rates have increased from 76% in 2004 to 88% in 2007, although considerable regional disparities persist, and girls' dropout rates and school performance tend to be worse than those of boys (African Development Fund, 2007; World Bank, 2008c)

Increased access to health services:

- Schemes that offer vouchers for antenatal and postnatal care and institutional deliveries have raised the number of assisted deliveries and antenatal and postnatal visits (Witter, 2011)
- In Bangladesh, research shows that institutional deliveries among poor, pregnant women who received such vouchers rose from 2% to 18%, utilisation of antenatal care by professionals increased from 42% to 89%, and utilisation of postnatal care rose from 10% to 60% (Ubaidur et al., 2010)
- Evaluations of Cambodia's health equity fund found that half of targeted women would not have attended healthcare facilities without it, and for one-third of these, access to a facility proved life-saving (Annear, 2010)
- However, many barriers remain. In Tanzania, implementation of the health subsidy programme was marred by unequal access due to discrimination in healthcare centres against poor clients, particularly young and less well-educated women (Smithson, 2005, cited in Burns and Mantel, 2006)
- The findings are not wholly positive either in Kenya, where socio-cultural constraints restrict women's access to services to help them deal with gender-based violence, which are stigmatised by local norms (Bellows and Hamilton, 2009)

Subsidy programmes (childcare subsidies)

Evidence of impact at the individual level:

Positive impacts of childcare subsidies on women's labour force participation:

- Impact assessments of Mexico's *Estancias* (childcare subsidies to support working mothers) programme show positive effects on women's labour force participation. Single mothers in particular have benefited through access to stable, dependable childcare services. However, the types of jobs available have not changed substantially, and remain low-paid employment (Santibañez and Valdes, 2008, cited in Pereznieto and Campos, 2010). Similarly, many women must first negotiate their participation in *Estancias* with their husbands (Pereznieto and Campos, 2010)

Positive impacts on women's decision making and women's empowerment:

- In Mexico's *Estancias* programme, women reported having new-found space to negotiate some domestic activities as men became more helpful at home and supportive of their wives as income earners. However, Pereznieto and Campos (2010) argue that not enough evidence exists to indicate a deeper transformation of gender roles, women's empowerment, and changes in intra-household decisionmaking as a result of the programme

Evidence of impact at the household and intra-household level:

Mixed impacts on equity of intra-household division of labour:

- There is little evidence to support changes in intra-household caring labour as a result of childcare subsidies. Although such subsidies promote women as 'micro-entrepreneur' care workers, childcare is still perceived as low-value 'women's work' (Staab and Gerhard, 2010). Given the number of family members who remain involved in childcare, it is also difficult to determine whether net benefits of programmes for carers and their families are positive
- In Guatemala's childcare programme, carers reported the need to receive help from at least one and sometimes up to five other family members in managing the *hogar* (home), typically their own children (Staab and Gerhard, 2010). Moreover, men typically opt out of policy debates relating to childcare, so there has been little improvement in public policies aimed at increasing the equity of intra-household divisions of caring labour (Staab and Gerhard, 2010:25)

Evidence of impact at the community level:

Mixed impacts on increasing women's community participation:

- In the case of Mexico's *Estancias* programme, mechanisms have not been sufficiently implemented to actively foster networks among beneficiaries. As a result, although some support is provided by the creche directors, who act as community focal points for women, this is ad hoc and reliant on individual commitment, rather than being a formal mechanism. There is no evidence to suggest that women beneficiaries are more active in community-level decision making as a result of the programme (Pereznieto and Campos, 2010)

Limited involvement of men in policy debates:

- In Guatemala's childcare programme, men typically opt out of policy debates relating to childcare, so there has been little improvement in public policies aimed at increasing the equity of intra-household divisions of caring labour (Staab and Gerhard, 2010:25)

Subsidy programmes (integrated subsidies)

Evidence of impact at the individual level:

Positive impacts on girls' education:

- In Vietnam, the school fee exemption policy of the National Targeted Programme for Poverty Reduction (NTPPR) was also cited as a key resource for women, resulting in children (many of them girls) attending school for longer; they also began learning the Kinh (majority) language, which would make it easier to engage in trade and business later in life (Jones and Tran, 2010).

Positive impacts on women's decision making and women's empowerment:

- Beneficiaries of Vietnam's NTPPR note that access to credit has made a significant positive impact, facilitating new investment opportunities in productive assets such as livestock. Women are often able to take responsibility for the purchase of the livestock, enabling them to contribute in a meaningful way to the household economy while also gaining a greater say over the use of household resources (Jones and Tran, 2010)

Evidence of impact at the household and intra-household level:

Positive impacts on intra-household relations:

- Beneficiaries of the NTPPR in Vietnam report improvements in intra-household relations attributed in part to the programme, while also noting that couples are less likely to quarrel, due to some relief of the pressure on overstretched household resources. Women also noted several less tangible gains, especially in terms of more harmonious intra-household relations. New-found loan availability has also prompted more regular discussions between husbands and wives about the use of household resources. Women who used loans to engage in petty trade or received vocational training reported greater respect and less violence from their husbands (Jones and Tran, 2010)

Positive impacts on access to health services:

- Subsidies have encouraged greater uptake of healthcare facilities by women. In Vietnam, the NTPPR has had a positive impact on basic healthcare needs for poor women and children. Women reported that their health insurance cards were an important means of enabling access to reproductive health services and contraceptives – with or without their husband's agreement – as well as providing a means of taking less time off work to look after ill children (Jones and Tran, 2010)

Evidence of impact at the community level:

Mixed impacts on increasing women's community participation:

- In Vietnam, NTPPR women participants reported an increase in the number of community and women's association meetings they attended, due in part to their greater degree of economic participation in the community, which was made possible by new-found access to credit. This had also improved their bargaining power in the household, allowing them to negotiate their attendance at community meetings. However, poor women often remain wary about expressing their full opinion, while cultural gender roles and gendered education and literacy gaps impede women's contributions in public discussions (Jones and Tran, 2010)

Glossary

Beneficiaries	Direct recipients of support from (social protection) programmes
Cash transfer	Regular transfer of income to (poor) individuals and households by government or non-governmental organisations
Community targeting	Involvement of members of the community in identifying who should receive social protection benefits
Conditional cash transfer	Regular transfer of cash from the government to (poor) individuals or households, often with the aim of improving human capital development, on the condition that they undertake specified activities (e.g. that children attend school or that mothers attend primary health centres)
Disability grant	Regular cash transfer from the government that is paid to disabled people
Empowerment	The positive transformation of power relations; the expansion of individual or group freedom of choice and action
Fee waiver	Exemption from payment of fees (e.g. school fees, fees for medical treatment) for selected individuals or groups
Food for work	A programme that gives food to (poor) individuals or households in exchange for labour
Gender	Women's and men's socially constructed roles and responsibilities, often resulting in power differentials
Gender budgeting	Analysis of budget allocations and expenditure to ascertain level of investment in gender-related policies and programmes
Gender equality	Equal opportunities, power, resources and rewards for women and men
Gender equity	Fairness to women and men
Gender inequality	Disparity in opportunities, resources, power and status between men and women

Gender lens	A systematic approach to understanding gender-related differences and their implications for policy and programme design and implementation
Gender-sensitive	Taking into consideration gender-related differences and their equity implications
Geographical targeting	Selection of beneficiaries on the basis of their residence in poorer regions or locations
Gross domestic product	A measure of the value of all the resources produced by a country in a year
In-kind transfer	Regular transfer of non-cash items, often food, by a government or non-governmental organisation
Leakage	The extent to which a programme includes non-targeted beneficiaries (e.g. the non-poor)
Means or income test	A test applied to determine eligibility for programme benefits, usually based on the income or assets, or both, of the applicant and their immediate family
Micro-insurance	Contributory programmes, often implemented by institutions other than the government, that offer coverage against specific contingencies such as ill health, funeral expenses and economic losses
Poverty gap	The difference between the current income or expenditure of the poor and the defined poverty line
Poverty headcount	The proportion of a population who are poor
Proxy meanstest	A targeting method in which a score for applicant households is generated based on easy-to-observe household characteristics (e.g. the location and quality of the household's dwelling, ownership of durable goods, demographic structure, education)
Public works programme	A programme involving money or in-kind transfer given to (poor) individuals or a households in exchange for labour
Risk	Exposure to an adverse event (which can be rapid onset and unpredictable, or slower onset and more predictable)
Social audit	Stakeholder (e.g. beneficiary) assessment of a project or service
Social insurance	Usually financed by contributions, an insurance programme that provides support in the event of specific contingencies (e.g. employment-related injury or sickness, old age, disability, maternity)
Social pension	Cash transfers paid to older people

Social security   A system administered by the government that includes tax-financed social assistance and social insurance instruments

Unconditional cash transfer   Cash transferred by a government or non-governmental organisation to individuals and/or households without conditions or requirements

Vulnerability   Susceptibility of individuals or households to risk

Notes

Introduction

1 Except Pakistan, where only institutional stakeholders were interviewed.

Chapter 1

1 1975 was the First World Conference on Women, held in Mexico City. Five years after this, in 1980, a Second World Conference on Women was held in Copenhagen. In 1985, the 'World Conference to Review and Appraise the Achievements of the UN Decade for Women: Equality, Development and Peace' was convened in Nairobi. The Fourth World Conference on Women was held in Beijing in 1995.

2 Such as between gender oppression and oppression based on class, race and nationality.

Chapter 2

1 See 'UN Women (undated) Women, Poverty and Economics.'www.unifem. org/gender_issues/women_poverty_economics (accessed 19 June 2012).

2 It is assumed that more women earn a living in the informal economy than men, but statistics show wide variation across countries (International Labour Organization, 2010b). Among 12 countries surveyed, only in Ecuador, Mali and South Africa were women more likely to be engaged in the informal sector than men. However, in most countries, a greater proportion of women are involved in informal employment, which includes own-account workers (self-employed with no employees) in their own informal-sector enterprises, employers (self-employed with employees) in their own informal-sector enterprises, and contributing family workers.

3 Of the 796 million adults (those over 15 years of age) unable to read/write in 2008, 64% were female. Disparity was highest in South Asia (73% male literacy but only 51% female literacy), sub-Saharan Africa (71% male, 53% female) and Northern Africa (76% male, 58% female) (UNEducational, Scientific and Cultural Organization, 2010).

4 In the World Development Report 2012, the World Bank (2011b) notes that, in 21 of the 63 countries with data for more than 40 years, women face unequal inheritance rights in the absence of wills. Default inheritance rights tend to award less than half of the estate to the widow, with the usual share in sub-Saharan Africa being between 0% and 30%. In the 16 sub-Saharan African studies that were part of the World Development Report 2012 qualitative study, more than half of widows reported not inheriting any assets from their husbands, and only a third reported inheriting the majority of assets.

5 In Tanzania, women travel 85% of all miles travelled: '80 percent of all journeys are for transporting water and fire wood and travelling to the

grinding mills' and '95 percent of this transportation is done by foot and head-loading' (Joto Afrika, 2011).

6 Conversely, the expanding biofuels market may also be exerting an increasing downward pressure on fossil fuel costs, with a corresponding economic advantage for women at the household level (Hochman et al., 2010).

7 Indeed, Arora-Jonsson (2011) argues that, in the dominant discourse in high-level policymaking such as the UN Framework Convention on Climate Change (UNFCCC) process, women are conceptualised only as 'more vulnerable' to climate change than men, which constructs vulnerability as the problem, rather than inherent power imbalances and the ways in which that vulnerability is (re)produced. It should be noted, however, that there are a range of efforts to integrate a gender perspective into climate change debates, including those reflected in the UNFCCC's gender mainstreaming strategy (www.gendercc.net/policy.html). In addition, a women's caucus to represent women from diverse sectors in the UN climate change process was formed and recognised in 2009.

8 As disaster response strategies too frequently omit a gender lens from their design and implementation, they miss opportunities to address the impact of disasters on sexual and reproductive health and assistance for obstetric emergencies (e.g. mobile clinics) as well as gender-sensitive psychological counselling (Enarson, cited in Rodriguez et al., 2006; Villar, 2012, personal communication).

9 It is also important to note this burden is exacerbated by the fact that men in all regions of the world have higher average disease burden rates as measured by disability-adjusted life years (www.who.int/healthinfo/global_burden_ disease/estimates_regional/en/index.html).

10 www.unifem.org/gender_issues/women_poverty_economics/facts_figures. php#2

11 www.wateraid.org/uk/what_we_do/the_need/206.asp, www.wateraid.org/ uk/what_we_do/impact_of_our_work/341.asp

12 www.un.org/works/sub2.asp?lang=en&s=22

13 The 2011 World Development Report (World Bank, 2011b:23) emphasises that 'skewed sex ratios at birth are a problem in China, parts of India, and parts of the Caucasus and the Western Balkans. The underlying cause is son preference among households, which has been exacerbated in some of these places by rapid income growth. Higher incomes have increased access to ultrasound technologies that assist in sex selection at birth, with 1 million girls in China and 250,000 girls in India missing at birth in 2008.'

14 See also www.measuredhs.com/

15 http://southasia.oneworld.net/Article/indian-survey-highlights-spousal- abuse-no-pay-for-working-women

16 'With masculinity and sexuality being closely related, sexual manifestations and control over women—often acted out in violence and sexual aggressiveness—seem to have become fundamental to restore male self-esteem' (Silberschmidt, 2001:668).

17 www.ipu.org/wmn-e/world.htm

18 http://nidprodev.org/articles-a-research/rural-womens-development- strategies-when-excluded-from-community-decision-making

19 There are also, of course, important considerations in quota enforcement, which can be problematic in some contexts (Dahlerup, 2006).

20 The link between quotas and participation is so poorly formed in Madhya

Pradesh that only one in eight women believes that quotas are meant to facilitate political participation (Jayal, 2006).

21 Men's higher remittances appear to be linked more to the type of work they undertake when they migrate than to rates of migration (Kelly, 2010). Men are more likely to be found in industry or construction, whereas women are more likely to be involved in domestic or care work. So, for instance, whereas 59% of total migrants from the Philippines are women, Sernyonov and Gorodzeisky (2005) found that men still remit significantly more than women in absolute terms.

Chapter 3

1 Examples include CCT programmes in Bangladesh, Cambodia and Pakistan (Fiszbein and Schady, 2009).

2 Examples include Mexico's *Oportunidades* CCT (Fiszbein and Schady, 2009).

3 Exceptions include South Africa's old-age grant and Brazil's means-tested pension, which transferred $199 and $318 per month, respectively, in 2011 (Barrientos and Lloyd-Sherlock, 2012).

4 http://graduation.cgap.org/

5 Lump-sum cash transfers have been used – for example, for the purchase or construction of housing or assets and in post-emergency circumstances. For an assessment of their effects, see Farrington and Slater (2009).

6 CFPR and CLP assets are worth approximately $100 and $160, respectively. For CFPR households, this can average six times the wealth of the poorest households (Bandiera et al. 2009).

7 There is a significant gap in gender coverage of pensions globally. Women are less represented in the formal economy and live longer, but typically have fewer years of service and receive lower wages, rendering them disadvantaged in contribution-based schemes. However, many states are moving towards non-contributory minimum income guarantee-type schemes, whereby a pension is paid regardless of employment history (International Labour Organization, 2010a).

8 This section is drawn from Amuzu et al. (2010).

9 This is drawn from the qualitative and quantitative primary research by Amuzu et al. (2010)in six sites in two districts in Ghana's Northern Region, one of the poorest areas in the country, and research by Jones et al. (2009b).

10 In Kpatinga and Galwei, all those sitting on the five-member committees were male, and in Sala/Sampubga, the seven members were all male. Only in Nachem was there one female CLIC member (out of a total of six members).

11 This section draws on evidence from three sources. The first is qualitative research conducted by Vargas Valante (2010) in 2009 in Ayacucho, a South Andean region, in two districts where interventions took place in the programme's first stage (November 2005). Two sites were selected in each district –Chanquil and Manzanayocc in Los Morochucos, and Motoy and Liriopata in Chiara. The second source is research by Molyneux and Thomson (2011) in Espinar and Acomayo, which are 3 and 5 hours' drive, respectively, from Cusco, the regional capital. *Juntos* had been operational in these communities since 2007, and to date 540 households in Acomayo are recipients (out of a total of 843). The third source is a documentary analysis and fieldwork by Jones et al. (2007) in two communities in Ayachucho, the first region where the programme's pilot was implemented. Qualitative

research involving key informant interviews and focus group discussions in Arizona and Rosapata communities was carried out in July and August 2006.

12 There were 687 at the national level in 2010.

13 The women's organisation *Movimiento Manuela Ramos* developed two gender indicators – sexual and reproductive health, and women's autonomy and control over reproduction (it is also proposed to monitor aspects such as the number of women heads of household and the percentage of pregnant women beneficiaries who are victims of domestic violence). An indicator for teenage pregnancy was also proposed that would allow monitoring of the state's obligation to develop an integrated sex education policy.

14 The aim of this was to maintain or strengthen customary systems of social support, and also to provide more systematic community-level protection against the social and environmental risks that the rural ultra-poor characteristically face. Some authors support this approach, but others have been more critical of it. Moore and Braunholtz-Speight (2007:3) refer to it as the 'middle ground between extremes of patron–client exploitation on the one hand, and idealised free citizenship on the other.'

15 Here we focus on STUP, which is further divided into STUP I (the most deprived and highest poverty-concentrated 20 districts) and STUP II (20 moderately poverty-concentrated districts). We focus on STUP II.

16 Evidence on the effects of the CFPR on gender is drawn from Holmes et al. (2010), from primary qualitative research conducted in four research sites (villages) in two districts (Magura and Narail), and CFPR evaluation documents. These two districts were selected on the basis that STUP II was implemented in these areas.

Chapter 4

1 According to the International Labour Organization (2009b:27), 'vulnerable employment is a newly defined measure of persons who are employed under relatively precarious circumstances' and 'is calculated as the sum of contributing family workers and own-account workers as a percentage of total employment.' These types of workers 'are less likely to have formal work arrangements, access to benefits or social protection programmes and are more at risk to economic cycles.' This indicator is important as it is highly gender-sensitive, given that family workers are predominantly women, and as a large proportion of vulnerable workers may indicate widespread poverty.

2 Regional disparities are also significant, with the largest gender gaps observed in North Africa, sub-Saharan Africa and the Middle East. Women's share in vulnerable employment (including own-account and unpaid family workers) with high insecurity and low earnings is alarmingly high in South Asia and sub-Saharan Africa (International Labour Organization, 2010b).

3 Antonopoulos (2007) notes that public work programmes were used as early as the fourth and fourteenth centuries by Indian rulers to avert famine.

4 In middle-income countries, workfare programmes are typically initiated to cope with one-time large macroeconomic shocks. In low-income countries, they are typically motivated by concerns about poverty relief and seasonal unemployment (World Bank, 2009).

5 Subbarao (2003) argues that benefits need to be sufficient to make a difference to people's lives and not stigmatise participants. However, in low-income settings where the majority of households are poor, there may be little stigma associated with poverty targeting. In Ethiopia's PSNP, social

divisions between beneficiaries and non-beneficiaries were not the result of stigma associated with poverty (Slater and Farrington, 2009). Stigmatisation is more often observed where social proxies are used for targeting – for example, in support for orphans and other vulnerable children in sub-Saharan Africa, where HIV and AIDS orphans are clearly targeted, or in the targeting of female-headed households in South Asia.

6 If benefits are high, they may necessitate quotas, which are more complex to administer (Subbarao, 2003). However, that said, demand for PWP employment typically exceeds supply, so rationing in some form is usually present (McCord, 2012, personal communication).

7 More than half of women's non-agricultural jobs are in informal employment in the majority of developing countries. For example, in Bangladesh only 3% of rural women work in wage employment, compared with 24% of rural men. Even when women can get wage employment, this is more likely to be part-time, seasonal and low-paid. In Malawi, 90% of women work part-time, compared with 66% of men, and 60% of women are in low-wage employment, compared with 40% of men. In Bangladesh, 80% of women have low-paid jobs, compared with 40% of men (Food and Agriculture Organization of the United Nations, 2011).

8 Women's average wages in both urban and rural areas are lower than those of men in most cases. For example, in Ghana, male wages are 31% higher than female wages in urban areas and 58% higher in rural areas (Food and Agriculture Organization of the United Nations, 2011). In India, women have up to 30% lower earnings than men in casual labour, and 20% lower earnings even for the same task (World Bank, 2009).

9 According to Quisumbing and Yohannes (2004), Ethiopian women who are participating in wage labour markets earn 2.7 times less than men.

10 In the RMP, a fraction of women's daily wages was deducted and transferred to their individual savings accounts. Women were allowed to withdraw their savings only after completing the 4-year cycle, for use in an income-generating activity. During their time in the RMP they were also provided with life skills training, to help them to be self-reliant after they left the programme (Ahmed et al., 2007).

11 The OFSP included a credit instrument, the 'household package', comprising loans for agricultural and non-agricultural activities, to provide resources along with training and a supporting environment to enable investment and household graduation to sustainable livelihoods.

12 This is in contrast to employment guarantee schemes, such as the MGNREGS, which set wages at the minimum wage rate for the agricultural sector, and are critically important in terms of increasing the bargaining power of the unemployed (Song and Philip, 2010).

13 www.ghanadistricts.com/home/?_=37&sa=3674

14 Unless otherwise stated, this section draws on Jones et al. (2010b),where research was undertaken in four research sites (villages/*kebeles*) in two districts (*woredas*) in Tigray and two in Southern Nations, Nationalities and Peoples Region (SNNPR) in 2009. Our primary research used a mixed-methods methodology that combined a small household survey with qualitative research tools, including focus group discussions with beneficiaries and non-beneficiaries, life histories and key informant interviews at community, district and national levels.

15 There are approximately 8.3 million chronically (predictably) food-insecure people in the country,compared with 6.7 million transitory (unpredictably)

food-insecure people (Devereux and Guenther, 2009; Ministry of Agriculture and Rural Development, 2010).

16 Inadequate adult labour may also be an issue in the case of male-headed households with HIV or other debilitating diseases, but is not taken into consideration in programme design.

17 http://ethiopia.usaid.gov/programs/feed-future-initiative/projects/ productive-safety-net-program-psnp

18 The practice of '*hara*' cattle involves tending the cattle of others so that they have access to the animals' dung, which is used as a fuelwood source.

19 Quisumbing and Yohannes (2004), drawing on three rounds of the Ethiopian Rural Household Survey, found that 26% of men in rural Ethiopia participate in off-farm labour markets, compared with 14% of women. The difference is even greater in the wage labour market (9% of men vs. 2% of women).

20 Although Ethiopia has one of the highest ratios of agricultural extension staff to farmers globally (Davis et al., 2009), female access is relatively low, given a number of supply- and demand-side factors. However, in the OFSP, expenditure on men is up to three times as high as that on women in some regions (Regional Food Security Bureaus, 2005, cited in World Bank, 2008a).

21 In 2000–2001, the budget for gender machineries represented just 0.017% of the national budget (World Bank, 2008a).

22 Unless otherwise stated, this section draws on Holmes et al. (2010), where research was undertaken in four research sites (villages) in Khargone and Betul districts of Madhya Pradesh in 2009. This primary research used the same mixed-methods approach as that described in the case of the Ethiopian case study outlined in Note 4.14.

23 In January 2010 the Act was amended to the Mahatma Gandhi National Rural Employment Guarantee Act and Scheme, respectively.

24 nrega.nic.in

25 Introducing bank accounts for the rural 'unbanked' population is very important. Khera and Nayak (2009a) found that, when asked, almost 53% of women surveyed preferred to be paid through a bank or post office account rather than in cash, as bank accounts would increase the likelihood of accumulating savings, reduce the possibility of being cheated by those who provide the wages, lead to a reduction in payment delays, and constitute an effective tool for controlling the use of their wages. However, there are considerable logistical challenges, including limited availability of rural banking facilities, resulting in lengthy and expensive trips for villagers to receive their wages and significant delays in payments, difficulties for illiterate programme participants in filling out requisite paperwork (Sudarshan, 2010), and, despite an overall reduction in corruption, the emergence of some new forms of embezzlement, including collusion between programme-implementing agencies and bank officials (Adhikari, 2010).

26 Kerala has the highest female participation rate (88% in 2009–2010), but the total number of female working days is very low – lower than those in Uttar Pradesh, which has one of the lowest female participation rates (21.6%). By contrast, the other three high achievers in terms of female participation have also offered a higher number of total female working days.

27 Furthermore, emerging evidence from several states suggests that gender wage differentials have grown (Shah et al., 2010, cited in Pellissery and Jalan, 2011). Pellissery and Jalan (2011) created a Social Accounting Matrix to calculate the impact of works on the wage-earning potential of women and

men in Andhra Pradesh, and found that the 13 works in Manchala village had actually generated more additional wages for men ($4,356) than for women ($1,644) for the equivalent number of days of labour.

28 Gender-disaggregated data are collected on (1) whether registration is refused to female-headed households or single women,(2) the average proportion of women working on the MGNREGS in a village, and (3) whether there are different task rates for women and men. However, an important gap relates to monitoring community assets and assessing the appropriateness and benefits of these using a gender lens, as well as ensuring women's participation in social audits of the programme.

Chapter 5

1 Lloyds estimates demand at 1.5–3 billion policies, based on the number of low-income people in the developing world who currently have no insurance (although they omit to define 'low-income') (Lloyds 360 Risk Insight, 2009).

2 Only one-third of countries globally have comprehensive social protection systems (International Labour Organization, 2010a).

3 *Moral hazard* is 'where agents do not bear the full cost of their actions and are thus more likely to take such actions' (Organisation for Economic Co-operation and Development, 2001). For instance, those with car insurance may be less careful to guard against car theft because they will be compensated if the car is stolen. *Adverse selection* is when an individual's demand for insurance is correlated positively with their risk of loss (e.g. higher risks buy more insurance) and the insurer is unable to allow for this correlation in the price of insurance. This may be due to information asymmetry or regulations or social norms that prevent the insurer from using certain categories of known information (e.g. gender or ethnic origin, genetic test results) to set prices (Polborn et al., 2006). *Covariate risk* refers to the probability that a large number of people will experience the same event(e.g. drought, flood), but with the effect on different people likely to be distinct, based on other types of risks to which they are vulnerable (Dercon et al., 2007a).

4 Insurance policies are often designed for large commercial farmers; access for small-scale farmers–where women are disproportionately clustered–or those growing a variety of crops is scarcer (Holmes et al., 2007; Sabates-Wheeler et al., 2009).

5 Women constitute less than 20% of landowners, with lower rates in West and Central Africa and the Middle East and North Africa. Figures are as low as 5% in North Africa and West Asia, on average 15% in sub-Saharan Africa, 25% in Latin America, and as high as 50% in Central and Eastern Europe (Bird and Espey, 2010).

6 As Dercon (2012, cited in Qureshi and Reinhard, 2012:20) has argued, 'a particularly troubling outcome of these studies [on micro-insurance] is that the most risk-averse of the participants bought the least insurance.'

7 Grameen Kalyan and BRAC charge lower premiums to the microfinance clients of their sister companies than to the general public (Ahmed and Ramm, 2006).

8 Women account for 83% of all adult VimoSEWA members in rural areas and 80% of them in urban areas. Their lower claims rates may reflect difficulties in accessing hospitals (due to both inadequate funds for transport and long

travelling distances to hospital facilities), as well as women's reluctance to be hospitalised, given their household and care work responsibilities (Ranson et al., 2007).

9 In addition, as Sinha et al. (2007b) point out, more disaggregated monitoring and evaluation of bundled insurance schemes is neededin order to understand the relative contribution of different components to improving the well-being of women, men and children.

10 Morduch (1999) argues that the evidence base from Africa and Asia on the effectiveness of informal insurance in supporting the poor to cope with shocks—especially aggregate shocks, but also the idiosyncratic shocks a household is likely to face—is limited. In a similar vein, Lund and Fafchamps (1997), cited in Morduch (1999), found that informal insurance in the Philippines only addresses acute illness reliably for younger adults, with older adults far less likely to be helped. Informal insurance also helps with funerals but not with mild illness, unemployment of household members other than the head or the head's spouse, and poor harvests.

11 Kongolo (2007) found participation rates of over 85% in Moretele Township (South Africa). An estimated one in ten Indian households participates in a group (Kapoor et al., 2011).

12 Estimates range from 60% in Cameroon (Etang et al., 2010) to 90% in Kenya (Gugerty, 2003).

13 Neither of the analyses by Habtom and Ruys (2007) and Teshome et al. (2012) include an explicit gender analysis, and there are no suggestions that the groups are dominated by women as they are in the case of local *equbs* (ROSCAs).

14 In April 2012, the International Labour Organization, in partnership with Women in Informal Employment: Globalizing and Organizing, launched a new database on informal employment in more than 40 medium- and low-income countries worldwide, which offers country-specific gender-disaggregated data.

15 In Kenya, women account for 25% of National Social Security Fund members. In Ghana, women accounted for 29% of Social Security and National Insurance Trust active contributors and just 14.9% of its beneficiaries (Osei-Boateg, 2011).

16 In around a quarter of countries, maternity benefits should be paid directly by employers, which in practice does not always happen (International Labour Organization, 2010a).

17 In rural Gambia, for example, there is a very high level of miscarriage for women whose second trimester coincides with the busy agricultural season (Sabates-Wheeler and Kabeer, 2003).

18 Illness is a priority risk, especially because of generally poorer nutrition and access to quality food among poor and vulnerable populations, involvement in more hazardous occupations, and residence in cramped and often unhygienic housing (Walsh and Jones, 2009).

19 In the poorest 100 countries, 6.8 million lives are covered for health, 35.3 million are covered for life, 12.6 million are covered for accidental death and disability, and 7.8 million are covered for property loss (Roth et al., 2007).

20 The gendered nature of risk is particularly evident in health insurance, where adverse selection means that the policy holder has a higher than average chance of claiming. In Benin, a women's self-help organisation included antenatal visits and birth in its benefit package. Mainly women joined, and pregnant women became over-represented in the risk pool, putting the sustainability of the product at risk (Radermacher and Dror, 2006).

21 See www.jointlearningnetwork.org/countries

22 *Seguro Popular* was introduced in 2004, and by 2010 a total of 43.5 million people were affiliated, 54.2% of whom were women; 36.9% of those affiliated lived in rural areas (www.seguro-popular.gob.mx). Families enrolled in Mexico's social transfer programme, *Oportunidades*, have automatic access, although King et al. (2009) found that only 66% of *Oportunidades* respondents in treated areas were aware of this.

23 See www.unicef.org/infobycountry/mexico_statistics.html#82

24 These statistics are derived from Mensah et al. (2010), but there is some dispute about levels of coverage. Apoya and Marriott (2011) recently challenged the systems used to measure enrolment, claiming that 82% of the population remain excluded from the scheme, with 64% of the richest being registered, compared with 29% of the poorest. However, the Ghana National Health Insurance Authority and the World Bank claim that the scheme covers 82% of the population.

25 Women are believed to be more likely to repay loans and invest profits in their families' human development (Ahmed and Ramm, 2006). In 2007, microfinance institutions reached 154.8 million clients globally; 106.6 million were among the poorest when they took their first loan, with women accounting for 83.4% of this group (Daley-Harris, 2009).

26 *Vimo* means 'insurance' in Gujarati.

27 See https://promujer.org

28 See www.swwb.org/expertise/microinsurance

29 Shepherd is a network of self-help groups in Tamil Nadu, with around 15,000 beneficiaries by 2004, and it acts as an intermediary between these and formal financial institutions, including banks.

Chapter 6

1 During 1990–2008, 147 countries experienced declines in the maternal mortality rate, of which 90 countries experienced a decline of 40% or more. The Middle East and North Africa had the largest decline (59%), followed by East Asia and Pacific (56%) and South Asia (53%) (World Bank, 2011b).

2 Including motives of political patronage and social stability in times of crisis (Marcus and Pereznieto, 2011; Wiggins and Brooks, 2010).

3 This section draws heavily on the Indonesian *Raskin* case study, given data limitations in the international literature on the gender dimensions and impacts of food subsidies (Arif et al., 2010a).

4 This section draws on primary research conducted in Indonesia in four research areas in two districts –Tapanuli Tengah and Timor Tengah Selatan. The former is located in the western part of the country, in North Sumatra province, and the latter is located in East Nusa Tenggara (Nusa Tenggara Timur) province, a poor region in the eastern part of Indonesia. There is evidence that the western part of Indonesia is generally more food secure than the eastern part (as well as benefiting more from economic development) (Arif et al., 2010a). (For more detailed research methodology, see Introduction.)

5 For methodology, see Introduction.

6 Pressure from international financial institutions in the 1980s and 1990s on African governments to reduce spending on subsidies as a precondition for receiving structural adjustment loans led to their decline across African countries. However, subsidising agricultural inputs has tended to be

controversial, as in practice they are difficult to implement and often result in undesirable market and distributional effects (World Bank, 2007). Indeed they are characterised by ineffectiveness and inefficiencies (e.g. high costs associated with delivery, difficult targeting, high leakages and possible crowdingout of commercial sales), especially in Africa, contributing to government overspending and fiscal and macroeconomic problems (Dorward et al., 2008; World Bank, 2007). In addition, subsidies that also have the safety-net objective of reducing poverty and food security are often seen as an inefficient mechanism for achieving this (relative to other social protection mechanisms, such as cash) in contexts where markets are functioning effectively (Dorward et al., 2008; World Bank, 2007). Furthermore, large-scale farmers tend to have the capital necessary to buy subsidised inputs such as fertiliser, unlike small-scale farmers, and as such are more beneficial to the former (Dorward et al., 2008; World Bank, 2007).

7   In some contexts, boys are involved in the worst forms of child labour and work extremely long hours.

8   This section draws on primary research carried out in two localities where the *Estancias* programme is operating, each in a different municipality within San Luis Potosi state, Mexico (for detailed methodology, see Introduction) (Pereznieto and Campos, 2010).

9   In the Guatemalan programme, for instance, an impact evaluation conducted in 1998–1999 found that the caretakers who were interviewed raised the lack of linkage to healthcare programmes as one of their main concerns. The work plan, created in 2000 by the new administration in Guatemala, included fostering linkages to healthcare activities as one of the goals for the future development of the programme (International Food Policy Research Institute, 2008).

10 For detailed methodology, see Introduction.

11 This section draws on primary research carried out in Vietnam in four sites – two in Ha Giang province in the impoverished North-East Highlands of the country, and two in An Giang province in the Mekong River Delta region of southern Vietnam (for detailed methodology, see Introduction) (Jones and Tran, 2010).

Chapter 7

1   www.thepolicypracticelibrary.com/index.php?any=Search+any+ field&title =Search+by+word%28s%29+in+title&author=Search+ by+author&all=on &subject=blank&country=blank&region=blank&bsearch=search#IDS2010

2   This section draws on Pomares (2011).

3   Analyses of voting data in Organisation for Economic Co-operation and Development (OECD) countries over time suggest that women voters have shifted to the left in terms of their preferences, partly because they prefer social protection to a greater extent than men do (see Inglehart and Norris, 2003).

4   This section draws heavily on Green (2008:217–19).

5   In a public meeting in 2007, Jean Drèze, one of the drafters of the original act, stated that a key objective had been to promote women's empowerment, through participation in the programme as well as in social audit processes.

6   BRAC started as the Bangladesh Rehabilitation Assistance Committee in 1972, and in 1973 was renamed the Bangladesh Rural Advancement Committee. Over time, BRAC became a motto, 'Building Resources Across

Communities.' More recently, given its expansion into urban areas and also other continents, it ceased to be an acronym (www.brac.net/content/faq-0).

7 *Chile Solidario* had implemented an analogous approach. The Ministry of Planning, as a reflection of its multidimensional conceptualisation of poverty, collaborates with other agencies on issues of health, education, employment, housing and justice, with strong linkages to other social programmes.

8 http://nrega.nic.in/circular/So_Audit_I.pdf

9 See www.unicef.org/socialpolicy/files/CSSP_joint_statement_9.13.10.pdf and www.odi.org.uk/resources/download/4884.pdf

10 For more details, see www.ids.ac.uk/go/news/senior-brazilian-policymaker-outlines-challenges-of-social-technology-transfer). For a discussion of 'social policy diplomacy', see www.guardian.co.uk/global-development/poverty-matters/2010/nov/19/brazil-cash-transfer-scheme

11 Women's organisations in Peru have tried to improve the gender impact of *Juntos* by proposing indicators that measure specific, but often neglected, aspects of gender equality (e.g. intra-household bargaining) and developing linkages with other gender programmes, including anti-domestic violence initiatives run in the highlands (Vargas, 2010).

12 In India, poor women have participated in the struggles of unorganised workers and in women's rights movements. However, many of the leaders of these organisations are actually middle-class women activists, and some middle-class women who are involved in politics pursue their own interests with little connection to poor women's needs.

13 In 2009, the Ethiopian Parliament passed a law restricting activities and funding for civil society organisations, and banning organisations with more than 10% non-domestic funding from being involved in policy debates on a number of issues, including gender equality. Consequently, organisations such as the Ethiopian Women Lawyers' Association and the Network of Ethiopian Women Associations, which champion the need to address gender inequalities, are likely to face increased difficulty in their work (Jones et al., 2010b). In Vietnam, civil society is relatively weak. This has recently been exacerbated by a tightening of the list of activities classed as 'legitimate' for civil society to undertake. Excluded from the list are issues of human rights, minority rights, gender and access to information, which means that there is limited scope for non-governmental organisations to promote social justice, transparency in resource distribution and accountability (Jones and Tran, 2010).

14 There are exceptions. The Department for International Development funded a multi-country study on gender and social protection in 2008–2010 (see Holmes and Jones, 2010b). In Indonesia, the German Agency for International Cooperation, along with other agencies, has started to conduct studies on social protection and gender in order to implement advances in gender mainstreaming and budgeting (www.gtz.de/en/weltweit/asien-pazifik/indonesien/33860.htm). The World Bank has produced several gender impact evaluations of social protection initiatives (www-esd.worldbank.org/gapdatabase/index.cfm?Page=Search&RecordID=483&sr=1).

15 Sinha, 2012, personal communication.

16 See http://siteresources.worldbank.org/INTPHILIPPINES/Resources/4PsDSWD.pdf

17 Programmes seeking to accommodate gender-based constraints and roles may eventually be transformative. Bangladesh's family planning programme, which started off as a door-to-door initiative (reinforcing norms of *purdah*),

evolved into a more clinic-centred model. The acceptability of this shift can arguably be partly attributed to growing ease among populations with the programme and what it offered (Sinha, 2012, personal communication), although Arends-Kuenning (2002) argues that the shift was largely economically motivated, given declining donor willingness to fund family planning initiatives.

18 According to Molyneux (2006:430), however, conditional cash transfers are essentially a neoliberal programme, with co-responsibility among the 'ideas that gained resonance in the 1980s when the state was identified as a major cause of development failure and accused of nurturing a "dependency culture."'

Chapter 8

1 See http://south-south.ipc-undp.org andwww.africacsp.org/apsp/index.php?option=com_content&view=frontpage&Itemid=1

2 This includes analytical and communication work by the International Labour Organization, the Institute of Development Studies, the Overseas Development Institute, Save the Children, the UN Children's Fund and the World Bank.

3 The Overseas Development Institute's cross-regional work funded by the Department for International Development and the Australian Agency for International Development is an exception here (www.odi.org.uk/work/projects/details.asp?id=1020&title= gender-vulnerability-social-protection), as is a growing body of work by CARE in Latin America.

4 See http://data.worldbank.org/topic/labor-and-social-protection

5 See www.odi.org.uk/resources/details.asp?id=5093&title=design-implement-gender-sensitive-social-protection-programmes

References

Abrego, L. (2009) 'Economic Well-being in Salvadoran Transnational Families: How Gender Affects Remittance Practices.' *Journal of Marriage and Family* 71: 1070–85.

Adato, M. and Bassett, L. (2008) *What Is the Potential of Cash Transfers to Strengthen Families Affected by HIV and AIDS? A Review of the Evidence on Impacts and Key Policy Debates.* Washington, DC: International Food Policy Research Institute.

Adato, M. and Roopnaraine, T. (2010) 'Women's Status, Gender Relations, and Conditional Cash Transfers.' In: M. Adato and J. Hoddinott (eds) *Conditional Cash Transfers in Latin America.* Washington, DC: International Food Policy Research Institute/Baltimore, MD: Johns Hopkins University Press.

Adenew, B. and Abdi, F. (2005) *Land Registration in Amhara Region, Ethiopia.* Research Report 3. London: International Institute for Environment and Development.

Adhikari, A. (2010) 'NREGA Wage Payments through Banks: Taking Stock.' Blog post. http://accountabilityindia.blogspot.com/2010/05nrega-wage-payments-through-banks.html.

African Development Fund (2007) *United Republic of Tanzania: Program in Support of the Secondary Education Development Plan: Appraisal Report.* Dar es Salaam: African Development Fund.

Agarwal, B. (1997) *'Bargaining' and Gender Relations: Within and Beyond the Household.* Discussion Paper 27. Washington, DC: Food Consumption and Nutrition Department, International Food Policy Research Institute.

Ahmed, A.U., Quisumbing, A.R. and Hoddinott, J.F. (2007) *Relative Efficacy of Food and Cash Transfers in Improving Food Security and Livelihoods of the Ultra-poor in Bangladesh.* Washington, DC: International Food Policy Research Institute.

Ahmed, M. and Ramm, G. (2006) 'Meeting the Special Needs of Women and Children.' In: C. Churchill (ed.) *Protecting the Poor. A Microinsurance Compendium.* Geneva: International Labour Organization and Munich Re Foundation.

Akintola, O. (2005) 'Unpaid HIV/AIDS Care in Southern Africa: Nature, Contexts and Implications.' Global Conference on Unpaid Work and the Economy: Gender, Poverty, and the Millennium Development Goals. Annandale-on-Hudson, NY, 1–3 October 2005.

Alcázar, L. (2008) 'Asistencia y Deserción en Escuelas Secundarias Rurales del Perú. En Análisis de Programas, Procesos y Resultados Educativos en el Perú.' In: M. Benavides (ed.) *Análisis de Programas, Procesos y Resultados Educativos en el Perú: Contribuciones Empíricas Para el Debate.* Lima: GRADE.

Alcázar, L. (2009) "Algunas Reflexiones sobre Que Sabemos de *Juntos* y Que Pasos Se Deben Seguir." International Seminar on Políticas Sociales en el Perú: Nuevos Desafios, Lima, 3 August 2009.

Alderman, H. and Haque, T. (2007) *Insurance against Covariate Shocks. The Role of Index-Based Insurance in Social Protection in Low-Income Countries of Africa.* Washington, DC: World Bank.

Alkire, S. and Santos, M. (2010) *Acute Multidimensional Poverty: A New Index for Developing Countries.* OPHI Working Paper No. 38. Oxford: Oxford Poverty and Human Development Initiative, University of Oxford.

Ambec, S. and Treich, N. (2007) 'Roscas as Financial Agreements to Cope with Self-Control Problems.' *Journal of Development Economics* 82: 120–37.

Amuzu, C., Jones, N. and Pereznieto, P. (2010) *Gendered Risks, Poverty and Vulnerability in Ghana: To What Extent is the LEAP Cash Transfer Programme Making a Difference?* Report to the Department for International Development, UK. London: Overseas Development Institute.

Anderson, L., Locker, L. and Nugent, R. (2002) 'Microcredit, Social Capital and Common Pool Resources.' *World Development* 30(1): 95–105.

Anderson, S. (2007) 'The Economics of Dowry and Brideprice.' In: K. Basu (ed.) *Oxford Companion to Economics.* Oxford: Oxford University Press.

Anderson, S. and Baland, J.M. (2002) 'The Economics of Roscas and Intrahousehold Resource Allocation.' *Quarterly Journal of Economics* 117(3): 963–95.

Anderson, S., Baland, J.M. and Moene, K. (2003) *Sustainability and Organizational Design in Informal Groups: Some Evidence from Kenyan Roscas.* Durham, NC: Duke.

Anggraeni, L. (2009) 'Factors Influencing Participation and Credit Constraints of a Financial Self-help Group in a Remote Rural Area: the Case of ROSCA and ASCRA in Kemang Village West Java.' *Journal of Applied Sciences* 9(11): 2067–77.

Annear, P. (2010) *A Comprehensive Review of the Literature on Health Equity Funds in Cambodia 2001–2010 and Annotated Bibliography.* Health Policy and Health Finance Knowledge Hub Working Paper. Melbourne: University of Melbourne.

Antonopoulos, R. (2007) *The Right to a Job, the Right Types of Projects: Employment Guarantee Policies from a Gender Perspective.* Working Paper 516. Annandale-on-Hudson, NY: Levy Economics Institute of Bard College.

Antonopoulos, R. (2009) *Promoting Gender Equality through Stimulus Packages and Public Job Creation: Lessons Learned from South Africa's Expanded Public Works Programme.* Public Policy Brief 101. Annandale-on-Hudson, NY: Levy Economics Institute of Bard College.

Antonopoulos, R. and Floro, M.S (2005) *Asset Ownership along Gender Lines: Evidence from Thailand.* Working Paper 418. Annandale-on-Hudson, NY: Levy Economics Institute of Bard College.

Antonopoulos, R. and Fontana, M. (2006) 'Hidden Vacancies? From Unpaid Work to Gender-Aware Public Job Creation: Toward a Path of Gender Equality and Pro-Poor Development.' The Levy Institute Conference on Public Employment Guarantee: Theory and Policy. New York, 13–14 October 2006.

Apoya, P. and Marriott, A. (2011) *Achieving a Shared Goal. Free Universal Health Care in Ghana.* Oxford: Oxfam GB.

Ardener, S. (1995) 'Women Making Money Go Round: ROSCAs Revisited.' In: S. Ardener and S.

Burman (eds) *Money-Go-Rounds: the Importance of Rotating Savings and Credit Associations for Women.* Oxford: Berg.

Ardener, S. and Burman, S. (eds) (1995) *Money-Go-Rounds: the Importance of Rotating Savings and Credit Associations for Women.* Oxford: Berg.

Aredo, D. (1993) *The Informal and Semi-Formal Financial Sectors in Ethiopia: A Study of the Iqqub, Iddir, and Savings and Credit Co-operatives.* Research Paper 21. Nairobi: African Economic Research Consortium.

Arends-Kuenning, M. (2002) 'Reconsidering the Doorstep-Delivery System in the Bangladesh Family Planning Program.' *Studies in Family Planning* 33(1): 87–102.

Arif, S., Syukri, M., Holmes, R. and Febriany, V. (2010a) *Gendered Risks, Poverty and Vulnerability: Case Study of the Raskin Food Subsidy Programme in Indonesia.* Report to AusAID. London: Overseas Development Institute.

Arif, S., Syukri, M., Isdijoso, W., Rosfadhila, M. and Soelaksono, B. (2010b) *Is Conditionality Pro-Women? A Case Study of Conditional Cash Transfer in Indonesia.* Working Paper. Jakarta: SMERU Research Institute.

Arora-Jonsson, S. (2011) 'Virtue and Vulnerability: Discourses on Women, Gender and Climate Change.' *Global Environmental Change* 21(2): 744–51.

Arun, T. and Steiner, S. (2008) *Micro-insurance in the Context of Social Protection.* Working Paper 55. Manchester: Brooks World Poverty Institute.

Arur, A., Gitonga, N., O'Hanlon, B., Kundu, F. and Senkaali, M. (2009) *Insights from Innovations: Lessons from Designing and Implementing Family Planning/Reproductive Health Voucher Programs in Kenya and Uganda.* Bethesda, MD: USAID.

Arza, C. (2012) *Pension Reforms and Gender Equality in Latin America.* Gender and Development Paper 15. Geneva: UN Research Institute for Social Development.

Asfar, R. (2011) 'Contextualizing Gender and Migration in South Asia: Critical Insights.' *Gender Technology and Development* 15(3): 389–410.

Ashraf, N., Field, E. and Lee, J. (2010) *Household Bargaining and Excess Fertility: An Experimental Study in Zambia.* Cambridge, MA: Harvard.

Asian Development Bank (2005) Vietnam: Gender Situation Analysis. Tokyo: ADB.

Asian Development Bank (2009) *Investing in Children in Indonesia: A Step toward Poverty Reduction.* Social Protection Project Brief. Manila: Asian Development Bank.

Asian Development Bank and World Bank (2005) *India Post Tsunami Recovery Program: Preliminary Damage and Needs Assessment.* Manila and Washington, DC: Asian Development Bank and World Bank.

Bach, K. (2010) *Social Transfers: Stimulating Household-Level Growth.* CPRC Policy Brief 14. Manchester: Chronic Poverty Research Centre.

Baden, S. and Goetz, A.-M. (1997) 'Who Needs [Sex] When You Can Have [Gender]? Conflicting Discourses on Gender at Beijing.' *Feminist Review* 56: 3–25.

Bailey, S., Pereznieto, P. and Jones, N. (2011) *Child-Sensitive Social Protection in DRC: Diagnostic Study.* London: Overseas Development Institute.

Bain, K. and Hicks, N. (1998) 'Building Social Capital and Reaching out to Excluded Groups: The Challenge of Partnerships.' CELAM Meeting on the Struggle against Poverty towards the Turn of the Millennium. Washington, DC, 21 April 1998.

Baird, S., McIntosh, C. and Özler, B. (2009a) *Designing Cost-Effective Cash Transfer Programs to Boost Schooling among Young Women in Sub-Saharan Africa*. Policy Research Working Paper 5090. Washington, DC: World Bank.

Baird, S., Chirwa, E., McIntosh, C. and Özler, B. (2009b) *The Short-Term Impacts of a Schooling Conditional Cash Transfer Program on the Sexual Behavior of Young Women*. Policy Research Working Paper 5089. Washington, DC: World Bank.

Baird, S., McIntosh, C. and Özler, B. (2010) *Cash or Condition? Evidence from a Randomised Cash Transfer Program*. Policy Research Paper 5259. Washington, DC: World Bank.

Balachin, C. (2011) *Avoiding Some Deadly Sins: Oxfam Learnings and Analysis about Religion, Culture, Diversity, and Development*. London: Oxfam.

Bandiera, O., Burgess, R., Gulesci, S. and Rasul, I. (2009) *Community Networks and Poverty Reduction Programmes: Evidence from Bangladesh*. London: London School of Economics.

Banthia, A., Johnson, S., McCord, M. and Mathews, B. (2009) *Microinsurance That Works for Women: Making Gender-Sensitive Microinsurance Programs*. Geneva: International Labour Organization.

Barber, S. and Gertler, P. (2010) 'Empowering Women: How Mexico's Conditional Cash Transfer Programme Raised Parental Care Quality and Birth Weight.' *Journal of Development Effectiveness* 2(1): 51–73.

Barnett, B., Barrett, C. and Skees, J. (2008) 'Poverty Traps and Index-Based Risk Transfer Products.' *World Development* 36(10): 1766–85.

Barrientos, A. (2010) *Social Protection and Poverty*. Social Policy and Development Paper 42. Geneva: UN Research Institute for Social Development.

Barrientos, A. and Hulme, D. (2008a) *Social Protection for the Poor and Poorest in Developing Countries: Reflections on a Quiet Revolution*. Working Paper 30. Manchester: Brooks World Poverty Institute.

Barrientos, A. and Hulme, D. (eds) (2008b) *Social Protection for the Poor and Poorest, Concepts, Policies and Politics*. London: Palgrave Macmillan.

Barrientos, A. and Lloyd-Sherlock, P. (2012) *Pensions, Poverty and Wellbeing: The Impact of Pensions in South Africa and Brazil, a comparative study*. Pension Watch, Briefing 7. London: HelpAge International.

Barrientos, A. and Scott, S. (2008) *Social Transfers and Growth: a Review*. BWPI Working Paper 52. Manchester: Brooks World Poverty Institute, University of Manchester.

Barrientos, A., Niño-Zarazúa, M. and Maitrot, M. (2010) *Social Assistance in Developing Countries Database*. Version 5.0. Manchester: Brooks World Poverty Institute.

Baruah, B. (2010) *Women and Landed Property in Urban India: Negotiating Closed Doors and Windows of Opportunity*. Working Paper 2010/56. Helsinki: UNU-WIDER.

Bebbington, A. (2007) 'Social Capital and Development Studies II: Can Bourdieu Travel to Policy?' *Progress in Development Studies* 7(2): 155–62.

Bellows, B. and Hamilton, M. (2009) *Vouchers for Health: Increasing Utilization of Facility-Based FP and Safe Motherhood Services in Kenya*. Bethesda, MD: Abt Associates Inc.

Bentaouet-Kattan, R., and Burnett, N. (2004) User fees in primary education. Washington, D.C. The World Bank

Berdegue, J. and Escobar, G. (2001) *Agricultural Knowledge and Information Systems and Poverty Reduction*. AKIS/ART Discussion Paper. Washington, DC: Rural

Development Department, World Bank.

Berkhout, E. and Oostingh, H. (2008) *Health Insurance in Low-Income Countries. Where is the Evidence that It Works?* Joint Agency Briefing Paper. Oxford: Oxfam GB.

Besse, S.K. (1996) *Restructuring Patriarchy: The Modernization of Gender Inequality in Brazil, 1914–1940.* Chapel Hill, NC: University of North Carolina Press.

Beyeza-Kashesy, J. S. Neema, A., Ekstrom, A. M., Kaharuza, F., Mirembe, F. and Kulane, A. (2010) '"Not a Boy, Not a Child": A Qualitative Study on Young People's Views on Childbearing in Uganda.' *African Journal of Reproductive Health* 14(1): 71–81.

Bhatty, K. (2008) 'Falling through the Cracks.' *The Hindu*, 16 March. www.hinduonnet. com/mag/2008/03/16/ stories/2008031650040200.htm

Birchfield, Lauren and Jessica Corsi (2010), "Between starvation and globalization: realizing the right to food in India", Michigan Journal of International Law, 31(1): 691-764.

Bird, K. and Espey, J. (2010) 'Power, Patriarchy and Land: Examining Women's Land Rights in Uganda and Rwanda.' In: S. Chant (ed.) *The International Handbook of Gender and Poverty: Concepts, Research, Policy.* Cheltenham: Edward Elgar.

Blackden, C.M. and Wodon, Q. (eds) (2006) *Gender, Time Use, and Poverty in Sub-Saharan Africa.* Working Paper 73. Washington, DC: World Bank.

Bloom, K. (2009) 'Social Safety Nets: Learning from Best Practice.' Asian Development Bank presentation, 6 July 2009.

Bollard, A., McKenzie, D. and Morten, M. (2010) 'The Remitting Patterns of African Migrants in the OECD.' *Journal of African Economies* 19(5): 605–34.

Booth, D. (2011) 'Introduction: Working with the Grain? The Africa Power and Politics Programme.' *IDS Bulletin* 42(2): 1–10.

Boserup, E. (1970) *Woman's Role in Economic Development.* London: Earthscan.

Botero, F., Churchill, C., McCord, M.J. and Qureshi, Z. (2006) 'The Future of Microinsurance.' In: C. Churchill (ed.) *Protecting the Poor. A Microinsurance Compendium.* Geneva: International Labour Organization and Munich Re Foundation.

Bouman, F.J.A. (1994) 'ROSCA and ASCRA: Beyond the Financial Landscape.' In: F.J.A. Bouman and O. Hospes (eds) *Financial Landscapes Reconstructed: The Fine Art of Mapping Development.* Boulder, CO: Westview Press.

Bouman, F.J.A. (1995) 'Rotating and Accumulating Savings and Credit Associations: A Development Perspective.' *World Development* 23: 371–84.

Bramoulle, Y. and Kranton, R. (2007) 'Risk-Sharing Networks.' *Journal of Economic Behavior and Organization* 64: 275–94.

Bradshaw, S. (2002) *Gendered Poverties and Power Relations: Looking Inside Communities and Households.* Managua: Puntos de Encuentro.

Bradshaw, S. (2008) 'From Structural Adjustment to Social Adjustment: A Gendered Analysis of Conditional Cash Transfer Programmes in Mexico and Nicaragua.' *Global Social Policy* 8(2): 188–206.

Bramoullé, Y. and Kranton, R. (2007) 'Risk-Sharing Networks.' *Journal of Economic Behavior and Organization* 64: 275–294.

Britto, T.F. (2007) *The Challenges of El Salvador's Conditional Cash Transfer Programme, Red Solidaria.* Brazil: International Poverty Centre, UN Development Programme.

Brody, A. (2009) *Gender and Governance: Overview Report.*

BRIDGE Cutting Edge Pack. Brighton: Institute of Development Studies.

Brody, A., Demetriades, J. and Esplen, E. (2008) *Gender and Climate Change: Mapping the Linkages: A Scoping Study on Knowledge and Gaps.* Brighton: BRIDGE, Institute of Development Studies.

Bronner M. (2003) *Economic Growth, Crisis, and Health: a Malaysian Case Study.* LSE Health and Social Care Discussion Paper. London: London School of Economics.

Brown, S. (2006) 'Can Remittances Spur Development? A Critical Survey.' *International Studies Review* 8(1): 55–76.

Budlender, D. and Parenzee, P. (2007) *South Africa's Expanded Public Works Programme: Exploratory Research of the Social Sector.* Johannesburg: On Par Development Consultancy and Community Agency for Social Enquiry.

Building Resources Across Communities (2009) *Pathways out of Extreme Poverty: Findings from Round I Survey of CFPR II.* Dhaka: Research and Evaluation Division, BRAC.

Burns, M. and Mantel, M. (2006) *Tanzania: Review of Exemptions and Waivers. Report to the Ministry of Health and Social Welfare.* Søborg: Euro Health Group.

Cambridge Education (2010) *China: Southwest Basic Education Project (SBEP).* www.camb-ed.com/ International/ Internationalpresence/ Internationalprojects/ ChinaSouthwestBasic EducationProjectSBEP.aspx

Chakraborty, Lekha (2010) Gender-Sensitive Fiscal Policies: Experience of ex-post and ex-ante Gender Budgets in Asia-Pacific. UNDP Asia-Pacific Human Development Report Background Papers Series 2010/06. Available from: http:// www.snap-undp.org/elibrary/

Publications/APHDR-TBP_2010_ 06.pdf

Chambers, R. (1989) 'Editorial Introduction: Vulnerability, Coping and Policy.' *IDS Bulletin* 20(2): 1–7.

Chant, S. (1997) 'Women-Headed Households: Poorest of the Poor? Perspectives from Mexico, Costa Rica and the Philippines.' *IDS Bulletin* 28(3): 26–48.

Chant, S. (2008) 'The "Feminisation of Poverty" and the "Feminisation" of Anti-Poverty Programmes: Room for Revision?' *Journal of Development Studies* 44(2): 165–97.

Chant, S. (2010) *The International Handbook of Gender and Poverty: Concepts, Research, Policy.* Cheltenham: Edward Elgar.

Chiswick, B and Miller, P. (1995) 'The Endogeneity between Language and Earnings: International Analyses.' *Journal of Labor Economics* 13(2): 246–88.

Chitrakar, R. (2009) *Overcoming Barriers to Girls' Education in South Asia: Deepening the Analysis.* New York: UNICEF.

Chong, K. (2008) *Deliverance and Submission: Evangelical Women and the Negotiation of Patriarchy in South Korea.* Cambridge, MA: Asia Center, Harvard University.

Chorghade, G.P., Barker, M., Kanade, S. and Fall, C.H.D. (2009) 'Why Are Rural Indian Women so Thin? Findings from a Village in Maharashtra.' *Public Health Nutrition* 9(1): 9–18.

Chronic Poverty Research Centre (2009) *Chronic Poverty Report 2008–9.* Manchester: CPRC.

Churchill, C. (2006) 'What Is Insurance for the Poor?' In: C. Churchill (ed.) *Protecting the Poor. A Microinsurance Compendium.* Geneva: International Labour Organization and Munich Re Foundation.

Churchill, C. and McCord, M.J. (2012) 'Current Trends in Microinsurance.' In: C. Churchill and M. Matul (eds) *Protecting the Poor: A Microinsurance Compendium. Volume II.* Geneva: International Labour Organization and Munich Re Foundation.

Churchill, C. and Matul, M. (eds) (2012) *Protecting the Poor: A Microinsurance Compendium. Volume II.* Geneva: International Labour Organization and Munich Re Foundation.

Clarke, D. and Dercon S. (2009) *Insurance, Credit and Safety Nets for the Poor in a World of Risk.* Working Paper 81. New York: UN Department of Economic and Social Affairs.

Cleaver, F. (2005) 'The Inequality of Social Capital and the Reproduction of Chronic Poverty.' *World Development* 33(6): 893–906.

Clisby, S. (2005) 'Gender Mainstreaming or Just More Male-Streaming?' *Gender & Development* 13(2): 23–35.

Cohen, M. and Sebstad, J. (2006) 'The Demand for Microinsurance.' In: C. Churchill (ed.) *Protecting the Poor. A Microinsurance Compendium.* Geneva: International Labour Organization and Munich Re Foundation.

Colletta, N. and Cullen, M. (2000) *Violent Conflict and the Transformation of Social Capital: Lessons from Rwanda, Somalia, Cambodia, and Guatemala.* Washington, DC: World Bank.

Connell, R.W. (1987) *Gender and Power: Society, the Person and Sexual Politics.* Cambridge: Polity.

Conroy, K. (2009) *Social Development: Knowledge, Attitudes and Practice – a Short Beneficiary Review.* Bangladesh: Chars Livelihoods Programme.

Conroy, K., Goodman, A.R. and Kenwood, S. (2010) 'Lessons from the Chars Livelihoods Programme, Bangladesh (2004–2010).' Paper presented to Ten Years of 'War Against Poverty': What Have We Learned Since 2000 & What Should We Do 2010–2020? CPRC International Conference, University of Manchester, 8–10 September 2010.

Corbridge, S., Harriss, J. and Jeffrey, C. (2012) *India Today: Economy, Politics and Society.* Cambridge: Polity Press.

Cuberes, D. and Teignier-Baqué, M. (2011) *Gender Inequality and Economic Growth.* WDR Background Paper for the World Development Report 2012. Washington, DC: World Bank.

Cunguara, B., Langyintuo, A. and Darnhofer, I. (2011) 'The Role of Nonfarm Income in Coping with the Effects of Drought in Southern Mozambique.' *Agricultural Economics* 42(6): 701–13.

Dageid, W. and Duckert, F. (2008) 'Balancing between Normality and Social Death: Black, Rural, South African Women Coping with HIV/AIDS.' *Qualitative Health Research* 18(2): 182–95.

Dagnelie, O. and LeMay-Boucher, P. (2008) *Rosca Participation in Benin: A Commitment Issue.* Porto Novo: Ministry of Science and Innovation.

Dahlerup, D. (2006) 'Strategies to Enhance Women's Political Representation in Different Electoral Systems.' In: Dahlerup, D. and Francisco, J. (eds) *Gender, Governance and Democracy.* Manila: Isis International.

Daley-Harris, S. (2009) *State of the Microcredit Summit Campaign Report 2009.* Washington, DC: Microcredit Summit Campaign.

Daly, M. (2005) 'Gender Mainstreaming in Theory and Practice.' *Social Politics* 12(3): 433–50.

Danish International Development Agency (2009) *Joint Evaluation of the Secondary Education Support Programme.* Report for the Ministry of Education, Nepal, and

Danida Evaluation Department. Copenhagen: Danish International Development Agency.

Danish International Development Agency (2009) 'Joint Evaluation of the Secondary Education Support Programme'. Report for the Ministry of Education, Nepal, and Danida Evaluation Department, Ministry of Foreign Affairs of Denmark.

Das, N.C. and Misha, F.A. (2010) *Addressing Extreme Poverty in a Sustainable Manner: Evidence from CFPR Programme*. CFPR Working Paper No. 19. Dhaka: Building Resources Across Communities (BRAC).

Davies, M., Guenther, B., Leavy, J., Mitchell, T. and Tanner, T. (2008) ''Adaptive Social Protection': Synergies for Poverty Reduction', IDS Bulletin 39(4): 105-112

Davies, M. and McGregor, J.A. (2009) *Social Protection Responses to the Financial Crisis: What Do We Know?* In Focus Policy Briefing 7. Brighton: Institute of Development Studies.

Davin, D. (2004) 'The Impact of Export-Oriented Manufacturing on the Welfare Entitlements of Chinese Women Workers.' In: S. Razavi, R. Pearson and C. Danloy (eds) *Globalization, Export-Oriented Employment and Social Policy: Gendered Connections*. New York: Palgrave Macmillan/UNRISD.

Davis, K. Swanson, B. and Amudavi, D. (2009) *Review and Recommendations for Strengthening the Agricultural Extension System in Ethiopia*. Washington, DC: International Food Policy Research Institute.

de Brauw, A. and Hoddinott, J. (2008) *Must Conditional Cash Transfers Be Conditioned To Be Effective? The Impacts of Conditioning Transfers on School Enrolment in Mexico*. Discussion Paper 00757. Washington, DC: International

Food Policy Research Institute.

de Britto, T. (2008) 'The Emergence and Popularity of Conditional Cash Transfers in Latin America.' In: A. Barrientos and D. Hulme (eds) *Social Protection for the Poor and Poorest, Concepts, Policies and Politics*. London: Palgrave Macmillan.

de la Fuente, A. (2008) *Remittances and Vulnerability to Poverty in Rural Mexico*. Tokyo: United Nations University.

De Pee, S., Bloem, M. and Sari, M. (2000) 'Indonesia's Crisis Causes Considerable Weight Loss among Mothers and Adolescents.' *Malaysian Journal of Nutrition* 6(2): 203–14.

de Walque, D. (2004) *How Does the Impact of an HIV/AIDS Information Campaign Vary with Educational Attainment? Evidence from Rural Uganda*. Policy Research Working Paper 3289. Washington, DC: World Bank.

Deere, C.D. and León, M. (2001) 'Who Owns the Land? Gender and Land-Titling Programmes in Latin America.' *Journal of Agrarian Change* 1(3): 440–67.

Dejardin, A. (1996) *Public Works Programmes, A Strategy for Poverty Alleviation: The Gender Dimension*. Issues in Development Discussion Paper 10. Geneva: International Labour Organization.

Delaney, P.L. and Shrader, E. (2000) *Gender and Post-Disaster Reconstruction: The Case of Hurricane Mitch in Honduras and Nicaragua*. Washington, DC: World Bank.

Department for International Development (2009) *Designing and Implementing Financially Inclusive Payment Arrangements for Social Transfers Programmes*. London: DFID.

Department for International Development (2011) *Cash Transfers*. Evidence Paper. London: Policy Division, DFID.

Department for International Development, Bangladesh (2006)

Challenging the Frontiers of Poverty Reduction: Specially Targeted Ultra Poor Programme. Project Completion Report. Dhaka: DFID.

Department of Social Development (2006) Guidelines for Early Childhood Development Services. Pretoria: Department of Social Development.

Dercon, S. (2004) Insurance Against Poverty. Oxford: Oxford University Press.

Dercon, S., Bold, T., de Weerdt, J. and Pankhurst, A. (2004) Extending Insurance? Funeral Associations in Ethiopia and Tanzania. Paris: Organisation for Economic Co-operation and Development.

Dercon, S., de Weerdt, J., Bold, T. and Pankhurst, A. (2006) 'Group-Based Funeral Insurance in Ethiopia and Tanzania.' World Development 34(4): 685–703.

Dercon, S., Bold, T. and Calvo, C. (2007a) Insurance for the Poor? Oxford: Global Poverty Research Group. Dercon, S., Hoddinott, J. and Woldehanna, T. (2007b) Growth and Poverty in Rural Ethiopia: Evidence from 15 Communities 1994–2004. Background Paper for CPRC. Manchester: Chronic Poverty Research Centre.

Dercon, S., Hoddinott, J., Krishnan, P. and Woldehanna, T. (2008) Collective Action and Vulnerability: Burial Societies in Rural Ethiopia. CAPRi Working Paper No. 83. Washington, DC: International Food Policy Research Institute.

Dessallien, R.L. (1999) Review of Poverty Concepts and Indicators. Poverty Programme. New York: UN Development Programme.

Devadasan, N., Manoharan, S., Menon, N., Menon, S., Thekaekara, M. and Thekaekara, S. (2007) 'Indian Community Health Insurance Schemes Provide Partial Protection Against Catastrophic Health Expenditure.' BMC Health Services Research 7: 43.

Devereux, S. (2009) Social Protection for Agricultural Growth in Africa. Growth and Social Protection Working Paper 06. Brighton: Future Agricultures and Centre for Social Protection.

Devereux, S. and Guenther, B. (2009) Social Protection and Agriculture in Ethiopia. Future Agricultures Consortium (FAC) Working Paper No. SP03. Brighton: Institute of Development Studies.

Devereux, S. and Sabates-Wheeler, R. (2004) Transformative Social Protection. Working Paper 232. Brighton: Institute of Development Studies.

Devereux, S. and Solomon, C. (2006) Employment Creation Programmes: The International Experience. Issues in Employment and Poverty Discussion Paper 24. Geneva: International Labour Organization.

Dimitrijevics, A. (2007) Mainstreaming Gender into Disaster Recovery and Reconstruction. Washington, DC: World Bank.

Division for the Advancement of Women (2009) World Survey on the Role of Women in Development. Women's Control over Economic Resources and Access to Financial Resources, Including Microfinance. New York: Division for the Advancement of Women.

Dollar, D. and Gatti, R. (1999) Gender Inequality, Income, and Growth: Are Good Times Good for Women? Policy Research Report on Gender and Development, Working Paper 1. Washington, DC: World Bank.

Donaldson, M., Howson, R. and Pease, B. (2009) Migrant Men: Critical Studies of Masculinities and the Migration Experience. New York: Routledge.

Donoso, S.B., Altunba, Y. and Kara, A. (2011) 'The Rationale Behind Informal Finance: Evidence from ROSCAs in Bolivia.' Journal of Developing Areas 45: 191–208.

Dorward, A., Chirwa, E. and Jayne, T. (2008) Evaluation of the 2006/7

Agricultural Input Supply Programme, Malawi. Final Report for the Ministry of Agriculture and Food Security.

Doss, C.R. 2006. 'The Effects of Intrahousehold Property Ownership on Expenditure Patterns in Ghana.' *Journal of African Economics* 15(1): 149–80.

Drimie, S. and Casale, M. (2009) 'Multiple Stressors in Southern Africa: The Link between HIV/AIDS, Food Insecurity, Poverty and Children's Vulnerability Now and in the Future.' *AIDS Care* 21(S1): 28–33.

Econometría (2006) *Informe Final de la Evaluación de Impacto de Familias en Acción*. Bogotá: Econometría.

Economic Commission for Latin America and the Caribbean (2007) *Teenage Motherhood in Latin America and the Caribbean: Trends, Problems and Challenges*. Challenges 4, January.

Economic and Social Commission for Asia and the Pacific (2007) *Economic and Social Survey of Asia and the Pacific, 2007: Surging Ahead in Uncertain Times*. Bangkok: ESCAP.

Ellis, F. (1992) *Agricultural Policies in Developing Countries*. Cambridge: Cambridge University Press.

Ellis, F., Devereux, S. and White, P. (eds) (2009) *Social Protection in Africa*. Cheltenham: Edward Elgar.

Elson, D. (1998) 'The Economic, the Political and the Domestic: Businesses, States and Households in the Organisation of Production.' *New Political Economy* 3(2):189–208.

Elson, D. and Cagatay, N. (2000) 'The Social Content of Macroeconomic Policies.' *World Development* 28(7): 1347–64.

Emmett, B. (2006) *In the Public Interest: Health, Education and Sanitation for All*. Oxford: Oxfam GB.

Engle, P.L. (1989) 'Mothers' Income Control: Consequences for Mothers and Their Children.' Paper presented to the Association of Women and Development.

Eriksen, S. and Silva, J. (2009) 'The Vulnerability Context of a Savanna Area in Mozambique: Household Drought Coping Strategies and Responses to Economic Change.' *Environmental Science and Policy* 12(1): 33–52.

Erulkar, A. and Chong, E. (2005) *Evaluation of a Savings and Micro-Credit Program for Vulnerable Young Women in Nairobi*. Nairobi: Population Council.

Erulkar, A.S., Mekbib, T.A. and Tegegne, M. (2008) *Biruh Tesfa: Creating a 'Bright Future' for Migrant Girls in Urban Areas of Ethiopia*. Transitions to Adulthood Brief 21. New York: Population Council.

Etang, A., Fielding, D. and Knowles, S. (2010) 'Trust and ROSCA Membership in Rural Cameroon.' *Journal of International Development* 23: 461–75.

Evers, B., Wondilimu, A., Garsonnin, J. and Aberra, A. (2008) *Contextual Gender Analytical Study of the Ethiopia Productive Safety Nets Programme*. Addis Ababa: Government of the Federal Democratic Republic of Ethiopia.

Ewig, C. (2010) *Second Wave Neoliberalism: Gender, Race and Health Sector Reforms in Peru*. Philadelphia, PA: Pennsylvania State University Press.

Ewig, C. and Bello, A.H. (2009) 'Gender Equity and Health Sector Reform in Colombia: Mixed State-Market Model Yields Mixed Results.' *Social Science and Medicine* 68: 1145–52.

Fang, H. and Ke, R. (2006) 'The Insurance Role of Rosca in the Presence of Credit Markets: Theory and Evidence.' Unpublished paper.

Fang, Z. and Sakellariou, C. (2011) 'A Case of Sticky Floors: Gender Wage Differentials in Thailand.' *Asian Economic Journal* 25(1): 35–54.

Farah, M. (2009) 'Social Policy for Poor Rural People in Colombia: Reinforcing Traditional Gender Roles and Identities?' *Social Policy and Administration* 43(4): 397–408.

Farid, H. (2011) 'Culture, Religion, and Female Agency: Birth in Pakistan.' *International Journal of Childbirth Education* 26: 11.

Farrington, J. (2005) *Recognising and Tackling Risk and Vulnerability Constraints to Pro-Poor Agricultural Growth*. Paris: Organisation for Economic Co-operation and Development.

Farrington, J. and Slater, R. (2009) *Lump Sum Cash Transfers in Developmental and Post-Emergency Contexts: How Well Have They Performed?* London: Overseas Development Institute.

Farrington, J., Slater, R. and Holmes, R. (2007) *Linking Social Protection and the Productive Sectors*. Briefing Paper 28. London: Overseas Development Institute.

Faur. E. (2008) *The 'Care Diamond': Social Policy Regime, Care Policies and Programmes in Argentina*. Geneva: UN Research Institute for Social Development.

Federation of Free Workers (2009) *Global Financial Crisis May Worsen Child Labor Situation*. www.ffw. org.ph/2009%20UPDATES/ JUNE%202009%20UPDATE/Glo bal%20Financial%20Crisis%20may %20worsen%20child%20labor%20si tuation.htm

Fernandez, B. (2010) 'Cheap and Disposable? The Impact of the Global Economic Crisis on the Migration of Ethiopian Women Domestic Workers to the Gulf.' *Gender & Development* 18(2): 249–62.

Fiszbein, A. and Schady, N. (2009) *Conditional Cash Transfers: Reducing Present and Future Poverty*. Washington, DC: World Bank.

Fleischman, Janet (2009) Making Gender a Global Health Priority: A Report of the CSIS Global Health Policy Center. Washington DC: CSIS. Available from: http://csis. org/files/publication/091124_ Fleischman_MakingGender_WEB. pdf

Fletschner, D. and Kenney, L. (2011) *Rural Women's Access to Financial Services: Credit, Savings and Insurance*. ESA Working Paper 11–07. Rome: Food and Agriculture Organization of the United Nations.

Folbre, N. (1994) *Who Pays for the Kids? Gender and the Structures of Constraint (Economics as Social Theory)*. London: Routledge.

Folbre, N. (2006) 'Gender, Empowerment and the Care Economy.' *Journal of Human Development* 7(2): 183–99.

Folbre, N. (2008) 'Reforming Care.' *Politics and Society* 36(3): 373–87.

Folbre, N. (2009) *Greed, Lust and Gender: a History of Economic Ideas*. Oxford: Oxford University Press.

Food and Agriculture Organization of the United Nations (2010) *Gender and Land Rights*. Rome: FAO.

FAO (2011). "Constitutional and Legal Protection of the Right to Food around the World", Rome: FAO.

Food and Agriculture Organization of the United Nations (2011) *The State of Food and Agriculture 2010–11: Women in Agriculture: Closing the Gender Gap for Development.*' Rome: FAO.

Food and Agriculture Organization and Organization for Economic Co-operation and Development (2011) *Price Volatility in Food and Agricultural Markets: Policy Responses*. Policy Report. Rome and Paris: FAO/OECD.

Forum for African Women Educationalists (2011) *Tuseme Youth Empowerment* www.fawe.org/ activities/interventions/tuseme/ index.php

Fraser, N. (1994) 'After the Family Wage: Gender Equity and the

Welfare State.' *Political Theory* 22; 591–618.

Fraser, N. (1997) 'From Redistribution to Recognition? Dilemmas of Justice in a "Post-Socialist" Age.' In: *Justice Interruptus: Critical Reflections on the 'Postsocialist' Condition*. London: Routledge.

Freire, S. (2004) *HIV/AIDS, Funeral Costs and Wellbeing: Theory and Evidence from South Africa*. www.csae.ox.ac.uk/conferences/2004-GPRaHDiA/papers/1h-Freire-CSAE2004.pdf

Friedman, J. and Thomas, D. (2007) *Psychological Health Before, During and After an Economic Crisis: Results from Indonesia, 1993–2000*. Policy Research Working Paper 4386. Washington, DC: World Bank.

Fuller, N. (1998) 'Reflexiones sobre el Machismo en el Peru.' Regional Conference on La Equidad de Género en America Latina y el Caribe: Desafíos desde las Identidades Masculinas. Santiago de Chile, 8–10 June 1998.

Galasso, E. and Ravallion, M. (2003) *Social Protection in a Crisis: Argentina's Plan Jefes y Jefas*. World Bank Policy Research Working Paper. Washington, DC: World Bank.

Gardener, J. and Subrahmanian, R. (2006) *Tackling Social Exclusion in Health and Education: Case Studies from Asia*. Summary Report for DFID. Brighton: Institute of Development Studies.

Gaunt, J. and Kabeer, N. (2009) *Rights, Responsibilities and Social Protection: The Dynamics of Supply and Demand*. Issues Paper. Brighton: Institute of Development Studies.

Government of Ghana (2007) *Livelihood Empowerment Against Poverty (LEAP) Social Grants Pilot Implementation Design*. Volume 1. Final draft. Accra: MESW (MMYE).

Grace, J. (2005) *Who Owns the Farm?*

Rural Women's Access to Land and Livestock. Kabul: Afghanistan Research and Evaluation Unit.

Green, D. (2008) *From Poverty to Power: How Active Citizens and Effective States Can Change the World*. Oxford: Oxfam International.

Green, D. (2011) 'Religion and Development: What are the Links? Why Should We Care?' Blogpost: www.oxfamblogs.org/fp2p/?p=7348

Grindle, M.S. (2011) 'Good Enough Governance Revisited.' *Development Policy Review* 29(S1): S223–51.

German Agency for International Cooperation (2004) *Social Health Insurance – Systems of Solidarity: Experiences from German Development Cooperation*. Eschborn: German Agency for International Cooperation.

Guenther, B., Huda, K. and Macauslan, I. (2007) 'Broadening Social Risk Management: Risks, Rights and the Chronic Poor. Debating Social Protection.' *IDS Bulletin* 38(3): 17–19.

Gugerty, M.K. (2003) *You Can't Save Alone: Testing Theories of Rotating Savings and Credit Associations*. Seattle, WA: University of Washington.

Guhan, S. (1994) 'Social Security Options for Developing Countries.' *International Labour Review* 133(1): 35–53.

Guha-Sapir, D., Parry, L., Degomme, O., Joshi, P.C., Singh, M.M. and Marx, M. (2006) *Risk Factors for Mortality and Injury: Post-Tsunami Epidemiological Findings from Tamil Nadu*. Brussels: Catholic University of Louvain.

Gunawardena, D. (2006) *Exploring Gender Wage Differentials in Sri Lanka: A Quantile Regression Approach*. PMMA Network Session Paper. www.pep-net.org/fileadmin/medias/pdf/files_events/5th_ethiopia/Gunawardena.pdf

Gupta, S. (2009) 'Women in India's National Rural Employment Guarantee Scheme.' In: S. Ravazi (ed.) *The Gendered Impacts of Liberalization. Towards 'Embedded Liberalism'?* London: Routledge.

Gwatkin, D.R. and Deveshwar-Bahl, G. (2001) *Immunization Coverage Inequalities: An Overview of Socioeconomic and Gender Differentials in Developing Countries.* Washington, DC: World Bank.

Habtom, M.K. and Ruys, P. (2007) 'Traditional Risk-Sharing Arrangements and Informal Social Insurance in Eritrea.' *Health Policy* 20: 218–35.

Haddad, L. (1992) 'The Impact of Women's Employment Status on Household Food Security at Different Income Levels in Ghana.' *Food and Nutrition Bulletin* 14(4): 341–433.

Hagen-Zanker, J., McCord, A., Holmes, R., Booker, F. and Molinari, E. (2011) *Systematic Review of the Impact of Employment Guarantee Schemes and Cash Transfers on the Poor.* London: Overseas Development Institute.

Haggblade, S., Hazell, P. and Brown, J. (2001) 'Farm-Nonfarm Linkages in Rural Sub-Saharan Africa.' *World Development* 17(8): 1173–201.

Haider, S., Todd, C. et al. (2008) 'Childbearing and Contraceptive Decision Making Amongst Afghan Men and Women: A Qualitative Analysis.' *Contraception* 78: 184.

Hancock, P. (2001) 'Women Earning Income in Indonesian Factories: The Impact on Gender Relations.' *Gender and Development* 9(1): 18–24.

Hanlon, J., Barrientos, A. and Hulme, D. (2010) *Just Give Money to the Poor: The Development Revolution from the Global South.* Sterling, VA: Kumarian Press.

Haque, M.S. (2008) 'Decentering the State for Local Accountability through Representation: Social Divides as a Barrier in South Asia.' *Public Administration Quarterly* 32(1): 33–58.

Harper, C. and Jones, N. (2011) 'Impacts of Economic Crises on Child Well-Being.' *Development Policy Review* 29(5): 511–526.

Harriss, J. (2002) *Depoliticizing Development: The World Bank and Social Capital.* London: Anthem Press.

Hashemi, S.M. (2006). *Graduating the Poorest into Microfinance: Linking Safety Nets and Financial Services.* CGAP Focus Note 34. Washington, DC: Consultative Group to Assist the Poor.

Hashemi, S.M. and Umaira, W. (2011) *New Pathways for the Poorest: the Graduation Model from BRAC.* CSP Research Report 10. Brighton: Institute of Development Studies.

Hastuti, N. (2008) *The Effectiveness of the Raskin Program.* Research Report. Jakarta: SMERU Research Institute.

Hattori, M.K. and DeRose, L. (2008) 'Young Women's Perceived Ability to Refuse Sex in Urban Cameroon.' *Studies in Family Planning* 39(4): 309–20.

Heemskerk, M., Norton, A. and de Dehn, L. (2004) 'Does Public Welfare Crowd Out Informal Safety Nets? Ethnographic Evidence from Rural Latin America.' *World Development* 32: 941–55.

Helmke, G. and Levitsky, S. (2004) 'Informal Institutions and Comparative Politics: A Research Agenda.' *Perspectives on Politics* 2(4): 725–40.

HelpAge (2009) *The Social Pension in India: A Participatory Study on the Poverty Reduction Impact and Role of Monitoring Groups.* HelpAge Briefing. London: HelpAge International.

Heyzer, N. (2009) 'The Impact of the Economic Crisis on Women and Children.' Lecture to the Secretary-General of the UN and the

Executive Secretary of UNESCAP. Kuala Lumpur, 11 May 2009.

Hickey, S. (2007) *Conceptualising the Politics of Social Protection in Africa.* Working Paper 4. Manchester: Brooks World Poverty Institute.

Hickey, S. (2008) 'Conceptualising the Politics of Social Protection in Africa.' In: A. Barrientos and D. Hulme (eds) *Social Protection for the Poor and Poorest: Concepts, Policies and Politics.* London: Palgrave Macmillan.

Hickey, S. (2009) 'The Politics of Protecting the Poorest: Moving Beyond the "Anti-Politics Machine."' *Political Geography* 28(8): 473–83.

Hickey, S. and Bracking, S. (2005) 'Exploring the Politics of Chronic Poverty: From Representation to a Politics of Justice?' *World Development* 33(6): 851–65.

Hicks, J. (2011) 'Strengthening Women's Participation in Local Governance: Lessons and Strategies.' *Community Development Journal* 46(S1): 136–50.

Hill, M.A. and King, E. (1995) 'Women's Education and Economic Well-Being.' *Feminist Economics* 1(2): 21–46.

Hirway, I., Saluja, M.R. and Yadav, B. (2008) *India – Reducing Unpaid Work in the Village of Nana Kotda, Gujarat: An Economic Impact Analysis of Works Undertaken under the National Rural Employment Guarantee Act (NREGA).* Annandale-on-Hudson, NY: UNDP/Levy Economics Institute.

Hoare, J and Gell, F. (2009) *Women's Leadership and Participation: Case Studies on Learning for Action.* Oxford: Oxfam.

Hochman, G., Sexton, S. and Zilberman, D. (2010) 'The Effects of Biofuels on Crude Oil Markets.' *Journal of Agrobiotechnology Management and Economics* 13(2): 112–18.

Hoddinott, J. and Haddad, L. (1995)

'Does Female Income Share Influence Household Expenditures? Evidence from Côte D'Ivoire.' *Oxford Bulletin of Economics and Statistics* 57(1): 77–96.

Holmes, R. and Jones, N. (2009) *Putting the Social Back into Social Protection: A Framework for Understanding the Linkages between Economic and Social Risks for Poverty Reduction.* Background Note. London: Overseas Development Institute.

Holmes, R. and Jones, N. (2010a) *Rethinking Social Protection Using a Gender Lens.* Working Paper 320. London: Overseas Development Institute.

Holmes, R. and Jones, N. (2010b) *Social Protection Programming: The Need for a Gender Lens.* Briefing Paper 63. London: Overseas Development Institute.

Holmes, R. and Jones, N. (2010c) *How to Design and Implement Gender-Sensitive Social Protection Programmes.* ODI Toolkit. London: Overseas Development Institute.

Holmes, R., Farrington, J. and Slater, R. (2007) 'Social Protection and Growth: The Case of Agriculture.' *IDS Bulletin* 38(3): 95–100.

Holmes, R., Mannan, F., Dhali, H. and Parveen, S. (2010) *Gendered Risks, Poverty and Vulnerability in Bangladesh: Case Study of the Challenging the Frontiers of Poverty Reduction Programme (CFPR), Specially Targeted Ultra Poor II (STUP II).* Report to DFID. London: Overseas Development Institute.

Holzmann, R. and Jørgensen, S. (2000) *Social Risk Management: A New Conceptual Framework for Social Protection, and Beyond.* Social Protection Discussion Paper 06. Washington, DC: World Bank.

Hopkins, J., Levin, C. and Haddad, L. (1994) 'Women's Income and Household Expenditure Patterns: Gender or Flow? Evidence from Niger.' *American Journal of Agricultural Economics* 76(5): 1219–25.

Hopkins, S. (2006) 'Economic Stability and Health Status: Evidence from East Asia Before and After the Economic Crisis.' *Health Policy* 75(3): 347–57.

Hossain, N. (2007) *The Politics of What Works: The Case of the Vulnerable Group Development Programme in Bangladesh.* Working Paper 92. Manchester: Chronic Poverty Research Centre.

Hossain, A. and Blackie, R. (2011) *Summary of CLP Output Targets and Expected Gender Access.* Bangladesh: Chars Livelihoods Programme, IML.

Hossain, N., Eyben, R. et al. (2009) *Accounts of Crisis: Poor People's Experiences of the Food, Fuel and Financial Crises.* Report on a Pilot Study in Bangladesh, Indonesia, Jamaica, Kenya and Zambia. Brighton: Institute of Development Studies.

Hsiao, W.C. and Shaw, R.P. (eds) (2007) *Social Health Insurance for Developing Nations.* World Bank Development Studies. Washington, DC: World Bank. http://siteresources.worldbank. org/SAFETYNETSAND TRANSFERS/Resources/ EthiopiaPSNP LessonsLearnedLite. pdf

Hulme, D. and Moore, K. (2007) *Assisting the Poorest in Bangladesh: Learning from BRAC's 'Targeting the Ultra Poor' Programme.* Working Paper 1. Manchester: Brooks World Poverty Institute.

Human Rights Watch (2009) *'Are You Happy to Cheat Us?': Exploitation of Migrant Construction Workers in Russia.* New York: Human Rights Watch.

Hunter, N. and May, J. (2002) *Poverty, Shocks and School Disruption Episodes Among Adolescents in South Africa.* CSDS Working Paper 35. Durban: University of Natal.

Hurst, E., Hsieh, T.-S., Jones, C. and Klenow, P. (2011) *The Allocation of Talent and Economic Growth.* Chicago: Chicago Booth.

Inglehart, R. and Norris, P. (2003) *Rising Tide: Gender Equality and Cultural Change around the World.* Cambridge: Cambridge University Press.

Institute for Integrated Development Studies (2004) *Review and Design of the Incentive and Scholarship Programmes for Primary and Secondary Education.* Research Report for DoE. Nepal: IIDS.

International Center for Research on Women (2006) *Child Marriage and Domestic Violence.* New York: ICRW.

International Center for Research on Women (2007) *How to End Child Marriage.* New York: ICRW.

International Food Policy Research Institute (2008) *The Guatemala Community Day Care Program: An Example of Effective Urban Programming.* Research Report 144. Washington, DC: International Food Policy Research Institute.

International Fund for Agricultural Development (1999) *Assessment of Rural Poverty in West and Central Africa.* Rome: IFAD.

International Fund for Agricultural Development (2011) *The Face of Rural Poverty in Peru: Rural Poverty Report 2011.* Rome: IFAD.

International Institute for Population Sciences and Macro International (2007) *National Family Health Survey (NFHS-3), 2005–2006: India: Volume 1.* Mumbai: IIPS.

ILO (nd) New rural cooperative medical scheme in China (NRCMS), downloaded at: HYPERLINK "http://www.ilo. org/gimi/gess/RessFileDownload. do?ressourceId=16913" www.ilo. org/gimi/gess/RessFileDownload. do?ressourceId=16913.

ILO (nd) New rural cooperative medical scheme in China

(NRCMS), downloaded at: HYPERLINK "http://www.ilo. org/gimi/gess/RessFileDownload. do?ressourceId=16913" www.ilo. org/gimi/gess/RessFileDownload. do?ressourceId=16913.

International Labour Organization (2007a) *ABC of Women Workers' Rights and Gender Equality.* 2nd edition. Geneva: ILO.

International Labour Organization (2007b) *Health Microinsurance Schemes: Monitoring and Evaluation Guide. Volume 1: Methodology.* Geneva: ILO/STEP.

International Labour Organization (2008) *Social Health Protection: An ILO Strategy Towards Universal Access to Health Care.* Geneva: ILO.

International Labour Organization (2009a) *Global Employment Trends for Women.* Geneva: ILO.

International Labour Organization (2009b) *Guide to the New Millennium Development Goals Employment Indicators: Including the Full Set of Decent Work Indicators.* Geneva: ILO.

International Labour Organization (2010a) *World Social Security Report 2010/2011: Providing Coverage in Times of Crisis and Beyond.* Geneva: ILO.

International Labour Organization (2010b) *Women in Labour Markets: Measuring Progress and Identifying Challenges.* Geneva: ILO.

International Labour Organization (2010c) *Maternity at Work: A Review of National Legislation, Findings from the ILO Database of Conditions of Work and Employment Laws.* Geneva: ILO.

International Labour Organization (2011) *Social Protection Floor for a Fair and Inclusive Globalization. Report of the Social Protection Floor Advisory Group.* Geneva: ILO.

International Trade Union Confederation (2008) *The Global Gender Pay Gap.* Brussels: ITUC.

Iraola, V.P. and Gruenberg, C. (2008)

'Clientelism, Poverty and Gender: Cash Conditional Transfers on the Loop.' GTZ Workshop on Gender and Corruption in Development Co-operation. Eschborn, 10–11 November 2008.

Isham, J., Kelly, T. and Ramaswamy, S. (2002) 'Social Capital and Well-Being in Developing Countries: An Introduction.' In: J. Isham, T. Kelly and S. Ramaswamy (eds) *Development: Well-Being in Developing Countries.* Cheltenham: Edward Elgar.

Islam, M.M., Siwar, C. and Karim, M.A. (2007). 'The Impact of the Financial Crisis on the Living Standard: An Empirical Investigation.' *UNITAR E-Journal* 3(1): 52–75.

Jacquier, C., Ramm, G., Marcadent, P. and Schmitt-Diabate, V. (2006) 'The Social Protection Perspective on Microinsurance.' In: C. Churchill (ed.) *Protecting the Poor. A Microinsurance Compendium.* Geneva: ILO and Munich Re Foundation.

Jan, M. and Akhtar, S. (2008) 'An Analysis of Decision-Making Power among Married and Unmarried Women.' *Studies on Home and Community Science* 2(1): 43–50.

Jandu, N. (2008) 'Employment Guarantee and Women's Empowerment in Rural India.' www.righttofoodindia.org/ data/navjyoti08_employment_ guarantee_and_women's_ empowerment.pdf

Jayachandran, S. and Kuziemko, I. (2011) 'Why Do Mothers Breastfeed Girls Less than Boys? Evidence and Implications for Child Health in India.' *Quarterly Journal of Economics* 126(3): 1485–538.

Jayal, N. (2006) 'Engendering Local Democracy: The Impact of Quotas for Women in India's Panchayats.' *Democratization* 13(1): 15–35.

Jenson, J. (2009) 'Lost in Translation: The Social Investment Perspective and Gender Equality.' *Social Politics* 16(4): 446–483.

Jewkes, R., Dunkle, K., Nduna, M. and Shai, N. (2010) 'Intimate Partner Violence, Relationship Power Inequity, and Evidence of HIV Infection in Young Women in South Africa.' *The Lancet* 376(9734): 41–8.

Jha, S. and Ramaswami, B. (2010) *How Can Food Subsidies Work Better? Answers from India and the Philippines.* Economics Working Paper Series 221. Manila: Asian Development Bank.

Jha, R., Bhattacharyya, S., Gaiha, R. and Shylashri, S. (2009) '"Capture" of Anti-Poverty Programs: An Analysis of the National Rural Employment Guarantee Program in India.' *Journal of Asian Economics* 20(4): 456–64.

Johnson, C. (2004a) *Final Evaluation Report of the Labour-Intensive Works Programme.* Kabul: CARE Afghanistan.

Johnson, S. (2004b) 'Gender Norms in Financial Markets: Evidence from Kenya.' *World Development* 32(8): 1355–74.

Johnsson-Latham, G. (2004) 'Understanding Female and Male Poverty and Deprivation. In: G. Johnsson-Latham (ed.) *Power and Privileges: Gender Discrimination and Poverty.* Stockholm: Regerinskanliet.

Joint UN Programme on HIV/AIDS (2008) *2008 Report on the Global AIDS Epidemic: Executive Summary.* Geneva: UNAIDS.

Jones, N. and Baker, H. (2008) *Untangling Links between Trade, Poverty and Gender.* Briefing Paper. London: Overseas Development Institute.

Jones, N. and Holmes, R. (2010) *Gender, Politics and Social Protection: Why Social Protection is 'Gender Blind.'* Briefing Paper 62. London: Overseas Development Institute.

Jones, N. and R. Holmes, with H. Marsden, S. Mitra and D. Walker (2009), Gender and Social Protection in Asia: What Does the Crisis Change? Background Paper for Conference on the Impact of the Global Economic Slowdown on Poverty and Sustainable Development in Asia and the Pacific, Hanoi, 28-30 September

Jones, N. and Marsden, H. (2009) *Assessing the Impacts of and Policy Responses to the 1997–1998 Asian Financial Crisis through a Child Rights Lens.* Report commissioned by UNICEF. London: Overseas Development Institute.

Jones, N. and Tran, T.V.A. (2010) *Gendered Risks, Poverty and Vulnerability in Viet Nam: A Case Study of the National Targeted Programme for Poverty Reduction.* Report to AusAID. London: Overseas Development Institute.

Jones, N., Vargas, R. and Villar, E. (2007) *Conditional Cash Transfers in Peru: Tackling the Multi-Dimensionality of Poverty and Vulnerability.* London: Overseas Development Institute.

Jones, N., Vargas, R. and Villar, E. (2008) 'Cash Transfers to Tackle Childhood Poverty and Vulnerability: An Analysis of Peru's *Juntos* Programme.' *Environment and Urbanization* 20(1): 255–73.

Jones, N., Jones, H., Steer, L. and Datta, A. (2009a). *Improving Impact Evaluation Production and Use.* London. Overseas Development Institute.

Jones, N., W. Ahadzie and D. Doh (2009b) *Social Protection and Children in West and Central Africa: Opportunities and Challenges in Ghana.* Country case study for UNICEF/WCARO. London: Overseas Development Institute.

Jones, N., Harper, C. and Watson, C. (2010a) *Stemming Girls' Chronic Poverty: Catalysing Development*

Change by Building Just Social Institutions. Manchester: Chronic Poverty Research Centre.

Jones, N., Woldehanna, T. and Tafere, Y. (2010b) *Gendered Risks, Poverty and Vulnerability in Ethiopia: To What Extent is the Productive Safety Net Programme Making a Difference?* Report to DFID. London: Overseas Development Institute.

Jones, N., Samuels, F., Gisby, L. and Presler-Marshall, E. (2011) *Rethinking Cash Transfers to Promote Maternal Health: Good Practice from Developing Countries.* Background Note. London: Overseas Development Institute.

Joto Afrika (2011) 'Women as Key Players in Climate Adaptation.' *Joto Afrika* Issue 6.

Kabeer, N. (1994) *Reversed Realities: Gender Hierarchies in Development Thought.* London: Verso Books.

Kabeer, N. (1995) 'Targeting Women or Transforming Institutions?' *Development in Practice* 5(2): 108–16.

Kabeer, N. (1997) 'Editorial: Tactics and Trade-Offs: Revisiting the Links Between Gender and Poverty.' *IDS Bulletin* 28(3): 1–13.

Kabeer, N. (1999) 'Resources, Agency, Achievements: Reflections on the Measurement of Women's Empowerment.' *Development and Change* 30(3): 435–64.

Kabeer, N. (2008) *Mainstreaming Gender in Social Protection for the Informal Economy.* London: Commonwealth Secretariat.

Kabeer, N. (2010) *Gender and Social Protection Strategies in the Informal Economy.* Abingdon: Routledge.

Kabeer, N. and Subrahmanian, R. (1996) *Institutions, Relations and Outcomes: Framework and Tools for Gender-aware Planning.* Discussion Paper 357. Brighton: Institute of Development Studies.

Kabeer, N., Kabir, A. and Huq, T. (2010) *Quantifying the Impact of Social Mobilisation in Rural Bangladesh: Donors, Civil Society and*

'The Road not Taken.' IDS Working Paper 333. Brighton: Institute of Development Studies.

Kamanga, I. (1998) 'Zambia Recovery Project—Evaluations and Perspective of the Central Government.' In: A. Bigio (ed.) *Social Funds and Reaching the Poor: Experiences and Future Directions.* Washington, DC: World Bank.

Kamerman, S. B. (1984) 'Women, Children, and Poverty: Public Policies and Female-Headed Families in Industrialized Countries.' *Signs* 10(2): 249–71.

Kapoor, M., Schoar, A., Rao, A. and Buteau, M. (2011) 'Chit Funds as an Innovative Access to Finance for Low-income Households.' *Review of Market Integration* 3(3): 287–333.

Kelkar, G. (2009) *Gender and Productive Assets: Implications of National Rural Employment Guarantee for Women's Agency and Productivity.* New Delhi: UNIFEM.

Kelly, P.F. (2010) 'Filipino Migration and the Spatialities of Labour Market Subordination.' In: S. McGrath-Champ, A. Herod and A. Rainnie (eds) *Handbook of Employment and Society.* Chichester: Edward Elgar.

Kenya National Bureau of Statistics (2009) *Statistical Abstract 2009.* Nairobi: Kenya National Bureau of Statistics.

Khan, M. and Ara, F. (2006) 'Women, Participation and Empowerment in Local Government: Bangladesh Union Parishad Perspective.' *Asian Affairs* 29(1): 74–92.

Khan, S. and Qutub, S. (2010) *The Benazir Income Support Programme and the Zakat Programme: A Political Economy Analysis of Gender in Pakistan.* Report to DFID. London: Overseas Development Institute.

Khandkar, S.R. (1998) *Fighting Poverty with Microcredit: Experience in Bangladesh.* Washington, DC: World Bank.

Khera, R. and Nayak, N. (2009a)

'Women Workers and Perceptions of the National Rural Employment Guarantee Act.' *Economic and Political Weekly* 44(43): 49–57.

Khera, R. and Nayak, N. (2009b) 'What Works against Women.' *Frontline* 26: 3–16.

Kimani, M. (2008) 'Women Struggle to Secure Land Rights.' *Africa Renewal* 22(1): 10–13.

Ki-Moon, B. (2007) 'Remarks at the International Women's Day Inter-agency Event on Ending Impunity for Violence against Women and Girls.' www.un.org/apps/news/infocus/sgspeeches/search_full.asp?statID=69

King, G. et al. (2009) 'Public Policy for the Poor? A Randomised Assessment of the Mexican Universal Health Insurance Programme.' *The Lancet* 373(9673): 1447–54.

Kishor, S. and Johnson, K. (2004) *Profiling Domestic Violence – A Multi-Country Study*. Calverton, MD: ORC Macro.

Klasen, S. and Lamanna, F. (2009) 'The Impact of Gender Inequality in Education and Employment on Economic Growth: New Evidence for a Panel of Countries.' *Feminist Economics* 15(3): 91–132.

Kloos, H., Wuhib, T., Haile Mariam, D. and Lindtjorn, B. (2003) 'Community-Based Organizations in HIV/AIDS Prevention, Patient Care and Control in Ethiopia.' *Ethiopian Journal of Health Development* 17 (Special Issue): 3–31.

Knowles, J.C., Ernesto, M.P. and Racelis, M. (1999) *Social Consequences of the Financial Crisis in Asia*. Economic Staff Paper 60. Manila: Asian Development Bank.

Köhler, G., Cali, M. and Stirbu, M. (2009) *Social Protection in Asia: A Review*. Kathmandu: UNICEF ROSA.

Koenig, M. et al. (2003) 'Domestic Violence in Rural Uganda: Evidence from a Community-Based Study.' *Bulletin of the World Health Organization* 81(1): 53–60.

Kongolo, M. (2007) 'Women and Informal Credit: Lessons from Moretele, South Africa.' *Journal of International Women's Studies* 3: 121–32.

Kumar, S. (2010) '*Gender, Livelihoods and Rental Housing Markets in the Global South: The Urban Poor as Landlords and Tenants.*' In: S. Chant (ed.) *The International Handbook of Gender and Poverty: Concepts, Research and Policy.* Cheltenham: Edward Elgar.

Kunz, R. (2006) 'Remittances are Beautiful? Unpacking the Gender Dimensions of the Global Remittance Trend.' International Studies Association Convention, San Diego, CA, 22–25 March 2006.

Kwon, W.J. and Skipper, H. (2007) *Risk Management and Insurance: Perspectives in a Global Economy.* London: Wiley-Blackwell.

Laddey, R., Kumamoto, M. and Treichel, P. (2011) *Gender and Climate Change: Advancing Development through an Integrated Gender Perspective*. Discussion Paper. New York: UNDP.

Lamadrid-Figueroa, H., Angeles, G., Mroz, T., Urquieta- Salomo'n, J., Hernandez-Prado, B., Cruz-Valdez, A. and Tellez-Rojo, M. (2010) 'Heterogeneous Impact on the Social Programme Opportunidades on Use of Contraceptive Methods by Young Adult Women Living in Rural Areas.' *Journal of Development Effectiveness* 2(1): 74–86.

Lampietti, J. and Stalker, L. (2000) *Consumption Expenditure and Female Poverty: A Review of the Evidence.* Working Paper 11. Washington, DC: World Bank.

Larrañaga, O., Huepe, R.F.M. and Marinho, M.L. (2009) *Chile Solidario y Género*. Santiago: UNDP.

Latortue, A. (2006) 'The Role of Donors.' In: C. Churchill (ed.) *Protecting the Poor. A Microinsurance Compendium*. Geneva: International Labour Organization and Munich Re Foundation.

Leatherman, S., Jones Christensen, L. and Holtz, J. (2012) 'Innovations and Barriers in Health Microinsurance.' In: C. Churchill (ed.) *Protecting the Poor. A Microinsurance Compendium*. Geneva: International Labour Organization and Munich Re Foundation.

Lee, J. (2000) 'Income Assistance and Employment Creation through Public Works in Korea.' Paper presented at the international conference on 'Economic Crisis and Labour Market Reform: The Case of Korea,' Seoul, 7 May 2000.

LeMay-Boucher, P. (2007) *Insurance for the Poor: The Case of Informal Insurance Groups in Benin*. Discussion Paper. Edinburgh: Centre for Economic Reform and Transformation.

LeMay-Boucher, P. (2009) 'Beninese and Ethiopian Informal Insurance Groups: A Comparative Analysis.' *Development Policy Review* 27(3): 333–47.

Leturque, H. and Wiggins, S. (2009) *Biofuels: Could The South Benefit?* Briefing Paper. London: Overseas Development Institute.

Lévesque, M. and White, D. (2001) 'Capital Social, Capital Humain Et Sortie De L'Aide Sociale Pour Des Prestataires De Longue Durée.' *Canadian Journal of Sociology/Cahiers Canadiens* de Sociologie 26: 167–92.

Lim, S., Dandona, L., Hoisington, J.A., James, S.P., Hogan, M.C. and Gakidou, E. (2010) 'India's Janani Suraksha Yojana, A Conditional Cash Transfer Programme to Increase Births in Health Facilities: An Impact Evaluation.' *Lancet* 375 (9730): 2009–23.

Lin, N. (2000) 'Inequality in Social Capital.' *Contemporary Sociology* 29(6): 785–95.

Lind, A. and Farmelo, M. (1996) *Gender and Urban Social Movements: Women's Community Responses to Restructuring and Urban Poverty*. Discussion Paper 76. Geneva: UNRISD.

Lindley, A. (2007) *The Early Morning Phonecall: Remittances from a Refugee Diaspora Perspective*. Oxford: Centre of Migration, Policy and Society.

Liu, H., Zhang, L., Summerfield, G. and Shi, Y. (2009) 'A Gendered View of Reforming Health Care Access for Farmers in China.' *China Agricultural Economic Review* 1(2): 194–211.

Lloyd, C. and Young, J. (2009) *The Power of Educating Adolescent Girls*. New York: Population Council.

Lloyds 360 Risk Insight (2009) *Insurance in Developing Countries: Exploring Opportunities in Microinsurance*. London: Lloyds.

Lokollo, J (1999). 'Community Participation and Gender Sensitivity: Irrigation, Forestry and Environmental Protection in Nepal.' *ASIST Bulletin* No. 8: 7–8.

Loster, T. and Reinhard, D. (2012) 'Microinsurance and climate change' in Churchill, C. and Matul, M. (eds) Protecting the Poor: A Microinsurance Compendium. Volume II. Geneva: International Labour Organization and Munich Re Foundation.

Lourenço-Lindell, I (2002) *Walking the Tight Rope: Informal Livelihoods and Social Networks in a West African City*. Stockholm Studies in Human Geography 9. Stockholm: Stockholm University, Department of Human Geography.

Lovell, P. (2006) 'Race, Gender, and Work in São Paulo, Brazil, 1960–2000.' *Latin American Research Review* 41(3): 63–87.

Lund, F. (2006) 'Working People and Access to Social Protection.' In: S. Razavi and S. Hassim (eds) *Gender and Social Policy in a Global Context: Uncovering the Gendered Structure of 'the Social.'* Social Policy in a Development Context Series. London: Palgrave Macmillan/UNRISD.

Lund, F. (2009a) 'Social Protection and the Informal Economy: Linkages and Good Practices for Poverty Reduction and Empowerment.' In: *Promoting Pro-Poor Growth: Social Protection.* Paris: Organisation for Economic Co-operation and Development.

Lund, F. (2009b) *The Provision of Care by Non-Household Institutions: South Africa.* Research Report 3. Geneva: UNRISD.

Lund, S. and Fafchamps, M. (1997) *Risk-Sharing Networks in Rural Philippines.* Stanford, CA: Stanford University, Department of Economics.

McCord, A. (2004) *Policy Expectations and Programme Reality: The Poverty Reduction and Labour Market Impact of Two Public Works Programmes in South Africa.* ESAU Working Paper 8. London: Overseas Development Institute.

McCord, A. (2005) 'A Critical Evaluation of Training within the South African National Public Works Programme.' *Journal of Vocational Education and Training* 57(4): 565–88).

McCord, A. (2008) 'The Social Protection Function of Short-Term Public Works Projects in the Context of Chronic Poverty.' In: A. Barrientos and D. Hulme (eds) *Social Protection for the Poor and the Poorest: Concepts, Policies and Politics.* London: Palgrave.

McCord, A. (2009) *Cash Transfers: Affordability and Sustainability.* Project Briefing 30. London: Overseas Development Institute and the Swiss Agency for Development and Cooperation.

MacDonald, M. (1998) 'Gender and Social Security Policy: Pitfalls and Possibilities.' *Feminist Economics* 4(1): 1–25.

MacDonald, R. (2005) 'How Women Were Affected by the Tsunami: A Perspective from Oxfam.' *PLoS Med* 2(6): e178.

Macours, K., Schady, N. and Vakis, R. (2008) *Cash Transfers, Behavioural Changes, and the Cognitive Development of Young Children: Evidence from a Randomised Experiment.* Washington, DC: World Bank.

Magnoni, B. and Zimmerman, E. (2011) *Do Clients Get Value from Microinsurance? A Systematic Review of Recent and Current Research.* Appleton, WI: Microinsurance Centre.

Mahler, A. and Pessar, P. (2006) 'Gender Matters: Ethnographers Bring Gender from the Periphery Towards the Core of Migration Studies.' *International Migration Review* 40(1): 27–63.

Maitra, S. (2007) 'Dowry and Bride Price.' Prepared for the *International Encyclopaedia of the Social Sciences*, 2nd edition. Toronto: York University.

Maman, S., Cathcart, R., Burkhardt, G., Omba, S. and Behets, F. (2009) 'The Role of Religion in HIV-Positive Women's Disclosure Experiences and Coping Strategies in Kinshasa, Democratic Republic of Congo.' *Social Science and Medicine* 68(5): 965–70.

Mamdani, M. and Bangser, M. (2004) 'Poor People's Experiences of Health Services in Tanzania. A Literature Review.' *Reproductive Health Matters* 12(24): 138–53.

Marcus, R. with Gavrilovic, M. (2010) *The Impacts of the Economic Crisis on Youth: Review of Evidence.* London: Overseas Development Institute.

Marcus, R. and Pereznieto, P. with Cullen, E. and Jones, N. (2011) *Children and Social Protection in the Middle East and North Africa: A*

Mapping Exercise. London: Overseas Development Institute.

Mariam, D. (2003) 'Indigenous Social Insurance as an Alternative Finance Mechanism for Health Care in Ethiopia (the Case of *Eders).' Social Science and Medicine* 56(8): 1719–26.

Masika, R., de Haan, A. and Baden, S. (1997) *Urbanisation and Urban Poverty: A Gender Analysis*. Brighton: Institute of Development Studies.

Mathauer, I. Schmidt, J.O. and Wenyaa, M. (2008) 'Extending Social Health Insurance to the Informal Sector in Kenya. An Assessment of Factors Affecting Demand.' *International Journal of Health Planning and Management* 23(1): 51–68.

Mathur, S., Greene, M. and Malhotra, A. (2003) *Too Young to Wed: The Lives, Rights and Health of Young Married Girls*. Washington, DC: International Center for Research on Women.

Matin, I. (2002) *Targeted Development Programmes for the Extreme Poor: Experiences from BRAC Experiments*. Working Paper 20. Manchester: Chronic Poverty Research Centre.

Matin, I., Sulaiman, M. and Rabbani, M. (2008) *Crafting a Graduation Pathway for the Ultra Poor: Lessons and Evidence from a BRAC Programme*. Working Paper 109. Manchester: Chronic Poverty Research Centre.

Mayoux, L. (2001) 'Tackling the Down Side: Social Capital, Women's Empowerment and Micro-Finance in Cameroon.' *Development and Change* 32: 435–64.

Mayoux, L. and Anand, S. (1995) 'Gender Inequality, ROSCAs and Sectoral Employment Strategies: Questions from the South Indian Silk Industry.' In: S. Ardener and S. Burman (eds) *Money-Go-Rounds: The Importance of Rotating Savings and Credit Associations for Women*. Oxford: Berg.

McManus, J. (2012) Thailand's Universal Coverage Scheme: Achievements and Challenges, An independent assessment of the first 10 years (2001-2010) Synthesis Report, Thailand: Health Insurance System Research Office.

Mechler, R. Linnerooth-Bayer, J. and Peppiatt, D. (2006) *Microinsurance for Natural Disaster Risks in Developing Countries: Benefits, Limitations and Viability*. Draft. Vienna: International Institute for Applied Systems Analysis.

Mechler, R. and Linnerooth-Bayer, J. with Peppiatt, D. (2006) Disaster Insurance for the Poor? A review of microinsurance for natural disaster risks in developing countries, A ProVention/IIASA Study, International Federation of Red Cross and Red Crescent Societies, ProVention Consortium and IIASA, downloaded at: http://bvpad.indeci.gob.pe/download/eventos/CD_RPNCCP/2008-10-20%20al%2022-%20Reuni%C3%B3n%20Plaraformas%20Nacionales%20y%20Cambio%20Clim%C3%A1tico%20en%20%20Panam%C3%A1/PRESENTACIONES%20LUNES%2020%20OCT/Docs%20for%20Toolkit%20presentation/Risk%20Insurance/1.4.10%20PCMicroinsurance.pdf.

Meinzen-Dick, R. and Zwarteveen, M. (1997). 'Gendered Participation in Water Management: Issues and Illustrations from Water Users' Associations in South Asia.' Paper Prepared for Women and Water Workshop, International Irrigation Management Institute, 15–19 September 1997, Sri Lanka.

Meinzen-Dick, R., Johnson, N., Quisumbing, A., Njuki, J., Behrman, J., Rubin, D., Peterman, A. and Waitanji, E. (2011) *Gender, Assets, and Agricultural Development Programs: A Conceptual Framework*. CAPRi Working Paper 99. Washington, DC: International Food Policy Research Institute.

Meinzen-Dick, R., Quisumbing, A., Behrman, J., Biermayr-Jenzano, P., Wilde, V., Noordeloos, M., Ragasa, C. and Beintema, N. (2010) *Engendering Agricultural Research*. Discussion Paper 973. Washington, DC: International Food Policy Research Institute.

Mendoza, R. (2011) 'Why Do the Poor Pay More? Exploring the Poverty Penalty Concept.' *Journal of International Development* 23(1): 1–28.

Mensah, J., Oppong, J.R., Bobi-Barimah, K., Frempong, G. and Sabi, W. (2010) *An Evaluation of the Ghana NHIS in the Context of the Health MDGs*. Washington, DC: Global Development Network.

Mensah, K. (2007) 'Funeral Celebration: Costly to the Economy.' *GhanaWeb*, 18 January. www.ghanaweb.com/ GhanaHomePage/features/artikel. php?ID=117472

Mequanent, G. (1998) 'Community Development and the Role of Community Organisations: A Study in Northern Ethiopia.' *Canadian Journal of African Studies* 32(3): 494–520.

Mesa-Lago, C. (2008) 'Social Protection in Chile: Reforms to Improve Equity.' *International Labour Review* 147(4): 378–402.

Microinsurance Network (2010) 'The Microinsurance Trilogy.' *Microinsurance Network Newsletter*, Winter 2010.

Miller, A. (1995) 'Risk and Religion: An Explanation of Gender Differences in Religiosity.' *Journal for the Scientific Study of Religion* 34(1): 63–75.

Miller, B. (2001) *Empowering Women to Achieve Food Security*. Washington, DC: International Food Policy Research Institute.

Ministry of Agriculture and Rural Development (2010) *Productive Safety Net Programme: Programme Implementation Manual (Revised)*. Addis Ababa: MoARD.

Ministry of Education and Vocational Training (2010) 'Education Sector Development Programme: Secondary Education Development Programme II (July 2010–June 2015).' Dar es Salaam, United Republic of Tanzania: Ministry of Education and Vocational Training.

Ministry of Finance and Economic Development (2002) *Ethiopia: Sustainable Development and Poverty Reduction*. Addis Ababa, Federal Democratic Republic of Ethiopia: Ministry of Finance and Economic Development.

Ministry of Finance and Economic Development (2005) *Ethiopia Participatory Poverty Assessment 2004–05*. Addis Ababa, Federal Democratic Republic of Ethiopia: Ministry of Finance and Economic Development.

Ministry of Labour, Invalids and Social Affairs and UN Development Programme (2009) *Support for the Improvement and Implementation of the National Targeted Programme for Poverty Reduction*. Mid-Term Evaluation Report. Hanoi: MOLISA and UNDP.

Ministry of Rural Development (2008) *National Employment Guarantee Act 2005 (NREGA) Operational Guidelines*, 3rd edition. New Delhi: Government of India.

Miraftab, F. (2010) 'Contradictions in the Gender–Poverty Nexus: Reflections on the Privatisation of Social Reproduction and Urban Informality in South African Townships.' In: S. Chant (ed.) *The International Handbook of Gender and Poverty: Concepts, Research, Policy*. Cheltenham: Edward Elgar.

Mishra, I. and Jhamb, B.Y. (2009) 'An Assessment of UPA-I Through a Gender Budgeting Lens.' *Economic and Political Weekly* 44(35): 61–68.

Molefe, S.P. (1989) 'Welfare Provision by Selected Self-Help Organizations: An Exploratory

Study.' PhD thesis, University of the North.

Molyneux, M. (1985) 'Mobilisation Without Emancipation? Women's Interests, the State and Revolution in Nicaragua.' *Feminist Studies* 11(2): 227–54.

Molyneux, M. (2002) 'Gender and the Silence of Social Capital.' *Development and Change* 33(2): 167–88.

Molyneux, M. (2006) 'Mothers at the Service of the New Poverty Agenda: Progresa/Oportunidades, Mexico's Conditional Transfer Program.' *Social Policy and Administration* 40(4): 425–49.

Molyneux, M. (2007) *Change and Continuity in Social Protection in Latin America: Mothers at the Service of the State?* Gender and Development Programme Paper No 1. Geneva: UNRISD.

Molyneux, M. (2011) 'Cash Transfers, Gender Equity and Women's Empowerment in Peru, Ecuador and Bolivia.' *Gender & Development* 19(2): 195–212.

Molyneux, M. and Razavi, S. (eds) (2002) *Gender Justice, Development, and Rights.* Oxford: Oxford University Press.

Molyneux, M. and Thomson, M. (2011) *CCT Programmes and Women's Empowerment in Peru, Bolivia and Ecuador.* Policy Paper. London: CARE International.

Moore, K. and Braunholtz-Speight, T. (2007) *What Works for the Poorest? Knowledge, Policies and Practices.* CPRC Research Summary 1. Manchester: Chronic Poverty Research Centre.

Morduch, J. (1999). 'Between the State and the Market: Can Informal Insurance Patch the Safety Net?' *World Bank Research Observer* 14(2): 187–207.

Morrison, A. and Sabarwal, S. (2008) *The Economic Participation of Adolescent Girls and Young Women: Why Does It Matter?* PREM Notes 128. Washington, DC: World Bank.

Morrison, A., Schiff, M. and Sjöblom, M. (2008) *The International Migration of Women.* Washington, DC: World Bank.

Moser, C. and van Bronkhorst, B. (1999) 'Youth Violence in Latin America and the Caribbean: Costs, Causes and Interventions.' LCR Sustainable Development Working Paper 3. Washington, DC: World Bank.

Mostafa, J. and da Silva, K.C. (2007) 'Brazil's Single Registry Experience: A Tool for Pro-poor Social Policies.' www.ipc-undp.org/doc_africa_brazil/Webpage/missao/Artigos/CadastroUnicoJoanaMostafa.pdf

Munich Re Foundation (2005) *Annual Review: Natural Catastrophes 2004.* Munich: Munich Re Foundation.

Mwangi, M. (2009) 'Gender and Drought Hazards in the Rangelands of the Great Horn of Africa. Is Gender Equity the Only Solution?' *Women and Environments International Magazine,* 1 April.

Namsomboon, B. and Kusakabe, K. (2011) 'Social protection for women homeworkers: a case of healthcare services in Thailand', International Journal of Sociology and Social Policy 31(1): 123 - 136.

Narayan, D. et al. (2000) *Voices of the Poor: Can Anyone Hear Us?* New York: World Bank, with Oxford University Press.

Narayanan, S. (2008) 'Employment Guarantee, Women's Work and Childcare.' *Economic and Political Weekly,* March Commentary.

Näslund-Hadley, E. and Binstock, G. (2010) *The Miseducation of Latin American Girls: Poor Schooling Makes Pregnancy a Rational Choice.* Washington, DC: Inter-American Development Bank.

National Alliance of Women (2008) *Engendering the 11th Five-year Plan*

2007–2012: Removing Obstacles, Creating Opportunities. New Delhi: NAWO.

National Food Policy Capacity Strengthening Programme, BRAC Research and Evaluation Division and BRAC Development Institute (2009) Study on the First Phase of the 100-Day Employment Generation Programme. Dhaka: BRAC.

Nelson, V. (2011) Gender, Generations, Social Protection and Climate Change: A Thematic Review. London: Overseas Development Institute.

Neumayer, E. and Plümper, T. (2007) 'The gendered nature of natural disasters: the impact of catastrophic events on the gender gap in life expectancy, 1981–2002', Annals of the Association of American Geographers 97 (3): 551-566

Nino-Zarazua, M. and T. Addison. "Redefining Poverty in China and India". United Nations University. 4th October, 2010. Helsinki. http://unu.edu/publications/articles/redefining-poverty-in-china-and-india.html

Ngaira, J. (2007) 'Impact of Climate Change on Agriculture in Africa by 2030.' Scientific Research and Essays 2(7): 238–43.

Nooteboom, G. and White, B. (2006) Through Turbulent Times: Experiences of Crisis in Indonesia. Singapore: ISEAS Press.

Norton, A., Conway, T. and Foster, M. (2001) Social Protection Concepts and Approaches: Implications for Policy and Practice in International Development. Working Paper 143. London: Cape and Overseas Development Institute.

Nussbaum, M.C. (1995) 'Human Capabilities, Female Human Beings.' In: M. Nussbaum and J. Glover (eds) Women, Culture and Development: A Study of Human Capabilities. Oxford: Clarendon Press.

O'Donnell, I. (2009) Global Assessment Report - Practice Review on Innovations in Finance for Disaster Risk Management, A Contribution to the 2009 ISDR Global Assessment Report on Disaster Risk Reduction, downloaded at: http://www.preventionweb.net/english/hyogo/gar/background-papers/documents/Chap6/ProVention-Risk-financing-practice-review.pdf.

Ogden, J., Esim, S. and Grown, C. (2006) 'Expanding the Care Continuum for HIV/AIDS: Bringing Carers into Focus.' Health Policy and Planning 21(5): 333–42.

Oliveira, A.M.H. et al. (2007) 'The First Results of the Baseline Impact Evaluation of Bolsa Família.' In: J. Vaitsman and R. Paes-Souza (eds) Evaluation of MDS Programs and Policies – Results. Brazil: SAGI/MDS.

Oostendorp, R. (2009) 'Globalization and the Gender Wage Gap.' World Bank Economic Review 23(1): 141–61.

Organisation for Economic Co-operation and Development (2001) Glossary of Statistical Terms. Paris: OECD. http://stats.oecd.org/glossary/detail.asp?ID=1689

Organisation for Economic Co-operation and Development (2012) Social Institutions and Gender Index. http://genderindex.org

Orloff, A.S. (2009) 'Gendering the Comparative Analysis of Welfare States: An Unfinished Agenda.' Paper presented at the Annual Meeting of RC19 Montreal, 20–22 August 2009.

Orozco, M., Lowell, B. and Schneider, J. (2006) Gender-Specific Determinants of Remittances: Differences in Structure and Motivation. Report to the World Bank. Washington, DC: World Bank.

Ortiz, M. E. (2009). Cuenta Pública Junji Gestión 2006–2009. www.Junji.Cl/Junjijoomla/Index.Php?Option=Com_Remository&Itemid=176&Func=Startdown&Id=78

Osaki, K. (1999) 'Economic Interactions of Migrants and their

Households of Origin: Are Women More Reliable Supporters?' *Asian and Pacific Migration Journal* 8: 447–71.

Osei-Boateg, C. (2011) *Engendering Social Security and Protection: The Case of Africa*. Bonn: FES Global Policy and Development Department.

Øvstegård, R., Bioforsk, K., Kakumanu, R., Lakshmanan, A. and Pannuswami, J. (2010) *Gender and Climate Change Adaptation in Tamil Nadu and Andhra Pradesh*. Oslo: Bioforsk.

Oxfam (2005) *The Tsunami's Impact on Women*. Briefing Note. Oxford: Oxfam.

Palriwala, R. and Neetha, N. (2009) *The 'Care Diamond': State Social Policy and the Market. India*. Research Report 3. Geneva: UNRISD.

Pankaj, A. and Tankha, R. (2010) 'Empowerment Effects of the NREGS on Women Workers: A Study in Four States.' *Economic and Political Weekly* 45(30): 45–55.

Pankhurst, A. (2009) 'Rethinking Safety Nets and Household Vulnerability in Ethiopia: Implications of Household Cycles, Types and Shocks.' World Conference of Humanitarian Studies. Groningen, 4–7 February 2009.

Pankhurst, A., and Mariam, D.H. (2004) 'The Iddir in Ethiopia: Historical Development, Social Function and Potential Role in HIV/AIDS Prevention and Control.' *Northeast African Studies* 7(2): 35–57.

Pasha, H.A., Jafarey, S. and Lohano, H.R. (2000) *Evaluation of Social Safety Nets in Pakistan*. Research Report 32. Karachi: Social Policy and Development Centre.

Pathways of Women's Empowerment (2010) *What Would a Feminist CCT Programme Look Like?* Pathways Middle East Case Study. Brighton: Institute of Development Studies.

Paxson, C. and Schady, N. (2007) *Does Money Matter? The Effects of Cash Transfers on Child Health and Development in Rural Ecuador*. Policy Research Working Paper Series 4226. Washington, DC: World Bank.

Pearson, R., Whitehead, A. and Young, K. (1984) 'Introduction: The Continuing Subordination of Women in the Development Process.' In: K. Young, C. Wolkovitz and R. McCullagh (eds) *Of Marriage and the Market*. London: Routledge and Kegan Paul.

Pellissery, S. (2008) 'Process Deficits in the Provision of Social Protection in Rural Maharashtra.' In: A. Barrientos and D. Hulme (eds) *Social Protection for the Poor and Poorest: Concepts, Policies and Politics*. London: Palgrave Macmillan.

Pellissery, S. and Jalan, S.K. (2011) 'Towards Transformative Social Protection: A Gendered Analysis of the Employment Guarantee Act of India (MGNREGA).' *Gender & Development* 19(2): 283–94.

Pereznieto, P. and Campos, M. (2010) *Gendered Risks, Poverty and Vulnerability in Mexico: Contributions of the Estancias Infantiles para Apoyar a Madres Trabajadoras Programme*. Report to DFID. London: Overseas Development Institute.

Pereznieto, P. and Diallo, V. (2009) *La Protection Sociale et les Enfants en Afrique de l'Ouest et du Centre: le Cas du Mali.'* Bamako: UNICEF, Overseas Development Institute and Ministère du Développement Social, de la Solidarité et des Personnes Agées.

Perova, E. and Vakis, R. (2009) *Welfare Impacts of the Juntos Program in Peru: Evidence from a Non-Experimental Evaluation,* Washington, DC: World Bank.

Peterman, A. (2010) 'Widowhood and Asset Inheritance in Sub-Saharan Africa: Empirical Evidence from 15 Countries.' CPRC/ Overseas Development Institute Roundtable: Inheritance and the Intergenerational Transmission of Poverty, London, 11 October 2010.

Peterman, A., Behrman, J. and Quisumbing, A. (2010) *Review of Empirical Evidence on Gender Differences in Nonland Agricultural Inputs, Technology, and Services in Developing Countries.* IFPRI Discussion Paper 00975. Washington, DC: International Food Policy Research Institute.

Pierro, R. and Desai, B. (2008) 'Climate insurance for the Poor: Challenges for Targeting and Participation', IDS Bulletin 39(4): 123-129

Pierro, R. (2010) 'Does disaster insurance have a role in climate change adaptation?' Time for Climate Justice Series No. 3, London: Christian Aid.

Pitt, M.M. and Khandkar, S.R. (1998) 'The Impact of Group-Based Credit Programs on Poor Households in Bangladesh: Does the Gender of Participants Matter?' *Journal of Political Economy* 106(5): 958–96.

Plan (2008) *Paying the Price: the Economic Cost of Failing to Educate Girls.* Woking, UK: Plan.

Planning Commission (2008) *11th Five-Year Plan (2007–2012): Agriculture, Rural Development, Industry, Services and Physical Infrastructure.* New Delhi: Government of India.

Polborn, M.K., Hoy, M. and Sadanand, A. (2006) 'Advantageous Effects of Regulatory Adverse Selection in the Life Insurance Market.' *Economic Journal* 116 (508): 327–54.

Pomares, J. (2011) *A Gendered Political Economy Analysis: A Literature Review.* Mimeo.

Porter, C. with Dornan, P. (2010) *Social Protection and Children: A Synthesis of Evidence from Young Lives Longitudinal Research in Ethiopia, India and Peru.* Policy Paper 1. Oxford: Young Lives.

Posel, D., Fairburn, J.A. and Lund, F. (2004) 'Labour Migration and Households: A Reconsideration of the Effects of the Social Pension on Labour Supply in South Africa.' *Economic Modelling* 23(5): 836–853.

Prata, N. Passano, P., Sreenivas, A. and Gerdts, C.E. (2010) 'Maternal Mortality in Developing Countries: Challenges in Scaling- Up Priority Interventions.' *Women's Health* 6(2): 311–27.

Putnam, R. (1993) *Making Democracy Work: Civic Traditions in Modern Italy.* Princeton, NJ: Princeton University Press.

Quisumbing, A. and McClafferty, B. (2006) *Using Gender Research in Development: Food Security in Practice.* Washington, DC: International Food Policy Research Institute.

Quisumbing, A. and Maluccio, J. (2000) *Intrahousehold Allocation and Gender Relations: New Empirical Evidence from Four Developing Countries.* Discussion Paper 84. Washington, DC: Food Consumption and Nutrition Division, International Food Policy Research Institute.

Quisumbing, A.R. and Yohannes, Y. (2004) *How Fair is Workfare? Gender, Public Works, and Employment in Rural Ethiopia.* Washington, DC: International Food Policy Research Institute.

Quisumbing, A.R., Estudillo, J.P. and Otsuka, K. (2004). *Land and Schooling: Transferring Wealth across Generations.* Baltimore, MD: Johns Hopkins University Press.

Quisumbing, A., Meinzen-Dick, R. and Bassett, L. (2008) *Helping Women Respond to the Global Food Price Crisis.* Policy Brief 7. Washington, DC: International Food Policy Research Institute.

Quisumbing, A.R., Kumar, N. and Behrman, J. (2011) *Do Shocks Affect Men's and Women's Assets Differently? A Review of Literature and New Evidence from Bangladesh and Uganda*. Discussion Paper 01113. Washington, DC: International Food Policy Research Institute.

Qureshi, Z. and Reinhard, D. (eds) (2012) 'Conference Report.' 7th International Microinsurance Conference 2011: Making Microinsurance Work for the Poor, Rio de Janeiro, 8 10 November 2011.

Rabbani, M., Prakash, V. and Sulaiman, M. (2006) *Impact Assessment of CFPR/TUP: A Descriptive Analysis Based on 2002–2005 Panel Data*. CFPR/TUP Working Paper 12. Dhaka: RED BRAC, Aga Khan Foundation Canada and CIDA.

Raday, F. (2003) 'Culture, Religion, and Gender.' *International Journal of Constitutional Law* 1(4): 663–715.

Radermacher, R. and Dror, I. (2006) 'Institutional Options for Delivering Health Microinsurance.' In: C. Churchill (ed.) *Protecting the Poor: A Microinsurance Compendium*. Geneva: International Labour Organization and Munich Re Foundation.

Radermacher, R., McGowan, H. and Dercon, S. (2012) 'What is the Impact of Microinsurance?' In: C. Churchill and M. Matul (eds) *Protecting the Poor: A Microinsurance Compendium. Volume II*. Geneva: International Labour Organization and Munich Re Foundation.

Rai, S.M. (2008) *The Gender Politics of Development: Essays in Hope and Despair*. London: Zed Books.

Ranson, M., Sinha, T., Gandhi, F., Jayswal, R. and Mills, A. (2006) 'Helping Members of a Community-Based Health Insurance Scheme Access Quality Inpatient Care Through Development of a Preferred Provider System in Rural Gujarat.' *National Medical Journal of India* 19(5): 274–282.

Ranson, M.K., Sinha, T., Chatterjee, M., Gandhi, F., Jayswal, R., Patel, F. and Mills, A.J. (2007) 'Equitable Utilization of Indian Community-Based Health Insurance Scheme Among Its Rural Membership: Cluster Randomised Controlled Trial.' *British Medical Journal* 334(7607): 1309–12.

Rao, V. and Walton, M. (2004) *Culture and Public Action*. Stanford, CA: Stanford University Press.

Rastogi, M. and Therly, P. (2006) 'Dowry and its Link to Violence against Women in India.' *Trauma, Violence and Abuse* 7(1): 66–77.

Ravallion, M. (1992) *Poverty Comparisons: A Guide to Concepts and Methods*. LSMS Working Paper 88. Washington, DC: World Bank.

Ravindran, T.K.S. (2012) 'Universal access: making health systems work for women', BMC Public Health 12(Suppl. 1): S4.

Razavi, S. and Miller, C. (1995) *From WID to GAD: Conceptual Shifts in the Women and Development Discourse*.' Occasional Paper. Geneva: UNRISD.

Razavi, S., Arza, C., Braunstein, E., Cook, S. and Gouding, K. (2012) *Gendered Impacts of Globalization: Employment and Social Protection*. Gender and Social Development Paper 16. Geneva: UNRISD.

Reddy, D.N., Tankha, R., Upendranadh, C. and Sharma, A.N. (2010) 'National Rural Employment Guarantee as Social Protection.' *IDS Bulletin* 41(4): 63–76.

Reddy, D.N., Upendranadh, C., Tankha, R. and Sharma, A.N. (2011) *Institutions and Innovations in the Implementation Process of the Mahatma Gandhi National Rural Employment Guarantee Scheme in India*. CSP Research Report 09.

Brighton: Institute of Development Studies.

Roberts, J. and Waylen, G. (1998) 'Towards a Gendered Political Economy.' *New Political Economy* 3(2): 181–9.

Rodriguez, H., Quarantelli, E.L. and Dynes, R. (eds) (2006) *Handbook of Disaster Research*. New York: Springer.

Roeder et al. (2008) 'Integrating Gender Responsive Budgeting into the Aid Effectiveness Agenda' Peru Country Report. September 2008. UNIFEM.

Rosendorff, B.P. (2005) 'Ideas, Interests, Institutions and Information: Bhagwati and the Political Economy of Trade Policy.' Conference in Honour of Jagdish Bhagwati on his 70th Birthday. New York, 5–6 August 2005.

Roth, J. (1999) *Informal Micro-Finance Schemes: The Case of Funeral Insurance in South Africa*. Geneva: International Labour Organization.

Roth, J., Churchill, C., Ramm, G. and Namerta (2005) *Microinsurance and Microfinance Institutions: Evidence from India*. Washington, DC: CGAP Working Group on Microinsurance.

Roth, J., McCord, M. and Liber, D. (2007) *The Landscape of Microinsurance in the World's 100 Poorest Countries*. Appleton, WI: Microinsurance Centre.

Roy, A.K. (2011) *Distress Migration and 'Left Behind' Women*. Jaipur: Rawat Publications.

RSBY (2011) RSBY Gender Analysis, downloaded at: http://www.rsby. gov.in/Documents.aspx?ID=14.

Sabates-Wheeler, R. and Devereux. S. (2008) 'Transformative Social Protection: The Currency of Social Justice.' In: A. Barrientos and D. Hulme (eds) *Social Protection for the Poor and Poorest: Concepts, Policies and Politics*. London: Palgrave Macmillan.

Sabates-Wheeler, R. and Kabeer, N. (2003) *Gender Equality and the Extension of Social Protection*. Extension of Social Security Paper 16. Geneva: International Labour Organization.

Sabates-Wheeler, R. and Koehler, G. (2011) '(Re)distribution and Growth: What is the Role of Social Protection?' *IDS Bulletin* 42(6): 86–8.

Sabates-Wheeler, R., Devereux, S. and Guenther, B. (2009) *Building Synergies Between Social Protection and Smallholder Agricultural Policies*. Brighton: Future Agricultures Consortium.

Saggurti, N., Mahapatra, B., Swain, S.N. and Jain A.K. (2011) 'Male Migration and Risky Sexual Behavior in Rural India: Is the Place of Origin Critical for HIV Prevention Programs?' *BMC Public Health* 11(Suppl. 6): 1471–2458.

Sahni, M. et al. (2008) 'Missing Girls in India: Infanticide, Feticide and Made-to-Order Pregnancies? Insights from Hospital-Based Sex-Ratio-at-Birth over the Last Century.' *PLoS One* 3(5).

Samarthan Centre for Development Support (2007) *Status of NREGA Implementation. Grassroots Learning and Ways Forward*. Second Monitoring Report. New Delhi: PACS.

Samson, M. et al. (2004) *The Social and Economic Impact of South Africa's Social Security System*. Report for the Department of Social Development. Cape Town: EPRI.

Samuels, F. and Jones, N. (2011) *Cash Transfers for Maternal Health: Design Opportunities and Challenges in Low-Resource Settings*. ODI Project Briefing 68. London: Overseas Development Institute.

Santhya, K., Haberland, N., Ram, F., Sinha, R. and Mohanty, S. (2007) 'Consent and Coercion: Examining Unwanted Sex among Married Young Women in India.'

International Family Planning Perspectives 33: 124–32.

Santibañez, L. and Valdes, C. (2008) *Estudio de Supervisión de las Estancias Infantiles de la Red del Programa de Guarderías y Estancias Infantiles para Apoyar a Madres Trabajadoras.* Mexico City: CIDE.

Santos, P. and Barrett, C.B. (2006) *Heterogeneous Wealth Dynamics: On the Roles of Risk and Ability.* Ithaca, NY: Cornell University.

Sassen, S. (2008) 'Two Stops in Today's New Global Geographies: Shaping Novel Labor Supplies and Employment Regimes.' *American Behavioral Scientist* 52(3): 457–96.

Satkunasingam, E. and Shanmuga, B. (2006) 'Underground Banking in Malaysia: A Case Study of ROSCAs.' *Journal of Money Laundering Control* 9(1): 99–111.

Saxena, N.C. (2001) *How Have the Poor Done? Mid-term Review of India's Ninth Five-Year Plan.* Natural Resource Perspectives 66. London: Overseas Development Institute.

Schech, S. and Vas Dev, S. (2007) 'Gender Justice: The World Bank's New Approach to the Poor?' *Development in Practice* 17(1): 14–26.

Schultz, T.P. (2000) School subsidies for the poor: Evaluating a Mexican strategy for reducing poverty. June. Report submitted to PROGRESA. International Food Policy Research Institute, Washington, D.C.

Sebastian, M, Grant, M, Mensch, B. (2004) *Integrating Adolescent Livelihood Activities Within a Reproductive Health Programme for Urban Slum Dwellers in India.* New Delhi: Population Council.

Sederlof, H. (2008) *Program Keluarga Harapan – PKH: Two Case Studies on Implementing the Indonesian Conditional Cash Transfer Program.* Pro-Poor Planning and Budgeting Project Working Paper 5. Jakarta: Hickling.

Seebens, H. (2006) 'Bargaining over Fertility in Rural Ethiopia.'

Proceedings of the German Development Economics Conference.

Seebens, H. (2011) *Intra-Household Bargaining, Gender Roles in Agriculture and How to Promote Welfare-Enhancing Changes.* ESA Working Paper No. 11–10. Rome: Agricultural Development Economics Division, Food and Agriculture Organization of the UN.

Self-Employed Women's Association (2009) *Financial Crisis Based on Experiences of SEWA.* Draft. Gujarat: SEWA.

Sen, A.K. (1985) *Commodities and Capabilities.* Oxford: Oxford University Press.

Sen, A.K. (1999) *Development as Freedom.* Oxford: Oxford University Press.

Sen, G. (2008) 'Poverty as a Gendered Experience: The Policy Implications.' *Poverty in Focus* 13: 6–7.

Sen, G., Östlin, P. and George, A. (2007) *Unequal, Unfair, Ineffective and Inefficient. Gender Inequity in Health: Why It Exists and How We Can Change It.* Geneva: World Health Organization.

Sernyonov, M. and Gorodzeisky, A. (2005) 'Labour Migration, Remittances and Household Income: A Comparison between Filipina and Filipina Overseas Workers.' *International Migration Review* 39(1): 45–68.

Sethuraman, K., Gujjarappa, L. et al. (2007) 'Delaying the First Pregnancy: A Survey in Maharashtra, Rajasthan and Bangladesh.' *Economic and Political Weekly.* 3 November.

Shah, T. et al. (2010) *Asset Creation through Employment Guarantee? Synthesis of Student CaseStudies of 40 MGNREGA Works in 9 States of India.* IRMA-IWMI Faculty Student Collaborative Research 2009–10.

Sharma, R.B., Hochrainer, S. and Mechler, R. (2011) Impact Assessment of Disaster Microinsurance for Pro-Poor Risk Management: Evidence from South Asia, AIDMI, RRTI and ProVention Consortium downloaded at: http://webarchive.iiasa.ac.at/Admin/PUB/Documents/XO-1-059.pdf

Sharp, K., Brown, T. and Teshome, A. (2006) *Targeting Ethiopia's Productive Safety Net Programme.* London: Overseas Development Institute.

Silberschmidt, M. (2001) 'Disempowerment of Men in Rural and Urban East Africa: Implications for Male Identity and Sexual Behavior.' *World Development* 29(4): 657–71.

Silvey, R. and Elmhirst, R. (2003) 'Engendering Social Capital: Women Workers and Rural–Urban Networks in Indonesia's Crisis.' *World Development* 31(5): 865–79.

Sinha, D. (2006) 'Women Eat Least, and Last.' *InfoChange News and Features,* October issue.

Sinha, T., Ranson, M.K., Patel, F. and Mills, A. (2007a) 'Why Have the Members Gone? Explanations for Dropout from a Community-Based Insurance Scheme.' *Journal of International Development* 19(5): 653–65.

Sinha, T., Ransom, M.K. and Mills A.J. (2007b) 'Protecting the Poor? The Distributional Impact of Bundled Insurance Schemes.' *World Development* 35(8): 1404–21.

Skocpol, T. (1992) *Protecting Soldiers and Mothers. The Political Origins of Social Policy in the United States.* Cambridge, MA: Harvard University Press.

Skoufias, E. (2003) 'Economic Crises and Natural Disasters: Coping Strategies and Policy Implications.' *World Development* 31(7): 1087–102.

Slater, R. (2009) *Cash Transfers: Graduation and Growth.* Project Briefing Paper 29. London: Overseas Development Institute.

Slater, R. and Farrington, J. (2009) *Cash Transfers: Targeting.* Project Briefing 27. London: Overseas Development Institute.

Smith, L. and Haddad, L. (2000) *Explaining Child Malnutrition in Developing Countries: A Cross-Country Analysis.* Washington, DC: International Food Policy Research Institute.

Smithson, P. (2005) *Health in Tanzania. What Has Changed, What Hasn't, and Why: Reviewing Health Progress in Tanzania.* Report to DFID (Tanzania).

Soares, S., Osório, R.G., Soares, F.V., Medeiros, M. and Zepeda, E. (2007) *Conditional Cash Transfers in Brazil, Chile and Mexico: Impacts upon Inequality.* Working Paper 35. Brasilia: International Poverty Centre.

Social Institutions and Gender Index (2009) 'Gender Equality and Social Institutions in Ethiopia.' http://genderindex.org/country/ethiopia

Song, M. and Philip, K. (2010) *Mitigating a Job Crisis: Innovations in Public Employment Programmes (IPEP).* Employment Report No. 6. Geneva: International Labour Organization.

Staab, S. and Gerhard, R. (2010) *Childcare Service Expansion in Chile and Mexico: For Women or Children or Both?* Gender and Development Programme Paper 10. Geneva: UNRISD.

Steinmo, S., Thelen, K. and Longstreth, F. (eds) (1992) *Structuring Politics: Historical Institutionalism in Comparative Analysis.* Cambridge: Cambridge University Press.

Suarez, M. and Libardoni, M. (2008) 'The Impact of the Bolsa Família Program: Changes and Continuities in the Social Status of Women.'

In: Vaitsman, J. and Paes-Sousa, R. (eds) *Evaluation of MDS policies and Programs – Results. Volume 2. Ministry of Social Development and Fight Against Hunger.* Brasília: DF.

Subbarao, K. (2003) *Systemic Shocks and Social Protection: Role and Effectiveness of Public Works Programs.* Social Protection Discussion Paper 0905. Washington, DC: World Bank.

Subbarao, K. and Raney, L. (1995). 'Social Gains from Female Education: A Cross-National Study.' *Economic Development and Cultural Change* 44(1): 105–128.

Subrahmanian, R. (2005) 'Gender Equality in Education: Definitions and Measurements.' *International Journal of Educational Development* 25(4): 395–407.

Sudarshan, R.M. (2009) *Examining India's National Regional Employment Guarantee Act: Its Impact and Women's Participation.* SPA Working Paper. Brighton: Institute of Development Studies.

Sudarshan, R.M. (2010) 'Women's Participation in the NREGA: The Interplay Between Wage Work and Care.' Chronic Poverty Research Centre Conference. Manchester, 5–11 September 2010.

Sudarshan, R.M. (2011) *India's National Rural Employment Guarantee Act: Women's Participation and Impacts in Himachal Pradesh, Kerala and Rajasthan.* CSP Research Report 06. Brighton: Institute of Development Studies.

Sulaiman, M., Parveen, M. and Chandra Das, N. (2009) *Impact of the Food Price Hike on Nutritional Status of Women and Children.* Dakar: BRAC Research and Evaluation Division.

Suryahadi, A. et al. (2010) *Binding Constraints to Poverty Reduction in Indonesia.* Jakarta: SMERU Research Institute.

Swarup, A. (2012) 'Rashtriya Swasthya Bima Yojana: Providing Health Insurance Cover to the Poor in India', Presentation in UN Women Southeast Asia Expert Group Meeting on Gender Responsive Social Protection in Southeast Asia, Bangkok, 13-14 November 2012.

Taimo, N.V. and Waterhouse, R. (2007) *Food Subsidy Programme.* Maputo and Inhambane: National Institute for Social Action and the Regional Evidence Building Agenda of the Regional Hunger and Vulnerability Programme.

Teixeira, C. and Soares, F.V. (2011) 'How Effective are the Non-Monetary Components of CCT Programs?' *International Policy Centre for Inclusive Growth, One Pager,* No. 129.

Teshome, E., Zenebe, M., Metaferia, H. and Biadgilign, S. (2012) 'The Role of Self-help Voluntary Associations for Women Empowerment and Social Capital: The Experience of Women's Iddirs (Burial Societies) in Ethiopia.' *Journal of Community Health* 37(3): 706–14.

Thieme, S. (2003) *Savings and Credit Associations and Remittances: The Case of Far West Nepalese Labour Migrants in Delhi, India.* Working Paper 39. Geneva: International Labour Organization.

Thomas, D. (1990) 'Intra-Household Resource Allocation: An Inferential Approach.' *Journal of Human Resources* 25(4): 635–64.

Thomson, R.J. and Posel, D.B. (2002) 'The Management of Risk by Burial Societies in South Africa.' *South African Actuarial Journal* 2: 83–128.

Tickner, J.A. (1992) *Gender in International Relations: Feminist Perspectives on Achieving Global Security.* New York: Columbia University Press.

Tomalin, E. (2011) *Gender, Faith, and Development.* Oxford: Oxfam GB.

Tripp, A.M. (2001) 'The Politics of Autonomy and Cooptation in Africa: The Case of the Ugandan

Women's Movement.' *Journal of Modern African Studies* 39(1): 101–28.

Trommershäuser, S., Lindenthal, R. and Krech, R. (2006) 'The Promotional Role of Governments.' In: C. Churchill (ed.) *Protecting the Poor: A Microinsurance Compendium.* Geneva: International Labour Organization and Munich Re Foundation.

Tsai, K.S. (2000) 'Banquet Banking: Gender and Rotating Savings and Credit Associations in South China.' *The China Quarterly* 161: 142–70.

Ubaidur, R. et al. (2010) 'Using Vouchers to Increase Access to Maternal Healthcare in Bangladesh.' *International Quarterly of Community Health Education* 30(4): 293–309.

UN (2012) The Millennium Development Goals Report 2012. New York: UN. Available form: http://mdgs.un.org/unsd/mdg/Resources/Static/Products/Progress2012/English2012.pdf

UN Children's Fund (2001) 'Early Marriage. Child Spouses.' *Innocenti Digest 7.* Florence: UNICEF Innocenti Research Centre.

UN Children's Fund (2006a) *Behind Closed Doors: The Impact of Domestic Violence on Children.* New York: UNICEF.

UN Children's Fund (2006b) *Programme Experiences in Early Child Development.* New York: UNICEF.

UN Children's Fund (2007) *Rural Employment Guarantee Schemes and Their Impact on Children in South Asia Workshop.* Social Policy Cluster. New Delhi: UNICEF Rosa.

UN Children's Fund (2007) 'Social Inclusion: Gender and Equity in Education SWAPS in South Asia: Nepal Case Study'. Kathmandu: UNICEF.

UN Children's Fund (2010) *Social Protection: Accelerating the MDGs with Equity.* Social and Economic Policy Working Brief: UNICEF Policy and Practice. New York: UNICEF.

UN Children's Fund (2012) *Integrated Social Protection Systems: Enhancing Equity for Children.* Social Protection Strategic Framework. New York: UNICEF.

UN Development Fund for Women (2001) *Widowhood: Invisible Women, Secluded or Excluded.* New York: UN DAW, Department of Economic and Social Affairs.

UN Development Programme (2009) 'The Economic Crisis's Impact on Migrants and AIDS.' *UNDP News,* 12 August.

UN Development Programme (2010a) *Rights-Based Legal Guarantee as Development Policy: The Mahatma Gandhi National Rural Employment Guarantee Act.* Discussion Paper. New Delhi: UNDP.

UN Development Programme (2010b) *Women's Representation in Local Government in the Asia-Pacific.* New York: UNDP.

UN Development Programme (2011) *Social Services for Human Development: Viet Nam Human Development Report 2011.* Hanoi: UNDP.

UN Economic and Social Commission for Asia and the Pacific (2011) *The Promise of Protection: Social Protection and Development in Asia and the Pacific.* Bangkok: UN ESCAP.

UN Educational, Scientific and Cultural Organization (2010) *Adult and Youth Literacy: Global Trends in Gender Parity.* Paris: UNESCO.

UN General Assembly (1979) *The Convention on the Elimination of All Forms of Discrimination Against Women.* New York: UN General Assembly. www.un.org/womenwatch/daw/cedaw

UN International Strategy for Disaster Reduction (2009) *Making Disaster*

Risk Reduction Gender-Sensitive Policy and Practical Guidelines. Geneva: UNISDR, UNDP and IUCN.

UN Office for Disaster Risk Reduction (2011) 'Killer Year Caps Deadly Decade: Reducing Disaster Impact is "Critical" Says Top UN Disaster Official.' www.unisdr.org/archive/17613

UN Office on Drugs and Crime (2009) *Global Report on Trafficking in Persons.* Vienna: UNODC.

UN Office on Drugs and Crime (2011) *Global Study on Homicide.* Vienna: UNODC.

UN Population Fund (2010) *Exploring Linkages: Women's Empowerment, Microfinance and Health Education.* New York: UNFPA.

UN Women (2010) *Pakistan Floods 2010: Rapid Gender Needs Assessment of Flood Affected Communities.* New York: UN Women.

UN Women (2011) *Facts and Figures on Women, Poverty and Economics.* New York: UN Women.

UN Women (undated) 'Women, Poverty and Economics.' www.unifem.org/gender_issues/women_poverty_economics (accessed 19 June 2012).

UNDP (2009) 'Gender and Climate Change: Impact and Adaptation', UNDP Asia-Pacific Gender Community of Practice Annual Learning Workshop, Workshop Highlights, Bangkok: UNDP

UNDP (2010) Gender, Climate Change and Community-Based Adaptation, New York: UNDP

UNDP (2011) Sharing Innovative Experiences: Successful Social Protection Floor Experiences, Vol. 18, New York: UNDP, Special Unit for South-South Cooperation and ILO.

UNFPA and UNIFEM (2006) Gender Responsive Budgeting and Women's Reproductive Rights: A Resource Pack. New York: UNFPA. Available from: http://www.unfpa.org/webdav/site/global/shared/documents/publications/2006/gender_responsive_eng.pdf

UNIFEM (2010) Gender Responsive Budgeting and Aid Effectiveness: Knowledge briefs. Available from: http://www.gender-budgets.org/index.php?option=com_joomdoc&view=documents&path=suggested-readings/gender-responsive-budgeting-and-aid-effectiveness-knowledge-briefs-eng-unifem-2010&Itemid=587

US Department of State (2009) *Trafficking in Persons Report.* Washington, DC: US Department of State.

Van der Lugt, R. and Kuby, T. (1997). *Senegal – AGETIP: Public Works and Employment Projects.* Washington, DC: World Bank.

Vanwey, L. (2004) 'Altruistic and Contractual Remittances between Male and Female Migrants and Households in Rural Thailand.' *Demography* 41(4): 739–75.

Varadharajan, S. (2004) *Explaining Participation in Rotating Savings and Credit Associations (RoSCAs): Evidence from Indonesia.* Ithaca, NY: Cornell University.

Varga, C. (2003) 'How Gender Roles Influence Sexual and Reproductive Health Among South African Adolescents.' *Studies in Family Planning* 34(3): 160–72.

Vargas, R. (2010) *Gendered Risk, Poverty and Vulnerability in Peru: A Case Study of the* Juntos *Programme.* Report to DFID. London: Overseas Development Institute.

Vargas, R. and Salazar, X. (2009) *Concepciones, Expectativas y Comportamiento en Población Pobre Beneficiaria del Programa Juntos en Huancavelica, Andahuaylas y Huánuco.* Lima: CIES.

Varley, A. (2007) 'Gender and Property Formalization: Conventional and Alternative Approaches.' *World Development* 35(10): 1739–53.

Soares, F.V. and Silva, E. (2010) *Conditional Cash Transfer Programmes and Gender Vulnerabilities: Case Studies of Brazil, Chile and Colombia.* Brasilia and London: International Policy Centre for Inclusive Growth and Overseas Development Institute.

Wagman, J., Baumgartner, J. et al. (2009) 'Experiences of Sexual Coercion among Adolescent Women: Qualitative Findings from Rakai District, Uganda.' *Journal of Interpersonal Violence* 24: 2073–95.

Walsh, C. and Jones, N. (2009) *Maternal and Child Health. The Social Protection Dividend.* Dakar: UNICEF WCA.

Ward, B. and Strongman, J. (2011) *Gender-Sensitive Approaches for the Extractive Industry in Peru.* Washington, DC: World Bank.

Warnecke W.G.G. (1994) 'Burial Societies, African Religion and the Church.' MTh dissertation, University of Natal.

Watson, M.W., Fischer, K.W., Andreas, J.B. and Smith, K.W. (2004) 'Pathways to Aggression in Children and Adolescents.' *Harvard Educational Review* 74(4): 404–30.

Waylen, G. (1997) 'Gender, Feminism and Political Economy.' *New Political Economy* 2(2): 205–16.

Weiser, S.D. et al. (2007) 'Food Insufficiency Is Associated with High-Risk Sexual Behavior among Women in Botswana and Swaziland.' *PLoS Med* 4(10): e260.

Wiggins, S. and Brooks, J. (2010) 'The Use of Input Subsidies in Developing Countries.' Global Forum on Agriculture, Paris, 29–30 November 2010.

Williams, G., Thampi, B.V., Narayana, D., Nandigama, S. and Bhattacharyya, D. (2010) 'The Politics of Defining Poverty and Its Alleviation: Questioning State Strategies Through Grassroots Voices in Kerala.' Chronic Poverty Research Centre Conference. Manchester, 5–11 September 2010.

Willman, A. (2008) *Valuing the Impacts of Domestic Violence: A Review by Sector.* Washington, DC: World Bank.

Wilopo P. (1999) *Country Assistance Strategy Update on the Health Sector.* Washington, DC: World Bank.

Witter, S. (2011) *Demand-Side Financing for Strengthening Delivery of Sexual and Reproductive Health Services: An Evidence Synthesis Paper.* Washington, DC: World Bank.

Wolffers, I., Fernandez, I., Verghis, S. and Vink, M. (2002) 'Sexual Behaviour and Vulnerability of Migrant Workers for HIV Infection.' *Culture Health & Sexuality* 4(4): 459–73.

Woolcock, M. (1997) 'Social Capital and Economic Development: A Critical Review.' *Theory and Society* 27: 151–208.

Woolcock, M. and Narayan, D. (2000) 'Social Capital: Implications for Development Theory, Research, and Policy.' *World Bank Research Observer* 15(2): 225–49.

World Bank (2005a) *Agricultural Growth for the Poor: An Agenda for Development.* Directions in Development Series. Washington, DC: World Bank.

World Bank (2005b) *Evaluating a Decade of World Bank Gender Policy: 1990–99.* Washington, DC: Operations Evaluation Department, World Bank.

World Bank (2006) *Social Safety Nets in Bangladesh: An Assessment.* Bangladesh Development Series Paper 9. Dhaka: World Bank.

World Bank (2007) *Agriculture for Development: World Development Report 2008.* Washington, DC: World Bank.

World Bank (2008a) *Ethiopia Agriculture and Rural Development Public Expenditure Review 1997/98–2005/06.* Washington, DC: World Bank.

World Bank (2008b) *Implementation and Completion and Results Report on a Loan in the Amount of US$500 Million to the Republic of Turkey for a Social Risk Mitigation Project.* Washington, DC: World Bank.

World Bank (2008c) *Implementation Completion and Results Report (IDA-39150 IDA-H0930).* Report No. ICR0000744, Eastern Africa 2. Washington, DC: World Bank Africa Regional Office.

World Bank (2009) *Agriculture and Rural Development. Gender in Agriculture: Sourcebook.* Washington, DC: World Bank.

World Bank (2010) *Pakistan Floods 2010: Preliminary Damage and Needs Assessment.* Washington, DC: World Bank.

World Bank (2011) Vietnam Country Gender Assessment. Available from: http://www-wds. worldbank.org/external/default/ WDSContentServer/WDSP/ IB/2011/11/14/000333038_ 20111114003420/Rendered/PDF/ 655010WP0P12270sessment.0Eng. 0Final.pdf

World Bank (2011a) *Gender-Based Violence, Health and the Role of the Health Sector.* Washington, DC: World Bank.

World Bank (2011b) *World Development Report 2012: Gender Equality and Development.* Washington, DC: World Bank.

World Food Programme (2008) *Vulnerability Analysis and Review of Food Subsidy in Egypt.* Rome: World Food Programme.

World Food Programme (2010)

Enabling Livelihoods, Nutrition and Food Security' Evaluation Report of Egypt Country Programme 10450.0 (2007–2011). Office of Evaluation of the World Food Programme. Rome: World Food Programme.

WHO (2009) WHO calls for action beyond the health sector to improve the health of girls and women. Available from: http:// www.who.int/mediacentre/news/ releases/2009/women_health_ report_20091109/en/index.html

World Health Organization (2002) *World Report on Violence and Health.* Geneva: WHO.

World Health Organization (2010) *The World Health Report: Health Systems Financing: The Path to Universal Coverage.* Geneva: WHO.

Yablonski, J. and O'Donnell, M. (2009) *Lasting Benefits: The Role of Cash Transfers in Tackling Child Mortality.* London: Save the Children Fund.

Young Lives (2010) *The Impact of Social Protection on Children.* Policy Brief 10. Oxford: Young Lives.

Zlotnik, H. (2003) *The Global Dimensions of Female Migration.* Washington, DC: Migration Information Source.

Zucco, C. (2008) 'The President's "New Constituency": Lula and the Pragmatic Vote in Brazil's 2006 Presidential Elections.' *Journal of Latin American Studies* 40(1): 19–49.

Zucco, C. (2009) *Cash-Transfers and Voting Behaviour: An Empirical Assessment of the Political Impacts of the Bolsa Família Program.* Washington, DC: World Bank.

Index

Note: *f* following a page number denotes a figure and *t* denotes a table.